UNDERSTANDINGS
OF
RUSSIAN FOREIGN
POLICY

Edited by Ted Hopf

UNDERSTANDINGS OF RUSSIAN FOREIGN POLICY

The Pennsylvania State University Press
University Park, Pennsylvania

Library of Congress Cataloging-in-Publication Data

Hopf, Ted, 1959–
    Understandings of Russian foreign policy / edited by Ted Hopf.
        p.   cm.
    Includes bibliographical references and index.
    ISBN 0-271-01914-X (cloth : alk. paper)
    ISBN 0-271-01915-8 (paper : alk. paper)
    1. Russia (Federation)—Foreign relations.   I. Title.
DK510.764.H67   1999
327.47—dc21   98-43067
                                                                      CIP

Published by The Pennsylvania State University Press,
University Park, PA 16802-1003

It is the policy of The Pennsylvania State University Press to use acid-free paper for
the first printing of all clothbound books. Publications on uncoated stock satisfy
the minimum requirements of American National Standard for Information Sciences—Permanence of Paper for Printed Library Materials, ANSI Z39.48–1992.

Contents

Figures and Tables

Figures

Tables

Preface

In 1995, the Finnish Institute of International Affairs launched a multinational research project on post–Cold War Russian foreign policy. We began the project with three goals in mind. First, we wanted to bridge the gap between the study of Russian foreign policy and contemporary international relations theory. Second, we wanted to make a contribution to the still sparse literature on post–Cold War Russian foreign policy. Third, we wanted to bring together scholars of Russian foreign policy from different parts of the world in order to transcend the usual agenda that dominates Western studies on post-Soviet affairs.

This book summarizes the most important arguments and conclusions of the project. Each chapter approaches empirical issues of Russian foreign policy through a theoretical prism. In addition to mainstream approaches, such as neorealism, neoliberalism, and democratic peace theory, the chapters include applications of "critical" theoretical approaches, such as constructivism, postmodernism, and psychoanalysis. As a result, the study offers a wide variety of conclusions and explanations, sometimes contradictory and incommensurable with one another. The book produces, both empirically and theoretically, a rich basis for future debates and research, making it especially useful for students of post-Soviet affairs as well as students of international relations theory.

The articles range from detailed case studies to more comprehensive treatments of the basic tenets of Russian foreign policy. Nevertheless, all the chapters tell us something about how outside powers can influence the behavior of Russia in the international arena. Compared with most other studies on Russian foreign policy, the book gives systematic attention to how the social construction of political issues affects Russian foreign policy. In this it sheds new light on the role played by culture, identity, and norms in Russia's relations with other countries.

Eight experts from five countries—Finland, Russia, the United States, Japan, and Korea—took part in the project. Ted Hopf's role as research director of the project and editor of this book was invaluable. He performed excellently in the unenviable task of coordinating the efforts of a group of people with different cultural backgrounds, theoretical orientations, and academic credentials. I also wish to thank all members of the project's steering committee—Gregory Flynn, John Lewis Gaddis, Bae Ho Hahn, Seppo Härkönen, Vilho Harle, Max Jakobson, Hiroshi Kimura, Andrei Kortunov, Pekka Sutela, and Raimo Väyrynen—whose expertise contributed significantly to the success of the project and the related conferences. The project would not have been possible without generous grants from the Academy of Finland, the Kone Corporation, the Neste Group, the Nippon Foundation, and the Nokia Corporation, and the support of the United States Information Agency. Finally, I would like to thank the editors of The Pennsylvania State University Press for their support in the process of preparing this book for publication.

Tapani Vaahtoranta, Director
Finnish Institute of International Affairs

Introduction

Russian Identity and Foreign Policy After the Cold War

Ted Hopf

The need to explain and understand a new Russia's foreign policy comes at the juncture of two significant, and not unrelated, changes in the world. The first and most obvious change is the collapse of the Soviet Union, the disappearance of a world Communist system centered in Moscow, which has led to the emergence of the new state of Russia. Like any new state, Russia is enduring an identity crisis, not unlike those of the other fourteen constituent republics of the former Soviet Union. Each state has in common a discredited Communist past, an often unbearable and confusing present, and a seemingly irresistible, but not universally acclaimed, democratic capitalist future.

The second great change in the world is the end of the Cold War, in its multifarious manifestations. Clearly, the most momentous outcome has taken place on the world stage: U.S. military unipolarity; the virtual end to all great power conflict, most notably in the developing world; an end to the nuclear, and a diminishing of the conventional, arms races; the continuing expansion of Europe, in the form of the European Union (EU) and the North Atlantic Treaty Organization (NATO); and the relative political democratization and economic liberalization of much of the world, particularly Africa and Latin America, all in less than a single decade.

The manifestation of the Cold War's passing most interesting to us is the effect on the study of international relations. The change is perhaps most marked in the United States. As the other end of the bipolar competition that constituted the Cold War, U.S. study of international relations theory and Soviet foreign policy was fixated on the struggle with Communism, the political use of nuclear weapons, and the prevention of nuclear war. Realism dominated early postwar U.S. thinking, both in academic and policy-making circles. By the late 1950s and early 1960s, theorists of arms control had suggested various accounts of how to end the nuclear arms race with more than enough security to go around for both sides.[1] Scholars, sometimes the same scholars (for instance, Thomas Schelling), developed arguments for using the unusable—how to make nuclear weapons an instrument of political power, through either their limited use or their mere existence.[2]

In the 1960s, there were efforts to achieve arms control: the antiballistic missile treaty and the first Strategic Arms Limitation Talks (SALT I) are the most notable products. In the late 1960s and early 1970s, a new school of international relations thought arose in the United States and Europe: transnational interdependence.[3] Its fundamental insights about the mutual vulnerability of states to one another's economic policies crystallized just

1. Bernard Brodie, *Strategy in the Missile Age* (Princeton: Princeton University Press, 1959); Hedley Bull, *The Control of the Arms Race* (New York: Praeger, 1961); Thomas C. Schelling and Morton Halperin, *Strategy and Arms Control* (New York: Twentieth Century Fund, 1961); Charles E. Osgood, *An Alternative to War or Surrender* (Urbana: University of Illinois Press, 1962).

2. For example, see Henry A. Kissinger, *Nuclear Weapons and Foreign Policy* (New York: Council of Foreign Relations, 1957); Robert Osgood, *Limited War* (Chicago: University of Chicago Press, 1957); Thomas C. Schelling, *The Strategy of Conflict* (Cambridge: Harvard University Press, 1960); Herman Kahn, *On Thermonuclear War* (Princeton: Princeton University Press, 1961); Glenn Snyder, *Deterrence and Defense* (Princeton: Princeton University Press, 1961).

3. The most important works here may be Robert O. Keohane and Joseph S. Nye, eds., *Transnational Relations and World Politics* (Cambridge: Harvard University Press, 1972), and Keohane and Nye, *Power and Interdependence: World Politics in Transition* (Boston: Little, Brown, 1977).

as two events catalyzed a rethinking of power in world politics. First, the Vietnam War was coming to be seen in the United States as a complete strategic, political, economic, and human disaster. Second, the Organization of Petroleum Exporting Countries (OPEC) was fashioning its first successful price increase. These two events made it clear to many that power traditionally understood as nuclear superiority could not explain outcomes in world politics.

Recognition of interdependence as a defining feature of world politics set off a debate that continues today, albeit in different forms. Just as Robert O. Keohane and Joseph S. Nye began the exploration of how states construct institutions to manage problems of mutual vulnerability, Kenneth Waltz declared all such theorizing reductionist triviality.[4] According to Waltz, the real, or neorealist, understanding of world politics must come through structure, which Waltz reduced to the distribution of traditionally understood power.

Neorealism arrived on the scene in the late 1970s, at a time when it was clear that the détente of 1971–78 was coming to a close. I think it is impossible to understand neorealism's appearance, and its allure to academics, independently of the debate about U.S.–Soviet relations unfolding in the United States from the mid-1970s until the end of the Cold War. Although it might seem paradoxical in view of its emphasis on bipolar stasis, neorealism was in fact the progressive alternative at the time. The collapse of détente did not begin on the sands of Somalia, as Zbigniew Brzezinski, then national security adviser to President Jimmy Carter, gravely intoned in his memoirs. The death of détente began with its birth, particularly with the unrequited expectations of both sides.

Détente was sold to the American people by the team of Nixon, Kissinger, and Ford as a package deal: the United States would accept post–World War II realities in Europe in exchange for mutual restraint in the nuclear arms race, observance of human rights codes in the Helsinki Final Act's "Basket Three," and unilateral Soviet renunciation of "adventurism" in the Third World. Such an agreement would have ushered in a far safer world had either party observed its terms to the satisfaction of the other. Although the U.S. government complained about Soviet military aid to its allies in Angola in 1975, in Ethiopia in 1977, and in Afghanistan in 1979, it refused to apply the same standard to itself in China, Chile, and Egypt.

During the 1976 Republican presidential primaries, Ronald Reagan argued that "détente was a one-way street," and then-President Ford, reflect-

4. Kenneth A. Waltz, *Theory of International Politics* (Reading, Mass.: Addison-Wesley, 1979).

ing growing popular opposition to Soviet conduct, declared the word
détente inadmissible in official utterances. Because both sides were building
new nuclear weapons and both were engaged in the search for unilateral
advantage among developing countries, the issue became Soviet intentions. Whoever believed them to be benign was an advocate of détente;
whoever believed them to be expansionist advocated the adoption of a
hard line.[5]

On these grounds, neorealism was a dovish theory in that its structuralism moved the debate about U.S.–Soviet relations from a discussion of how
to determine Soviet intentions to a discussion of how to manage an inevitable relationship of conflict and confrontation. Instead of figuring out how
to deter nuclear war or how to encourage a more amicable relation with
Moscow or thinking of an alternative way of understanding how the world
works, the central issue became managing an unavoidable enmity.

This stasis characterized the study of international relations and Soviet
foreign policy until the Gorbachev revolution. My non-U.S. colleagues have
reminded me, and I think appropriately, that this description characterizes
the *American* study of international relations theory. On the other hand, in
Europe, since the late 1970s, no doubt partly because of the neorealist
dominance of discourse in the United States, a lively departure from structuralism has been under way, including both the English society school
associated with Hedley Bull and more critical theoretical approaches, such
as the constructivism explored in Pursiainen's account of Russian actions
in Chechnya and the postmodern offerings of both Medvedev and Heikka.

Just as Russia is experiencing an identity crisis today, so too is the study
of international relations theory in the world. As we are called on to make
sense of Russia's foreign policy, neorealism is under attack from neoliberal
institutionalists, the heirs to Keohane and Nye's early understandings of
interdependence and institutions, and from conventional and critical constructivists.[6] All these flavors of international relations theory are represented in this book. Moreover, as our Soviet colleagues used to utter more

5. On the importance of attributed intentions to the other, see Robert Jervis, *Perception
and Misperception in International Politics* (Princeton: Princeton University Press, 1976); Glenn
Snyder and Paul Diesing, *Conflict Among Nations* (Princeton: Princeton University Press, 1977);
Robert Jervis, "Cooperation Under the Security Dilemma," *World Politics* 30 (January 1978):
167–214.

6. Emanuel Adler, "Seizing the Middle Ground: Constructivism in World Politics," *European Journal of International Relations* 3.3 (1997): 319–63; Jeffrey T. Checkel, "The Constructivist Turn in International Relations Theory," *World Politics* 50 (January 1998): 324–48; Ted
Hopf, "The Promise of Constructivism in International Relations Theory," *International Security* 23 (Summer 1998): 171–200.

than occasionally, it is no accident that the collapse of the Soviet Union and the fall of the Berlin Wall were accompanied by the popularization of the nostrum of a democratic peace. The statistical regularity that democracies rarely fight each other was noted in 1976, but attracted little interest then.[7] Some twenty years later, democratization has become not only the subject of hundreds of books and articles but also the declared foundation for such nontrivial policies as expanding NATO.

Both Russia and the community of scholars who specialize in international relations theory and Russian foreign policy are experiencing one aspect of the Cold War's end that is a boon for both: all seemingly fixed viewpoints have been under critical assault for the last ten years.

For example, in the world of international relations theory, the structuralism of neorealism, its reification of the state, anarchy, self-help, identicality of units, and material power are all being called into question. Neoliberal institutionalism's failure to present an account for the origin of preferences, to capture individual or group agency, and to deconstruct the state are also being challenged. Constructivism's failure to specify some theory of politics to animate its account of process, its apparent methodological flabbiness, and its persistent systemic bias are being assailed. Critical theory's failure to avoid epistemological nihilism, to depoliticize its truth claims, and to establish usable methodological criteria are under attack.

The end of the Cold War has brought to the study of international relations the end of the implicit a priori privileging of some accounts of world politics at the expense of others. We are experiencing one of those all too rare, potentially transformative moments when thousands of serious people are open to the vigorous and rigorous critical analysis of their own work. Let us hope that in the future we do not regret having wasted this opportunity. I think that the contents of this volume reflect the promise of the moment.

This book brings together a variety of understandings of contemporary Russian foreign policy. The views expressed here vary along two dimensions. First, they vary according to how unique the writers believe Russia to be. Medvedev and Heikka see Russia as a particular social, political, cultural, and geographical phenomenon. Lopez, Kimura, and Chung treat Russia as a state like other states. Pursiainen serves as a conceptual hinge

---

7. Melvin Small and J. David Singer, "The War-Proneness of Democratic Regimes, 1816–1965," *Jerusalem Journal of International Relations*, no. 1 (1976): 50–69.

between these two poles, arguing that Russian particularities require attention, but do not account for everything Russia does.

The second dimension of difference is how the authors regard current international relations theory and its usefulness for interpreting Russian foreign policy. Medvedev and Heikka advocate discursive and psychoanalytic accounts of Russian foreign policy. Kimura and Chung are satisfied with variations of realism and neorealism, respectively. Pursiainen and Lopez, as transitional figures, combine accounts from traditional neorealism, neoliberalism, and the democratic peace with more reflectivist or constructivist understandings of Russian identity.

PREVIEWS

Russia is unique for its vastness. This space has conventionally been seen as a major asset for Russia, as a strategic reserve, but it has another aspect. Sergei Medvedev shows that space has always represented an absence of control for Russian rulers, and this pattern continues to this day. Medvedev sees Russia as an agglomeration of different cultures: European, Mediterranean, and Near Eastern Christian cultures along with Near and Middle Eastern Islamic, Buddhist-Mongolian, Chinese cultures, and more. Although he does not explicitly say so, cultural diversity and vastness may make the issue of control very salient to Moscow. The control of vastness has always required vast resources, and the accumulation of power has always been vested in a hypertrophying state, with obvious consequences for the fate of liberalism and markets in Russia.

Medvedev applies the insights of Jean Baudrillard to explain the symbolic control that the Russian state has always had to exercise over such a vast land and variegated population, although these insights are perhaps true for all relations between states and societies. The exercise of power through semiotic control is an important regularity for Russian rule. As Medvedev deftly puts it: "Russia continues to be managed by textual means. Russian space remains plain text: the Great Russian plain."

In a vast space, tension emerges between the people who want to spread out into that terrain and the state that wants to control their movements and fix their positions. This tension underlies historical cycles of spread and fixation. Urbanization itself may somehow be an accomplice of the state in fixing the population. Medvedev applies the insights of Vladimir

Paperny to generate a cyclical account of Russian relations with its vastness. In periods of "Culture One," there is movement, the beginning, horizontal openness or internationalization and Westernization, and struggle against hierarchies. "Culture Two" sees fixity, the end, vertical institutionalizations of authority, and hierarchy. Medvedev provides a table tracing these cultural alternations back to early Muscovy, but he provides an incisive understanding of the last decade as well.

Since 1985, Russia has undergone a complete cycle: from the expansion of Culture One under Gorbachev and early Yeltsin to the post–1993 closure of Culture Two under late Yeltsin. The achievement of a utopian goal under Culture One requires a sacrifice, which explains the extraordinary Soviet and Russian concessions that characterized Gorbachev's and early Yeltsin's foreign policy. These concessions were not a strategic move, but an act of self-denial for the sake of the utopian harmony of a democratic peace of modern civilized states.

The turn away from Culture One in 1993 has domestic roots. By late 1993, those who had benefited from the privatization of space wanted to refix the hierarchy to provide a guaranteed stability to enjoy the fruits of Culture One. Since 1993, Russia has seen a re-establishment of hierarchy: of presidential authority in Moscow; of financial clout in Moscow; of industrial, export, and natural-resource capital concentrated in Moscow; of a hierarchical criminal network articulated throughout Russia; of a new alliance between church and state; of a common ideology of Great Russia; and of a vertical architecture, both public and private. According to Medvedev, the turn toward an increasingly assertive Russian foreign policy after 1993 can be understood in the metasocial cycling back to Culture Two.

Henrikki Heikka agrees that there was a turn in Russian foreign policy in 1993. He proposes to assess the relative merits of neorealist, constructivist, and psychoanalytic discursive accounts. He claims that neither neorealist structure nor constructivist interaction can account for the 1993 turn. He uses a text of Sergei Kortunov, a Russian foreign policy analyst, as the body of evidence to be placed on the couch. According to Heikka, both neorealism and constructivism commit the same sin: they ignore the relation between "decentered subjectivity and the origins of nationalism and threat perceptions."

Through a close reading of Waltz and Jean-Jacques Rousseau, Heikka shows that Waltz's use of Rousseau is truncated and misleading. Although Waltz concluded that international anarchy is sufficient to promote conflict through security dilemmas, Rousseau explicitly asserted that structure is insufficient to account for state behavior, and the nature of states themselves must be included in any satisfactory account. Neorealism has an implicit theory of identity, based on its assumption of self-regarding units, which drives the model in the direction it assumes.

If neorealism's treatment of identity is simultaneously incidental and overdetermining, then constructivism's account is underspecified. Heikka points out that ego's perception of alter—even on their first encounter—cannot be separated from the way in which the actors deal with the internal split constituting their own identities. A Lacanian reading of nationalism is one of individuals sacrificing part of themselves to become citizens to recover themselves in a larger collective entity and enterprise. To paraphrase Heikka's sophisticated and nuanced prose, hypernationalist discourse is characterized by the identification of an inferior Other who signifies what Russia lacks, the possibility of becoming a collective whole. Without this displacement onto the other, a society (in this case Russian) would have to deal with its own impossibility, rather than obscuring it under the illusion of nationalism. Heikka hypothesizes that the role of others in identity construction becomes especially acute in times of turmoil, when the borders defining the collective's identity are called into question. Russia's search for identity after the Soviet collapse would of course be such a period.

In Kortunov's essay on a new grand strategy for Russia, Heikka finds much that can be understood from a Lacanian discursive perspective. Heikka concludes that the suppression of the split inherent in any identity and the consequent neglect of the desire of the other, not the nature of the West or international structure, transmute Kortunov's search for Christian and humanistic ideals into an identity based on hate and fear. The solution, according to Heikka, is to replace the illusion of wholeness, such as that of Organic Russia, by a coexistence with an uncomfortable truth. This move makes self–other relationships impossible. In a specific policy implication, Heikka argues the West should not try to teach Russia that NATO enlargement is no threat, but should engage in a critical dialogue on all totalizing identity moves of both sides.

Neoliberal institutionalism is often said to be weakest in explaining interstate cooperation on security issues. The Russian military intervention in Chechnya, which violated a number of Conference on Security and Cooperation in Europe (CSCE) norms and rules, appears to vindicate the neorealist position, but the evidence is not so clear-cut. After the initial military action, Russia acceded to a number of CSCE demands that resulted in institutionalized constraints on subsequent Russian conduct in Chechnya. Why did Russia choose to violate one set of norms, only to adhere to another?

In a rich historical account of Russian decision making on Chechnya, Christer Pursiainen assesses the relative merits of neorealist, neoliberal, and constructivist understandings of Russian conduct. Structural realism is supported by the Russian decision to crush the Chechen rebellion, but subsequent Russian willingness to endure CSCE supervision seems less susceptible to such an understanding. There is no evidence that Russian decision makers considered CSCE norms when planning the military action; the only norms and rules they discussed were those in the Russian constitution. Russia allowed an institution, the CSCE, to interfere in the Chechen situation. Constructivism would differentiate between Russian violation of the CSCE rule requiring prenotification of troop movements, which was not a genuine violation because the CSCE members lacked any intersubjective understanding that the rule was meant for such contingencies, and Russia's violation of human rights in Chechnya, which was understood as a violation by all. In addition, the international community unanimously constructed Chechen actions as an internal rebellion against a sovereign state with rights to its own territorial integrity. Indeed, the institutional mechanisms deployed by the CSCE for early warning and preventive diplomacy went unused because of the understanding that the Chechnya situation was an internal sovereign matter of Moscow. Pursiainen's conclusion is that no single approach has a monopoly on Russia's decisions on Chechnya, although exploring intersubjectively constructed understandings of rules and norms is imperative.

The democratic peace, a perfect example of how closely intertwined the study of international relations theory is to current political practice, proves too broad a brush to account for different Russian reactions to events in former Soviet republics. Andrea Lopez finds that regard for democratic norms does not stay the hand of Moscow but rather the way that Russian decision makers understand the legitimacy of the other government shapes Moscow's Choices. To the extent that the other is regarded as legitimate, the Russian government refrains from intervening on behalf of a putative ally.

Lopez may have put her finger on a serious weakness in the democratic peace. If indeed intersubjectively experienced legitimacy, rather than democracy, drives pacific relations between states, then democratic peace has cast its theoretical net too narrowly. After all, legitimacy may be understood in many nondemocratic ways. This fact might explain, for example, why there have for centuries been oases of peace in Africa and Latin America among many different groups of states. In other words, the notion of democratic peace, by ignoring legitimacy, may also obscure from view the authoritarian peace that has been characteristic of much of the rest of the world much of the time. Lopez's work is consistent with that of Ido Oren's, which suggests that democracy is what states make of it.[8] Intersubjective understandings of identities drive actions chosen regarding one another; a priori labeling of states as democracies and observations of expected correlated behavior are not sufficient.

In a nicely chosen pair of cases, Russia intervenes in the less democratic Moldova, but not in the more democratic Estonia. Yet an analysis of the decision-making process suggests that this consideration did not drive a differentiated Russian approach. One of the more significant contributions of this work is to refuse to conflate correlation with cause. Democracies do not necessarily *not* fight one another because they are democracies. Lopez's work demonstrates that it is critical to keep this caveat in mind at all times.

The dispute over the Kuril Islands remains a major impediment to the development of normalized relations between Japan and Russia. According to Hiroshi Kimura, the differences, at least in part, persist because of different understandings of how to resolve the issue of the islands' sovereignty. Russian proposals defer the settlement of the issue of ultimate sovereignty into an indefinite future, with the hope that a number of joint economic projects will help promote an amicable resolution. Japan understands a willingness to develop cooperative economic projects on the islands as signaling a willingness not only to defer discussions of sovereignty, but to entertain an outcome of less than full Japanese sovereignty over the territories. In a seeming game of deadlock, what one side, Russia, sees as an act of cooperation—joint economic projects—the other side, Japan, sees as its own unilateral concession.[9] A deadlock occurs when both parties prefer conflict to cooperation, but effective deadlock may ensue if, as here, one party construes cooperation as a sucker's payoff, and the other, in this case Russia, sees the rejection of its offer as Japan's refusal to cooperate.

Although this elaboration of preferences helps us understand the stalemate in the relationship, it still remains to unravel why the seemingly natural marriage of Japanese capital and technology and Russian natural resources in the Far East, and the promised economic windfall from such a union, has not overwhelmed any Japanese concerns about Etorofu, Kunashiri, Shikotan, and the Habomai. One compelling answer advanced by Kimura is that the economic dividends for collaborating with Russia are

8. Ido Oren, "The 'Subjectivity' of the Democratic Peace," *International Security* 20 (Summer 1995): 147–84.

9. See Snyder and Diesing, *Conflict Among Nations*, esp. 124–27.

less than negligible for Japanese investors. This lack of economic interest implies that Japan will not become economically interdependent with Russia any time soon.

Lack of economic interest makes it much easier for Japan to remain insistent on the return of full sovereignty over the Kurils; so too does Japanese popular antipathy for Russia. No Japanese politician need fear being called too hard on Moscow. Japan's obviously different economic relationship with China rests on its different self-understandings with respect to Russia and China. Soviet Russia was seen as an untrustworthy aggressor, but China is seen as a victim of Japanese aggression. The continued Russian occupation of the Kurils only reproduces Japanese conceptions of their relationship with Russia. So long as Russian economic realities remain unattractive and the Japanese continue to understand Russia as an aggressive occupier of Japanese territory, this aspect of the Cold War shows no signs of melting.

According to Eunsook Chung, realism is better than neoliberal institutionalism at explaining Russian efforts to develop security regimes in East Asia and the negative reactions of most East Asians to those Russian initiatives. Repeated and recent Russian proposals to create regional security institutions in East Asia can be understood through neoliberalism. Russia seeks to create a managed security environment to avoid any unrestrained military competition with states with military forces in the region. Chung describes an array of regional actors who prefer to watch Russia unilaterally decline and disarm rather than participate in an institutionalized process that might require any of them to make concessions. In this realist view, Russia aims to use regional institutions to prop up its own atrophying power.

MAKING CONNECTIONS

A major theme of these contributions is how states find their own identities in others. Perhaps this theme appears most clearly in the relation between Russia and Europe, Russia and the West. On the one hand, to build on Heikka's theorization of the issue, the West becomes a demonized other as part of the effort of Russians to retain an illusory wholeness. This typification of the Russian relation with the West is complicated by the findings of several of the other authors. For example, Pursiainen shows that the CSCE's ability to represent the West and Europe allowed that institution to be seen in Moscow as a legitimate actor in Russia's most internal matters of self-definition: in Chechnya. Lopez as well points out that the critical difference between Russian nonintervention in Estonia and sanctioning of military force in Moldova was the fact that Russia did not understand Moldova as European, but it did see Estonia as such. Because Russia wants, needs to, and does see itself as European, it also constructs Estonia, in part at least, as part of itself.

Which one of these two broad understandings of identity construction people choose to believe has direct consequences for their view of the future of Russian foreign policy. Both Heikka and Medvedev starkly state that since 1993 there has been a turn in that policy toward a harder line. Heikka writes that the West has become the other, and Medvedev notes that Culture One includes a Russian desire to become a civilized state and join the West, which implies a reversal of such desires once Culture Two takes over by 1993. Perhaps, however, this putative turn might not have occurred, or it might not have occurred in the manner described.

The latter suggestion is a less ambitious alternative, but one implicit in some of the other authors' selections. If Heikka's account is true, then it is also true that Western behavior had no effect on how Russia constructed its most recent foreign policy identity. Is it true that the West did nothing to alter Russia's view of itself or the West? Although the contributions to this volume do not provide a certain answer, we should not reject the possibility. The expansion of NATO; continual complaints and threats from the United States about Russian weapons sales while the United States becomes the largest exporter of weapons in the world; continued U.S. dominance of all global political and economic institutions; U.S. obstruction of pipeline projects in Central Asia and the Caucasus all at least raise the possibility that Western conduct helped construct the West as partially other for Russia.

I wrote *partially other* to stress the complexity of this process. The constitution of the Russian self is not the product of a single binary relation—Russia-the West, Russia-Europe—but is more complicated. First, there is more than a single Russian identity, as shown by Pursiainen's account of the differential effects of Western human rights concerns on the Russian government. Andrei Kozyrev, new Russian foreign minister, immediately understood this intervention as an issue of Russia's identity as Western, European, and civilized. Presumably, other members of the presidential council did not share this interpretation of Western sensibilities. Moreover, there are multiple others, each with different meanings for Russian selves. Kimura's analysis of how Japan and Russia construct each other is surely different from the story we would tell about the United States as other, Germany as other, and so on.

The process of Russian identity construction, marked in this volume as a central part of any understanding of Russian foreign policy, is itself a multifaceted challenge to understanding. The turn of 1993, the move from Culture One to Culture Two, from West as partner to West as other, is, in fact, not so much a turn as a return. There are two parts to the story. First, Russia's conduct since 1993 is misleadingly read against Gorbachev's policies of unilateral retreats across the globe. Second, too much attention is paid to what Russia does, and not enough to what it does not do.

What is usually enumerated as Russian behavior constituting a turn away from the West is noticeable only against the background of a completely compliant and conciliatory Russia of Culture One. The bill of particulars includes nuclear technology sales to Iran; military hardware sales to China and other countries; continued occupation of the Kurils; opposition to NATO expansion; military interventions in Abkhazia, Tajikistan, Georgia, Azerbaijan, Moldova, and Chechnya; and opposition to Nato's war against Serbia. Although the West would presumably prefer that none of these decisions had been made in Moscow, they hardly constitute evidence of a turn in Russian foreign policy against the West. It is difficult to construe any of these events as particularly anti-Western.

After all, Germany and France continue to annoy the United States over their economic ties to Iran; the United States has assumed global leadership in weapons exports; Culture One under Gorbachev and early Yeltsin did not return the Kurils; even the most liberal politicians in Russia oppose NATO expansion; with the exception of Abkhazia and perhaps Moldova (see Lopez), Russian armed forces were invited into the foreign territories in question.

Finally, Russia has done far less than it could have done to effect a turn away from the West. For example, it continues down the road of International Monetary Fund (IMF)-mandated economic reform; it is a weak democracy, according to Lopez; it has not responded with even the merest hint of the use of military force with respect to the twenty-five million Russians living abroad; and it supports U.S. foreign policy positions on the Middle East peace process, the Koreas, nuclear nonproliferation, and arms control in general. In other words, there has been far more "self-denial" of the type Medvedev ascribes to Culture One than is perhaps appreciated.

The open question that this volume clearly asks, but necessarily only partially answers, is whether a turn toward Culture Two at home, toward nationalism to control the unruly vastness of Russia, to the ideology of *derzhavnost'* ("centralized power"), necessarily and inevitably implies an equally abrupt reconceptualization of others abroad.

1

Power, Space, and Russian Foreign Policy

Sergei Medvedev

Oak is a tree. Rose is a flower. Deer is an animal.
Sparrow is a bird. Russia is large. Death is inevitable.
—Pierre Smirnoff, *Russian Grammar,* 1897

Russia is large, larger than life, superior to a man. Apart from qualifying for the Guinness Book of Records, this geographical fact is a starting point for much speculation. The problem of Russia's enormity is traditionally welcome in a number of historical and culturological discourses; but the field of political studies often seems to neglect the amount of raw space granted to Russia and embodied in its people, politicians, and politics

This chapter is based on a presentation at the conference on Center–Periphery Relations in Russia organized by the Center for Russian Studies of the Norwegian Institute of International Affairs in November 1996 in Oslo. It is a substantially enlarged and updated version of an article titled "A General Theory of Russian Space: A Gay Science and a Rigorous Science," published in *Alternatives: Social Transformation and Humane Governance* 22 (October–December 1997): 523–54.

proper. In a humble attempt to fill this spatial gap, this chapter addresses the phenomenon of Russian space in its relation to the state authority, policy making, and foreign policy.

Space is generally considered to be a major Russian asset, but is it not also a major pain in the back? True, it shapes a "mysterious Russian soul," with its breadth and depth, its abysses, and the ideal of Madonna living side by side with the ideal of Sodom like ebony and ivory, as Dostoyevsky testified. True, Russia borrowed from Byzantium its imperial seal of a double-headed eagle with one head looking east and the other west. True, Russia, with its vastness, "cannot be embraced by mind,"[1] as Tyutchev observed, and as many have repeated for over a century as an ultimate justification for everything that happens in Russia.

The same space has prevented Russia from developing civil institutions, civic society, and the rule of law (*Rechtsstaat*)—from developing the entire concept of civility, from *civitas*, as a European fashion of development by urbanization. In Russia, there has been little necessity to settle down and work at a land plot. Endless space is forgiving and undemanding, irresponsible and undiscriminating; its human embodiment is a weak-willed and dreamy Iliya Iliych Oblomov in Ivan Goncharov's novel, a Russian archetype. If we accept the German differentiation between culture and civilization, space is about culture, not civilization. Russia has good literature and bad roads. To paraphrase a Russian saying, space is like a suitcase without a handle: it is not too easy to carry, but it would be a shame to throw it away.

RUSSIAN SPACE AS A BURDEN

Russia's territory is not just quantitatively vast, it is qualitatively infinite, amorphous, and contradictory. As pointed out by the geographers Leonid

---

1. The whole quatrain cited by Russophiles everywhere is:

> *Russia cannot be embraced by mind*
> *Or measured by common measure*
> *It is a thing in its own right*
> *One can only believe in Russia.*

A century later, the poet Dmitry Alexandrovich Prigov somewhat demystified the national symbol:

> *Papua-New-Guinea cannot be embraced by mind*
> *Or measured by a common measure*
> *It is a thing in its own right*
> *One can only believe in Papua-New-Guinea.*

Smirnyagin and Vladimir Kagansky,[2] Russia's immensity involves the follow-ing equivocal properties:

1. *Low population density.* As a result, there are difficulties in implement-ing reciprocal action, and overcoming huge distances is costly.

2. *Savage nature.* Russia is located in the northeastern corner of the Eurasian land mass. Three-quarters of its territory lies in the tundra or taiga, always in the grip of permafrost. Barely one-fifth of the territory is suitable for plowing, and one-half of this area lies in the so-called zone of risky agriculture. Nearly all the surrounding seas freeze over, and most of the frontiers are unpopulated; these frontiers run across mountains and through dense forests. Rather like the Tsar Bell that never rang and the Tsar Cannon that was never fired, Russia possesses the longest roads that lead nowhere, the greatest number of seas on which no one sails, and the longest frontiers along which no one lives and that scarcely anyone crosses.

3. *Boundless space.* Amorphous Russian space tends to spread; there are no natural limits and barriers and no single mother region (Eurasia can hardly be regarded as a single region). At the same time, although natural confines are lacking, the space is bound together by external isolation, internal repression, or both; one can speak of integration by coercion.

4. *A great polyperiphery.* Russian space is a conglomeration of periph-eries. It includes peripheries of European cultures, Mediterranean and Near Eastern Christian cultures, Near and Middle Eastern Islamic cultures, Buddhist-Mongolian culture, Chinese culture, and so on. The same is true of the ethnic and language groups represented in the Russian space and having their historical centers outside it. Even Russian nature is in a sense peripheral: the landscape of the East European plain was formed mostly during the Ice Age by glaciers from Scandinavia, and weather in most parts of Russia is defined by Atlantic cyclones and Pacific monsoons.

At the same time, Russian space is young. Elements of different and sometimes contrasting peripheries have not yet melted together into a co-hesive cultural landscape, but have been arbitrarily combined by the state. Russian space is like a suspension that has not yet settled.[3]

5. *Contrasts in population distribution.* Three-quarters of the population

2. A. Yu. Livshits, A. V. Novikov, and L. V. Smirnyagin, "Regional'naya strategiya dlya Rossii" [A regional strategy for Russia], *Region: Ekonomika i sotsiologiya* 2, 3 (1994): 32–52; Vladimir Kagansky, "Sovetskoye prostranstvo: Konstruktsiya i destruktsiya" [Soviet space: Construction and destruction], in Sergei Chernyshov, ed., *Inoe: Khrestomatiya novogo rossiskogo samosoznaniya* [The other: Anthology of the new Russia's self-consciousness], vol.1: *Rossiya kak predmet* [Russia as an object] (Moscow: Argus, 1995), 125.

3. Kagansky, "Sovetskoye prostranstvo," 125.

is concentrated in the European part of the country, which itself makes up only one-quarter of the total territory. In the other three-quarters, only one-quarter of the population lives. Most of the abundant resources for which Russia is known are situated far from the main industrial centers, mainly in the far north.

All capitals of the Russian space have been historically situated either on the western border or close to it (Novgorod, Kiev, Moscow, St. Petersburg); Moscow is twenty times closer to the western border than to the eastern. The centers and nuclei of the Russian space are essentially eccentric, almost on the frontier; the country looks like a hollow shell without a middle.

6. *The one-dimensional factor.* The developed part of the country is squeezed down toward the southern frontier and stretches west to east in a ten-thousand-kilometer-long strip. Beyond the Urals, it has barely any thickness and is situated within reach of the Trans-Siberian Railroad. As in the case of the contrasts in population density, this factor simply adds to the problem of huge distances.

7. *Geographical contradictions.* Here, contrasting qualities combine. The monotonous, low-lying settled belt is cut by great Siberian rivers and mountain ranges (such as the Urals), which make for difficulties in communications. A patchwork of nationalities (150, as proudly claimed by Soviet propagandists) once lived under the overwhelming dominance of one of them, "the most prominent."[4] A rigid monocentric culture (in the Soviet Union, over 60 percent of all economic links went by way of Moscow) coexists with traditional autonomous, distant regions. Finally, there is a disproportion in the level and nature of economic development from pre- to postindustrial.

8. *The complexity of the territorial structure.* In this area, two rules reign supreme: first, the regularity of the center–periphery relation; the concentration of life in the biggest cities; the fall in population density, economic activity, innovation, and much else—in proportion to the distance from the major centers. This distribution is particularly obvious throughout the country, but it also shows up in individual oblasts. For these reasons, the map takes on the appearance of a disorderly mosaic. Second, the medium scale is frequently lacking. It is easy enough to identify the large areas of the Russian territory, such as East or West Siberia or the Urals (macro-

---

4. Russian supremacy was proclaimed in a famous toast pronounced by Stalin to "the most prominent of all nations of the Soviet Union," to "the leading Russian people" at a dinner celebrating victory over Germany in May 1945. *Bolshevik,* no 10 (1945): 1–2.

scale). Each inhabitant knows very well the area that he or she inhabits (microscale). Areas on the middle level, however (e.g., Meschera east of Moscow, south of Vladimir and north of Ryazan; Polessie on the territories of the Bryansk Oblast of Russia, Chernigov Oblast of Ukraine, and Gomel Oblast of Belarus), are rarely known. Both factors add to the complexity of territorial organization of social life.

9. *The ossification of administrative/territorial divisions.* All forms of social life were crammed together in the confines of oblasts and republics of the Soviet Union, and regional borders were transformed into "Chinese walls." These borders are easily seen even from outer space on a good day; a network of roads opens up and changes the specialization of agriculture, and almost all borders are overgrown by thick forest.[5]

10. *A lack of spatial sense.* This notion may sound ironic in a nation living under the spell of space, but there is a relatively vague sense of distances, borders, and places. In this sense, Russia is not a utopian, but rather an *atopic* culture. In part, this vagueness is linked to the particularities of natural conditions—distances are too great, and natural boundaries are not delineated. This characteristic reconciles Russians to centralized government, and they have become accustomed to define their geographical surroundings according to administrative and territorial divisions, rather than according to historical and cultural regions, as do the majority of the world's nations. (Therefore, the prevailing global trend is *regionalism*—the emergence of historical and cultural regions—whereas the former Soviet Union tries to cope with *regionalization*—disintegration along administrative lines.) All these factors have helped Russians widen the area of their settlement but at the same time have prevented them from mastering it.

This is the basic dilemma faced by any extensive culture: the more it expands, the less it controls. A heterogeneous, diversified, paradoxical space has been, and remains, a major challenge for authorities and for authority in general. It is not just center against periphery; it is order against anarchy, cosmos against chaos, structure against entropy. According to the second law of thermodynamics, entropy prevails. Titans defeat Olympic gods, Valhalla perishes in flames.

In the Russian language, the opposition between power and space is conveyed by grammatical gender. Spatial phenomena are essentially feminine; often the word *matushka* (affectionate for "mother") is used: *zemlya-matushka* (land-mother), *Rossiya-matushka* (Russia-mother), *Volga-matushka* (the Volga is in a way synonymous to the length and breadth of Russia).

---

5. Livshits, Novikov, and Smirnyagin, "Regional'naya strategiya," 35.

This feminine line culminates (with Freudian overtones) in Alexander Blok's exclamation: *O Rus' moya, zhena moya!* ("O my Russia, O my wife!").

The attributes and locations of power, on the contrary, are never given feminine names and epithets.[6] There is an instructive difference between *rodina* ("motherland," also a common Slavic root for "family") and *otchizna* or *otechestvo* ("fatherland"). *Rodina* expresses a natural, organic, family-type belonging; *otechestvo* has overtones of citizenship and state affiliation. The incarnations of power and space into figures of father and mother, husband and wife can also be seen in the Russian rite of coronation (*venchaniye na tsarstvo*, "marriage to a tsardom"), which since the time of Ivan IV literally repeats the wedding ceremony, with the tsar symbolizing the husband and Russia the wife.

For centuries, Russian culture has identified itself with the feminine part of this dichotomy: Russian Orthodoxy is very much a cult of Our Lady, and the feast of the Protection of the Virgin (*Pokrov*) is perhaps the most "Russian" of local religious holidays. *Ewig Weibliche* was hardly attainable for a German Goethe (there is no "motherland" in German, only *Vaterland*), but it is quite identifiable in Russia. Nikolai Berdyaev wrote somewhat disdainfully on the "always womanish" in the Russian soul (O *vechnobabiem v russkoi dushe*).[7] Later in the century, the same argument was effectively used by the Germans in their *Drang nach Osten*: the manliness of the Aryan race had to subdue the soft, womanish nature of the Slavs.

Russia as a wife has always been obstinate, however, unwilling to submit to foreign invaders and native rulers alike. Napoleon's army died in the snow. Bold reformers became corrupted bureaucrats. The space is vast, amorphous, and frightening; power has to seek compromise with it. In fact, most Russian history is about the standoff, interplay, and compromise between power and space, between state and territory. Their relation is a permanent Taming of the Shrew, and much too often, Love's Labour's Lost.

In its present form, the interplay between authority and territory goes back to the mid-sixteenth century, during the reign of Ivan IV. With his conquest of the Tartar capital of Kazan, *Rus'* expanded beyond its original

6. One of the few exceptions is "Moscow, the mother of Russian cities"; but this is a common idiom used by many nations: cf. Czech *Praha, matka měst* (Prague, the mother of cities), etc.

7. Nikolai Berdyaev, "O vechno-babiem v russkoi dushe" [On the always-womanish in the Russian soul], in *Sud'ba Rossii* [The destiny of Russia] (Moscow: Sovetsky pisatel', 1990), 36–40. Originally, *baba* referred to a married, especially an older, peasant woman, and in many cases this word has a humiliating meaning, as contrasted with the neutral *zhenshina*, "woman."

confines, eastward beyond the Volga River and the Urals, and became *Russia*. The Moscow Prince became the Tsar, the Metropolitan of Moscow became the Patriarch, and the country started turning into an empire (although the term "Russian Empire" was codified almost two centuries later, under Peter the Great). At this point, an uneasy relation between the state authority and a vast, heterogeneous, and ungovernable space emerged as a key contradiction of Russian history and politics.

THE ART OF SPACE GOVERNANCE

Statecraft in Russia can thus be interpreted as authority's permanent quest for compromise with territory, with inexplicable, desirable, and unattainable Russia. Any political action, including foreign policy, has a spatial meaning, but politics is not the only field of power–space relations; the intercourse between authority and territory takes place simultaneously at several levels, including

- *The economic level.* Authority, obliged by long borders to defend, numerous neighbors to combat (until the eighteenth century, Russia had to wage two wars a year on average), and a vast territory to develop and sustain, had to withdraw a large portion of product for the purpose of controlling space. Driven by the empire's increasing military power, the state acted as a main customer of agricultural and industrial output. Through the treasury (*Kazna*) acting as a main buyer, the state directly controlled production without any necessity of worrying about the circulation sphere. The national economic model has thus emphasized producers to the detriment of merchants and relations of distribution (basically distribution in kind) to the detriment of exchange. Over the centuries, the Russian state has therefore emerged as a key economic agent, a manager of the nation's capital, and since 1917, as the legal proprietor of all this capital (on behalf of the "people").[8]

  Today, the situation remains essentially unchanged: the treasury (the federal budget) still has the responsibility of upholding distant territories

8. For an analysis of Russia's national economic model from a spatial perspective, see Vladimir Chervyakov, "The Russian National Economic Elite in the Political Arena," in Klaus Segbers and Stephan de Spiegeleire, eds., *Post-Soviet Puzzles: Mapping the Political Economy of the Former Soviet Union*, vol. 1: *Against the Background of the Former Soviet Union* (Baden-Baden: Nomos, 1995), 205–82.

and decaying industries. The space takes a heavy toll, and the hypertro-
phied role of the state prevents effective liberalization and privatization,
providing for corporatism, corruption, and the emergence of a bureaucratic state capitalism in Russia. The spatial factor, exogenous from the
viewpoint of canonical economic theory, again proves to be decisive.

The administrative level. Power tries to master space by setting up a
system of multifunctional institutional districts: *gubernias* in Russia and
oblasts in the Soviet Union. Just as the *gubernias* were originally planned
to suppress possible peasant uprisings, the Soviet administrative-territo-
rial division (ATD) was created to control Soviet space with all its "contents," to organize the operation of state institutions as well as people's
everyday lives. The spectrum of state activities (law enforcement, military
draft, ideology, education, health care, housing, day-to-day management
of local industry and agriculture) was carried out entirely on the regional
level and almost never beyond it. All state functions were concentrated
in the regions, which became focal points, vital centers, and principal
institutions of the state.[9]

This logic of administrative subordination contradicted and suppressed the natural logic of territorial relations. Instead of an organic
regional system, which respected all geographical, historical, ethnic, demographic differences and in which local communities interacted in a
natural manner, there was an artificial system of ATD in which any territorial or ethnic differences and natural interaction of localities were disregarded, and regions became functional units, agents of the universal
state. Instead of promoting unity by nature, the system imposed unity
by order that turned out to be superficial and nonresistant to future
transformations of the Soviet system. In this sense, the centralization imposed on the Soviet territory contained seeds of disunity, and today's
regionalization of Russia is a "revenge of the territory."[10]

• *The socio-political level.* The economic and territorial forms of power–
space relations combine to yield a specific Russian phenomenon of the
"administrative market." The dual alienating–distributing relation be-

9. For an analysis of the administrative and territorial structure and concepts of "bour-
geois revolution of regions," "society of regions," and phenomenology of the Soviet space,
see Kagansky, "Sovetskoye prostranstvo," 89–127; Kagansky, "Russian Regions and Territories," in Segbers and de Spiegeleire, eds., *Post-Soviet Puzzles*, vol. 2: *Emerging Geopolitical and
Territorial Units: Theories, Methods, and Case Studies* (Baden-Baden: Nomos, 1995), 49–56; Sergei
Medvedev, "Post-Soviet Developments: A Regional Interpretation: A Methodological Review,"
in Segbers and de Spiegeleire, eds., *Post-Soviet Puzzles*, vol. 2, 5–48.
10. Kagansky, "Sovetskoye prostranstvo," 92.

tween center and periphery, coupled with hierarchical subordination of territories (ATD), results in a situation in which any two adjoining levels of the administrative and territorial hierarchy are in a state of permanent bargaining (especially in Soviet times). This bargaining, which pertained essentially to the proportions between the industrial, alimentary, and raw material goods alienated from a lower level and distributed by a higher one, constituted the administrative market, another form of coexistence between authority and territory.[11]

- *The semiotic level.* Authority tries to master territory in symbolic form by producing and circulating signs of power and control.[12] Historically, the Russian Empire was a consequence of and hostage to its geography: the boundless, insuperable, and heterogeneous space lent itself not to practical (highly impractical, in fact) but rather to symbolic assimilation. The growth of Russia was not an act of economic, strategic, or metaphysical necessity—it was a spatial and symbolic act. The "Russian Empire" and the "Soviet Union" were simply words written down in the blank spaces on the map, and no one questioned whether they represented any feasible political, economic, and ethnic reality. Russia has always been a playground for nonreferential semiotics, symbolic exchange, and simulation.

These principles were elevated to a norm during the Soviet period. Authority, unable to practically control the space in accordance with ideology,

11. The concept of "administrative market" in the Soviet Union, together with the notion of "administrative currency," was developed by Vitaly Naishul' and Simon Kordonsky. See Vitaly Naishul', "Vysshaya i poslednyaya stadiya sotsializma" [The highest and ultimate stage of socialism], in *Pogruzheniye v tryasinu* [Sinking into a quagmire] (Moscow: Progress Publishers, 1991); Naishul', "Liberalizm i ekonomicheskiye reformy" [Liberalism and economic reforms], *Mirovaya ekonomika I mezhdunarodniye otnosheniya* 30 (August 1992): 35–54; Simon Kordonsky, "Nekotorye sotsiologicheskiye aspekty izucheniya khozyaistvennykh otnoshenii" [Some sociological aspects of studying economic relations], in *Teoreticheskiye problemy sovershenstvovaniya khozyaistvennogo mekhanizma* [Theoretic aspects of improving economic mechanisms] (Moscow: VNIISI, 1986); Kordonsky, "Paradoksy realnogo sotsializma" [Paradoxes of the real socialism], *Voprosy filisofii* 60 (March 1991): 75–94; Kordonsky, "The Structure of Economic Space in Post-Perestroika Society and the Transformation of the Administrative Market," in Segbers and de Spiegeleire, eds., *Post-Soviet Puzzles*, vol. 1, 157–204.

12. Jean Baudrillard, *In the Shadow of the Silent Majorities or the End of the Social and Other Essays* (New York: Sémiotext(e), 1983), 10; Baudrillard, *Selected Writings* (Stanford: Stanford University Press, 1988), 179–80. For application of the simulationist paradigm for the analysis of Soviet/Russian space, see Boris Groys, *The Total Art of Stalinism* (Princeton: Princeton University Press, 1992); Groys, *Utopia i obmen* [Utopia and exchange] (Moscow: Znak, 1993); Mikhail Ryklin, *Terrorologiki* [Terrorologics] (Tartu-Moscow: Eidos, 1992); Medvedev, "USSR: Deconstruction of the Text: At the Occasion of the 77th Anniversary of Soviet Discourse," in Segbers and de Spiegeleire, eds., *Post-Soviet Puzzles*, vol. 1, 83–120.

translated its revolutionary ambition into the symbolic sphere, deploying a self-sufficient Soviet discourse. Everything external to this discourse was driven out of life. In retrospect, the Soviet power could have written on its banners the maxim of Jacques Derrida: "There exists nothing beyond text"—because everything actually *became* text. The Soviet Union as a form of social, state, economic, and cultural organization was a space of total textuality, a purely semiotic form of relation between authority and territory.

In the post-Soviet period, especially in the mid-1990s, authority expanded resources of symbolic exchange by introducing new designators (nation, territory, religion, fatherland, heritage, historical justice, great power, national interest) that pretend to have a national, organic character but are as nonreferential as their Soviet internationalist predecessors. In other words, Russia continues to be managed by textual means. Russian space remains plain text: the Great Russian plain.

LIVING WITH SPACE:
CULTURE ONE AND CULTURE TWO

Finally, there is *a level of social anthropology*. Here one must examine specific forms of coexistence of the Russian population with space and the government's reactions. Analyzing Russian history, the nineteenth-century historians of the Russian state school observed an inherent contradiction between the population's desire to spread across the territory and efforts of authority to settle people. Sergei Soloviev described this contradiction in terms of a "habit of spread in the population" (*privychka k raskhodke v narodonaselenii*) and of government's desire "to catch and attach" (*lovit' i prikreplyat'*). Soloviev vividly depicted the inherent rootlessness of the Russians:

> In this structure of space, there are no firm houses that would be hard to abandon, that would be inhabited by generations . . . ; there is so little immovable property that everything can be carried away, and building a new house is easy because materials are cheap. . . . That is why ancient Russians so easily left their homes, their cities and villages: they escaped from the Tartars or from the Lithuanians, from heavy taxes or from a bad *voivode* [local governor] or *podyachy* [local state official]; the Russians did not mind walking along be-

cause everywhere one found the same, everywhere one could smell Russia.[13] (my translation)

Moreover, according to Vassily Klyuchevsky, spread and stopovers are not just two trends but *periods*.[14] In this sense and with a considerable degree of approximation, Russian history can be roughly interpreted as a sequence of twin cycles of spread or spillover (when space and chaos take the upper hand) and fixation or hardening (when government temporarily takes over) (see Appendix).

Periods of spread (like the late fifteenth century; the late seventeenth century, with its movement of schismatics [*raskolniki*] into the northwest; the 1860s and 70s, following the abolition of serfdom; the 1920s; Khrushchev's late 1950s and 60s, with millions going to the virgin lands of Kazakhstan [*tselina*] or to the Komsomol construction sites or joining the subculture of mass tourism; the Gorbachevian late 1980s) can be interpreted as sociospacial phenomena. Moving along becomes an act of free will, often an act of protest. The inherent Russian desire to move along the plain created a special institute of wanderers (*stranniki*) and was reflected in the novels of Andrei Platonov, which displayed the specific "strolling spirit" of the 1920s. In this context, one can speak of a specific Russian "democracy in space," like the American frontier, which expanded democracy in the United States. In Russia, however, this population spread did not contribute to democratic institutions: when people stopped (or were stopped), instead of forming local communities, they were turned into subjects of the state.

The state, for its part, sometimes tended to ride the wave of migration for the purpose of exploring and developing new lands and even institutionalized it as a state service (cf. the institution of Cossackdom, used to protect the southern and eastern borders of Russia from the Great Steppe or to explore Siberia and the Far East [the expeditions of Yermak Timofeevitch]; Peter Stolypin's policy of support to peasants moving to Siberia in the early twentieth century; or the 1950s *tselina* movement). More often than not, however, the Russian state tended to settle its subjects in control-

---

13. Sergei Soloviev, *Istoriya Rossii s drevneishikh vremen* [The history of Russia from ancient times], 7 (Moscow: Nauka, 1962), 46. The idiom "it smells of Russia" (*Rusiyu pakhnet*), originating in the folklore and taken up by Russian literature (cf. Gavrila Derzhavin's *dym otechestva* ["the smoke of fatherland"]), appears to be important for a culture lacking a spatial sense. Russia is so immeasurable and plain and there are so few landmarks that it is better smelled than seen.

14. Vassily Klyuchevsky, *Sochineniya* [Works], vol. 4 (Moscow: Nauka, 1958).

lable units, like landlords' estates, or on controllable administrative (not historical or cultural!) territories, like *gubernias* in Russia and oblasts in the Soviet Union. There is a striking similarity in the language of the Council Code of 1649 establishing full serfdom in Russia; the decrees of Peter the Great forcibly bringing people to St. Petersburg for its construction; and the laws of the Supreme Soviet in the 1930s, instituting the granting of residence permits by local authorities (*propiska*).[15]

The tendencies of spread and settlement can be further described as horizontality and verticality, centrifugal force and centripetal force, spill-over and crystallization, femininity and masculinity (see above), heterarchy and hierarchy of Russian space, Russian chaos and Russian cosmos. In a study undertaken in the mid-1970s, the architect and designer Vladimir Paperny made an impressive attempt to project this dichotomy onto the history of Soviet architecture and of Soviet culture at large.[16] He called the culture accompanying the period of spread *Culture One* and that corre-sponding to the period of settlement *Culture Two* and argued that the for-mer ruled between the 1917 revolution and approximately 1930 and the latter from the early 1930s to the mid-1950s.

Following a simple yet effective method devised by the German art his-torian Heinrich Wölfflin in his work on Renaissance and Baroque art,[17] Paperny unraveled his theory of two cultures by constructing binary opposi-tions. Thus, Culture One is about *beginning*, and Culture Two is about *end*. Culture One imagines that it stands at the origin of history and looks into the future; therefore, it is often futuristic (as in the 1920s) and technocratic (in the 1920s and 1960s). It thoroughly abolishes the past: in the 1920s, in a zealous attempt to eradicate the legacy of tsarism, it also intended to "throw away from the ship of modernity" all Russian classical culture, in-cluding Alexander Pushkin, Leo Tolstoy, Peter Tchaikovsky. Characteristi-cally, after the 1917 revolution, together with private property, the right of heritage was abolished in the Soviet Union.[18]

15. In today's Moscow, the practice of *propiska* is being revived by the mayor Yuri Luzhkov; most Muscovites readily welcome this move.

16. Vladimir Paperny, *Kultura dva* [Culture Two] (Moscow: Novoye literaturnoye obozren-iye, 1996). For the interplay of "horizontal" and "vertical" in Russian architecture, see I. E. Grabar', *Istoriya russkogo iskusstva* [History of Russian art], vol. 3 (Moscow: Knebel, 1912), 5–199.

17. Heinrich Wölfflin, *Renaissance und Barock* [Renaissance and baroque] (Munich, 1907).

18. Cf. Nikita Khrushchev's battle with the cult of personality and his promise of a radiant future in 1960: "The present generation of the Soviet people will live under Communism." The official propaganda prognosticated the coming of Communism in the Soviet Union in 1980. For an extensive analysis of Culture One of the Khrushchev period, see Petr Weil and

Present at the creation, Culture One is about improvisation and innovation; its element is fire. It is interesting that in the postrevolutionary decade the institution of inhumation and cemeteries in general were regarded as too conservative and were replaced by cremation. In fact, not only human bodies but many material objects of the old culture (books, pianos, antique furniture) were burned as firewood in small stoves (*burzhuiki*) during the fierce winters of 1918, 1919, and 1920. Alexander Blok, who in his revolutionary poem "The Twelve" beatified "world fire in blood," saw the peasants on his estate burn his own library.

Rejecting corporeality and burning material embodiments of the old culture (including human bodies) for the sake of the future have a long tradition in Russian history. In the seventeenth century, schismatics known as *raskolniki* were forced, after the 1654 schism in the Russian church, to move to the virgin forests of the Russian Northeast where they led a sectarian life, anticipating the Second Coming. At times, the *raskolniki* thought that the Second Coming was so near that they stopped sowing and mowing, did not care about food, and, wearing white gowns, slept in coffins. Pursued by government troops, many sects ended in self-immolation (see the finale of Modest Mussorgsky's *Khovanshchina*): over twenty thousand people burned themselves in the end of the seventeenth century alone! In these fires, the schismatics proved an essential Russian archetype (which probably has much to do with traditional Russian masochism): modernization through self-denial, a suicidal spurt into the future.[19]

On the contrary, Culture Two, with its specific feeling of the end, preserves things for eternity. When Lenin died in January 1924, his body was placed in a temporary wooden sarcophagus in Red Square in Moscow for those thousands of people who wanted to mourn him. Later, the body was embalmed, and better wood was used for the sarcophagus; finally, the newly arrived Culture Two built a mausoleum of granite and marble over Lenin's body in 1930. This story is one of gradual hardening and settlement, culminating in conservation (and glorification) of the body, in preservation of history.

Alexander Genis, *60e: Mir sovetskogo cheloveka* [The 1960s: The world of the Soviet Man] (Moscow: Novoye literaturnoye obozreniye, 1996).

19. N. I. Kostomarov, *Ocherk domashnei zhizni i nravov velikorusskogo naroda v XVI i XVII stoletiyakh* [Study of the domestic habits and ways of the Great Russian people in the 16th and 17th centuries] (St. Petersburg: Tipografia Karla Wolfa, 1860); P. N. Milyukov, *Ocherki po istorii russkoi kultury* [Essays in the history of Russian culture], vol. 2 (St. Petersburg: M. O. Wolf, 1897), 67–69; A. I. Klibanov, *Narodnaya sotsial'naya utopia v Rossii: Period feodalizma* [Popular social utopia in Russia: The period of feudalism] (Moscow: Nauka, 1977).

In Culture Two, hardening and imprinting occur simultaneously with construction; it tries to immortalize itself instantly. The first line of the Moscow metro was opened in May 1935, and by June a book entitled *How We Built the Metro* was out of print: this achievement is remarkable in light of the publishing capacities of the 1930s. A great number of books published in the 1930s and 1940s start with the word "How" and commemorate the acts of Soviet power: *How We Rescued the Icebreaker* Cheliuskin, *How We Flew over the North Pole.*[20]

The obsession of Culture Two with history (the main book of the period was Stalin's *Brief Course of History of the VKP[b]*[21]) culminates in the idea of Rome. The idea of Russia as Rome, an ultimate empire and God's city on earth, haunted the rulers of the country since the early sixteenth century when the monk Philotheus proposed that Moscow was the third Rome (the first two being imperial Rome and Constantinople) as the basis for an ideology for expanding the Grand Duchy of Moscow.[22] In another period of Culture Two, Catherine the Great invited Giacomo Quarenghi and other Roman architects to St. Petersburg to crown her glorious reign in architecture. In the 1930s, Soviet architects again sought to follow the spirit of imperial Rome (the neoclassicism of Ivan Zholtovsky), and the writer laureate Alexis Tolstoy was sent by the Soviet government to the Eternal City to write the novel *Rome*. Rome is a symbol of Culture Two: all roads lead there, and history ends there; Rome terminates time and, most important, space.

The end means loss of motion. Another binary opposition analyzed by Paperny is *movement and immobility*,[23] reflecting cycles of spread and settlement in the Russian space. People of Culture One are permanently on the move; they are restless, rootless, and socially active. After the revolution, communes became popular (at least, people were squeezed into communal flats); the ideas of free love, communal wives, and communal children found many followers. Private cooking was replaced by public catering. Citizens enjoyed greater freedom of movement, and no passports were

---

20. Paperny, *Kultura dva*, 45–46.

21. VKP(b) stands for the All-Union Communist Party (of the Bolsheviks).

22. In a 1511 letter to the Grand Duke Vasily III, the monk Philotheus (Starets Filofey) wrote: "And now, I say unto thee: take care and take heed, pious Tsar; all empires of Christendom are united in thine, two Romes have fallen, and the third exists, and there will not be a fourth." Cited in Dimitri Strémooukhoff, "Moscow the Third Rome: Sources of the Doctrine," *Speculum* 28 (January 1953): 84–101. See also Iver B. Neumann, *Russia and the Idea of Europe: A Study in Identity and International Relations* (London and New York: Routledge, 1996), 7.

23. Paperny, *Kultura dva*, 60–71.

needed for travel inside the country. Architects experimented with ideas of deurbanization and movable houses; some designed individual "shell houses" that could be moved by trains or ships along with their dwellers. The Swiss-born architect Le Corbusier found a fertile ground for his functionalist theories in Soviet Russia. Among other projects, he erected an office building "on legs" on Myasnitskaya Street in the center of Moscow: the general impression was that the building had "walked in" from somewhere.[24]

From 1930 on, the Soviet authorities began to limit people's mobility. First came decrees of the Supreme Soviet aimed at controlling labor fluidity; in 1932, passports were reintroduced; in 1937, passport photos became obligatory; later the same year, personal files and labor books were introduced for each employee in the country, and these exist until now. In 1938, the Supreme Soviet passed a law taking away passports from peasants. Leaving the kolkhoz became a criminal offense, which could entail death (a stipulation more severe than pre-1861 serfdom in Russia).[25] According to another law of January 1941, employees faced trial for being over twenty minutes late to work. These laws, along with the introduction of *propiska*, local residence permits, firmly fixed people to their farms, factories, and places of residence. During the same period, streets in medium and small cities were paved with asphalt (a symbolic conquest of soil/land/territory), and fences were built around Le Corbusier's structure in Moscow to conceal its provocative "legs" and to anchor the building in the cityscape.[26]

Culture Two makes no difference between cities, buildings, and people: all are subjects of the state and must be fixed in space. Peter the Great not only built new cities (Azov, Taganrog, St. Petersburg), but also ordered people to live there, not only virtually enslaved workers, but even the higher classes. During the construction of St. Petersburg, Peter issued ordinances that forced the nobility to leave their homes and estates and to build houses in the new capital.[27] Later, the tsar demanded that houses be

24. Paperny, *Kultura dva*, 66–67.
25. Passports were returned to *kolkhozniks* only during Khrushchev's "thaw."
26. In the same manner, Russian villagers still put boxes under their beds or drape their bed legs: furniture, like houses, should grow directly from the land (or from the floor).
27. A Soviet anecdote from the 1930s tells of a Party activist sent to the countryside to organize a kolkhoz. After several days, he sent a telegram reading: "The kolkhoz is organized. Send in the farmers." Another anecdotal dialogue from the later Soviet period: "Can we build a Swedish model of socialism in the Soviet Union?" "Of course we can, but where can we find so many Swedes?" As with St. Petersburg, we see a purely semiotic approach to reality (which Baudrillard called a "precession of the model"): first comes an abstract institution, a

built of stone, not wood (an analogue to the Lenin mausoleum), and that they should "conform to architecture." Buildings that were not in accordance with "architecture" were to be torn down.

Architecture in Russia is largely a function of authority and a phenomenon of Culture Two. Power seeks to bring everything into conformity and to mark its subjects, and their dwellings, with signs of belonging to the state. Architecture is essentially a spatial art (it exists in three dimensions) and therefore is a political, not a private, issue, a manifestation of authority. In 1839, the Marquis de Custine, a critic of old Russia, described the Moscow Kremlin thus: "Art does not have a term to characterize the architecture of the Kremlin. The style of its palaces, prisons, and cathedrals is neither Moorish nor Gothic, neither Roman, nor even purely Byzantine. The Kremlin does not have a prototype; it is like nothing in the world. It bears an imprint of, so to say, architecture of the Tsarist style" (my translation).[28]

The third binary opposition is *horizontal and vertical*: a flat horizontal territory against vertical institutions of authority. In Paperny's analysis,[29] horizontal intentions of Culture One mean spread beyond the borders, not only beyond conventions and social barriers but also beyond state boundaries, a spatial impulse translated into greater openness and internationalization of the system. In Russia, horizontal periods of Culture One are accompanied by feelings of backwardness and inferiority and by looking to the West for examples. The reforms of Peter the Great, driven by his vision of Russia as the "new Holland," resemble Khrushchev's call to "catch up and overtake America" or Gorbachevian westernization.

On the contrary, Culture Two builds a vertical state in national limits and seeks to curb foreign contacts. As if fighting with boundless space, it is particularly sensitive about borders. In 1934, the Supreme Soviet passed a law making the escape of a Soviet citizen abroad a capital crime. From the social sphere (a conflict between the proletariat and the bourgeoisie), the border between good and evil moved into the geographical sphere and coincided with the state frontier: Good was inside the Soviet Union, and

---

form, and only afterward authority fills it with human contents. In fact, the entire Russian space can be interpreted as an ideal form, an intention of authority—but people have not yet been sent in.

28. Marquis de Custine, *Nikolayevskaya Rossiya* [Russia under Nicholas I; original title *La Russie en 1839*] (Moscow: Izdatel'stvo vsesoyuznogo obshchestva politkatorzhan i ssyl'noposelentsev, 1930), 210.

29. Paperny, *Kultura dva*, 72–99.

evil was outside.[30] Correspondence with abroad was restricted and thoroughly inspected: it could take several months or a year for bureaucrats in the Soviet secret police to decide whether a letter from abroad should be delivered to an addressee. In some cases, inspectors returned the letter to the sender with inscriptions like "Of no interest for us"[31] if they did not discard it altogether. The same xenophobic attitude was extended to foreign languages (in the 1940s, foreigners felt uncomfortable speaking their native languages in public) and even to foreign alphabets. In 1929, the declining year of Culture One, Central Asian states could switch from Arabic to the Roman alphabet, but ten years later, Culture Two made them change into the Cyrillic alphabet.

Finally, there is a dichotomy between *even (homogeneous)* and *hierarchical*. Culture One seeks to return things to their primordial spatial condition and fights any economic, social, or territorial hierarchy. In conformity with the Communist ideology in its basic form, the postrevolutionary reforms were aimed at equally sharing land in the villages among peasants and at sharing dwelling space in the city. One of the first decrees of the Soviet power in March 1918 expropriated the so-called apartments of the rich; by Lenin's definition,[32] which followed that of Friedrich Engels,[33] in these apartments, the number of rooms exceeded or equaled the number of residents. In other words, no one was entitled to a room of his or her own. This decree initiated the infamous Soviet institution of communal apartments in which every room was occupied by one (sometimes more than one) family, and which brought the principle of spatial homogeneity into everyday life.

The same principle was applied on the municipal level; for instance, an attempt was made to redraw the historical circular structure of Moscow. Traditionally, the upper class dwelled in the center of the city, inside the boulevard ring, the middle class in a larger garden ring, and the lower classes in the outskirts. The new authority tried to move the proletarians into luxurious central apartments, but because the factories were in outer districts, workers had to undergo long commutes to work.

30. This is an interesting parallel with Ronald Reagan's rhetoric about the Soviet Union as the evil empire.

31. Paperny, *Kultura dva*, 83.

32. Vladimir Ilyich Lenin, *Polnoye sobraniye sochinenii* [Complete works], 5th ed., vol. 54 (Moscow: Politizdat, 1975), 380.

33. Friedrich Engels, *Sochineniya* [Collected works], vol. 18 (Moscow: Politizdat, 1965), 239.

Just as Culture One opposed the hierarchy of places, it did away with the hierarchy of people. First, it "undressed" people and stripped them of all social marks, status symbols, grade, and rank. In most areas of the state service, uniforms were abolished. Schools abolished marks; in fact, there were no longer humanitarian, vocational, or military schools—only comprehensive secondary education. Universities did not require attendance or entrance and graduation examinations and issued no diplomas. After death, citizens were equal; all were entitled to the same civil funeral. Even Lenin's body and brain were submitted for scientific examination after his death in 1924 like those of ordinary citizens: culture had not yet made the leader sacred.

From the early 1930s, however, the hierarchy of places and people made a gradual comeback. An instructive case was the hierarchy of cities. Traditionally, as in any monocentric culture (e.g., Paris in France), Moscow occupies a focal place in Russian mythology, as epitomized by the yearning call "To Moscow! to Moscow!" in Anton Chekhov's *Three Sisters*. In the 1930s, this special role of Moscow, far exceeding that of a national capital, was administratively sanctioned by Culture Two through the institution of passports and residence permits. Passports were initially introduced in Moscow, Leningrad, and Kharkov; those living in Moscow could live everywhere in the country; those in Leningrad could live everywhere except Moscow; and those in Kharkov everywhere except Moscow and Leningrad. People from the rest of the country could not live in those cities without obtaining a special permit from the authorities.[34]

Later, this hierarchy was extended to the capitals of the union republics and to oblast centers (in the countryside, passports were taken away), so that by the late 1930s, the entire population of the Soviet Union was settled in territorial cells of the administrative hierarchy. A person registered in Minsk (capital of the republic of Belorussia) could move to live in Gomel or Vitebsk (oblast centers), but not to Moscow or Leningrad. Soviet court sentences included formulas like "minus three," "minus ten," "minus forty," meaning the prohibition to live in Moscow, Leningrad, and Kharkov (and within a one-hundred-kilometer zone outside these cities), in the republican capitals, in the oblast centers, and so on.[35] The hierarchy of places in Culture Two thus implied the hierarchy of people, in which the "good" were living in the centers and the "bad" on the periphery.

---

34. A joke from the 1930s divided the Soviet population into three categories: those living in Moscow, those on their way to Moscow, and those dreaming of living in Moscow.

35. Paperny, *Kultura dva*, 110.

Simultaneously, other forms of the status hierarchy were reintroduced, starting with entrance examinations in the universities in 1933 and marks and uniforms in schools in 1935. In 1934, academic degrees were established, together with the titles of Hero of the Soviet Union and Master of Sports; in 1935, the military ranks of major, colonel, and marshal were returned; the title of People's Artist was instituted in 1936, and the Stalin Prize in 1941.

Culture Two completely codified people and places, turning the Russian territory into a space of total etiquette. In this sense, the Soviet civilization of the period of Culture Two can be compared to other highly codified cultures like the Jewish or the Chinese, which created strict rules for all occasions in life. Thus, we read in the Mishnah that on Saturday night a tailor must not go out with a needle; in the Book of Rituals, it is written that a guest must drink the first glass with a serious look and the second one with a respectful and happy face. The same strict etiquette can be found in Soviet practices. During Lenin's lifetime and later in the 1920s, names of members of the Politburo were listed in alphabetical order, but starting from Joseph Stalin's fiftieth birthday in December 1929, his name appeared first and was followed by the others in alphabetical order.[36] In the same manner, lists of literature in Soviet academic works, defying rules of the alphabet, strictly followed ideological etiquette. First came Marx and Engels, then Lenin, then the incumbent general secretary of the Communist Party of the Soviet Union and Politburo members, then Russian authors in alphabetical order, and finally names in unwelcome Roman typeface.

By the same token, rules of applause at Party congresses and meetings were codified: junior Politburo members were met by "long applause," middle rank were greeted by "stormy applause," top people deserved "long stormy applause; everyone rises to their feet," and the general secretary got "long stormy applause turning into an ovation. Everyone rises to their feet and shouts 'Hooray! Long live our leader comrade Stalin!' " These ritual formulas were reproduced by newspapers over decades; the tradition continued with Nikita Khrushchev and Leonid Brezhnev, in the 1980s under Yuri Andropov, Konstantin Chernenko, and early Gorbachev. It seemed as fundamental as the cobblestone in Red Square.

One morning in 1987, the country woke up to read the newspaper tran-

---

36. Abdurakhman Avtorkhanov, *Tekhnologia vlasti: Protsess obrazovaniya KPSS: Memuarno-istoricheskiye ocherki* [Technology of power: Process of formation of the CPSU: Memoirs and historical essays] (Munich: Isdanie tsentral'nogo ob'edineniya politicheskikh emigrantov iz SSSR, 1959), 156.

script of the previous day's plenary session of the Central Committee and found the usual italicized remarks missing. There was plain ("horizontal") text of Mikhail Gorbachev's speech, but it was no longer marked by *applause, stormy applause,* or *shouts* that would provide clues for correct interpretation. The general secretary was not greeted by a *standing ovation* (at least the paper did not say so), and the singing of the "International" was not reported. The country was puzzled, bemused, disturbed. The signal system suddenly did not work; the usual codes were falling apart. Then it all started.

PERESTROIKA AND BREAKUP
OF THE SOVIET UNION

It is fascinating to trace the interplay of Cultures One and Two during the last decade, from 1987, the first year of perestroika (before 1987, the official name for Gorbachev's reform was "acceleration"[37]) to the present. In a remarkable compression of history, Russia has undergone a full cycle of power–space relations in only ten years, from spatial chaos of the late 1980s and early 1990s to post-Soviet restoration of the mid-1990s, with corresponding changes in domestic and foreign policies.

Perestroika was essentially a Culture One phenomenon: horizontal, open (glasnost was also translated as "openness"), destroying all hierarchies. Black government Volgas (Soviet executive automobiles) were scorned on Moscow streets; Boris Yeltsin was once spotted going to work on a trolley. As restrictions were progressively removed, a horizontal civil society started to emerge: in fact, in 1987–91, the Soviet/Russian civil society, as well as the free press, had had their day and are eventually fading away in post-Soviet Russia. The population enjoyed greater social and territorial mobility, and all barriers to emigration were removed on the Soviet side (tragically, some years later, we have seen the other side of this mobility, with millions of migrants and refugees escaping from Chernobyl, civil wars, and genocide). The ultimate acts of Culture One were the destruction of the Soviet Union in 1991 (with the subsequent ban on the Communist Party), of the socialist economy through shock liberalization and

---

37. Mikhail Sergeevich Gorbachev, *Perestroika i novoye myshlenie dlya nashei strany i dlya vsego mira* [Perestroika and new thinking for our country and for the whole world] (Moscow: Politizdat, 1987).

privatization in 1992, and finally, of the institutions of the Soviets in 1993. Gods were dislodged, and the old world of all things Soviet was engulfed in flames.

The Soviet/Russian foreign policy of perestroika was essentially a Culture One phenomenon: innovation at the cost of breaking with the past. It was fundamentally opportunistic, aimed at rejecting old values and structures. Gorbachev's "new thinking" was very much about the denial of the ideological confrontation of previous decades, especially of the late 1970s and early 1980s. As for Russian foreign policy, it originated as a semiclandestine enterprise, with Andrei Kozyrev and a few aides sitting for several months in almost complete isolation in a small mansion in Moscow's Prospekt Mira representing the foreign ministry of a virtual state, which was Russia in 1991. It took the August coup, the Belovezhskaya Pushcha agreements, and the breakup of the Soviet Union for Russia to become a full state and for Kozyrev to move into the Ministry of Foreign Affairs high-rise on Smolenskaya Square—but the Russian foreign policy of the early 1990s carried on this somewhat conspiratorial and revolutionary spirit born during the months of opposition and neglect. As if contesting the image of the late Soviet Foreign Minister Andrei Gromyko who was for several decades a "Mr. No" for the West[38] and even outdaring his successor Eduard Shevardnadze, Andrei Kozyrev became a "Mr. Yes" in the years 1991–93.

In the spirit of Culture One, the foreign policy of the Gorbachev and early Yeltsin periods was largely improvised. Improvisation started as early as November 1986, at the Reykjavík summit, when Mikhail Gorbachev and President Ronald Reagan struck an unexpected deal on strategic arms limitation and started a decade of major arms control agreements. In general, improvisation was largely due to the "personal" style of big politics introduced with the new Soviet "openness" and egalitarian flair of Culture One. One of the most important decisions of the decade—the reunification of Germany in the summer of 1990—was reached in the same improvisational and personal manner: Mikhail Gorbachev invited Chancellor Helmut Kohl to his native town of Stavropol where he took his guest for a walk along the small streets filled with childhood memories; later, the two went by helicopter to a distant mountain residence. As testified by aides, there was virtually no talk about the future of the North Atlantic Treaty Organization (NATO) and the Warsaw Treaty, about economic guarantees and military aspects of

38. Gromyko's role in endorsing the leadership of Mikhail Gorbachev at the April 1985 plenary session of the CPSU Central Committee should not be forgotten; he proposed and advocated his candidacy and oversaw a peaceful transfer of power from the old guard to the new guard.

reunification; this deal was between two friends, involving little analysis and legal commitments (once again, a feature of Culture One, which disregards documents). Later, the role model of "friend Mikhail" was inherited by "friend Boris," who enjoyed a personal relationship with "friend Bill" and "friend Helmut."

Interesting parallels to this improvisatory and personal superpower relationship are to be found in the previous period of Culture One, in post-Stalinist Soviet foreign policy, during Nikita Khrushchev's "thaw" and the first détente. Following the Geneva Soviet-American summit in July 1955, Khrushchev strongly adhered to the spirit of Geneva where he looked into the eyes of President Dwight Eisenhower and unilaterally withdrew Soviet troops from Finland and China, signed a peace treaty with Austria, and cut down the size of the army. Leonid Brezhnev, known for his sentimentality, also tried improvisational diplomacy during the summit with President Richard Nixon in June 1973. In Nixon's San Clemente residence, he stayed in a small room prepared for Nixon's daughter. After a day of negotiating, late in the evening, he knocked at Nixon's door, presented a handmade scarf for Nixon's wife, and proposed to talk in full candor to reach a solution on the Middle Eastern problem.[39]

Improvisation in Soviet and Russian foreign policy of the late 1980s to early 1990s, its spatial magnitude (the unification of Germany, withdrawal from Eastern Europe and Afghanistan, shifts in the Russian position on the Kurils during the early Yeltsin administration, etc.), and a somewhat lighthearted and playful, if not altogether irresponsible, manner of decision making had much to do with a specific feeling typical of Culture One. This foreign policy was aimed at the future, which looked like a liberal utopia in the spirit of Francis Fukuyama's end of history. The inherent utopian zeal of Russian culture found a perfect (yet unintentional and accidental) match in Fukuyama's millenarian phraseology and theories of "democratic peace." The ultimate goal of late Soviet foreign policy was joining the community of the civilized nations (or returning to the civilized world); for early Russian foreign policy, it was strategic partnership with the West.

In terms of traditional Russian culture, especially Culture One, achievement of a utopian goal requires a sacrifice. All Russian modernizations and revolutions, including perestroika and the anti-Communist revolution of the late 1980s–early 1990s, also involved sacrifice, not simply a rejection of

---

39. Richard Nixon, *The Memoirs of Richard Nixon*, vol. 2 (New York: Warner Books, 1978), 429–31.

the past, but a passionate self-denial. Against this cultural background, a radical change in Soviet/Russian foreign policy of the period can be interpreted as a willful sacrifice. Some concessions were inevitable (Afghanistan, arms control); the Soviet Union, and later Russia, got rid of the unbearable burden of being a superpower for economic reasons. In many cases, however, the Soviet Union/Russia gave up more than the West expected (a hasty reunification of Germany, voluntary withdrawal from the Middle East, refusal of support for leftist movements in Central America and Communist parties all over the world, retreat from the arms markets in Eastern Europe and in the Third World, etc.). This result was not a strategic retreat, but a ritual sacrifice, a passionate gesture of self-denial. This ascetic line of Russian foreign policy was summarized in Andrei Kozyrev's repeated pronouncement that Russia has no national interests as such—a statement that can also be interpreted as relinquishment of personal identity for the sake of common salvation, in this case, for the sake of the utopian harmony of democratic peace.

Yet another trait of Culture One was a horizontal, egalitarian approach in late Soviet and early Russian foreign policy, as symbolized by the idea of a "common European home."[40] Treating all subjects of European politics as equals, this political design denied the old Yalta–Potsdam hierarchy of European states and, instead of vertical structures of domination, offered a horizontal mode of cooperation. The most important change occurred with respect to East European countries; in a way, the common European home was intended to replace the "Brezhnev doctrine," but a gradual reform of Soviet imperial rule was cut short by instant East European revolutions.

In this failed attempt of reform, the strategic goal of the "common European home" was preserving socialism in Eastern Europe by adding to it democratic and European features. In fact, this goal was a belated variation on the theme of socialism with a human face and the ideas of the 1968 Prague Spring; in a sense, the "common European home" was rooted in the idealism and historical optimism of Culture One of the 1960s. (During his postgraduate years at the law school of Moscow University in the mid-1950s, Mikhail Gorbachev was a roommate and friend of the Czech student Zdenek Mlýnař, who was to become one of the architects of the Prague Spring.)

The same horizontal intentions of Soviet/Russian foreign policy of the period can be found in the so-called Burbulis doctrine, named after Boris Yeltsin's close counselor in the first year of his presidency. This doctrine

---

40. In Soviet texts, *dom* was translated as a welcoming "home"; mainstream Western political discourse favored a more cautious "house."

implied refusal of direct control over the neighboring states and resulted in the creation of the Commonwealth of Independent States (CIS); in calls to join the European Community (EC) and NATO, quite popular in Russia in 1991–92; and in far-reaching Soviet and Russian proposals for the Conference on Security and Cooperation in Europe (CSCE) and enthusiastic support of the Paris Charter for the New Europe. President Gorbachev's idealist globalism as summarized in his United Nations speech in December 1988 was not reiterated by his successors.

Summing up, many elements in Soviet/Russian foreign and domestic policy in 1987–92 can be ascribed to the influence of space and to a specific horizontal mentality in decision making. When Boris Yeltsin, running for the Russian presidency in June 1991, told Russia's regions to take as much sovereignty as they can digest, he was saying this to the entire Russian space, calling it back into existence. Apart from emancipation of the Russian space proper, this trend spilled beyond the borders of the Soviet Union, removing structures of Soviet domination in Eastern Europe and other regions of the world.

Emancipation of space involved not only the liberation of East European states and Soviet republics; it was the comeback of territory as a principle, of its inherent cultural, ethnic, and social diversity. The policy of perestroika was largely based on a vague romantic idea (once again, in the spirit of the Prague Spring): unleashing chaotic forces of space ("natural" or "healthy" forces, in Gorbachev's lexicon), and putting them to the service of a socialist state. These forces turned out to be as ungrateful as a Prague golem. Once brought to life, they turned against their creator and devoured the state that was supposed to control them.

POST-SOVIET RESTORATION

There was a certain social and economic logic behind the emancipation of space. A number of groups in the Soviet state and society, the territorial agents of the administrative market (regional and local elites, in some cases ethnic, clannish, and tribal groups), and its functional agents (elites in branches of the economy) had accumulated a certain administrative status that they sought to convert into private property and political power. They pursued vertical mobility, a chance to upgrade their status, to break out of the rigid political and administrative hierarchy of the late Brezhnev period.

These regional and economic elites, largely supported by the so-called Soviet middle class (up to thirty million of qualified labor force in major cities who also sought to convert their educational, professional, and cultural assets into a higher social and economic status[41]) became the political army of perestroika and Culture One. The emancipation of space in the late 1980s–early 1990s was largely their work, and their chance to remove Brezhnev's antiquated feudalism, with its Party, Soviet, KGB, and economic mechanisms of control. In an atmosphere of innovation and mobility, they had an opportunity to enhance their status by getting access to property, rights, and political power.

In fact, many of them did. In the course of illegal (1987–91) and legal (1992–93) privatization of the Soviet economy, there were more losers than winners, but those who won (e.g., the financial sector, the oil and gas sectors, resource-rich regions like Tatarstan and Yakutia, the city of Moscow) became fully licensed proprietors of functional and territorial fragments of space. (At the end of the day, this phenomenon turned out to be *privatization of space*, because certain elites obtained full rights of property in their respective territories with all their contents including natural and human resources.) This process was mostly finished by 1993. Newly acquired property had to be protected against further redistribution. From 1993 onward, there has been an ever-increasing quest for stability in Russia.

Responding to this quest, authority once again attempted to control space. As much too often in Russian history, this meant reconstructing the hierarchy. Something in the optics of Russian space, and Russian mentality, makes authority believe that control means command and that building a territorial and administrative hierarchy is the only way to deal with space. Over centuries, a strong state in Russia has always meant a strong vertical, and this paradigm has never been called into question.[42]

According to the local logic, the hierarchy starts from the top, not vice

41. Andrei Fadin, "Modernizatsiya cherez katastrophu? (Ne bolee chem vzglyad)" [Modernization by catastrophe? (Just a point of view)], in Chernyshov, ed., *Inoe*, vol. 1, 325–27.

42. E.g., for Stephen Krasner a "strong state" means something completely different: "[T]he power of the state [is] in relation to its own society. This power can be envisaged along a continuum ranging from weak to strong. The weakest kind of state is one which is completely permeated by pressure groups. Central government institutions serve specific interests within the country, rather than the collective aims of the citizenry as a whole. . . . At the other extreme from a state which is completely permeated by political pressure groups is one which is able to remake the society and culture in which it exists; that is, to change economic institutions, values, and the pattern of interaction among private groups" (Stephen D. Krasner, *Defending the National Interest: Raw Materials Investments and U.S. Foreign Policy* [Princeton: Princeton University Press, 1978], 57, 60).

versa. The territory had to see a strong man in the Kremlin. A display of power followed in late September and early October 1993, when President Yeltsin disbanded the parliament, the parliamentary opposition took to the streets of Moscow, and the showdown culminated in President Yeltsin moving in tanks and bombarding the parliament. The walls of Jericho came tumbling down, and the reaction was almost unanimous relief. A large part of the intelligentsia praised the long-awaited solution in collective letters of support. Within one month of the shelling of the Russian White House, regions that had been reluctant to pay taxes for the last two years resumed their payments into the federal coffers. The wheels of Culture Two started moving.

By the mid-1990s, a new Byzantine symphony between the church and the state had been re-established, somewhat short of creating a holy synod, like that in imperial Russia. According to the original plan, canceled at the last minute, the inauguration of the re-elected Boris Yeltsin in 1996 should have taken place in the Cathedral Square of the Kremlin, like the coronation of Russian tsars. Rebuilding churches destroyed by the Soviets has become a matter of state priority. The institution of army chaplains has been reintroduced.

In the meanwhile, Russia rediscovered its symbols of statehood. The ideology of Great Russia now uniting democrats, Communists, and nationalists has become a basic legitimization of the new regime. Ideas of Great Russia are projected both externally and domestically, above all, to the Russian territory, denouncing Yeltsin's take as much sovereignty as you can digest. Although war in Chechnya had practical and down-to-earth reasons (oil, drugs, arms transfers, misappropriation of budgetary funds), its main legitimization was indivisible federal Russia. A new hierarchy of spaces has been born, this time based not on administrative rank, but on resources under local control (e.g., resource-rich Tatarstan and Yakutia-Sakha have special privileges).

In architecture, the new hierarchical ambitions of Culture Two are materialized by the new favorite of authority, the architect Zurab Tsereteli and his multimillion-dollar-worth and multihundred-meter-high monuments in Moscow, like the Monument of Victory on Poklonnaya Hill and the Monument to the Three Hundredth Anniversary of the Russian Navy (note the ideological context of both). In the district of Krasnaya Presnya, Moscow City is being built, with a number of high-rises to accommodate expanding businesses. The private architecture of the new rich, or New Russians, also reaches for the skies: in a display of wealth, people build three-, four-, or even five-floor country homes with elevators. Even more characteristically, their roofs are crowned with towers and spires, like Disneyland castles. The new hierarchy requires splendor and architectural dominance.

The culture in general now has all the features of Culture Two. Gone are the polycentrism and multiculturalism of the late 1980s and early 1990s. The inflow of money in Moscow once again makes it a cultural capital, despite a bitter financial crisis in late 1998. St. Petersburg is marginalized in the national cultural context, following the decay of the city's economy. The Russian culture of the late 1990s, tired of both rediscovering the Russian avant-garde of the 1910s and 1920s and of playing postmodernist games,[43] has developed a feeling of the end typical of Culture Two. Fin de siècle stylistics and bohemian decadence (fueled by a dramatic growth of drug abuse) become trendy. In contrast to repudiating all things Soviet in 1987–92, the past is now looked at with much warmth. This is not a conceptualist look of *soz-art*, but rather "this is our past and we don't have to be ashamed of it." The new ideology is indiscriminate about the past: the new Moscow monuments include busts of all Russian tsars, a statue of the Soviet marshal Georgi Zhukov, sculptures of the antiestablishment poets Sergei Yesenin and Vladimir Vysotsky; and a recent critically acclaimed biography of Stalin by Edvard Radzinsky (also screened as a television series) presents a fairly balanced perspective of this ruler, which would have been totally unimaginable just several years ago.

During Yeltsin's 1996 election run, Russian public television unraveled a high-quality social advertising campaign entitled The Russian Project. In short clips featuring favorite Russian actors, simple life situations were shown, concluded by a plain moral: "This is my city," "Everything will be OK," "Mother, don't cry," "Take care of love." These intelligent advertisements carefully conveyed feelings of stability and continuity (implicitly connected with the figure of Yeltsin), bringing peace and order, a basic hierarchy of values into the hearts and souls of the electorate.

A POWER IN SEARCH OF THE PAST

Finally, one must consider *new "vertical" trends in the Russian foreign policy*. These have emerged on a symbolic and ideological level, where Russia

43. Symptomatically, a brief and stormy period of Russian literary postmodernism, nourished by the underground conceptualism of the 1970s and 80s (Ilya Kabakov, Dmitri Alexandrovich Prigov, Vladimir Sorokin, et al.), and peaking in the late 1980s and early 1990s, seems to be almost over, giving way to the Culture Two-type "new sentimentalism" among many

turned from a horizontal policy of dissolving its own identity in the liberal environment of Western institutions to a vertical approach of constructing identity by elevating national values in foreign policy. This trend started in 1993 and was greatly accelerated by a landslide victory of nationalist and patriotic forces, including Vladimir Zhirinovsky's Liberal Democratic Party, in the December 1993 parliamentary elections. In the wake of the elections, one of the principal conditions of political stabilization (including amnesty to the leaders of the October 1993 riot in Moscow and the Treaty of Public Accord signed in March 1994) was the incorporation of national-ist discourse in the lexicon of authority.

The unifying ideology of the regime has thus become a moderate na-tionalism, but also something transcending nationalism: the ideas of *derz-havnost'* (aspirations of a strong state and a great power status). Although the ruling elite was initially reluctant to use this term for fear of too openly sounding like the former opposition, *derzhavnost'* finally became the basic legitimization of the new Russian regime. *Derzhavnost'* can be interpreted as a call to create a strong, paternalist, and to some extent expansionist state. Rather than nationalism, this ideology is a return to a traditional Russian form of legitimacy characteristic of the tsarist and Soviet periods, in which the idea of a strong state replaces that of a nation and the state is situated above society.[44]

Derzhavnost' has become a common foreign policy denominator for mainstream politicians (with the exception of uncompromising democrats like Yegor Gaidar, Konstantin Borovoy, Boris Fedorov, Valeria Novodvor-skaya) as well as major elites. An instructive example was the evolution of Andrei Kozyrev in 1993–95. Kozyrev sought to follow the national-interest consensus and tried to play on Zhirinovsky's field, but was considered too pro-Western and was replaced in the wake of the 1995 parliamentary elec-tions by Yevgeny Primakov, a figure much more appealing to *derzhavniki*. Indeed, Primakov's policy of national interests in 1996–98 won him the support of the Duma and propelled him to the post of prime minister in September 1998.

As far as elites are concerned, even liberal groups have drifted toward the nationalist side of the political spectrum. One can speak of a certain

---

former conceptualists (e.g., Timur Kibirov). Referring to the well-known battery advertise-ment ("they keep going, and going, and going"), the critic Vyacheslav Kuritsyn ironically commented on this new development, "*Energizers* of the postmodernist bunny have become critically low."

44. Thomas Graham, "Novyi rossiyski rezhim" [The new Russian regime], *Nezavisimaya gazeta*, 23 November 1995.

disillusionment in the Culture One idea of cooperation with the West among liberal elites. It has yet to be decided who (if anyone) is to blame for this—the West, which did not live up to the challenge to devise a strategy of engaging Russia comparable to the Marshall Plan; Russia itself, which could not create even an acceptable, let alone favorable, normative environment for Western investment; or the uniqueness of Russian space, Russia's *Sonderweg*, which prevented large-scale and long-term cooperation and application of models successfully used elsewhere. Whatever the answer, by 1994, even the most ardent advocates of systemic cooperation had to recognize that the West "had lost Russia,"[45] or, like Mikhail Leontyev, that the liberal period of 1991–93 "had ended in the defeat of the West that had almost completely missed the opportunity of a 'soft' integration of Russia into the Western world and placed the political forces in Russia, that had been counting on the Western perspective, in the position of political outsiders."[46]

The public, too (to the extent that common people care about foreign policy), has become skeptical. A total of 72 percent of today's respondents link Russia's dramatic production slump and the decline in its standards of living with the attempts to emulate Western economic practices. This segment of the voters believes that Russia has its own road to take, whereas 75 percent of the population say that this country can do without Western assistance altogether.[47]

In short, *derzhavnost'*, as a typical Culture Two phenomenon, is a vertical axis of the new Russian foreign policy. It is the construction of identity by distinguishing itself from the other, attributing the role of the other to the West.[48] In the mid-1990s, Russia's national interests are largely formulated by seeking points of divergence with the West. (Of course, some of Russia's interests converge with those of the Western states, e.g., certain aspects of

45. Viktor Kremenyuk, "Teryaet li Zapad Rossiyu" [Is the West "losing" Russia?], *Nezavisimaya gazeta*, 1 December 1995. "The potential positions which the West had had in Russia after the breakup of the Communist regime disappeared one after another without being realized. In general, an opinion emerged in Russia, that its readiness to open up frontiers and the society by changing economic and political regimes and to become an integral part of the modern world was coldly received in the West and that the only thing the West is seeking is to bring it down to the level of a regional power without its own say in decisions on global matters." See also Galina Sidorova, " 'Prezumptsiya vinovnosti' i 'osobost' Rossiyi" ["Presumption of guilt" and the "specialness" of Russia], *Nezavisimaya gazeta*, 3 December 1994.

46. Mikhail Leontyev, "Teni stabilizatsii nad tenevym gosudarstvom" [Shadows of stabilization over the shadow state], *Segodnya*, 6 January 1995.

47. Stanislav Kondrashov, "Elections Won't Change Foreign Policy," *Passport to the New World* (January–February 1996): 27.

48. See Chapter 2 in this volume.

arms control, but the very concept of national interest in post-Soviet Russia was nourished by anti-Western rhetoric.)

The first year of such conflict-type construction of foreign policy identity was 1994. Despite a number of cooperative endeavors (Russia's participation in the Naples Group of Seven [G-7] summit, joining NATO's Partnership for Peace), Russia for the first time in many years refused to join the coordinated Western stance and pursued its own policy in Bosnia, Iraq, the Middle East, and in the CSCE Minsk Group on Nagorno-Karabakh. It also went ahead with rocket engine sales to India despite multiple protests from the United States. Tension built up for the whole year and resulted in the near-complete diplomatic isolation of Russia at the CSCE/ Organization on Security and Cooperation in Europe (OSCE) summit in Budapest in December 1994. Failing to get any of its proposals adopted, Moscow blocked the resolution against the Bosnian Serbs. The same thing happened several days later during the vote on sanctions against the Kraina Serbs in the United Nations (UN) Security Council: for the first time since the late 1980s, Moscow used the right of veto.

The advent of Culture Two, ideas of *derzhavnost'*, and assertion of Russia's national interests have had an impact on most areas of Russian foreign policy. *In the "near abroad,"* there has been a rather sharp transfer from the Burbulis doctrine mentioned above to a more interventionist policy, euphemistically called by Sergei Karaganov an "enlightened postimperial course." This new policy, presupposing an open projection of Russia's interests and power in the CIS and aimed at partial reintegration of the post-Soviet space, was stated in President Yeltsin's address to the UN General Assembly in October 1994 and one year later, in the presidential directive "On Russia's Strategic Course with the CIS Countries." If in the early 1990s Russia was rather apathetically and reluctantly involved in Abkhazia, Transdnestria, and South Ossetia, escalation of the conflict in Tajikistan in 1994 prompted a more resolute military action from Russia. By the same token, although the conclusion of a "contract of the century" to develop the Tenghiz oil fields in Kazakhstan by a consortium of Western companies in 1992–93 passed almost without Russia's involvement, a similar deal by Azerbaijan to develop the oil shelf of the Caspian Sea in 1994–95 caused heated protests from the Russian Foreign Ministry and attempts of power pressure on Azerbaijan.[49]

---

49. In fact, Russia participates in the Caspian oil consortium, but it was the *Lukoil* company that obtained a 15 percent share in it, not the state structures. This was a point of conflict between Lukoil and the Foreign Ministry.

After a horizontal dissolution of the Soviet Union, Russia now attempts to recreate a hierarchical vertical of post-Soviet space. Efforts at post-Soviet reintegration were facilitated by a comeback of ex-Communist leaders in some CIS states in the summer of 1994 (Leonid Kuchma in Ukraine, Alexander Lukashenko in Belarus), a weakening of the national-democratic popular fronts that have become mostly oppositional (in Moldavia and Azerbaijan), the emergence of new concepts of reintegration (Eurasian Union of the Kazakh President Nursultan Nazarbaev), the consolidation of Russian diasporas in the "near abroad" (e.g., in North Kazakhstan), and a number of other factors.

Among many elements of this new course were the announcement of new Russian military bases in Transcaucasia, a forward defense strategy in Tajikistan, undercover arms supplies to Armenia, conclusion of a favorable treaty with Ukraine in May 1997, which seems to solve the Black Sea Fleet issue and to guarantee Russia a dominant strategic position in Sevastopol for the next twenty years, and the conclusion of a union treaty with Belarus the same month (and its ratification by the Russian Duma in June 1997), which stops short of forming a confederation. As a result, a new Russian hegemony and hierarchy of reintegration emerge in the post-Soviet space, with Russia as a center, Belarus as a "small brother," Kazakhstan, Kirgizia, and Armenia in the first circle of integration, Ukraine (as a whole, or part of it), Georgia, Azerbaijan, and Moldova in the second circle, and Uzbekistan, Tajikistan, and Turkmenistan as its most remote components.[50]

At the European front, horizontal and liberal intentions of the common European home and strategic partnership with the West have been replaced by a more realistic (and Realist) perspective.[51] Because of economic crisis, political instability, and sheer size, Russia is not likely to join the European Union (EU) or NATO "early or at all" (as stated in the 1995 NATO Enlargement Study). Consequently, idealist concepts of integration (Culture One) gave way to principles of damage limitation, which can be interpreted as a Culture Two phenomenon.

Damage limitation emerged in 1993–96 as a compromise between the political ambitions of the new regime (*derzhavnost'*, etc.) and the Western-dominated economic environment in which it exists and on which it is

50. See the theses of the Council for Foreign and Defense Policy: "Will the Union Revive in 2005?" in *Nezavisimaya gazeta*, 23 May 1996.

51. As a matter of discussion, Culture One can be associated with a Liberal Internationalist perspective, and Culture Two with a Realist perspective.

dependent. According to this argument, Russia should act to protect its own interests and to minimize the alleged negative effects of Western policies while remaining in the general framework of dialogue with the West on security issues and using all available institutional mechanisms, first of all the OSCE. As seen in Moscow, damage limitation is based on four pillars:

- Unsentimental and realistic cooperation with the West.
- Limiting the alleged effects of expansion of Western institutions.
- A better differentiation among Russia's foreign policy partners both in the West and in Central and Eastern Europe.
- Consolidating Russia's leadership in the post-Soviet area (see above); the decline of Russia's European engagement should be offset by increased engagement in the "near abroad"; a popular argument goes that "the European policy of Russia is carried out primarily in the CIS."

Damage limitation is a strategy that postpones Russia's European engagement. Underlying this argument is a long-term strategic consideration aimed at the new European balance of the twenty-first century. Russia, currently in a phase of geopolitical and economic decline, must prevent the fixation of this unfavorable status quo by any treaty, agreement, or security system. Russia is objectively interested in maintaining the current uncertain and unstructured security arrangement that took shape in Europe in the wake of the Cold War as long as possible—preferably until the economic upsurge in Russia expected by the middle of the next decade. Russia is therefore instinctively opposed to any institutional upgrade of European security, NATO enlargement included; it would prefer to see European security not as an institution, but as an open-ended process (much like the former CSCE: hence the current impact of Moscow on the OSCE) and would like to dissolve it in various pan-European collective security proposals, reminiscent of old Soviet designs of the 1930s

Damage limitation can thus be seen as yet another period of Russia's concentration (but this time not isolation) and increased awareness (but not hostility) in relations with the West typical of Culture Two, as yet another stop on its endless way into Europe (see Fig. 1.1).

Finally, dealing with the *Third World and China*, Russian foreign policy, in the spirit of Culture Two, turns to old allies and modes of engagement in world affairs. Slowly returning to the Middle East, developing relations with Iraq, reinforcing military and technical cooperation with India and Southeast Asia, making a steady comeback to the global arms markets, and,

Figure 1.1   Russia on the way into Europe.

most important, proclaiming a strategic partnership with China (a striking change from the early 1990s, when for the democratic leaders in the Kremlin post-Tiananmen China was synonymous with Communist authoritarianism) are to a certain extent acts of reconstruction of the Soviet foreign policy from the period of superpower rivalry.

Building links to the past, asserting Russia as the heir to a great power, and using historical arguments for legitimization of Russia's rights (e.g., in the Balkans) create a feeling of continuity and unity in foreign policy. If the foreign policy of Culture One was fixed on the romantic liberal future (the end of history), the foreign policy of Culture Two is fixed on the past, recreating and celebrating history.

CONCLUSION: BETWEEN THE SWIMMING POOL AND THE CHURCH

One of the ultimate symbols of Culture Two and the current reassembly of Russian space is the reconstruction of the Church of Christ the Savior in the center of Moscow. Its story is captivating and instructive. In the beginning there was a swamp: a marshy, low place some half a mile from the Kremlin upstream from the Moskva River called Devil's bog (*Chertovo boloto*). On this place, it was decided to build a church consecrated to the Russian victory over Napoleon in 1812. The task was accomplished in 1832–83, the project of Konstantin Ton, and the Church of Christ the Savior stood as one of the biggest churches in the Orthodox world. After the revolution of 1917, it became an unwanted symbol, and one of the last ritual acts of Culture One was the destruction of the church in 1931, along with hundreds of other churches and historical monuments in Moscow, as part of the "Plan of the General Reconstruction of the City." The place was cleared for the greatest construction in history, the Palace of the Soviets, which was to become the highest building in the world—eight meters taller than the Empire State Building, crowned with a one-hundred-meter-high statue of Lenin. Culture Two had to immortalize itself in a vertical structure symbolizing and subjugating the entire Russian space and built strictly in the hierarchical canon (the palace was to consist of several tiers, with each one taller than the preceding one).

The construction never went beyond the basement level: unlike the granite of Manhattan, the boggy low place would not hold the enormous structure. Other reasons cited were the lack of metal and fears that Lenin's statue would be almost permanently obscured by clouds. (These are all practical explanations, but in the highly impractical terms of Culture Two, the palace was so ideal and sacral that it could not be built in reality. In iconoclastic terms, the palace was so symbolically intensive as to prevent its material embodiment, and its construction was unnecessary; in a way, the Palace of the Soviets *has been* built. It still stands in the center of Moscow, rising proudly above the clouds. Whoever believes in it strongly enough can see it.)

With the death of Stalin, the project was abandoned, and the newly arrived Culture One with its horizontal and egalitarian intentions built in its place an enormous swimming pool: a pure triumph of space and entropy, a return to primordial protoplasm, apotheosis of the elements. History makes a full cycle, however, and with another advent of Culture Two in the mid-1990s, the swimming pool was destroyed as an impious symbol, and the Church of Christ the Savior was reconstructed on that very place. The president of Russia, the prime minister, and the mayor of Moscow supervised its construction. The Second Temple is due to be finished in 1999.[52]

This story seems symbolic if not archetypal. Above all, it tells the sad truth that Russia is doomed to a vicious cycle of change between destruction and construction, Culture One to Culture Two, determined by cycles of expansion and hardening in space. In general, the binary paradigm seems unavoidable in Russia. In his late work *Culture and Explosion,* Yuri Lotman identified Russia with a cultural form for which binary structures

52. Following the logic of change between Cultures One and Two and the metaphor of Jewish history, the Second Temple will be ruined as well. In its place, triumphant Chechens will build a mosque, and Russians will be left with a Wailing Wall by the Moskva River (Sergei Medvedev, "Svyato mesto pusto . . ." [The holy place is empty . . .], *Nezavisimaya gazeta,* 15 January 1997).

are typical.[53] A binary way of thinking, imaginary alternatives (but, in fact, the ultimatum nature of the either–or choice) considerably narrow the political and cultural choices for Russia. Furthermore, according to Lotman, binary structures are doomed to settle conflicts by way of catastrophes; their extreme components are preprogrammed for mutual destruction, for the demolition "to the basement." Transition from the old to the new is perceived in the explosive terms of binaryism.[54]

This observation of Lotman adds a further perspective to the problem of Culture One and Culture Two. A change of paradigms often involves ideal deconstruction and physical destruction of the preceding culture: the First Church of Christ the Savior, the ground level of the Palace of the Soviets, and the swimming pool were all consecutively demolished, but there is a difference. Culture Two is about the end and eternity, and at a certain point it begins to care about preservation. On the contrary, Culture One is about the beginning and the future; it implies an uncompromising break with the past and a suicidal rush toward the future.

Many periods of Culture One turned out to be destructive and incurred heavy human losses: Peter the Great's reforms; the postrevolutionary decade and Stalinist collectivization of agriculture; and finally, the breakup of the Soviet Union, which caused ethnic violence, wars, and impoverishment of a large fraction of the population. The ultimate symbol of Russia's Culture One are seventeenth-century schismatics, *raskolniki*, dying in self-immolation, in a radical Russian utopia, a rush to the future through self-denial. The same spirit can be found in the revolutionary millenarianism of the 1910s and 20s, and, in a weaker form, in the mentality of perestroika, as well as in the Soviet/Russian foreign policy of the period that resulted in the demise of all structures of Soviet domination in the world (the Warsaw Treaty, the Council for Mutual Economic Assistance [COMECON], the Soviet Union proper, national liberation movements, and Communist parties in the Third World), and of all physical signs of a superpower.

In this sense, modernization in Russia (Peter the Great, Stalin, the pe-

53. Yuri M. Lotman, *Kultura i vzryv* [Culture and explosion] (Moscow: Gnozis, 1992), 257–60.

54. "The process that we witness can be described as switching from the binary to a ternary system. However, one cannot but notice the peculiarity of the moment: this transition is being understood in the binary sense. In practice, two possible ways are being worked out. One of them, which had led to Gorbachev's loss of power, lay in substituting reforms by declarations and plans and leading the country into a dead end fraught with the most gloomy forecasts. The other one, which expressed itself in various plans like 'five hundred days' or other projects for the fast transformation of the economy, is aimed at 'curing like by like,' at curing explosion by explosion" (Lotman, *Kultura i vzryv*, 264–65).

riod of 1987–92) almost always takes the form of a catastrophe: it denies
the past, the existent material culture, corporeality proper. Andrei Fadin
calls the period of 1991–92 an attempted variant of a "modernization by a
catastrophe,"[55] of hitting the bottom to get the energy of a breakthrough
(this line of development has been terminated by post-1993 Yeltsin's "restoration"), a description that perfectly fits the cultural history of Russia.

Why is radical modernization that would preserve the material culture
of the past, like the Meiji modernization in Japan, not possible? The answer, perhaps, is the same Russian space, its extensive nature, as compared
with intensive space in Japan. The vastness and amorphous nature of Russian space, "in which there are no firm houses" (Soloviev), together with
the lack of spatial sense among the population mean the lack of practical
sense and reason. The space contributes to the inherent irresponsibility of
decision making in Russia, as reflected in a popular saying: "It is easier to
knock things down than to build them up" (*Lomat'—ne stroit'*). In fact,
Russian space possesses a great destructive potential, and Culture One simply releases and sublimates it. A perpetual choice between Culture Two
and Culture One is a choice between dictatorship and anarchy, binding by
force and destroying by force, between the authoritarianism of power and
the ruthless vigor of space, a snowstorm in the steppe.

APPENDIX:
Russian History in Twenty-Two Periods, with an End

Acknowledgment: The author hates any systematic discourse and binary op-
positions; however, the temptation of squeezing Russian history into a strict
scheme like Mendeleev's periodic table was irresistible. This is not history
as a rigorous science, but rather a glass bead game on the themes of Russian history.

Years	Culture One: Horizontal (Spread, spillover)	Culture Two: Vertical (Hardening, structuring, fixation)
1480s–90s	Nil Sorsky, "nonseekers" (*nestyazhateli*).	
1500–1520s		Council of 1503: victory of Joseph Volotsky. Conquest of Pskov and Smolensk, growth of the Moscow state. Ideology of

		Moscow the Third Rome. Construction of brick wall around the Kremlin.
1530s–50s	Political turmoil. Infant Ivan IV, Yelena Glinskaya, riots and fires in Moscow. Early reign of Ivan: The Chosen Council, reforms, looking at the West. Russia spreads beyond the Volga: capture of Kazan.	
1560s–90s		Ivan after Kazan and coronation: "Grozny." Conquest of Tver. *Oprichnina.* Terror. Construction of St. Basil's, white stone and earthen walls around the Kremlin. 1589—Installation of Patriarchate.
1600–1613	Instability after Grozny. 7 boyars, Godunov, Poles and Lithuanians, fire of Moscow in 1611; irregular troops of Minin and Pozharsky.	
1613–1650s		Council of 1613, installation of the Romanov dynasty. Increasing stability under Mikhail and Alexei, a powerful hierarchy, Naryshkin baroque.
1650s–70s	1654—schism of the church. *Raskolniki* (schismatics) spread over northeastern Russia, fires, self-immolation, Avvakum, *Khovanshchina.*	
1680s–1700s	Popular movements precede the shock of Peter the Great. Reforms of early Peter. Russia spreads in the west and south, fights wars. New cities (St. Petersburg, Azov, Taganrog).	
1710s–20s		Late Peter. Russia turns into empire (1721). Church is part of a new state as a holy synod. The Table of Ranks:

		codification of civil service. The origins of the Russian bureaucracy. Ordinances to build with stone in St. Petersburg.
1730s	Catherine I, Anna, and the rule of Biron. The inflow of Westerners.	
1740s–50s		Elizabeth—new state hierarchy. High baroque of Rastrelli (Smolny monastery, Winter Palace, Peterhof Palace). Lomonosov and Barkov.
1760s–70s	Early Catherine II, "the Northern Semiramis," correspondence with Voltaire and Diderot, enlightened reforms.	
1780s–90s		Late Catherine, high Russian absolutism, imperial grandeur.
1800–1825	Paul I (mason and Knight of the Maltese Order), Alexander I, spirit of enlightenment, plans of reform, Speransky. Napoleonic wars, Moscow fire in 1812, popular mobilization. Russia moves into Europe, Cossacks roam in Paris, young officers smell Europe and decide to reform the Russian monarchy: 1825 December uprising.	
Late 1820s–1850s		Coronation of Nicholas I and the Decembrists' trial (1825–26). "The dark years of reaction." Professionalization of Russian literature.
1860s–mid-1880s	Alexander II: reforms. Abolition of serfdom, judicial reform. Egalitarian trends in the educated classes, People's Will (narodovoltsy), nihilists, Chernyshevsky. Continued under early Alexander III.	

Mid-1880s, 90s and early 1900s		Alexander III since mid-1880s: a turn to conservative ways. Oppression of the revolutionary movement, industrial revolution reaches Russia: peasants move to factories and settle there. Imperial trends of Nicholas II.
Early 1900s	Emergence of egalitarian, deconstructivist, horizontal trend in Russian popular movements (workers' socialism, social democracy) and art (avant-garde, futurism). Revolution of 1905.	
1917–1920s	Popular Culture One culminates in revolutions of 1917 and postrevolutionary decade: egalitarianism and communes, abolition of heritage, class, rank, diplomas, school marks; mass migrations due to wars, famine, etc.; mass emigration until 1922; avant-garde, futurism, constructivism, deurbanism in architecture.	
1930s–mid-1950s		The Soviet Union between late 20s and mid-50s: the acme of Stalinism and triumph of Culture Two. *Gesamtkunstwerk* Stalin. Centralized state socialism. Final settlement of the Soviet people in administrative regions and cities (institution of *propiska*). Emergence of strict hierarchy of spaces and people. Deification of the leader. Socialist realism, "grand style," Palace of the Soviets and Moscow skyscrapers.
Late 1950s–early 1970s	Khrushchev and early Brezhnev: fighting the past, Stalinism, and the cult of the personality. 20th Party Congress. Population starts to move across the territory: prisoners return from	

Gulag, youngsters go to Siberia
to develop new territories, build
railroads (Baikal–Amur
Railway), or as tourists. Gagarin
in space. Looking at the West:
1957—the Moscow Youth
Festival, Khrushchev's desire to
"catch up with and overtake
America." Massive cheap
housing construction.

Mid-1970s–mid-1980s		Mature Brezhnev: "feudal socialism," "stagnation," new socialist baroque. The era of ceremonies and jubilees. Strict rules of social etiquette. In literature and art, epic prevails over lyric. By late 70s, détente gives way to confrontation with the West: Afghanistan, Moscow Olympics, euromissiles. Attempts of Andropov to further harden the regime: labor discipline, etc. Early Gorbachev's antialcohol campaign, although he was to become a man of a different culture.
1986–1991	Gorbachev: "acceleration" and perestroika. Unleashing the forces of space, greater social and territorial mobility, including unprecedented emigration. Honeymooning with the West: "new thinking," "common European home," Nobel prize. Fighting the party hierarchy, preparing the new union treaty ("the Novo-Ogarevo process"). Emergence of civil society and free press, the winds of change. Breakup of the WTO, CPSU, Soviet Union.	
1991–1992	Early Yeltsin: continuation of horizontal trends. Fighting communist structures and	

soviets, letting Russia's regions
"take as much sovereignty as
they want to." Gaidar's reforms:
destruction of the socialist
economy. 1993—abolition of
the soviets.

1993–???

October 1993—a watershed.
Post-Soviet restoration. New
authoritarianism, new verticals.
Derzhavnost'. Great Russia.
National interests. War in
Chechnya. Presidential
elections and "Tzar Boris." New
bureaucratic hierarchy. Culture:
feeling of the fin de siècle.
Architectural verticals: new
Moscow monuments, houses of
the "new Russians."
Reconstruction of Church of
Christ the Savior: the Second
Temple.

The End of History:
Not with a bang, but a whimper.
(T. S. Eliot, "The Hollow Men")

2

Beyond Neorealism and Constructivism

Desire, Identity, and Russian Foreign Policy

Henrikki Heikka

> I remind you of the famous statement of Pascal that
> the history of the world would have been different
> had Cleopatra's nose been a bit shorter. How do you
> systemize that?
> —Hans Morgenthau, "International Relations:
> Quantitative and Qualitative Approaches"

> If Cleopatra's nose changed the course of the world,
> it was because it entered the world's discourse, for
> to change it in the long or short term, it was
> enough, indeed, it was necessary, for it to be a
> speaking nose.
> —Jacques Lacan, *Écrits*

Understanding the change in the basic orientation of Russian foreign policy from the initial pro-Western liberalism prevalent during 1991–92 to a more assertive postimperialism in the following years provides one of the most interesting puzzles related to East–West relations in the post–Cold War era. Was the change an unavoidable return to normality caused by socialization to the system, as neorealists would claim, or was it caused by a

Previous drafts of this chapter have been presented at seminars at the University of Helsinki, the University of Tampere, the Finnish Institute of International Affairs (UPI), and the 1996 ISA Conference in San Diego. For helpful comments and advice, I am grateful to Tuomas Forsberg, Ilkka Heiskanen, Ted Hopf, Vivienne Jabri, Raimo Lintonen, Sergei Medvedev, Renée de Nevers, Heikki Patomäki, Christer Pursiainen, Wynne Russell, Helena Rytövuori-Apunen, Mike Shapiro, Christine Sylvester, as well as two anonymous reviewers.

less deterministic sequence of interaction where changes in the social structure of Russian-Western relations led to changes in the identities and interests of the actors and resulted in a situation that could have been avoided, as constructivists would argue? The answers for these questions are significant both for Western decision makers trying to formulate the most efficient policies for dealing with Russia in the future and for scholars of international relations assessing the relative merits of different theoretical approaches.

In this chapter, I argue that both neorealism and constructivism provide inadequate guides for explaining the development of post–Cold War Russian foreign policy, because their theoretical presumptions ignore the relation between the dialectical nature of subjectivity and the variables that drive the causal mechanisms implied by the theories. An alternative approach, integrating psychoanalytic identity theory with discourse analysis, is offered to provide a methodology for analyzing the relation between national identity construction and conflictual ("predationist") definitions of interstate relations. The methodology is then used to analyze a proposal for a new Russian grand strategy and to show that psychoanalytic theory can help us understand—and deal constructively with—the anti-Western-ism inherent in "enlightened patriotist" discourse.[1]

The argument of the chapter proceeds through three steps. First, to highlight problems in explaining the change in Russian foreign policy as socialization to the system, I look at the origins of neorealist theory and show that the possibility of understanding the role that the dialectic of identification plays in the construction of political order is stifled in neorealist theory by Kenneth Waltz's attempt to interpret Jean-Jacques Rousseau and Sigmund Freud—on whom Waltz relied in constructing his "third-image" theory—by means of a social ontology that contradicts Rousseau's and Freud's dialectical ontology. This misinterpretation, I argue, leads neorealists to treat dilemmas of international security as consequences of anarchy instead of following Rousseau and Freud in tracing the causal roots to

---

1. In this chapter, I do *not* make definitive causal claims about the relation between, on the one hand, Russian foreign policy behavior, and, on the other hand, the immensely complex topic of national identity in Russia. I simply suggest, first, that in theory such a relation necessarily exists and that without a dialectical understanding of identity we can neither understand that relation nor deal effectively with the problems it poses, and, second, that Lacanian psychoanalysis can help us gain a deeper understanding of that relation—especially the role of extreme nationalism in it—than contemporary constructivist theories permit. A comprehensive causal narrative on the subject would have to deal with hundreds of texts, as well as include an inquiry into the domestic struggle between competing blueprints. Such an analysis is obviously beyond the scope of one chapter.

the interplay of identification processes, which connect all three levels of Waltz's analysis. This ontological conflation, I conclude, forces neorealists to interpret as "normal" changes that are actually driven by perceptions of self–other relations.

Second, I argue that attempts to explain Russian foreign policy through a constructivist theory of identification are questionable because the theory's causal claims rest on a modernist account of agency, which omits the tension between identity and representation in the development and decentering of the self.[2] By *modernism*, I refer to the philosophical and cultural project that became the central theme of thinkers of the Engligtenment during the eighteenth century. A modernist account of agency presumes an essential self—a self-conscious locus of true subjectivity— whose existence as an ontological category is not questioned. An alternative account of the emergence of the self in human development, based on Jacques Lacan's psychoanalytic theory, is offered to show that the self as a linguistic representation is not the original self, as constructivism suggests, but the result of a cultural process by which the first understanding of the self, constructed through visual identification, becomes subordinate to the covenant of representation and to the basic rules on which social and political order is based. Lacan's theory is then used to open up the black box of agency in constructivist international relations theory and to construct a methodological toolbox for analyzing the cultural origins of nationalism and threat perceptions and their relation to the innermost desires and fears of modern selves.

Finally, relying on the framework developed in my critique of Waltz and Alexander Wendt, I show that the causal origins of an anti-Western construction of Russian national interests can be traced to cultural identification processes and discursive strategies rather than to current Russian-Western interaction or to the structure of international relations. In a case study on the thinking of Sergei Kortunov, a prominent Kremlin strategist working on Russian national security policy, I analyze the logic that leads him from the search for a national idea in Russian philosophy and litera-

2. The term *decentered self* ("decentered subject") refers to the ontological assumption that human consciousness does not have a stable point of true subjectivity, where the *I* or the *self* is located. In this chapter, the concept is used in the Lacanian sense, which implies that the self is a product of a continuous identification process, in which subjects seek to gain an identity by taking signifiers ("I," "liberal," "female," "rationalist," etc.) as their representative, while creating a loss ("lack-of-being"), which remains outside the expressive potential of systems of representation, which in turn arouses the desire for ever more alienating identifications. See Lacan, "The Agency of the Letter in the Unconscious or Reason Since Freud," in *Écrits* (New York: Norton, 1977), 146–78.

ture to enlightened patriotism and a tough geopolitical realist vision of foreign policy. The anti-Westernism inherent in Kortunov's enlightened patriotism, I conclude, is not so much a reaction to Western actions or to the structure of the international system as it is a symptom of a discursive structure where the split inherent in identity based on representation is displaced to the Western other to rescue the fantasy of an organic Russia from its own impossibility. The article closes with a digression into Dostoyevsky's meditation on the problem of theodicy and suggests that Kortunov's anxiety about the fate of Russia may be better solved through a Dostoyevskyan interpretation of the Russian idea (one where the split signifying one's alienation is assumed as representative of the self) rather than by drastic changes in Western policy or in the organizing principles of the international system.

NEOREALISM, CONSTRUCTIVISM, AND RUSSIAN FOREIGN POLICY

Stories in Western publications about the evolution of Russian foreign policy in the post–Cold War world are surprisingly uniform in content.[3] According to the prevailing narrative, the initial phase of Russian foreign policy, characterized by a more or less unqualified Westernism, was called into question during 1992 by eurasianist, moderate-conservative, and pragmatic nationalist views. In the second phase, a minimum consensus was reached with the adoption of the new foreign policy conception of the Russian Federation in spring 1993. The beginning of the third phase of Russian foreign policy is usually timed around the parliamentary crisis of October–December 1993, which is viewed as polarizing the foreign policy

---

3. See, e.g., Alexei Arbatov, "Russian Foreign Policy Thinking in Transition," in Vladimir Baranovsky, ed., *Russia and Europe: The Emerging Security Agenda* (Oxford: Oxford University Press, 1997), 135–59; Neil Malcolm and Alex Pravda "Introduction," in Neil Malcolm, Alex Pravda, Roy Allison, and Margot Light, *Internal Factors in Russian Foreign Policy* (Oxford: Oxford University Press, 1996), 21–25; Richard Sakwa, *Russian Politics and Society* (London: Routledge, 1996), 275–80. Leon Aron, "A Different Dance: From Tango to Minuet," *National Interest*, no. 39 (Spring 1995): 27–37; Leszek Buszynski, "Russia and the West: Toward Renewed Geopolitical Rivalry?" *Survival* 37 (Autumn 1995): 104–25; Alexei K. Pushkov, "Letter from Eurasia: Russia and America: The Honeymoon's Over," *Foreign Policy* 93 (Winter 1993–94): 76–90; Bruce D. Porter, "Russia and Europe After the Cold War: The Interaction of Domestic and Foreign Policies," in Celeste Wallander, ed., *The Sources of Russian Foreign Policy After the Cold War* (Boulder, Colo.: Westview Press, 1996), 131–41.

debate, especially about the "near abroad," into the geopolitical realist line of moderate conservatives and the even tougher line of nationalist opposition. Later developments, such as the uniform opposition to North Atlantic Treaty Organization (NATO) enlargement and the enlightened imperialism of constructing a Russian sphere of influence, are usually seen as reflecting the dominant position of the moderate conservatives, who seek to pursue the Russian national interest in a realist fashion under pressure from the hard-line opposition.

Analysts clearly disagree, however, about explaining the causes of these developments and consequently about their long-term implications for Western states and policies. Underlying these disagreements are differing views of the origins of foreign policy behavior in general. From the various theories used by scholars to inject causality into the narrative described above, I concentrate on two well-known and politically relevant ones—neorealism and constructivism.[4]

Neorealist theory, as formulated by Kenneth Waltz, is based on the observation that the international system is anarchic by nature because it lacks a central authority. For Waltz, the imperative of survival in an anarchic environment ensures that all actors are like units—they do not perform functionally differentiated tasks.[5] From the neorealist perspective, the relationship between us and them in international relations is always stable: states that do not perceive the relation as competitive are severely punished for their idealism. The violent nature of international history in its Waltzian interpretation teaches those states that survive that their primary interest is to ensure their survival also in the future.

According to neorealism, the emergence of a tougher and more assertive Russian foreign policy was a natural, indeed, a positive, consequence of the pushing and shoving created by the structural pressures of the international system.[6] In Waltzian terms, the adoption of a realist outlook on for-

4. On the role of neorealism and constructivism in contemporary international relations theory discourse, see John Mearsheimer, "The False Promise of International Institutions," *International Security* 19 (Winter 1994–95): 5–49; Alexander Wendt, "Constructing International Politics," *International Security* 20 (Summer 1995): 71–81. The third major approach identified by Mearsheimer, neoliberal institutionalism, has so far not played a major role in explanations of post–Cold War Russian foreign policy.

5. Kenneth N. Waltz, *Theory of International Politics* (Reading, Mass.: Addison-Wesley, 1979), 88–97.

6. Waltz called this "socialization to the system." As an example of the tendency, he described how the Bolsheviks, soon after their rise to power, had to conform to the conventions of diplomacy and the rules of the game, because doing otherwise would have made it harder for Russia to achieve "working deals" with other states whom they could balance against the hegemonic powers (127–28).

eign policy can be seen merely as an acceptance of Russia's role as a great
defensive power (as opposed to the role of a global superpower or an ally
of the West), arising from the relation of its economic and technological
capabilities to those of other states.[7] From this perspective, a Western policy
of hoping for the best but preparing for the worst would be the most morally virtuous one.[8] The policy recommendations for Western decision makers, which can be derived from the analyses sharing this logic, stress the
importance of policies based on cool calculations rather than on wishful
thinking or deterministic Russophobia and remind us that peace is an effect of the balance, rather than the identity, of interests.

In contrast to neorealists, constructivists argue that the fact that the
international system is anarchic does not mean that it is a self-help system.
The central claim of constructivist international relations theory has been
summarized by Alexander Wendt in his argument that international security systems can vary between competitive and cooperative, depending on
"the extent to which and the manner in which the self is identified cogni-
tively with the other."[9] Constructivists thus maintain that the construction
of Russian national interests depends largely on how the identities of Russia and other states—for historical and cultural reasons, especially the identities of Russia and the West—relate to one another.

Examples of causal arguments about the origins of Russian foreign policy based on constructivist logic are abundant.[10] In explaining the evolution

7. Waltz, "The Emerging Structure of International Politics," *International Security* 18 (Fall
1993): 52. See also Sergei Kortunov and Andrei Kortunov, "From 'Moralism' to 'Pragmatics':
New Dimensions of Russian Foreign Policy," *Comparative Strategy* 13, 3 (1994): 261–76. Sher-
man Garnett, "Russian Power in the New Eurasia," *Comparative Strategy* 15, 1 (1996): 31–40.

8. Waltz himself leaves no room for collective identity construction between Russia and
the West: "The Soviet Union created NATO, and the demise of the Soviet threat 'freed'
Europe, West as well as East. But freedom entails self-reliance. In this sense, both parts of
Europe are now setting forth on the exhilarating but treacherous paths of freedom. In the
not-very-long run, they will have to learn to take care of themselves or suffer the consequences" (Waltz, "The Emerging Structure of International Politics," 76). See also Stephen
Sestanovich, "Geotherapy: Russia's Neuroses and Ours," *National Interest*, no. 45 (Fall 1996):
3–13.

9. Alexander Wendt, "Anarchy Is What States Make of It: The Social Construction of
Power Politics," *International Organization* 46 (Spring 1992): 399–400.

10. "Russian leaders define the 'directions and priorities' of Russian foreign policy in
light of expectations based on Russia's previous interactions with the international environment, expectations that are institutionalized in decision-making procedures as part of Russia's
'developed statehood.' . . . To understand how internal and external pressures converge upon
the politics of national identity in Russia, I examine how liberal, statist, and extremist images
of Russian identity serve to organize politicians' preferences for domestic and international
order" (James Richter, "Russian Foreign Policy and the Politics of Identity" in Wallander, *The*

of Russian foreign policy from a position where Russia's interests were seen as almost identical to those of the West toward a more independent and assertive position, analysts relying on constructivist arguments can point to changes in the intersubjective relation between Russia and the West, especially the processes by which expectations of a collective security system turned to discursive understandings of the self and other as competitors. The emergence of a disillusioned perception of the Western other in Russian discourse can be explained, for example, by inflated expectations of Western aid, leading to a feeling of betrayal by the West; by too idealistic expectations about Western cooperation in the building of a new European security system, leading to feelings of being isolated and threatened by the West; and by false expectations of being treated and respected as a great power, leading to feelings of being humiliated by the West and other major powers. Consequently, the analysis emphasizes that avoiding a slide into a world of strict relative gains calculations and spheres of interests is still possible, if the right policies are followed.[11]

Thus, to make the correct assessment about the implications of the developments in Russian foreign policy during recent years, especially with respect to the question of the possibility of Russian and Western interests

---

Sources of Russian Foreign Policy, 77). "[W]hether this once and sure-to-be future great power will cast its lot with the West will depend in large measure on which among the competing national identities emerges as the most salient" (Robert G. Herman, "Identity, Norms, and National Security: The Soviet Foreign Policy Revolution and the End of the Cold War," in Peter J. Katzenstein, ed., *The Culture of National Security: Norms and Identity in World Politics* [New York: Columbia University Press, 1996], 315). "When we turn to today's Russia, however, the problem of historical self-identification reaches a level of acuity perhaps unparalleled elsewhere. . . . The answer to this question is a crucial factor in determining the institutions that Russia seeks to build and upon which the country's future and its domestic and foreign policies depend" (Douglas W. Blum, "Conclusion: Is Disintegration Inevitable, and Why Should We Care?" in Douglas W. Blum, ed., *Russia's Future: Consolidation or Disintegration?* [Boulder, Colo.: Westview Press, 1994], 5–6).

11. For examples of such arguments, see, e.g., Richter, "Russian Foreign Policy," 88–89; Margot Light, "Foreign Policy Thinking," in Malcolm, Pravda, Allison, and Light, *Internal Factors,* 84–85; Blum, "Conclusion," 155–56; S. Neil MacFarlane, "Russia, the West, and European Security," *Survival* 35 (Autumn 1993): 20–22; Herman, "Identity, Norms, and National Security," 315. Even Alexei Arbatov, in an otherwise realist-oriented analysis of Russian national interests, explained the development of Russian foreign policy from Westernism to a more assertive stance by feelings of "disappointment," "shame," and "humiliation" among the Russian elite caused by Western policies, especially the "arrogance and shortsightedness" of U.S. policy and unfulfilled promises related to Western involvement in Russian political and economic affairs. In his policy prescriptions, he called for the West to display "understanding and flexibility." Alexei Arbatov, "Russian National Interests," in Robert T. Blackwill and Sergei A. Karaganov, eds., *Damage Limitation or Crisis* (CSIA Studies in International Security, no. 5; Cambridge: Harvard University Press, 1994), 75.

colliding in a violent manner, one must examine international relations theory, whether or not one wants to. In the following, I seek to shed light on some fundamental problems inherent in both neorealist and constructivist interpretations of Russian foreign policy by focusing on the logic of the theories themselves. This strategy is chosen because it permits me to construct an alternative theoretical framework for analyzing Russian foreign policy discourse, which is used in the case study.

Through a close reading of the theoretical origins of neorealism, I first show that Waltz's presumption that zero-sum competition between states is the norm in international relations is based on an implicit identity agenda, which is constructed by omitting the importance of Rousseau's writings on the relation between individual and state. Using Freudian identification theory, I show that Rousseau's views on political order, nationalism, and international relations imply a dialectical understanding of citizenship and the consequent decentering of identities. After providing a hypothesis about the relation between decentered subjectivity and the origins of nationalism and threat perceptions, I show that the same theme is also found in constructivist international relations theory, which claims to capture the causal relevance of the dynamic of identification for international relations. Finally, drawing on psychoanalytic identity theory, I introduce an alternative methodology for analyzing the cultural roots of nationalism and threat perceptions in foreign policy discourse and show that such an approach can enhance our understanding of Russian foreign policy.

IDENTITY AND ORDER IN WALTZIAN NEOREALISM

Measured in citations, Waltzian neorealism is the most influential and arguably also the most criticized theory in modern international relations. By focusing solely on the structure of the international system in explaining outcomes of international interaction, neorealism has provided a solution to two great identity problems. On the one hand, it has relieved its followers from studying the role of identity issues in generating conflict and cooperation by implying that order is created by the threat of the use of force in both hierarchic and anarchic systems. On the other hand, Waltz's exclusive focus on the international system has provided international relations scholars with an identity distinct from other political scientists.

A closer look at how domestic and international order is constructed in neorealism raises doubts about how justified and universally applicable

Waltz's main claims are. Although a theoretical digression into the neorealist classic dealing with the causes of war may not seem to be the most logical
first step to take to shed light on the origins of Russian foreign policy, it is
a practical way to understand the process by which the self–other problem
is frozen into a situation of perpetual antagonism, leading to a world where
predation—not security maximization as Waltz claimed—is what states expect from one another.

From Nature to State: Waltz on Rousseau

In his classic treatise on the causes of war, Waltz first analyzed the first
image, individual human beings. He described the individuals that inhabit
the domestic political space as imperfect and slowly learning actors and
gave credit to "first-image pessimists"—a label referring to Hans Morgenthau, Reinhold Niebuhr, Saint Augustine, and Benedict de Spinoza—for
"descrying the limits of possible political accomplishment."[12] Citing Sigmund Freud, Waltz noted the slow pace of changes in the human psyche:
"Those who would have peace await changes in men 'conjure up an ugly
picture of mills which grind so slowly that, before the flour is ready, men
are dead of hunger.'"[13] In a similar tone, Waltz criticized nineteenth-
century liberals for an "assumption of the infinite perfectibility of man."[14]

According to Waltz, difficulties of cooperation between people lie not
only in human imperfectability, but also in the situations that people face.
To illustrate this, Waltz relied on Rousseau's example of the stag hunt,
where men in an imagined "state of nature," realizing the need for cooperation to satisfy their hunger, team up to catch a stag. The story has an
unhappy ending; one of the hunters defects from the team on seeing a
hare and thus permits the stag to escape.[15] Political order, Rousseau concluded, is created from the state of nature when men realize the economic
advantages of cooperation and set up rules as well as organize the means

12. Waltz, *Man, the State, and War* (New York: Columbia University Press, 1959), 30–31.
13. Waltz, *Man, the State, and War*, 71.
14. Waltz, *Man, the State, and War*, 103.
15. Waltz, *Man, the State, and War*, 165–71. See "A Discourse on the Origin of Inequality,"
in Jean-Jacques Rousseau, *The Social Contract and Discourses* (London: Dent, 1973), 87. Rousseau's example, Waltz argued, "is the point of departure for the establishment of government
and contains the basis for his [Rousseau's] explanation of conflict in international relations
as well" (Waltz, *Man, the State, and War*, 167). Rousseau's position was also the one Waltz
himself used as the main source for his own "third-image" theory (172–86).

for enforcing them.[16] Waltz's explanation for the peacefulness of the domestic political space rests on an analogous interpretation: "domestically disputes are settled by institutions that combine reason with force."[17]

Relying on the stag hunt metaphor, Waltz argued that Rousseau's worldview implies that the peaceful settlement of international disputes requires a world government with powers similar to domestic courts. Again, the idea is parallel to Freud's, which Waltz cited earlier: "There is but one sure way of ending war and that is establishment, by common consent, of a central control, which shall have the last word in every conflict of interests. For this, two things are needed: first, the creation of such a supreme court of judicature; secondly; its investment with adequate executive force."[18] Nevertheless, Waltz warned that creating a world government was not only an unattainable goal, but that the attempt to create it might cause death or lead to a "life worse than death."[19] Thus Waltz opted for a realist theory where anarchic competition is taken as an unquestioned reality and where the use of force is seen as a legitimate instrument for creating order in the political space outside the boundaries of states. To describe the nasty and brutish nature of international relations in a world without a global sovereign, Waltz resorted again to Freud's authoritative formulation: "So long as there are nations and empires, each prepared callously to exterminate its rival, all alike must be equipped for war."[20]

Although the only unit-level events of interest to neorealists should be changes in the material capabilities of states (resulting in changes in the distribution of capabilities in the system), a closer look at Waltz's reading of Rousseau reveals that Waltz recognized other relevant processes inside the billiard ball in addition to material preparations for war. When discuss-

16. Waltz, *Man, the State, and War*, 171. For a full description of Rousseau's narrative about the emergence of order from the state of nature, see Rousseau, *The First and Second Discourses and Essay on the Origins of Languages* (New York: Harper and Row, 1986), 170–99.

17. A similar Waltzian assumption about the origins of order in the domestic political space can be found in a recent influential study of the threat of proliferation of Russian nuclear weapons, which contrasts the authoritarian control of all aspects of Soviet society with the present unstable situation, in which "nothing valuable can be secured from loss, theft, or sale," leading to a possibility of a "nuclear anarchy." Graham T. Allison, Owen Coté, Jr., Richard A. Falkenrath, and Steven E. Miller, *Avoiding Nuclear Anarchy: Containing the Threat of Loose Russian Nuclear Weapons and Fissile Material* (Cambridge: MIT Press, 1996), 2.

18. Waltz, *Man, the State, and War*, 71.

19. Waltz, *Man, the State, and War*, 228.

20. Waltz, *Man, the State, and War*, 187; see also Jean Bethke Elshtain, "Freud's Discourse of War/Politics," in James Der Derian and Michael Shapiro, eds., *International/Intertextual Relations: Postmodern Readings of World Politics* (Lexington, Mass.: Lexington Books, 1989), 60–61.

ing the third image (the international system), Waltz, following in Rousseau's footsteps, admitted that because of the complexities of modern states, an additional factor is needed to achieve the unity that a good state needs. This factor is the "public spirit" or "patriotism" that acts as the mediator between the first and second images (men and the state) amid the complexities of the modern state.[21] Patriotism ensures that instinct-driven men in the state of nature are transformed into citizens through surrendering to a sovereign and identifying themselves as part of the body politic. Rousseau himself described this relation by arguing that "the words *subject* and *sovereign* are identical correlatives whose meaning is conjoined in the single word *citizen*."[22]

For Waltz, the consequences of this move seem to be relatively unproblematic: the social contract is a guarantor of equality, and identification with the sovereign is a necessary condition for a good state, where the population agrees with the government's foreign policy.[23] When citing Rousseau to describe the ideal seedbed for patriotism, however, Waltz implicitly acknowledged that people's identification with the state does not take place in a psychological vacuum, but is dependent on their previous identifications:

> If children are brought up in common in the bosom of equality; if they are imbued with the laws of the State and the percepts of the general will; if they are taught to respect these above all things; if they are surrounded by examples and objects which constantly remind them of the tender mother who nourishes them, of the love she bears them, of the inestimable benefits they receive from her, and of the return they owe her, we cannot doubt that they will learn to cherish one another mutually as brothers, to will nothing to the contrary to the will of the society, to substitute the actions of men and citizens for the futile and vain babbling of sophists, and to become in time defenders and fathers of the country of which they have been so long the children.[24]

21. Waltz, *Man, the State, and War*, 174.
22. Rousseau, *Political Writings* (Madison: University of Wisconsin Press, 1986), 100.
23. Waltz, *Man, the State, and War*, 174–79.
24. Cited in Waltz, *Man, the State, and War*, 175. The passage is an excellent reflection of the way political and psychic constitutions are treated as interdependent in Rousseau's work. Elsewhere, Rousseau called the family "the most ancient of societies, and the only natural one," and said that "it may be taken, therefore, as the prototype of political societies; the ruler represents the father, the people the children." Rousseau, *Social Contract*, 4–5. When talking about the nature of the "people," Rousseau resorted to analogies between the develop-

This quotation suggests that Rousseau understood the sovereign–
subject relationship like the child–parent relationship, as characterized by
ambivalence: to become a citizen, one must surrender to the power of the
sovereign and be empowered by identification with it, just as children on
the one hand respect the state above all things and surrender to the general will and on the other hand are imbued with its authority through law
to become "fathers of the country" and to cherish the other citizens as
equal brothers. In other words, Rousseau apparently saw citizenship as an
identity characterized by ambivalence, which he traced to the nature of the
subject and the sovereign.[25] Rousseau's political writings, including those
cited by Waltz, reflected his concerns about the tensions this ambivalence
creates in collectives and the need he perceived for means to control it for
the sake of political order.[26] The reason that Waltz did not make much out
of the political consequences of this ambivalence is that he read Rousseau
through a social ontology that presupposes a sovereign subject. Waltz's interpretation of domestic order simply as a result of the hierarchical relation
between the state and people is a logical consequence of his presupposed
differentiation between the three images, which is a premise that Rousseau,
for example in the above quotation, desperately attempted to transcend.

The consequences of Waltz's ontological conflation for international
relations theory are huge. Rousseau, although not denying the importance
of the use of force by the sovereign in the construction of domestic order,
did not base his pessimistic view of international relations only on the absence of a sovereign at the international level, but also on a belief in the
existence of unit-level attributes leading to the emergence of states seeking
nonsecurity expansion.[27] This belief, in turn, was not meant to be a univer-

---

mental stages of human beings and society, between individual crisis and social revolutions
(46–47).

25. See also Rousseau, *Social Contract*, 14–20.

26. See, e.g., Rousseau's advice to the government of Poland. "Considerations on the
Government of Poland," in Rousseau, *Political Writings*, especially 176–78.

27. Rousseau explicitly denied that maximizing the security of the state was the main goal
of rulers: "The whole life of Kings, or of those on whom they shuffle off their duties, is
devoted solely to two objects: to extend their rule beyond their frontiers and to make it more
absolute within them. Any other purpose they may have is either subservient to one of these
aims, or merely a pretext for attaining them." Rousseau, "Judgment on Saint-Pierre's Project
for Perpetual Peace," in M. G. Forsyth, H. M. A. Keens-Soper, and P. Savigear, eds., *The Theory
of International Relations: Selected Texts from Gentili to Treitschke* (London: George Allen and
Unwin Ltd., 1970), 158. Consider also the following description: "There have been states so
constituted that the need for conquest was part of their very constitution and that in order to
maintain themselves, they were forced to grow ever large" (Rousseau, *Social Contract*, 50).
Citing the same passage, Waltz categorized it among immediate causes of war, not seeing how

sally valid fact, but a parallel to Rousseau's critique of the corrupt state of the governments of Europe at his time. Thus, Waltz's third-image theory, which he claimed to ground in Rousseau's observations about security dilemmas arising in an anarchic space populated by rational security maximizers, is very different from Rousseau's own skepticism about international cooperation, which is primarily a historically specific critique of the naïveté Rousseau perceived in his contemporaries' plans for a free and voluntary association of European states.[28] Waltz's ontological presumptions blinded him to the intimate connection between domestic and international order in Rousseau's discourse and led Waltz to deduce the danger of predation from international anarchy, whereas Rousseau traced its origins also to domestic factors.[29]

From this perspective, one could argue that whether the causal mechanisms of a neorealist world actually start to influence the relations between Russia and other major powers depends on whether the states involved have a reason to fear predationist behavior from one another. Many modifications of neorealist theory have sought to make the theory more compatible with reality by integrating the causes and effects of this fear through variables like threat perceptions and hypernationalism, but none of them has provided a rigorous methodology for analyzing such social constructions.[30] In the following, I move in that direction by deepening Rousseau's

---

constitutive the fear of nonsecurity expansion is of Rousseau's description of the logic of international anarchy (Waltz, *Man, the State, and War*, 184–85, n. 51).

28. On the role of corrupt statesmen, tyrant kings, and dishonest ministers in Rousseau's critique of Abbé de Saint-Pierre's Project for Perpetual Peace, see Rousseau, "Judgment," 157–66. Rousseau explicitly defined his critique as bound to the historical context of his time and noted that Saint-Pierre's project might be a "reasonable proposal" if wise enough statesmen were found to implement it (166). See also Michael C. Williams, "Rousseau, Realism, and Realpolitik," *Millennium* 18, 2 (1989): 185–203.

29. Randall Schweller, criticizing neorealism's status quo bias from another viewpoint, has come to a similar conclusion: "[N]eorealism overlooks the importance of revisionist goals (nonsecurity expansion) as the driving force—indeed, sine qua non—behind most of its theoretical concepts. . . . What triggers security dilemmas under anarchy is the possibility of predatory states existing among the ranks of the units the system comprises" (Randall Schweller, "Neorealism's Status-Quo Bias: What Security Dilemma?" in Benjamin Frankel, ed., *Realism: Restatements and Renewal* [London: Frank Cass, 1996], 91, 92). Mark Kauppi, in his reading of Thucydides' classic, has pointed out that Thucydides regarded states' perceptions of the "national character" of others as an important cause of war: "[T]he emphasis in the phrase 'growth of Athenian power' should be as much on the adjective 'Athenian' as it is on the noun 'power.' In particular, Spartan fear of Athens was a result of the actual and perceived special character of Athenian society" (Mark V. Kauppi, "Thucydides: Character and Capabilities," in Frankel, ed., *The Roots of Realism* [London: Frank Cass, 1996], 142–43).

30. Stephen Walt's balance of threat theory is a good example of such an attempt. Walt's analysis of threat perceptions lacks a methodology in any real sense, and conclusions about

idea of the ambivalence of citizenship through the identification theory of Sigmund Freud, whom, like Rousseau, Waltz used in painting a pessimistic view of international relations and whose arguments about the relation between war and the dialectical nature of authority structures suffered equally from Waltz's ontological presumptions.

The Dialectics of Freud and Rousseau

As noted earlier, Waltz credited Freud for both first- and third-image pessimism. Freud, however, explicitly grounded his explanation of the origins of war in collective feelings of hate toward others, which cannot be separately attributed to any of Waltz's three levels. Freud did not create a comprehensive theory of the origins of such feelings (his main interests were elsewhere), but his writings on the theme, largely inspired by the First World War, clearly indicate that he considered domestic factors, such as the immaturity of nation states as organizations, part of the picture. The parallel with Rousseau—and the contradiction with Waltz—is clear in Freud's argument that major war is made possible not because states have a rational interest in survival, but because deeper passions (the fact that collectives so often "despise, hate, and detest one another") are rationalized as national interests, leading to the breakdown of the community of interests established by commerce.[31] In other words, Freud's belief in the likelihood of predationist tendencies of states—not a bad insight from an Austrian Jew writing in the interwar period—was an integral part of his pessimism about international affairs.

---

the impact of intersubjective relations between states on national decisions (eighty-six of them!) are made on the basis of secondary literature, often backed up with a few quotes from the heads of states. Stephen Walt, *The Origins of Alliances* (Ithaca: Cornell University Press, 1987). Similarly, John Mearsheimer gave the concept of "hypernationalism," which he defined as "the belief that other nations or nation-states are both inferior and threatening and must therefore be dealt with harshly," a significant role in explaining German aggression in the World Wars, but did not provide a scientific theory about its origins or a methodology for uncovering signs of resurgent nationalism. John J. Mearsheimer, "Back to the Future: Instability in Europe After the Cold War," *International Security* 15 (Summer 1990): 20–21, 25. For a critique of neotraditional and other attempts to "fix" neorealism, see John A. Vasquez, "The Realist Paradigm and Degenerative Versus Progressive Research Programs: An Appraisal of Neotraditional Research on Waltz's Balancing Proposition," *American Political Science Review* 91, 4 (1997): 899–913. See also the replies by Waltz and other prominent realists in the same issue, which testify to the metatheoretical and theoretical inconsistency in the (neo)realist "research program."

31. Sigmund Freud, "Thoughts for the Times on War and Death," *Standard Edition of the Complete Psychological Works of Sigmund Freud*, vol. 14 (London: Hogarth Press, 1989), 275–88.

Freud's pessimism about relations between states originated in his path-breaking work on the concept of identification, which he defined as the process by which an individual makes someone or an aspect (e.g., behavior, attitude, or values) of someone a part of him- or herself.[32] Freud saw identification as a universal phenomenon arising from the tendency of the human psyche to strive for stability and consistency amid needs and desires that could not be fulfilled.[33]

One of Freud's most important contributions was to shed light on the ambivalent nature of identification. When studying oedipal identification, Freud concluded that introjection of the attributes of the object of identification (e.g., the little boy's attempts to be like his father or other figures sharing similar traits) arose from children's desire to replace the object by themselves, to revolt and overthrow the object that was perceived threatening to the primary identification with the biological source of life. Freud thus understood the son's identification with the father figure as a defense mechanism, a way of coping with the loss of the struggle over "ownership" of the primary object, and as a necessary step for the son to become a mature individual. Freud's real "discovery" resulting from this formulation was that oedipal identification results in a decentering of the subject by giving birth to a new agency in the child's psyche. This is the ego ideal, which consists of the internalized values and attributes of the parents, and which functions as an agency of "self-observation, moral conscience, the censorship of dreams, and the chief influence of repression."[34]

Armed with an understanding of the ambivalent nature of identification and the resulting decentering of the subject, Freud constructed a theory about group behavior where authority structures in the mind and in society are connected by a dialectic ontology.[35] To describe the way identification processes produce and reproduce order at the level of society, Freud resorted to the same technique as Rousseau—describing the transi-

32. For a summary of the main schools of identification theory, see William Bloom, *Personal Identity, National Identity, and International Relations* (Cambridge: Cambridge University Press, 1990), 25–53.

33. In the context of childhood development, Freud defined identification as the "earliest expression of an emotional tie with another person," which evolves into "a substitute for a libidinal object tie" and may later "arise with any new perception of a common quality shared with some other person who is not an object of the sexual instinct." See Freud, *Group Psychology and the Analysis of the Ego* (New York: Norton, 1959), 37.

34. See Freud, *Group Psychology*, 37–42.

35. The following discussion is drawn mainly from Freud's *Totem and Taboo* (London: Routledge & Kegan Paul, 1975) and *Group Psychology*, which are usually considered representative of Freud's theory of collective behavior.

tion from a state of nature to society. Although metaphoric, Freud's state of nature was not a purely imagined construction, as Rousseau's was, but a scientific reconstruction, based on his contemporaries' anthropological studies as well as on Darwin's hypotheses about the similarities between the behavior of higher apes and primitive people.

In Freud's state of nature, primitive people live in "primal hordes" each dominated by a powerful male, who rules the group through violence, keeping all the females to himself and driving his sons away as they grow up.[36] When explaining the origins of order in such a group, Freud argued that not only violence, but a social construction created by the interaction of violence and human needs, explains the unity of the group. The young males not only hated their despotic father but also, as a way of coping with their desire to have what the father had, identified with him. Using his theory of oedipal identification, Freud concluded: "The primal father is the group ideal, which governs the ego in the place of the ego ideal."

In Freud's account, the rule of the strongest turns into an order based on community (although a very limited one) in two phases. The first phase—a revolution—is captured in Freud's metaphorical story about the murder of the father, in which the sons, unwilling to live under the rule of the despot, team together to overthrow their father, killing and—savages as they were—devouring him.[37] For Freud, the devouring of the primal father was a ritual of introjection, where the sons, who had envied their father's power and position, finally accomplished full identification with him, each acquiring (symbolically) a portion of his strength.[38] The introjection of the sovereign's attributes into the subject's ego ideal made the murder—the revolution—a starting point for future identifications with symbols representing the sovereign.[39]

36. Freud, *Totem and Taboo*, 125–26, 141–46.

37. The roots of this revolution lie in the competition of ownership (for the females). This struggle arose from what Freud perceived as natural needs and desires related to the human condition. Rousseau believed that wars occur because of things, not because of men, and that relations between things are a necessary condition for wars to occur. In Rousseau's world, war cannot occur either in the state of nature, where there is no settled property, or in the domestic realm, where property relations are governed by law. Rousseau, *Social Contract*, 10.

38. To understand the cultural and historical context of Freud's controversial hypothesis, see the lengthy footnote in *Totem and Taboo* (142–43), where Freud sought support for his hypothesis in anthropological studies. The dialectics of identification in Freud's theory work well without the ritual meal scene, which to a contemporary armchair anthropologist might seem a far-fetched interpretation of later ritual meals, such as the Eucharist.

39. Freud, *Totem and Taboo*, 140–55. Freud argued that we can deduce this observation even from contemporary Christian doctrine: "If the Son of God was obliged to sacrifice his

Freud's explanation for order among the rival brothers after the sovereign is gone is derived from their former identification with the sovereign. Freud believed that the revolting against the ego ideal that had first united the group was a traumatic experience and created a feeling of guilt among those who had taken part in it. This guilt, Freud argued, reflected first in the worship of symbols representing the former object of common identification, such as totem animals and symbols of gods, made the father even more powerful when absent than when present and provided the basis for understanding the nature of divine monarchs and charismatic leaders in society.[40] The emergence of a Hobbesian state of nature in the anarchical political space created by the death of the father is thus prevented because of the former dialectic of identification between the son and the father, which was then institutionalized into the culture of the community through two taboos—one forbidding murder and the other forbidding incest—corresponding to the two wishes that the son during the oedipal phase has to repress.[41]

The significance of Freud's theory is not to refute the importance of other factors, such as economic pressures, in explaining the origins of political order, but to show that constructing unity through the consumption of an object of common identification results not in coherence but in ambivalence in the individual. This leads to the conclusion—similar to that made by Rousseau—that order in collectives can be achieved only at the price of a split in the identity of the citizens of the collective, just as the child in Freudian theory can gain control of instinct-driven desires only through the ambivalent process of identification, during which the dialectic of revolution and subjugation becomes constitutive of the psyche through the ego-ego ideal tension.

In this light, patriotism, the spirit uniting the subject and the object of identification in the ambivalence of citizenship, can be seen as structurally similar to people's desire to overcome the split in their own psyches. In the

---

life to redeem mankind from original sin, then by the law of talion, the requital of like by like, that sin must have been a killing, a murder. Nothing else could call for the sacrifice of a life for its expiation. And the original sin was an offense against God the Father, the primal crime of mankind must have been a parricide, the killing of the primal father of the primitive human horde, whose mnemic image was later transfigured into a deity" (Freud, "Thoughts for the Times," 292–93).

40. On the role of the Renaissance prince in forging a metaphorical connection between people and the state, see Erik Ringmar, "On the Ontological Status of the State," *European Journal of International Relations* 2, 4 (1996): 443–46.

41. "Whoever contravened those taboos became guilty of the only two crimes with which primitive society concerned itself" (Freud, *Totem and Taboo*, 143).

words of Anne Norton: "The citizen seeks to complete himself in politics. Conscious of his incompletion, he surrenders himself to a more comprehensive identity, thereafter regarding his individuality as a shameful partiality only partly overcome. Split in the ambivalence of subject and Sovereign, the citizen acquires not an unambiguous unity, but the capacity to govern himself."[42] According to such a view, the dialectic of identification per se is the ontological entity to be studied, and people and the state are treated as the effects of the process. Methodologically, such an ontological shift provides a way to understand how harmonious resolution of dilemmas of common interests among individuals may not arise from the convergence of interests among individuals or from the existence of a Waltzian institution combining reason with force, but from a previous relationship of domination, which has been embedded in cultural constructions of identity. Conversely, behavior leading to violation of norms may be understood not as arising simply from material self-interests, but from attempts to deal with the tensions arising from the dialectical nature of subjectivity.[43]

Freudian insights into the relation between identity and order provide at least two inputs that could be added to modify the third-image structural logic of neorealism. First, the structural similarity between the split characterizing the individual's psyche in Freudian theory and the ambivalence characterizing citizenship for Rousseau provides a potentially powerful explanation for hypernationalism in neorealist discourse. The cultural logic behind the explanation is summarized in Norton's reading of Rousseau: "The citizen, constant in his singularity, is individually greater in inverse proportion to his nation. He is diminished in his natural character insofar as his nation is great. This fraction expresses the relation of the citizen as subject to the nation that subjects him."[44] In other words, extreme nationalism can be seen as a collective attempt to provide a final solution to anxieties arising from the split inherent in citizenship and the psyche by total subjection to the sovereign.[45]

42. Anne Norton, *Reflections on Political Identity* (Baltimore: Johns Hopkins University Press, 1988), 34.

43. For explanations of the origins of the predationist behavior of Communist Russia and Nazi Germany along these lines, see Nathan Leites, *A Study of Bolshevism* (Glencoe, Ill.: Free Press, 1953); Klaus Theweleit, *Male Fantasies: Women, Floods, Bodies, History* (Oxford: Polity Press, 1987); Klaus Theweleit, *Male Bodies: Psychoanalyzing the White Terror* (Cambridge: Polity Press, 1989).

44. Norton, *Reflections on Political Identity*, 32.

45. This dynamic can of course lead to other identifications than the national one. The modern tendency for sentiments of national identification to be deeper and stronger than feelings of identification with, say, a political party, church, or local hockey team, is supported

Closely related to the phenomenon of nationalism are threat perceptions. If every identity is characterized by an internal ambivalence and a drive toward cohesion, as the Freudian approach suggests, then perceptions and fantasies of threatening others—whether external or internal— are intimately linked to attempts to construct a coherent and stable identity.[46] It can be hypothesized that the role of other in identity construction becomes especially acute in times of turmoil, when the borders defining the collective's identity are called into question—whether the borders are the external ones of the state or the prevailing construction of the subject-sovereign relationship that defines the boundaries of the identity of the individual citizen.

For a scientific study of this interaction, we need an ontology that is capable of recognizing politics and power in the spaces "between" all three images—in the conflicts about different discursive constellations of identity and otherness, which reify or modify the intersubjective reality between people and states, or in the textual battles that reconstruct or deconstruct state sovereignty in the domestic and international realms. Incorporating these issues into an analysis does not necessarily require a departure from a realist philosophy of science or from skepticism about the possibilities of collective identity construction at the level of interstate relations. It requires an engagement with theories about the social construction of identities and a methodology for analyzing the role language plays in self–other relations. Currently, research on these issues in international relations is pursued mostly under the label of constructivism.[47]

by the extreme constructions of self–other relations that individuals have experienced as parts of socially constructed national communities during history and is transferred to new generations through education and propaganda. For example, when seeking allegiance and loyalty among its supporters, a political party, at least in a democratic society, cannot resort to narratives of concentration camps and gulags where other parties send their opponents (but must settle instead for stories about corruption or marital infidelity). Churches cannot enlarge their congregations by stories about the nuclear missiles that a competing church is pointing at them, and the local hockey club cannot increase the level of commitment among its fans by stories about the brutal assassination of their top players by death squads of the competing team. Nation states are still the only organizations with a legitimate monopoly on collective violence. This fact connects the issue of national identity to security problems in a unique way.

46. The prevailing causal explanation in social identity theory for intergroup discrimination found in empirical experiments is based on an assumption that individuals have a universal desire for self-esteem, which they seek to enhance by maximizing the difference between their collective and other collectives. Jonathan Mercer, "Anarchy and Identity," *International Organization* 49 (Spring 1995): 239–43.

47. On constructivism in international relations, see Nicholas Onuf, *The World of Our Making: Rules and Rule in Social Theory and International Relations* (Columbia: University of South

Mainstream constructivism, exemplified by the work of Alexander Wendt, is especially interesting in the light of what has been argued above, because it claims to provide a systemic theory of international relations, capable of taking into account phenomena such as predation and threat perceptions, while pointing the way toward achieving a collective identity at the systemic level.[48] My next step is to engage the Freudian insights of decentered subjectivity with theories about the social construction of reality through a dialogue with Wendt's theory. My argument is that the main claim of Wendtian constructivism—that social constructions of identity precede interests—is misleading, if not totally false, because it neglects the tension between corporeal desires and the covenant of representation in the process of the formation of the self and leads constructivists to ignore the split in subjectivity, which is the prerequisite of socially constructed interests. This theme, as formulated by Jacques Lacan—a self-confessed Freudian—is then elaborated to deepen Rousseau's and Freud's insights on predation and to provide an explicit methodology for an identity agenda in structural realism.

IDENTITY AND REPRESENTATION: BEYOND CONSTRUCTIVISM

Anarchy is what states make of it, said Alexander Wendt. Wendt thus reversed Waltz's logic that the interest for maximizing security in an anarchic world forces states to behave in roughly similar ways by arguing that identities are the basis of interests. For Wendt, the social construction of reality comes first, and defining interests follows from it: "Actors do not have a portfolio of interests that they carry around independent of social context;

Carolina Press, 1989); Wendt, "Constructing International Politics," *International Security* 20 (Summer 1995): 71–81; Wendt, "Anarchy," 391–425; Wendt, "The Agent–Structure Problem in International Relations Theory," *International Organization* 41 (Summer 1987): 335–70.

48. At first sight the Freudian idea of psychoanalysis as a way to free people's egos from the shadow of the past (the ego ideal), by making them conscious of the way past identifications have distorted the understanding of reality seems strikingly similar to constructivists' attempts to construct a less violent international system by revealing that the pessimistic assumptions of dominant modes of thinking about international relations are based on questionable universalizations from past events and that positive interaction can change the intersubjective understandings and thus free communities from the shadow of their past traumas.

instead, they define their interests in the process of defining the situation."[49]

In describing the dynamics of construction and reconstruction of social identities through interaction, Wendt resorted to an analogy about the first meeting of ego and alter. In Wendt's scheme, which is actually his theory about the state of nature, the encounter is characterized by two actors who want to survive and have certain material capabilities, but "neither actor has biological or domestic imperatives for power, glory, or conquest (still bracketed), and there is no history of security or insecurity between the two." He then showed that the relation between the actors and their perceptions of each other is determined by their interaction, which can lead to conflict as well as cooperation, the latter culminating in a collective identity between the actors. Wendt noted that the analogy is "metaphorical," but claimed that such "first encounters" have actually happened in international relations when new states have been "discovered."[50]

Wendt's example is powerful and appealing because it seems to be so consistent with common sense. As constructivists frequently argue, however, metaphors carry with them many unsaid and unquestioned (sometimes unconscious) assumptions about reality. Wendt's example has at least two of them. First, Wendt assumed that the ego is a representation derived from a cognitive learning process, whereby people learn to treat themselves rationally as an object of knowledge through language. Second, Wendt assumed that the ego can be meaningfully treated separately from the material or biological entity of which it is a part—in other words, that the ego's interaction with the alter happens as a cognitive process without any significant distortions in the biological or "corporate" component of the actor.[51] Both claims are typically modernist and have fundamental implications for the way Wendtian theory treats the origins of political order.

49. Wendt, "Anarchy," 398.

50. Wendt, "Anarchy," 403–7. The "systematic empirical study about first contacts" that Wendt called for might be useful for constructivist theory. Such study would reveal that the entities "discovered" by European states, for example in Africa or America, were not in fact states, but communities organized along very different principles from the European states that "found" them. Such a study would also question the argument that the enmity created between the ego and the alter in such situations was just a social construction arising from the exchange of gestures, because the ego "discovering" new cultures often has a material interest in doing so and has good reasons for expecting the indigenous population to resist exploitation.

51. Wendt has further elaborated the relation between identity and interests (as well as the relation between the social and the corporeal) by making a distinction between "social identity" and "corporate identity." The former refers to "sets of meanings that an actor attributes to itself while taking the perspective of others—that is, as a social object," and the

Constructing Subjectivity: A Lacanian Reading

Wendt called his own theory about the construction of identities and interests a "mirror theory of identity formation."[52] Based on symbolic interactionism and theories about social cognition, his theory relies on an
assumption of the existence of a reflexive hard core of the self, around
which, and by which, identity is constructed through language and symbolic interaction.[53] Although such an approach does not deny the significance of the development of the ego's understanding of social reality, it
interprets historical narratives by assuming an intentional consciousness,
rather than by treating the ego as being at the mercy of conflicting impulses coming from the libido and the superego (Freud) or by assuming
that the ego is produced by cultural structures and mechanisms of articula-
tion that it can never be fully aware of (poststructuralism).[54]

latter to the "intrinsic qualities that constitute actor individuality," such as the body and
consciousness for people and constituent individuals, shared beliefs, and institutions for organizations. Wendt, "Identity and Structural Change in World Politics," in Yosef Lapid and
Friedrich Kratochwil, eds., *The Return of Culture and Identity in International Relations Theory*
(Boulder, Colo.: Lynne Rienner, 1996), 50–51.
    52. Wendt, "Anarchy," 407.
    53. According to David L. Morgan and Michael L. Schwalbe ("Mind and Self in Society:
Linking Social Structure and Social Cognition," *Social Psychology Quarterly* 53, 2 [1990]: 148–
64), "Sociologists typically define the self-concept as the total set of beliefs about and attitudes
toward the self as an object of reflection. These beliefs and attitudes, it is argued, arise in
early childhood contacts with the physical environment and in interactions with others
throughout life." An example of the constructivist leap from early childhood development to
the institutionalization of ego–alter relations through interaction can be found in Peter L.
Berger and Thomas Luckmann, *The Social Construction of Reality: A Treatise in the Sociology of
Knowledge* (Harmondsworth, England: Penguin Books, 1971), 65–85. Berger and Luckmann's
approach to childhood identification is reflected in their description of psychoanalytic transference as identical to any resocialization process and their belief in the possibility of always
making the unconscious reality of the subject conscious through phenomenological analysis
(130–34, n. 25, 231). However, Berger and Luckmann made no claims about the ontological
status of different theories of the unconscious. According to them, psychoanalysis is not qualitatively different from, e.g., Haitian voodoo psychology; both have empirically proved themselves effective forms of therapy only in one cultural context (194–200).
    54. In view of the magnitude of this difference, it is alarming how often French poststruc-
turalists and postmodernists are lumped under the label of *constructivism* in international
relations literature. "What I have come across under this designation [constructivism] has
not exactly evoked sentiments of kinship being rediscovered. Again, I may have missed something, but the 'constructivist' literature I have seen seems to come from the aforementioned
ideological cauldron with which I have no affinity whatever. The notion of the social construction of reality is here reinterpreted in neo-Marxist, 'critical,' or 'post-structuralist' terms and
it is radically altered in this translation" (Peter L. Berger, "Reflections on the Twenty-Fifth
Anniversary of 'The Social Construction of Reality,'" *Perspectives* 15 [April 1992]: 2). "A goodly
part of the 'success' of 'Social Construction' must have been due to inattentive reading. Occa-

Instead of entering into the philosophical abyss of epistemological and ontological differences between contending theories of the self,[55] I next point out problems in the assumptions underpinning Wendt's theory by providing a brief review of the development of the ego according to Jacques Lacan's identity theory and by contrasting it with Wendt's "mirror theory" of identity formation.[56] Although entering again into a theoretical discussion about the origins of identity at the level of the individual might seem to take us even farther from questions of Russian foreign policy, it is a necessary step in studying the role of identity questions in foreign policy in a theoretically rigorous manner. After all, socially constructed reality exists only in the minds of individuals, and if our theory of the individual is deficient, the rest of the theory is not of much use.[57]

---

sionally I have suspected that among those who purchased or cited the book there must have been some who only read the title, lightly skipping over the 'social' part of it. . . . In any case, whenever someone mentions 'constructivism' or even 'social constructionism,' I run for cover these days" (Thomas Luckmann, "Social Construction and After," *Perspectives* 15 [April 1992]: 4). Although Berger and Luckmann's views of the political underpinnings of post-structuralism are debatable, their frustration at the numerous superficial cocktails of constructivism proper and French social theory—increasingly common also in international relations discourse—is surely justified.

55. These are dealt with in more detail in Henrikki Heikka, "Decentred Subjectivity and the Logic of Anarchy: Theoretical Reflections on the Russian-Western Security Dilemma" (licentiate thesis, University of Helsinki, April 1999).

56. Accessible introductions to Lacanian theory include Slavoj Žižek, *Looking Awry: An Introduction to Jacques Lacan Through Popular Culture* (Cambridge: MIT Press, 1991); Anika Lemaire, *Jacques Lacan* (London: Routledge and Kegan Paul, 1977); Malcolm Bowie, *Lacan* (London: Fontana Press, 1991). On Lacan and politics/political science, see Norton, *Reflections on Political Identity;* Sherry Turkle, *Psychoanalytic Politics: Jacques Lacan and Freud's French Revolution* (London: Burnett Books, 1979); Slavoj Žižek, *The Sublime Object of Ideology* (London: Verso, 1989); Mark Bracher, *Lacan, Discourse, and Social Change: A Psychoanalytic Cultural Criticism* (Ithaca: Cornell University Press, 1993); F. M. Dolan, "Political Action and the Unconscious: Arendt and Lacan on Decentering the Subject," *Political Theory* (May 1995): 330–52; David Mertz, "The Racial Other in Nationalist Subjectivations: A Lacanian Analysis," *Rethinking Marxism* 8 (Summer 1995): 77–88. On Lacan and international relations, see Michael Shapiro, "That Obscure Object of Violence: Logistics and Desire in the Gulf War," in David Campbell and M. Dillon, eds., *The Political Subject of Violence* (Manchester: Manchester University Press, 1993), 114–36; Diane Rubenstein, "Hate Boat, National Identity, and Nuclear Criticism," in Derian and Shapiro, eds., *International/Intertextual Relations,* 231–55. For a useful summary of different schools of psychoanalysis, see Stephen A. Mitchell and Margaret J. Black, *Freud and Beyond: A History of Modern Psychoanalytic Thought* (New York: Basic Books, 1995).

57. Relying on Lacanian ideas when studying collective identities does not lead to a reductionist approach to international relations—one seeking to explain the behavior of collectives by the attributes of the individual. The role Lacan attributed to the other in the formation of the subject makes the individual and the social inseparable in his theory from the beginning.

From One to Two

In human development, every identity is preceded by a stage of noniden-
tity.[58] Newborn infants cannot understand what they are or will become.
According to psychoanalytical theory, through hunger and pain, through
physiological warning signs that survival is threatened, infants realize that
they are separate entities whose survival depends on another entity. This
first corporate identity emerging in the early months of human development is characterized by experiences of physiological needs and their satisfaction. The first desire is the desire for power over that which is not part
of the child, but which the child depends on for survival. Visual images of
the (m)other are not understood as symbolizing another human being,
but simply as something outside the infant's body, which satisfies the needs
created by hunger and other unpleasant feelings. The fact that what is
outside the corporate identity of infants is treated as an object does not
make it an alter to the infant any more than infants' bodily experiences
make them an ego to themselves.[59]

The point at which constructivism and Lacanian theory depart is in
their accounts of the birth of the ego, which both approaches see as related
to the child's ability to understand the idea of representation.[60] Whereas
constructivism views ego construction as a process in which subjects learn
to treat themselves as objects of knowledge, based on cognitive learning,
linguistic activity, and interaction with significant others,[61] Lacan interpreted the individual's ego as not only a linguistic representation, but as an
illusion, of which children's identification with their own corporeal image
is the archetypal form. Thus this process decenters people's self-conscious-
ness into three registers: one based on similarity (identity), one on differ-

58. George Herbert Mead, *Mind, Self, and Society* (Chicago: University of Chicago Press,
1950), 135, 171–72.

59. For a discussion, see Norton, *Reflections on Political Identity*, 11–13.

60. My discussion of the constructivist account of the ego draws on the following sources,
which are cited also by Wendt: Mead, *Mind, Self, and Society;* Berger and Luckmann, *The Social
Construction of Reality;* Morgan and Schwalbe, "Mind and Self in Society"; John Hewitt, *Self
and Society: A Symbolic Interactionist Social Psychology* (London: Allyn and Bacon, 1984); Sheldon
Stryker, *Symbolic Interactionism: A Social Structural Version* (Menlo Park, Mich.: Benjamin/Cum-
mings, 1980); Rob Farr and Serge Moscovici, "On the Nature and Role of Representation in
Self's Understanding of Others and of Self," in Mark Cook, ed., *Issues in Person Perception*
(London: Methuen, 1984), 1–27; Viktor Gecas, "The Self-Concept as a Basis for a Theory of
Motivation," in Judith A. Howard and Peter L. Callero, eds., *The Self–Society Dynamic: Cognition,
Emotion, Action* (Cambridge: Cambridge University Press, 1991), 171–87.

61. See, e.g., Mead, *Mind, Self, and Society*, 138; Hewitt, *Self and Society*, 12, 69–74, 96–102.
Stryker, *Symbolic Interactionism*, 33–40, 59–62.

ence (representation), and one arising out of the tension between these two, but remaining outside their expressive potential.[62]

Lacan distinguished two transformations that people must go through before a meeting of ego and alter can take place in the Wendtian sense. Both are of utmost importance to the relation between identification and political order, because they are concerned with the process by which norms, rules, and relations of dominance interact with the innermost needs and desires of individuals throughout their lives so that people assume various subjective dispositions vis-à-vis others, be they fellow citizens or foreigners. The first stage concerns the development of children's ability to comprehend themselves as an object of knowledge. The second stage concerns children's socialization into the world of language and laws and renunciation of the desire to transcend difference.

The Mirror Stage

The first stage takes place during the ages of six to eighteen months, when children acquire the knowledge and understanding that they are and look like a human. Lacan called this period of development "the mirror stage."[63] During the mirror stage, children's consciousness is captured and occupied by their image reflected in the mirror. In the mirror stage, the body, which was first experienced as a fragmented and disjointed entity characterized by hunger and pain when away from the nurturing parent, is reflected from the mirror as an integrated and coordinated image, which children can control through their gestures.[64]

At first, the experience is characterized by joyful comprehension. The separation between children and the other, earlier realized through need

62. It is ironic that although Wendt's view of the development of identity is based on the Meadian I/me distinction and his view about the relation between agents and structures draws mainly on Gidden's structuration theory, Giddens himself argued that compared with Lacan's perspective on the psychological development of human beings, Mead's approach "has major deficiencies." Giddens, in my view unjustly, argued that Lacanian theory does not adequately incorporate "the organic foundations of human motivation," but he still claimed that "in respect of interpreting the emergence of subjectivity, Lacan's Freud can be drawn upon with profit." Explicitly, Giddens mentioned the role that Lacanian theory attributes to *repression* in the insertion of the infant into the subject–object relation, an issue he claimed is treated too unproblematically in Meadian theory. Anthony Giddens, *Central Problems in Social Theory* (Berkeley and Los Angeles: University of California Press, 1979), 121–22.

63. See "The Mirror Stage as Formative of the Function of the I," in Lacan, *Écrits*, 1–7.

64. For Lacan, the mirror stage is not a specific, "scientific" theory about child psychology but an "exemplary function" that reflects the way the ego is first built around illusions and images of its own making.

and want, is overcome when they identify with their image. At this point, the difference between signifier and signified is blurred, just as early moments of satisfaction blurred the difference between children and the world. Children's first understanding of themselves as human beings, their first ego, is *imaginary*, both in the sense of being illusory (as an identification with the unitary image of the body, compared with the chaos within) and visual (based on visual identification). In other words, the idea of the ego is first conceived in the image—it is an image of the visual image.[65]

In Lacanian terms, this prelinguistic construction of reality and identity takes place in the imaginary ("image-inary") register.[66] The imaginary is a subjective realm characterized by projections, reciprocities, and identifications that transcend the difference between self and other. Throughout people's existence, the imaginary register provides the stage where the original identificatory procedures that brought the ego into being are enacted in the relation with the outside world. In Malcolm Bowie's words: "The imaginary is the scene of a desperate delusional attempt to be and to remain 'what one is' by gathering to oneself ever more instances of sameness, resemblance, and self-replication; it is the birthplace of the narcissistic 'ideal ego.' "[67] The imaginary is particularly important from the viewpoint of political science, because it is a metaphor for all processes by which people seek to construct, at a prelinguistic level, unity and coherence—"sovereignty"—from chaotic and inchoate impulses and sensations.

The birth of the ego is soon followed by children's understanding that the mirror image is at once identical to them and something other to their bodily experience. At this moment, children understand the idea of *representation*, of symbols that mean something that they themselves are not. This covenant makes it possible for children to understand the idea of language and brings into being the idea of the symbolic other—an other-

65. Mikkel Borsch-Jacobsen, *Lacan: The Absolute Master* (Stanford: Stanford University Press, 1991), 48–49. The idea that the child's understanding of the "ego" is born too soon for it to be a real ego is reflected in Berger and Luckmann's explicit acknowledgment of the "premature" birth of humans. However, Berger and Luckmann did not draw any conclusions with respect to the social construction of reality.

66. Lacan developed the concept of "imaginary" in numerous passages scattered through his work, but the essence of the concept in Lacanian identity theory—emphasizing the role of visual identification in mediating people's first relation to themselves, thus constructing the "authentic" (and alienated) ego as an "image-inary" function—can be grasped from the papers "Mirror Stage" and "Aggressivity in Psychoanalysis," Lacan, *Écrits*, 1–29.

67. Bowie, *Lacan*, 92. See also Lacan, *The Seminar of Jacques Lacan: Book 1, Freud's Papers on Technique 1953–1954*, ed. by Jacques-Alain Miller (Cambridge: Cambridge University Press, 1988), 116.

ness that remains other. Only after grasping the abstract idea of representation can children understand their identity as social—that is, attributing
meanings to themselves "while taking the perspective of the other," as
Wendt wrote. The first social identity is thus constructed in people's minds
through interaction with themselves, not with others (although mirroring
the newly acquired social identity from significant others is naturally also
part of the process).[68]

The split [*Spaltung*] between the body and the imaginary ego also
brings about a transformation in children's needs vis-à-vis the other. The
original need (or lack) through which separateness was first realized is
complemented by a *desire* arising from the presence of an absence created
by representation. This desire arises in the margin in which linguistically
articulated demand becomes separated from biological need (demand
here refers to a need where the object is raised [*aufgehoben*] via representation from particularity to the function of a signifier). It is a desire that seeks
to deny otherness, a desire for unconditional recognition of one's desire
by the other.[69]

Entry into the Symbolic

Symbolic interaction (on which Wendt's theory about social identity formation is based) can take place only after the renunciation of imaginary desire

68. Norton pointed out that this is people's first "collective identity" because during the
mirror stage children understand themselves to be part of the collective of humans, "one of
a kind." Norton, *Reflections on Political Identity*, 14. The degree that the mirror stage is merely
a metaphor in Lacanian theory is disputed, but Lacan's insistence on ego construction being
first based on visual identification can hardly be contested as one of the central themes distinguishing Lacanian theory from constructivism. In contrast to more behaviorist understandings of the mirror stage (such as the one presented by Norbert Wiley), Anthony Wilden has
argued that "[w]hat seems fairly clear is that the *stade du miroir* never 'occurs' at all—any
more than the genesis of the ego does." Wilden suggested that the mirror stage is a structural
or relational concept, which besides referring to a phase in development also reads as "a
symptom of or substitute for a much more primordial identification" (Anthony Wilden,
"Lacan and the Discourse of the Other," in Jacques Lacan, *Speech and Language in Psychoanalysis*, translated, with notes and commentary by Anthony Wilden [Baltimore: Johns Hopkins
University Press, 1991], 174; Norbert Wiley, *The Semiotic Self* [Cambridge: Polity Press, 1994],
172–73).

69. Lacan, *Écrits*, 19, 83, 287–89, 311. Another way to frame the effect of the signifier in
transforming need to demand concerns the differences in the aims of the two: "[W]here the
aim of need is the change in the organic status of the animal or person who needs (for
example, the satisfaction of thirst), the aim of demand is a 'transformation of the subject to
whom it is addressed'" (Jonathan Scott Lee, *Jacques Lacan* [Boston: Twayne Publishers, 1990],
75).

and after children can perceive themselves to be equal to others. This stage of development, which is in essence Lacan's explanation for the origins of political order, takes place after the mirror stage, and with it people pay a significant price to become a real subject in the community in which they are born.

Through their ability to understand representation, children enter the realm of the symbolic and begin to construct their self-identity through a system of fixed meanings, language. They acquire the power to communicate verbally and to think in terms of abstract rationality. The birth of the ego in the sense Wendt used it requires children's subjugation to the law of the signifier, the system of language. Lacan referred to these language-like structures by the term *symbolic* register, which is a closed order of differences (of which mathematical language is the most purified form), a realm of signifiers that acquire value in their mutual relations.[70]

Entry into the confines of the symbolic order means renouncing the desire to overcome difference. At this point in Lacan's theory, linguistics meets the Freudian oedipal triangle to form a basis for a unique explanation of the origins of social order. According to Lacan, children's first desire, to be one with the mother, is reflected in their desire to fulfill the desire of the (m)other, to be that which the (m)other lacks. Lacan described this as an imaginary identification with a signifier that signifies that which the (m)other lacks (termed *phallus* by Lacan, and not to be mistaken for Freudian biologisms). Entry into the symbolic means admitting defeat to the father (the third term in the self–other relationship) in the imaginary battle to be that which would fulfill the (m)other's desire and finding one's place in the symbolic system that constitutes the community into which one is born.

In theoretical terms, the move from the imaginary to the symbolic happens in relation to the paternal metaphor, which represents the organizing and controlling function of the symbolic over the imaginary.[71] The paternal metaphor refers both to the *No* of the father, signifying the negative prohibition of a child's wish to be that which the mother lacks, and the *name* of the father, signifying the positive potentialities opened by accession to the world of difference, the symbolic.[72] In this move, something is lost

70. Lacan, *Écrits*, 56–57; Lacan, *Seminar, 1*, 222–26; Lacan, *The Seminar of Jacques Lacan: Book 2, The Ego in Freud's Theory and in the Technique of Psychoanalysis 1954–1955* (Cambridge: Cambridge University Press, 1988), 27–31. See also *Écrits*, 146–78.

71. This move is described in Lacan, *Écrits*, 192–200; see also 66–67.

72. Borsch-Jacobsen has argued that although Freud believed that the ego ideal and the superego converged in the person of the father, causing the ambivalence characteristic of

forever, because the lived enjoyment of unity with the (m)other can never be expressed in the realm of the symbolic. With identification with the paternal metaphor, the desire to repair the imaginary bond between mother and child, to be the phallus, must be suppressed.

The place where desire speaks from thereafter is that which is other to the symbolically constructed self—the unconscious. Lacan's well-known one-liner "desire is always the desire of the other" highlights the nature of the ego as a social construction alienated from its own desire.[73] The ambivalence of representation, comprehended in the mirror stage, becomes constitutive of subjectivity, and alienation becomes a precondition for the formation of the self.[74] The true structure of the ego is thus paranoiac.[75] In taking the signifier as representative (as constructivism suggests), people replicate the delusional identification of the mirror stage while repressing the split caused by symbolization beyond reflection.[76] The dialectic between the conscious, "illusionary" ego and the unconscious discourse of the other is the *internal* ego–alter relationship making possible speech and symbolic interaction.[77] As children acquire what Wendt called

oedipal identification, Lacan claimed that this (the Oedipus complex) was a distinctively modern phenomenon. According to Borsch-Jacobsen, Lacan argued that in primitive societies, the repressive function of the real father (the taboo) was differentiated from the sublimating function of the totem (the symbol, or "name of the father"). Thus, in the Lacanian dialectic, the meaning of the parental imago is decomposed to a conscious ego ideal and an unconscious superego, which relate to each other differently in different phases of history. Borsch-Jacobsen, *Lacan*, 35–41.

73. Anika Lemaire has described the consequences of this alienation: "Caught up in the symbolic, where he is simply represented, obliged to translate himself through the intermediary of the discourse, the subject will become lost, lured away from himself, and will shape himself in accordance with the other's look. Identification with various ideals and rationalizing discourse upon oneself are so many forms in which the subject becomes fixed and betrays himself" (Lemaire, *Jacques Lacan*, 179).

74. Lacan feared that with its uncritical acceptance of selfhood, psychoanalysis was about to become a "right-thinking movement whose crowning expression is the sociological poem of the *autonomous ego*." Lacan, *Écrits*, 171. See also Lacan, *The Four Fundamental Concepts of Psycho-Analysis*, ed. by Jacques Alain Miller (London: Penguin Books, 1991), 127.

75. "Paranoia: Chronic psychosis characterized by a more or less systematized delusion, with a predominance of ideas of reference but with no weakening of the intellect and, generally speaking, no tendency towards deterioration" (Jean Laplanche and J.-B. Pontalis, *The Language of Psychoanalysis* [London: Hogarth Press and the Institute of Psycho-Analysis, 1973], 296).

76. Lacan, *Seminar*, 2, 49–52.

77. "The Other is, therefore, the locus in which is constituted the I who speaks to him who hears, that which is said by the one being already the reply, the other deciding to hear it whether the one has or has not spoken. But this locus also extends as far into the subject as the laws of speech, that is to say, well beyond the discourse that takes its orders from the ego,

the *ego* and become political subjects capable of meeting the alter on equal terms, they also become other to themselves and to their desire.[78]

Finally, that which is left completely beyond representation, that which can have effects only in the imaginary and the symbolic, is the real. The real in Lacanian theory refers not only to the material world and the corporeal body, but also to whatever in the mental world escapes signification. The former refers to the impossibility of ever fully capturing the real via the symbolic, and the latter is a logical consequence of the lack induced in the symbolic by the covenant of representation. In the context of identity construction through language, the real is at the same time that which is excluded in symbolization (the enjoyment sacrificed in assuming an identity in the symbolic) and that which is produced by the same process—the latter referring to a real lack-of-being that *would not exist* (and have effects in discourse) without symbolization. Thus the real is simultaneously "the remainder, leftover, scraps" of the process of symbolization and "the fullness of the inert presence, positivity" into which lack is introduced only by the signifier. In other words, it is a fullness without lack and "the lack around which the symbolic order is structured."[79]

"Ego" Meets "Alter": A Second Cut

How does the Lacanian interpretation of subjectivity relate to the constructivist understanding about the origins of political order? Most important, a Wendtian state of nature, where two states meet with only the need to survive, becomes impossible. The need to survive (as an interest, in Wendt's terms, and not as an instinctual drive) requires subjects who can conceive of themselves and their interests as objects of knowledge and can engage in interaction constructed in their minds in the symbolic register. The

---

as we have known ever since Freud discovered its unconscious field and the laws that structure it" (Lacan, *Écrits*, 141).

78. In fact, from the Lacanian perspective the illusion of an ego totally differentiated from the other is itself a reflection of people's alienation from their desire. The Wendtian interpretation of raising a reflexive self to the position of the transcendental signifier, which can control or own desire, is typical of late modernity. Previously, the notion of God was usually thought to occupy the same position. On the relation between the Christian God and ego identity, see also Jürgen Habermas, "On Social Identity," *Telos*, no. 19 (Spring 1974): 91–103.

79. The quotes are from Žižek, *The Sublime Object*, 169–70. Another way to formulate the definition is Lacan's one-liner: "[T]he real is that which always comes back to the same place—to the place where the subject in so far as he thinks, where the *res cogitans*, does not meet it" (Lacan, *The Four Fundamental Concepts of Psycho-Analysis* [London: Penguin Books, 1977], 49).

price to be paid for this possibility is decentering, the birth of an *internal* otherness, without which no speech and no identity are possible. Interests and desires in the symbolic are thus inevitably tied to the desire of the other, born simultaneously with a child's birth as a subject of language.

Ego's perceptions of alter—even on their first encounter—cannot be separated from the way in which people deal with the internal split constituting their identities. For example, if alter happens to deal with the dialectical nature of subjectivity in a way characteristic of psychopaths, the root cause of potential problems in ego–alter relations does not lie in the sphere of interaction between ego and alter, but in the way alter's own historically contingent understanding of the world distorts the interpretation of ego's gestures (e.g., interpreting ego's good-intentioned moves as a threat to alter's very existence), which may then be reflected in the interaction as violence. The analogy applies in the realm of international politics as well. When constructivists and neorealists seek to explain, for instance, the interaction leading to the Second World War, the hypernationalist identity of Nazi Germany and Hitler's drive toward nonsecurity expansion cannot be overlooked. Wendt, like neorealists, recognized this problem and referred to predator states and anarchy as "permissive cause," but like neorealists, he did not provide any theory about the origins of the phenomenon to which he attributed causal relevance.[80]

My argument is that to find the root cause of hypernationalism and predation, the move from one aggregate level to another, taken by Wendt and Mearsheimer as a purely metaphorical displacement,[81] has to be politicized by taking into consideration the role that the sovereign (the "third term") plays in mediating the relation between self and other. This leads me to abandon the billiard ball model of both constructivists and neorealists and focus on the interdependence of internal and external othernesses. Here the role of the real in identification processes as "the lack

80. "For whatever reasons—biology, domestic politics, or systemic victimization—some states may become predisposed to violence. The aggressive behavior of these predators or 'bad apples' forces other states to engage in competitive power politics, to meet fire with fire, since failure to do so may degrade or destroy them" (Wendt, "Anarchy," 408–9).

81. Wendt explicitly based his theory on an *analogy* of individuals and states. He claimed the analogy was justified because it is "an accepted practice in mainstream IR discourse" and because "states are collectivities of individuals that through their practices constitute each other as 'persons,' having interests, fears and so on" (Wendt, "Anarchy," 397, n. 21). Although one of the purposes of this chapter is to show that the latter criterion is problematic, the former criterion, which is strictly speaking no criterion at all, is at least interesting because it reveals how potentially extensive the reverberations of an immanent critique of the analogy can be.

around which the symbolic order is structured" is the key because it high-lights the fundamental impossibility at the core of every identity.[82] The fact that representation induces lack not only in the subject but also in the realm of the symbolic implies that coherent identities, collective or individ-ual, are possible only through a displacement of their impossibility and inconsistency onto that left outside their confines—the other—and pre-cisely this relation is mediated by the state and by political discourse.

Although this theme is discussed in more detail in the case study, the idea that a lack in the symbolic other is the prerequisite for any identity allows us to construct an alternative hypothesis about the phenomenon of hypernationalism, one adding a Lacanian twist to Freud's and Rousseau's criticism of corrupt polities. In hypernationalist discourse, the inferior other (the Communist, the imperialist, the Jew, the Black) is the signifier of the lack in the symbolic other, the displacement needed to hide the impossibility of the collective identity constructed in the symbolic. In other words, the other is the signifier of the symptom arising from the discrep-ancy between the illusion of collective corporeality and the fact of a society split by antagonisms.[83] Without this displacement, the society in question must deal with its own impossibility by a discourse questioning the split inherent in identity instead of one seeking to hide it under nationalist illusions.

In Lacanian theory, the key to unveiling the textual politics of hyperna-tionalism and predation lies in the concept of desire. Analyzing how desire in discourse operates in the registers of the imaginary, the symbolic, and the real to construct identities and interests makes it possible to trace their origins beyond the assumption of the existence of a self-reflexive ego. Be-fore demonstrating that our understanding of the origins of Russian for-eign policy can benefit from such an approach, I provide a brief methodological guide for analyzing the operation of desire in discourse.

DESIRE IN DISCOURSE: TOWARD A LACANIAN METHODOLOGY FOR READING IDENTITY POLITICS

Unlike constructivism, the Lacanian approach provides a methodology for analyzing how different forms of desire are evoked or promised satisfaction

82. Žižek, *Sublime Object*, 121–24.
83. Žižek, *Sublime Object, 126.*

in discourse and how these forms of desire lead people to identify with various positions in the larger collective constructed by discourse. Thus it is possible to uncover the discursive strategies by which perceptions of collective selves and others are used when turning people's innermost fears and desires into political interests and thus making possible certain forms of collective behavior. Because of the nature of the subject analyzed, the following taxonomy of six forms of desire, inspired largely by Mark Bracher's discussion,[84] concentrates only on how narcissistic desire in its active and passive forms is evoked and promised satisfaction in discourse. Anaclitic desire (the desire to possess or be possessed by the other) is given less attention.

Desire in the Imaginary, the Symbolic, and the Real

The first expression of desire is made possible by imaginary identification. It can take the form of loving and admiring the image of the other, as in the mirror stage when children invest their bodies with a new meaning by identifying with the image (active narcissistic form of imaginary desire), or it can take the opposite form of the desire to be the object of identification (passive narcissistic form of imaginary desire). The former desire is at work in discourse, for example when a student, reading a standard billiard ball textbook on international relations, identifies with the position, constructed by the author, in which a coherent visual image of an international system, reminiscent of the imagery of classical physics and economic microtheory, "emerges" from the complex coaction of the units and reflects the imaginary move from chaos to a safe and seductive visual gestalt.[85] An example of the latter desire—constructing the illusion of corporeal unity in the eyes of the other—can be evoked in identification with the narcissistic mirroring of men in uniform, whose rigid postures symbolize corporeal integrity and prestige, usually linked to feelings of national pride and power, in the eyes of the other.[86]

In the symbolic, desire operates in relation to language. Especially im-

84. Bracher, *Lacan*, 22–45.
85. Such a picture is painted for example in Waltz, *Theory of International Politics*, 91.
86. Lacan's thesis "Aggressivity is the correlative tendency of a mode of identification that we call narcissistic, and which determines the formal structure of man's ego and of the register of entities characteristic of his world" refers precisely to the close connection between a feeling of bodily coherence and security of the self, where imaginary challenges to the former (e.g., images of bodily fragmentation) give birth to aggressive feelings that seek to protect the imaginary unity of self from the bodily other (Lacan, *Écrits*, 12–25).

portant are master signifiers, which function as the bearers of people's identity.[87] They derive their power from people's relation to them (from being people's representatives in the symbolic) and from the ensuing split in people, which in turn arouses desire. In politics, master signifiers representing nationality, ethnicity, race, or sex are particularly important, as seen in people's reactions when such signifiers are used in a derogatory way. In its active narcissistic form, desire in the symbolic refers to identification with privileged signifiers, highly valued in the symbolic order. Although no two identities are completely identical with respect to the master signifiers representing them at one time, identification with certain master signifiers such as the one representing nationality is almost automatic.[88] People's aggression in defending their symbolic identities arises from the functional similarity of the roles of the mirror image and the cluster of master signifiers representing people in identity construction. These roles provide the illusion of an ego (ideal) that would let people be themselves (have a stable social identity in the eyes of the other) without the alienating effects caused by the desire of the other from within. Thus, interaction and identity construction in the symbolic are always tied to the dialectic of desire caused by the split that is the prerequisite for symbolic representation.[89]

The desperate and delusional effort to gain recognition from the symbolic other sets the stage for passive narcissistic desire in the symbolic. This desire seeks the other's approval by causing people to speak and act in ways consonant with the master signifiers occupying a privileged place in the symbolic. Words and deeds reflecting people's sometimes ridiculous attempts to tie their self-identity to signifiers like masculine, feminine, intellectual, realist are everyday reflections of this desire. In politics, such a desire can be used to discipline collective behavior by making people's ability to construct their identity in the symbolic, for instance, through

87. "Just as a nation can achieve unity and identity necessary for conducting its affairs with other nations only through its ambassadors, envoys, or elected officials—i.e., through its representatives—so too can an individual subject attain a unity and identity only through its representatives: signifiers" (Bracher, *Lacan*, 25).

88. People watching a hockey game between representatives of their nationality and another choose a side to support whether or not they know the individual players and whether or not they are interested in the game itself.

89. According to Bracher (*Lacan*, 25), "If, and when, I encounter another human subject, it is really our representatives, our signifiers, that are communicating and negotiating with each other, then whenever these representatives get together, my fate as a subject is in some way at stake."

discourses subordinate to collective master signifiers like God, the Party, the International Monetary Fund, conditional on behavior.

Desire in the real centers on what Lacan called "the object *a*," which reflects in discourse the being or enjoyment lost in taking the signifier for one's representative. The object *a* is thus the ultimate object, through which people in fantasy seek to restore their lack-of-being in the real. In its passive narcissistic form, desire in the real drives fantasies such as (hyper)-nationalism and racism, where people of a certain collective believe that they embody something extra (the object *a*), which raises them to a special position in the eyes of the other (resulting, e.g., in having to bear the "white man's burden" or in being a citizen of the "world's truly indispensable nation"[90]). Active narcissistic fantasy, on the other hand, is reflected in people's identification with figures possessing the object *a*. Such figures seem to have access to the enjoyment lost in symbolization; they seem to be outlaws in the world governed by the law-of-the-father. According to Bracher, such a desire can be seen in "the attempt of subjects (perhaps most overt in children and adolescents) to assume the voice, gaze, or certain mannerisms or styles of subjects who seem 'cool' or outrageous."[91]

Producing/Transforming Order Through Discourse

To provide a parsimonious account of the political effects (educating/in-doctrinating, governing/commanding, desiring/protesting, analyzing/transforming/revolutionizing) produced by discourse, it is necessary to seek to reveal the structure of the discourse analyzed.[92] According to Lacanian theory, differentiation among the effects of discourse is produced by differentiation in the positions occupied by four psychological elements in the discourse: knowledge, ideals, self-division, and *jouissance*. More precisely, the factors involved in the interaction between discourse and its receiver are the master signifiers (S1), the symbolic system of knowledge (S2), the lack in the real that the symbolic produces and around which it is structured (a), and the decentered subject ($), split in its identification

90. The dangers of such thinking can be seen in the way Secretary of State Madeleine Albright legitimized the use of force: "If we have to use force, it is because we are America. We are the indispensable nation. We stand tall. We see further into the future" (*New York Times*, 2 February 1998).

91. Bracher, *Lacan*, 45.

92. Again, as in the previous part, I follow closely in Bracher's footsteps, partly because Lacan's work on the above topic has not (to my knowledge) been translated into English. Bracher, *Lacan*, 53–80.

with master signifiers (S1) in the discourse and the desire to replace the enjoyment (a) lost in the process of identification.

The basic structure of the relation between a (decentered) author/ speaker and a (decentered) receiver of the discourse/message is shown in Figure 2.1:

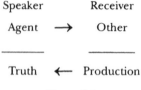

Figure 2.1

The upper-left-hand position, that of Agency, is occupied by the manifest, dominant, and obvious factor in discourse. An example is a totalizing system of knowledge, such as the dogmas taught in an introductory international relations course ("the international system is anarchic," "states are the most important actors"). The lower-left-hand position, in turn, is the place of that left latent or covert in the manifest factor, which is repressed by it, but without which the existence of the former is impossible, such as self-evident presumptions of reality, which are not called into question in the discourse. In the upper-right-hand corner, we find the other, the factor in the receiving subject called into action by the Agent. This factor is a prerequisite for receiving the symbolic message. In the international relations introductory course example, the receiving factor would be a nonarticulated position—the object a in the real—reflecting the subject's need to empty him- or herself of knowledge that interferes with the process of successful indoctrination. The desire that the discourse arouses in the Receiver leads us to the lower-right-hand corner, that which is latent in the other produced by the discourse. It represents the price that the Receiver has to pay in assuming the position (other) reserved to him or her in the discourse. In the case of a young international relations student, the price paid for assuming the position of the object a is repressing the split inherent in subjectivity beneath linguistic reflection, producing a person alienated from his or her true (split) self.[93]

To demonstrate that a deconstruction of the operation of desire in dis-

93. In reality, the speaker–receiver relation is never as perfect as the graph in Figure 2.1 indicates, because no receiver is ever totally "empty" and defined only by the discourse read. Especially the arrow leading from the receiver to the speaker, indicating a demand by the receiver for repetition of the original impetus to sustain the effect caused by the speaker's message, is often interrupted by other factors.

course can help us understand the relation between Russian identity and Russian foreign policy, I next turn to a focal point in the discourse of enlightened patriotism and show that an analysis of its structure can be used to link identification processes and the construction of national interests with one another.

CASE STUDY: DESIRE AND IDENTITY IN SERGEI KORTUNOV'S ENLIGHTENED PATRIOTISM

Sergei Kortunov's article "Natsional'naya sverkhzadacha; Opyt rossiyskoy ideologii" [National supertask: An essay in Russian ideology], published in *Nezavisimaya gazeta* in October 1995, is just one of the many attempts by Russian foreign policy experts to formulate a grand strategy for Russia based on Russia's presumed cultural uniqueness.[94] It is an especially useful text because during the time of its publication, Kortunov's work in Yeltsin's administration dealt with the development of the official Russian national security concept[95] and because the article's arguments about Russian identity and national interests are popular and unusually explicit and well articulated.

The main argument of Kortunov's article is that Russian foreign and domestic policy should be based on a unique national mission, ingrained in Russian culture and traditions, of leading all countries and civilizations to peaceful unity. Much of the article is devoted to interpreting the last millennium of Russian history as a preparation of this role. Because Kortunov's analysis of the post–Cold War policies of the West and his assessments of Russia's possibilities of taking the lead in world history in the near future are rather pessimistic, he ends up advocating "enlightened patriotism," which implies a strong state, a unilateral foreign policy, and a rejection of the Western way of development as the strategy through which Russia can secure her missionary role in the future.[96]

94. Sergei Kortunov, "Natsional'naya sverkhzadacha; Opyt rossiyskoy ideologii," *Nezavisimaya gazeta*, 7 October 1995. An English version of the article is available as Sergei Kortunov, "The Fate of Russia," *Comparative Strategy* 15, 2 (1996):183–91. Those who can read Russian should consult the original, because many of the most revealing passages have been either edited or shortened to a more politically correct form in the English version.

95. Interview with Sergei Kortunov, Moscow, December 1995. For an analysis of the Russian national security concept, see Henrikki Heikka, "The Evolution of Russian Grand Strategy and its Implications on Finnish Security," *Northern Dimensions* (1999): 27–44.

96. For more detailed articulations of Kortunov's policy prescriptions with respect to NATO enlargement, see Kortunov, "Potentsial'nye soyuzniki Rossii" [Potential allies of Rus-

Kortunov's description of Russian identity meets Mearsheimer's criteria of hypernationalism:[97] Russia is described not only as unique but also as being better than other countries, as having a privileged position in the eyes of God and a special role in world history. Kortunov's worldview and policy prescriptions imply that military power plays an integral part in the fulfillment of Russia's mission, because the survival of superethnicity is identical to the survival of the Russian state, which Kortunov believes to be threatened by the weapons as well as the exotic values of the West.

What is the cause of Kortunov's anti-Westernism? Is it really, as his arguments imply, a mixture of the deeds of Western governments and the effects of an anarchic international system composed of nation states, which leads him to advocate a rather tough foreign policy? In the following, Lacanian discourse analysis is applied to his article to show that an alternative logic is at work underneath what is said and that this logic compels Kortunov to end up in anti-Westernism no matter how reassuring, respectful, and constructive the deeds of Western governments.

The Search for Identity

The article begins by noting that both the formation of Russia's self-identity and her national security concept are still under way. Suggesting that these two processes are intimately related but that there is currently not even a common language for discussing the issue, Kortunov sets out to define a "metahistorical" concept of national security, based on the "Russian idea" instead of on rational calculations about Russia's strategic interests. A comprehensive, philosophical approach to national security, Kortunov argues, is needed because there is not even a subject of national security—an idea of Russia as a state—and because a national security concept must reflect ideas that transcend the political interests of different parties and political actors.

Kortunov starts his analysis of the Russian national idea by asserting that in the future Russian statehood is likely to be based on a "universal" model of development, which includes a competitive market economy, a civil society, and a legally organized state (*pravovoe gosudarstvo*). Having said

---

sia], *Nezavisimaya gazeta*, 1 March 1996; Kortunov, "Dogovor ne mozhet byt' platoy za rasshireni" [The treaty cannot be the price for enlargement], *Nezavisimaya gazeta*, 13 February 1997. See also Kortunov, "Rossiya ishchet soyuznikov" [Russia in search of allies], *Mezhdunarodnaya zhizn'*, no. 5 (1996): 17–30. In the article, Kortunov outlined a more "aggressive (i.e., active)" foreign policy to replace the present "reactive" one.

97. See note 29 above.

this, Kortunov argues that such assertions only shadow Russia's uniqueness and do not bring us closer to an understanding of the true national (Russian) idea. The real decisions, according to Kortunov, deal with Russia's role in world history. Will Russia follow its own pattern of development or copy the West? Will Russia be self-reliant or dependent on the outside world? Will Russia be a large European country or a global superpower? Was the disintegration of the Soviet Union a crime or a natural phase in the historical development of Russia? How should the Stalin-style state, Russian Communism, the Soviet Union, and attempts to revive it be treated? Most important: have the Russian people had their say in world history, or is their time yet to come?

The first rhetorical move is thus one where the desire for a comprehensive solution to the problem is created by describing the agency, Russia, as a split subject ($), unwilling to define its identity by the master signifiers offered by the currently available language. Under this split is placed the desire for unity (active narcissistic form of imaginary desire), which would satisfy the lack (a) of a national consensus. The satisfaction promised to the desire of the readers is linked to the desire (the active narcissistic form of symbolic desire) for new objects of identification, the master signifiers (S1), which help produce a system of knowledge (S2) underlying the new consensus. The structure produced by the first move is shown in Figure 2.2:

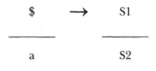

$$\frac{\$}{a} \quad \longrightarrow \quad \frac{S1}{S2}$$

Figure 2.2

This is the discourse of the hysteric, which is symptomatic of a situation in which a person is unwilling to accept the master signifiers offered by language. The language that Kortunov's Russia is unwilling to embody is of course the one offered by the West in the form of neoliberal economic discourse, demands of Western-style democracy, and a definition of Russia's role in global politics based on its current economic weakness. Kortunov's description of how the so-called New Russians (the representatives of neoliberal economic discourse in Russia) were "torn away" or "rejected" from the Russian national consciousness is almost identical to the bodily symptoms of the psychological state of hysteric neurosis. Both reflect an imaginary body torn between desire (a) and ideals (S1), which are not available in the dominant discourse, resulting in the dysfunction of the body and creating a desire for new master signifiers.[98]

Liminality

The bulk of the article is devoted to satisfying the "messianic anticipation" (Kortunov's words) created by the first move. Kortunov begins his construction of Russian subjectivity by citing Lev Gumilev and Daniil Andreev and arguing that although every nation has a mission in world history, only some are blessed with a supermission or supertask (*sverkhzadacha*). These nations are supernations (*sverkhnatsiya*) or superpeople (*sverkhnarod*), representing a group of nations united under a common culture. Implying that Russia is one of the chosen few, Kortunov describes how Russia has always been a center of cultural attraction to Slavs and other nations related to the Russian empire and how Russia itself has never been a nation inhabited only by ethnic Russians (*russkiy*) but always an empire of various peoples (*rossiyskiy*) united under the Russian state. Because of this, Kortunov says, the Russian national idea has never had any relation to Russian nationalism, but has always been immeasurably above it.

The argument that a special role in the construction of Russia's unique identity has throughout history been played by liminal groups who are neither ethnic Russians nor part of the other reflects a peculiar imaginary move, typical of Russian political discourse. Understanding the role played by liminal groups in Kortunov's vision of Russian identity is of utmost importance, because the way he sees Russia's relations to them is a microcosm of the structure of the long-term global geopolitical vision embedded in his reading of the Russian idea.

In the Lacanian perspective, the role of liminal groups in identity construction is similar to the role of the mirror in the move from imaginary identifications to a symbolic identity: providing an object with which the subject can identify while differentiating him- or herself from it. Just as the individual's birth into the symbolic order is preceded by a dialectic of imaginary identification and symbolic differentiation, so the construction of collective identities in the symbolic requires a dialectic where recogniz-

---

98. The organic metaphor of bodily dysfunction is also reflected in Kortunov's description of the intercourse of the different value systems of Russia and the West as analogous to giving a human being a transfusion of blood of the wrong type, resulting in death. Kortunov, "Rossiya: Natsional'naya identichnost' na rubezhe vekov" [National identity at the turn of the century], *Nauchnye doklady 37* (Moscow: Moskovskiy Obshchestvennyy Nauchnyy Fond, 1997), 56.

ing the likeness of the other is followed by a differentiation of self and other based on abstract principles. In the construction of nation states, the recognition of other states as like units is usually paralleled by differentiation based on comparison of the internal ordering principles of the units. Thus, the definition of states as well as the legitimacy of their internal organizations originates in the same triadic differentiation as individual identity.[99]

The way that Kortunov differentiates Russia from liminal groups and others reveals an understanding of geopolitics where even basic concepts, such as space, time, and otherness, are treated in a non-Western manner. To begin with, differentiation between Russia and the liminal groups is never clear or finished in Kortunov's world. His construction of Russia as a state parallels the view, which he attributes to Russian philosophers in general, that the nation state is only an intermediate stage in a process of historical development that eventually leads human civilization to unity (he cites Vladimir Soloviev's description of humanity as "some large organism"). In this context, the uniqueness of Russia and of her relations to neighboring states lies in Kortunov's claim that Russian policy has always been driven by a need to create an interculture—an undifferentiated, imaginary unity between Russia and those attracted to her. In other words, what is usually referred to as Russian imperialism or expansionism (subordination of the other to the will of the self) in the West is in Kortunov's world a reflection of Russia's attempt to overcome differentiation and to further the process of global cultural integration in as large a geopolitical space as possible.[100]

99. Norton, *Reflections on Political Identity*, 53–54. In practice, liminal groups can be any collectives of individuals at the verge of the symbolic order of a collective, whether defined in terms of territory, intellectual norms, wealth, class, gender, or ethnicity. Examples of territorial liminars include frontier people or outlaws in the history of North America (for an analysis of this phenomenon, see Norton, *Reflections on Political Identity*, 57–68) and the "pagans" living on the borders of the Russian civilization in the seventeenth century. See Iver B. Neumann, "Self and Other in International Relations," *European Journal of International Relations* 2, 2 (1996): 145–46.

100. What makes this idea particularly dangerous is Kortunov's claim that Russian imperialism has never been based on involuntary subordination of other nationalities. Kortunov's vision of the future Russia as a "responsible state" abiding with "universal values" should be seen in the light of his interpretation of history: If occupation of the Baltic states was a responsible policy in the past, why could it not be described as a responsible policy in the future? Especially worrisome from the perspective of the Baltic states is Kortunov's argument that although the fall of communism was "natural" and "inevitable," the disintegration of the Soviet Union was not. Kortunov also maintains that restoring the great power position of Russia is an "objective" and "natural" process and defines the sphere of interest of the future

Why should it be Russia, not the West with its crusade for democratization, who leads the world to unity? According to Kortunov, special spiritual
and cultural qualities are required from the leading supernation. These
include universal humanity, susceptibility to other cultures, tolerance, and
extensive spiritual qualities. Referring to great Russian authors, particularly
Fyodor Dostoyevsky and Nicholas Berdyaev, Kortunov claims that such
qualities are characteristic of Russian people. This leads Kortunov to envision Russia's future mission as a spiritual mission of creating an interculture or inter-religion, based on the vitality of Russian moral values.[101]

In this move, the dialectic of God and man comes into play, and Russia's role as the core of the future interculture is legitimized. Kortunov's
spiritual attributes place Russia in a unique position in the eyes of the symbolic other (God); Russia embodies those characteristics that the symbolic
other desires from those he loves. The desire at work here is the passive
narcissistic kind (in the real), where Russia is seen as embodying that special trait (the object a) that would heal the gap brought into being by
assuming the existence of the symbolic other (which is, as elaborated earlier, the precondition for linguistic identity construction). The role of Russians as the chosen people whose mission is to suffer for others is
structurally similar to the role of the son, the concrete embodiment of the
power of the symbolic other (the word as flesh), who acts as the mediator
between God and humanity, giving direction to the historical process leading to an eschatological utopia, where the principle of differentiation will
finally be erased by the second coming of Christ.[102] The Western understanding of time in geopolitics (related to variables such as growth or decline in population, gross national product, defense expenditures) is thus
subordinate to an eschatological vision of history, where cultural and spiritual strength, not material resources, is the determining force.

The same utopia colors Kortunov's understanding of geopolitical
space. His vivid description of the miraculous expansion of the Russian
state from Eastern Europe to the Bering Sea and all the way to California,
covering a "severe, cold, comfortless, almost deserted territory, rich only

---

great power (in economic *and* military relations) as "the Post-Soviet area." Kortunov, "Rossiya," 8, 34–38, 48, 50.

101. See also Kortunov, "Rossiya," 6–10, 65–67.

102. See also the first paragraph of page 63 in Kortunov's "Rossiya," which is a particularly good example of this move. On the current role of eschatological thinking in Russian
politics, see Assen Ignatow "Solowjow und Berdjajew als Geschichtsphilosophen: Ideen und
aktueller Einfluß," *Berichte des Bundesinstituts für ostwissenschaftliche und internationale Studien* 3
(1997).

in animals, birds, and fish,"[103] is explained by Russia's historical destiny of uniting the major civilizations of the world. In other words, Russia's geopolitical location in the Eurasian heartland is taken as a reflection and precondition of its role as the heart of the future interculture. The process itself is described by the author as one of assimilating, melting, and uniting other cultures into Russia until a planetary unity is achieved.

The move here is based on the active narcissistic form of imaginary desire, where the image of territory is taken over by the will of the collective (imagined) self, just as the image of the body is taken over by the will of the self in the first move of the mirror stage.[104] Just as the move at the individual level leads to an understanding of representation, so the collective self in Kortunov's text is defined by identification with that which is what it is not—captured in the passage where the deserted territory turns into an instrument for the actualization of the self's will. The price to be paid at the collective level is similarly the split instituted in the self, arising from the discrepancy between the assumed organic unity of the self and the objective identity acquired through representation. In other words, when Kortunov's Russia defines its boundaries and identifies with the territory under its will, it has become an alienated, split, and desiring self, fearful of losing something it never had.

The Imaginary Threat and the Symbolic Solution

In Kortunov's discourse, differentiation of the self from the threatening and degenerating other is done in the context of this utopian vision. The threat from the other is primarily an imaginary one, targeted on the presumed organic unity of the Russian interculture and the mission ingrained in the "genetical instinct of the nation." The past two thousand years of Russian history, writes Kortunov, have been a struggle for the preservation of the superethnos, which has been threatened by dissolution (*rastvorenie*) and disappearance (*ischeznovenie*) into otherness, and even attempts of out-

103. This vision of geopolitical expansion coupled with a moral mission has many similarities with the dominant American founding story. Michael J. Shapiro, "Sovereign Anxieties" (Paper presented at the University of Turku Seminar on State Regulations, Citizenship, and Democracy, May 1996): 11.

104. The parallel between the individual's and the collective's relation to their corporeal "bodies" is captured in Norton's description of the child's first visual identification: "Drawn to the image because it was other to himself, external, alien in texture and appearance, he does not mistake it for himself. He takes it as an army takes foreign territory, making it his own through occupation. The image signifies the success of this act of willful imperialism." Norton, *Reflections on Political Identity*, 14–15.

right destruction and extermination (*istreblenie, unichtozhenie*) by the other. The survival of Russia, he continues, "cost the flesh and blood of the supernation."[105] Imaginary identification with these images of bodily dissolution and extermination is possible only if one has first identified with the illusion of the existence of an organic collective self, where geopolitical territory plays the role of the mirror image.[106]

The clear and present danger now, according to Kortunov, is the "new world order" imposed by the West, based on materialism and the culture of consumption. The imaginary threat this time is not only annihilation of the supernation, but "a global ecological disaster," the real end of history following from policies animated by the idea that history has ended with the victory of Western ideas. Kortunov relates the master signifier "West" to the symbolic other in an opposite way from the position he attributes to Russia—a move typical of previous nationalist formulations of the self-other problem in Russian-Western relations.[107] Referring to Berdyaev, Kortunov describes Russia as being able to resist the "world of things." The dialectic of God and humanity is brought forward in the metaphor of the golden calf, the temptation that Russia (not the West) can resist, just as Christ resisted the temptations of Satan. The mission of the chosen people (*narod-bogonosets*), then, is to provide an alternative to the Western global political order, which Kortunov sees as based on choosing Antichrist instead of the real thing.[108]

To explain how to secure the supernation and its mission against the threatening other, Kortunov evokes the paternal images of past strong leaders, whom he, in a peculiarly Freudian tone, refers to as originators (*rodomysli*). These figures have a special place in the people's memory, including

105. These words are from the English version; the original talks only about "Russia" surviving a "bloody" war. Of interest here is especially the use of the singular, which dissolves the wars against the Mongols, the Nazis, NATO into one big war against the other. No wonder Kortunov calls it a "complex" war.

106. See also Kortunov, "Rossiya," 61–62.

107. Kortunov, for example, contrasts the Russian empire, a supernation consisting of various nationalities all "attracted" to the spiritual center of Russia, with Western imperialism, based on violence and subordination of the other. Kortunov, "Imperskie ambitsii i natsional'-nye interesy" [Imperial ambitions and national interests], *Nezavisimaya gazeta* 11 September 1997. Kortunov, "Rossiya," 59. On Russian dualism, see Yuri M. Lotman and Boris A. Uspenski, *The Semiotics of Russian Culture* (Ann Arbor: University of Michigan Slavic Contributions 11, 1984), 3–35, 53–67.

108. Elsewhere, Kortunov describes Russia as the "purifier" and "drainage pipe" of the West. If the West chokes this pipe, Kortunov claims, the West will only kill itself. Thus, he continues, the true Russian patriot (one defending Russia's unique role in world history) is also a patriot of the West! Kortunov, "Rossiya," 62.

the intellectual elite and the broad masses, Kortunov writes, even if their deeds sacrificed countless human lives. Their policies were seen as legitimate because they increased the "might and greatness of the supernation," he argues. In the context of this historical trajectory, Kortunov's *Endlösung* ("final solution") for Russia's identity crisis, "enlightened patriotism," receives its legitimacy.

Kortunov here seeks to satisfy the readers' desires evoked in the opening lines of the article by providing a stable identity for the self constructed in the article. The paternal master signifiers serve two functions. On the one hand, they act as objects of common identification, enabling the construction of an imaginary organic unity among the community united under their authority. On the other hand, they act as mediators between the collective self and Russia's historical mission by ensuring the continuity of Russia's privileged position in the eyes of the symbolic other.

The political significance of the first function arises from the fact that it deprecates the differentiation of subject and object. The symbolic-order abstract and objective structures separating the individual, the community, and the state in a rational legal regime all melt in identification with the charismatic figure representing authority, resulting in a feeling of unity resembling the *méconnaissance* (misrecognition) of the mirror stage, where the physical experience of the self is identified with its representation. In Kortunov's text, the legitimacy of the leader's authority is affirmed outside law and formal structures of representation, because it flows from the leader's instinctive understanding of the Russian mission, which, as Kortunov claims, is recognized in his deeds by all strata of society. Consequently, the move constructs an organic community, whose precondition, the split arising from representation and the sense of lack it creates, is repressed.

The latter function is especially important for political order because a strong leader, conscious of Russia's mission, signifies the continuity of Russian polity during periods of radical change. More precisely, the function attributed to the strong leader in Kortunov's text is maintaining the Russian idea (the object a) at the heart of Russian political culture and fighting—shrewdly, if needed—against external as well as internal enemies. In this context, the countless human lives sacrificed during this project are seen as morally justified because without the object a the Russians would not be the chosen people.

At the end of his essay, Kortunov reveals precisely what Russia's national survival requires if his analysis of Russian history and the Russian national idea is correct. The attempt to export a Western liberal model to Russia, Kortunov says, has failed. Instead of trying to follow the Western way of development, Kortunov argues, Russia should seek to protect its freedom and its technological potential, which is threatened by the attempts of the West and China to buy out Russian technology for their own benefit. What Russia needs is once again a powerful state, which has always been the guardian of Russia's independence, securing Russia from exotic values. According to Kortunov, the real political watershed in Russian politics is not between left and right, but between those who are for a strong state and those who are against it. Underlying this division, he claims, is a deeper split related to modernization: will Russia become just a raw material producer for the West, or will it seek its own solution, giving hope to the rebirth of a great power? According to Kortunov, the ideology leading Russia to the latter scenario is enlightened patriotism (*prosveshchennyy patriotizm*), which implies the idea of a strong and responsible state.

Governance Through Mastery

As noted earlier, Kortunov's vision of Russia's role in the world is based on master signifiers (S1), which describe its uniqueness. The desires evoked by Kortunov serve the purpose of constructing an organic, unitary self having a special position in the eyes of the symbolic other. This position, reflected in the Russian mission, explains the blurred differentiation between the self and liminal groups and the strict differentiation from signifiers representing the threatening other. The desires evoked previously by the discourse of the hysteric are satisfied by repressing the split (\$) arising from symbolic representation beyond reflection.

The role enacted by the other (the readers) in relation to the discourse is the function of a system of knowledge (S2) based on the master signifiers describing Russia's uniqueness. In assuming this system of knowledge (enlightened patriotism) as a representative of identity, readers gain access to a feeling of security and a sense of direction, which is lacking in the discourse of the hysteric. When identifying with this system of knowledge, readers lose something (a) for which there is no place in the master's subjectivity (S1/\$) or in the knowledge evoked in the other (S2/a). The price paid for constructing the self on the system of knowledge based on Kortunov's master signifiers is thus suppression of the desire (in the real) created by taking this position, beneath the bar. In Lacanian terms, Figure 2.3 depicts the discourse of the master:

The messianic anticipation of a Russian identity has been answered by constructing a position of mastery and governance, legitimizing the need for a strong state. In this position, the voice of the other is repressed, as

Figure 2.3

witnessed both in the speaker's repression of the split in his own identity ($), without which there could be no identity at all, and the denial of the desire of the receiver (a). It is precisely the neglect of the desire of the other that is the corrupting element in such a discourse, because it implies that the people, to whom the discourse is addressed, are reduced to a position of slavery. Their right to express their lack is suppressed by the master's (probably honest) ignorance of the split in his own identity.

Kortunov's anti-Westernism and general hostility toward the threatening and degenerating other is a logical consequence of this discursive structure. The fact that an organic Russian society does not exist any more than any other imagined community is masked by displacing the antagonisms of the Russian body politic onto signifiers like "the West," "the New Russians," and "NATO," which are described in terms (materialist, anti-Christian, antiecological) that are symptomatic of Russia's own current plight. In Kortunov's world, the West in its internal and external variants is the signifier that explains why the fantasy of Russia as an organic whole remains only a fantasy. This argument may be taken even further by arguing that Kortunov's fantasy of an organic Russia is a presupposition for his understanding of the degenerating, materialist Western other, but that this fantasy *could not exist* without the constant displacement of its own impossibility onto the Western other.[109] In other words, the element ($), which is repressed in the symbolic construction of the unitary Russian self, constantly returns in the real as a paranoid construction of the Western other.

I do not mean to imply that Kortunov is totally wrong in treating the West as a military threat to Russia or in defining the "New Russians" as a problem for Russian society, but hate toward the New Russians has an integral role in Kortunov's discourse regardless of the real nature of these others (such as the actual offensiveness of NATO, the degree of materialism in Western culture, or the corruption of the New Russians and their true role in Russia's economic problems). The suppression of the split inherent

109. It is no coincidence, then, that according to Kortunov "in a paradoxical way [*sic!*], the expansion of NATO stimulates Russia's search for national identity." Kortunov, "Dogovor."

in identity and the consequent neglect of the desire of the other, not the nature of the West or the structure of the international system, cause Kortunov's search for Christian and humanistic ideals to result in an identity based on hate and fear. One confronts this paradox whenever seeking to integrate the Christian idea of absolute freedom with an earthly form of governance based on a unitary identity. Because one of the first thinkers to foresee the dangers of the combination was, not surprisingly, a Russian, I will let Fyodor Dostoyevsky's Shigalyov have the last word on the issue: "I am perplexed by my own data and my conclusion is a direct contradiction of the original idea with which I start. Starting from unlimited freedom, I arrive at unlimited despotism. I will add, however, that there can be no solution to the social problem but mine."[110]

CONCLUSION: FOR(GET) IDENTITY

Neorealists maintain that cold wars arise from the structure of the international system, which they define by the distribution of capabilities across the units of the system. Constructivists argue that interaction among the poles, not anarchy itself, defines whether the system is characterized by cooperation, zero-sum competition, or something in between. In this chapter, I have argued that the phenomenon of predation, arising from extreme nationalism, makes possible cold-war type situations and that identification processes, cutting through all three levels of analysis, generate predation. Building on insights by Rousseau, Freud, and Lacan, I presented a methodology for tracing the origins of extreme nationalism and perceptions of threatening others in the interplay of desire and identity in foreign policy discourse.

Psychoanalytic identity theory does not tell us all we want to know about the origins of cold wars, but it can tell us a few important things and can do this relatively parsimoniously. Most important, it is one of the few theories that actually provide a methodology for distinguishing the structure of different identities from one another, and thus it eliminates at least some individual researchers' personal bias about these complicated and often highly political issues. As seen in the analysis above, Lacanian psychoanalysis is a rather complex and uncomfortable theory, because it does not locate the reasons for people's mutual fears in some predetermined simple

---

110. Dostoyevsky, *The Possessed.*

structures, but instead in the various ways in which individuals and collectives deal with the split in their own identity. Peace in politics among decentered nations is, according to such a view, not only a function of mutual deterrence but also, in systems free of predationist tendencies, a result of a long and multifaceted cultural process through which collectives have learned to deal with the problem of otherness in a constructive way. The case study above indicates that a cultural crisis of representation is intertwined with the crisis in political representation and that political discourse that represses the split caused by representation easily leads to a potentially dangerous view of otherness, one that makes possible a return to a cold war regardless of the deeds of the other.

Psychoanalytic theory can offer guidelines for dealing with potentially dangerous social constructions of reality in ways other than just preparing for the worst. In the field of international relations, a constructive alternative to pure realpolitik would involve a dialogue with the other itself, or more precisely, an engagement with the cultural process by which the other interprets the cultural artifacts on which its identity is based.[111]

To hint how a Lacanian intervention into the process of constructing Russian identity based on the Russian idea can lead us toward constructing a less nationalistic Russian identity, I end this chapter by showing that an alternative reading of one of the core texts of the tradition of thinking into which Kortunov places himself can reveal that all the seeds of peace already exist in the world of enlightened patriots. The text, Dostoyevsky's "Legend of the Grand Inquisitor," in his novel about parricide, *The Brothers Karamazov*, is often referred to as the heart of the dialectics of the Russian idea, because the themes of freedom and slavery, which are dealt with in the context of the theodicy problem, reveal the seductive power of enslaving forms of governance and the terrible burden that freedom of choice puts on humanity.[112]

The Legend, told by the revolutionary intellectual Ivan Karamazov to his brother, is set in Seville in the sixteenth century, one day after one hundred heretics have been burned by order of the Grand Inquisitor. A

111. In effect, this strategy is the cultural variant of the monitoring of teaching honest history to dampen hypernationalism. See Stephen Van Evera, "Primed for Peace: Europe After the Cold War," *International Security* 15 (Winter 1990–91): 52.

112. Dostoyevsky, *The Brothers Karamazov* (London: Penguin Books, 1993), 283–304; See also Kortunov, "Al'ternativy: Aksiologicheskie aspekty khristianstva, marksizma, i filosofii zhizni" [Alternatives: Axiological aspects of Christianity, Marxism, and the philosophy of life], *Nauchnye doklady* 10 (Moscow: Rossiyskiy nauchnyy fond, 1992). Nicholas Berdyaev, *Dostoyevsky* (New York: Meridian Books, 1959); Berdyaev, *The Russian Idea* (London, Centenary Press, 1947).

feast is interrupted by the quiet appearance of Christ, who is—strangely, as Ivan notes—recognized by everyone. At the end of the day, after bringing back to life a young child who had died, Christ is taken to the Inquisitor, who in a long monologue, accuses Christ of refusing to change world history when he resisted the temptations to use his power to solve the problems of the world. The Inquisitor reveals the impossibility of the human condition: being an imperfect creature in an imperfect world but having the freedom of choice between good and evil. Even slavery, which offers people peace, food, and other ingredients of a decent life, is preferable to the burden of having to live with the freedom of choice and the problem of theodicy. The poem ends with the silent Christ kissing the Inquisitor, who shudders, releases him, and tells him never to return.

Theoretically, the dialogue between the Grand Inquisitor and Christ involves the former as the speaker, who expresses his lack (a), derived from a system of knowledge (S2) representative of the reasoning of humanity, and the latter as the other who is present only through his silence. The identification process involved in the discourse is similar to psychoanalysis, whereby the silent presence of the other allows a speaker to become conscious of the split in his or her self. In Lacanian terms, the process can be described as a *dissolution of transference,* where the question "What does the other (God) want?" (Why do I have this mandate?"), which led Kortunov to identify with a mission, is resolved when the analysand realizes that the symbolic mandate given to him or her by the covenant of representation can never be fulfilled—that the subject's lack can never be filled by the subject's offering him- or herself to fulfill the other's (the analyst's) lack.[113] The Legend thus strikes a blow against all forms of governance that refuses to accept the effect of the real on the symbolic. Even the symbolic other itself contains no final answer, only a radical inconsistency arising from lack.[114]

Such a structure, in which the hysteric search for identity does not discharge itself into a discourse of the master, is called by Lacan the discourse of the analyst.[115] It is useful in promoting social change because it forces one in search of a new identity into a position in which what is left out (a) in taking the signifier as one's representative is recognized by assuming the signifier of one's alienation ($) as representative of the self (see Fig. 2.4):

113. On theodicy, see also Kortunov, "Al'ternativy," 5–25.
114. See Žižek, *Sublime Object,* 121–24.
115. Bracher, *Lacan,* 68–73.

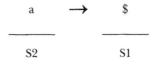

Figure 2.4

This move is one of radical disillusionment, after which the illusion of wholeness, whether reflected in the presumption of the existence of an organic "Russia" or of the autonomous ego, is recognized as what it is—a fantasy repressing the uncomfortable truth. From there on, the other has a voice through which to express its desire and consequently cannot be used as a locus onto which the inconsistency in the fantasy of wholeness is displaced. In other words, the move makes impossible such self–other relations as are the prerequisite for hypernationalism and predation.

To achieve and sustain such a cultural momentum between actors from the intrapersonal level to the international level, there is no other means than critical dialogue. The Lacanian contribution to the dialogue between an increasingly assertive Russia and an integrating West reminds both sides that dangerous illusions are broken not only by adjusting perceptions in line with "reality" (as reflected in the current Western strategy of trying to assure the Russians that NATO enlargement is not a threat to them), which overlooks the effects of the real on the symbolic, but by facing their internal inconsistency, the hidden truth in fantasies of nationalism and threatening others. This means, paradoxically, that we need to bring the theme of identification and desire into international relations discourse to help produce identities aware of their own impossibility.

3

The Impact of International Security Regimes on Russia's Behavior

The Case of the OSCE and Chechnya

Christer Pursiainen

> Everyone knows that we Russians do not like to obey
> all sorts of rules, laws, instructions, and
> directives—any kind of previously established
> regimentation of behavior. We are a casual sort of
> people and rules cut us like a knife.
> —Boris Yeltsin, *The Struggle for Russia*

The importance of institutions and international law in a world of anarchy has been one of the major watershed problems in the theoretical disputes in international relations since the time of the first grand debate about the juxtaposition of idealism and realism. Today, the problems related to institutionalized, norm-based cooperation between states or to the rules of the game are discussed in regime analysis through the prism of several approaches.[1] The fundamental problem, the promise of institu-

For very helpful comments on earlier versions of this chapter, I am especially thankful to Ted Hopf, Stephen Hanson, Henrikki Heikka, Raimo Lintonen, James Richter, Antti Turunen, and the anonymous reviewers of the publisher.

1. For a thorough survey, see Andreas Hasenclever, Peter Mayer, and Volker Rittberger, "Interests, Power, Knowledge: The Study of International Regimes," *Mershon International*

tions, has, however, remained one of the most important subjects of con-
tention in international relations in general.[2] These controversies are
interesting not only from the theoretical point of view; for practitioners
and decision makers involved in international politics, the questions over
which theoreticians wrestle are also the most crucial. Can institutions enhance cooperation between states? Do international norms and rules
matter? More to the point of this discussion, do they matter to Russia?
Can institutions prevent or contain Russia's unilateral behavior and make
Russia behave in a cooperative and nondiscordant way? Above all, is this
possible where it seems to be needed the most, in the field of military
security?

In answering these questions, I draw on the interparadigm debates in
international relations theory and examine the problems of international
cooperation and institutions with particular reference to security regimes. Later, however, I take a less abstract approach in terms of questions and empirical illustrations. I deal with norms and rules created in
one particular organization, the Conference on Security and Cooperation in Europe (CSCE)/Organization for Security and Cooperation in
Europe (OSCE)[3] focusing especially on its impact on Russia's policy
toward Chechnya from 1994–95. Why did Russia openly violate certain
commonly accepted OSCE rules? Why, after a period of negotiation, did
Russia nevertheless allow the OSCE to become a legitimate party in conflict management in its own territory in the form of a long-term permanent mission? Can international relations theory help us understand

---

Studies Review: Supplement to the International Studies Quarterly 40, Supplement 2 (October 1996):
77–228; for an extended version of the former, see Hasenclever, Mayer, and Rittberger, *Theo-
ries of International Regimes* (Cambridge: Cambridge University Press, 1997); see further Marc
A. Levy, Oran R. Young, and Michael Zürn, "The Study of International Regimes," *European
Journal of International Relations* 1, 3 (1995): 267–330; Rittberger, ed., with the assistance of
Mayer, *Regime Theory and International Relations* (Oxford: Clarendon Press, 1993); see also
James C. Hsiung, *Anarchy and Order: The Interplay of Politics and Law in International Relations*
(Boulder, Colo., and London: Lynne Rienner, 1997).

2. See, for instance, the following heated discussion: John J. Mearsheimer, "The False
Promise of International Institutions," *International Security* 19 (Winter 1994–95): 3–49; and
subsequently in the same issue of *International Security* 20 (Summer 1995): Robert O. Keohane
and Lisa L. Martin, "The Promise of Institutionalist Theory," 39–51; Charles A. Kupchan and
Clifford A. Kupchan, "The Promise of Collective Security," 52–61; John Gerard Ruggie, "The
False Promise of Realism," 62–70; Alexander Wendt, "Constructing International Politics,"
71–81; and Mearsheimer, "A Realist Reply," 82–93.

3. The Conference on Security and Cooperation in Europe (CSCE) has since January
1995 been known as the Organization for Security and Cooperation in Europe (OSCE). Hereafter in this chapter, it is referred to as the OSCE.

Russia's somewhat paradoxical behavior? What are the theoretical and practical implications of this problem?

WHY RUSSIA COOPERATES

It is usually accepted that "[i]nternational regimes form part of the more general set of phenomena known as international institutions."[4] Yet the concept of a regime can be used in numerous contexts. The definitions of a security regime, for instance, range from tacit understandings about spheres of influences via secret treaties or informal agreements to formally binding and publicly declared treaties and complicated networks of detailed agreements.[5] Although I do not argue the merits of any of these definitions now, I nevertheless start with the notion that there clearly exist many more or less formally and explicitly stated international security regimes that are constantly referred to as bases to describe the international security system and behavioral practices in security-related affairs. Russia is a key regime participant in many cases, and much of Russia's domestic and diplomatic activity in the field of security, as well as that of other regime participants, is connected with the formulation, implementation, and follow-up of these regime norms and rules. Moreover, from a purely legalistic point of view, Russia, as well as most countries in the world, recognizes the centuries-old international legal canon of *pacta sunt servanda*—obligations must be followed. Respect for international law and primacy of international obligations over domestic laws are emphasized in the 1993 constitution of the Russian Federation,[6] and the law on the international

4. John S. Duffield, "Explaining the Long Peace in Europe: The Contributions of Regional Security Regimes," *Review of International Studies* 20 (1994): 369–88, quotation 375.

5. For security regime definitions, see Harald Müller, "The Internalization of Principles, Norms, and Rules by Governments: The Case of Security Regimes," in Rittberger, *Regime Theory*, 361–88; Duffield, "Explaining the Long Peace in Europe," 378. For general regime definitions, compare the original "consensus definition" in Stephen D. Krasner, "Structural Causes and Regime Consequences: Regimes as Intervening Variables," in Krasner, ed., *International Regimes* (Ithaca and London: Cornell University Press, 1983), 1–22; the "new consensus definition" in Levy, Young, and Zürn, "The Study of International Regimes"; and the latter definition of that in Friedrich Kratochwil, "Contract and Regimes: Do Issue Specificity and Variations of Formality Matter?" in Rittberger, *Regime Theory*, 73–93. For further discussion, see Hasenclever, Mayer, and Rittberger, "Interests, Power, Knowledge"; and Robert O. Keohane, "The Analysis of International Regimes: Towards a European-American Research Programme," in Rittberger, *Regime Theory*, 23–45.

6. Article 15.4.

agreements of the Russian Federation, approved in 1995, is based on the conscientious fulfillment of obligations, on the *jus cogens* principle. This principle applies to agreements of all kinds, regardless of whether they are called agreements or conventions or protocols.[7]

Thus, at first sight, international norms and rules seem to be of great significance for Russia and for international politics on the whole, although as we know they are sometimes violated by regime participants. Still, the question is not whether regimes exist or whether they are celebrated and cited or not even whether they are adhered to. The crucial point is the reason that they are ever complied with. Why does Russia comply with jointly agreed-on international norms and rules, and why does it sometimes violate them? Why does it take its international commitments seriously, if it does, and why does it cooperate in the first place?

The international relations literature has produced several hypotheses as useful starting points. The most important theoretical differences are embraced by the three mainstream approaches of contemporary international relations theory: structural realism, neoliberal institutionalism, and constructivism. One can simplify the picture, in terms of their explanatory variables, by saying that structural realism focuses on power relations, neoliberal institutionalism bases its analysis on constellations of interests, and constructivism emphasizes knowledge dynamics, communication, and identities.[8] There is another well-known distinction between the two research programs of rationalism and reflectivism,[9] with the former emphasizing the potential gains from institutionalized cooperation calculated by states behaving rationally and the latter emphasizing the potentiality of changes in preferences by states generated during the intersubjective processes they are involved in. In terms of this typology, structural realism and neoliberal institutionalism are understood as rationalist approaches,

7. "Zakon o mezhdunarodnykh dogovorakh RF (15.7.1995): Vstupitel'naya stat'ya A. N. Talayeva" [The law on international agreements of the Russian Federation (July 15, 1995)], *Moskovskiy zhurnal mezhdunarodnogo prava*, no. 2 (1996): 251–77.

8. This typology follows that of Hasenclever, Mayer, and Rittberger, "Interests, Power, Knowledge," with some minor differences. For other typologies, see, for instance, Frank Schimmelfenning, "Arms Control Regimes and the Dissolution of the Soviet Union: Realism, Institutionalism, and Regime Robustness," *Cooperation and Conflict* 29 (June 1994): 115–48; Müller, "The Internalization of Principles, Norms, and Rules by Governments," especially 362.

9. The rationalism–reflectivism dispute was formulated by Keohane in his 1988 article "International Institutions: Two Approaches," reprinted in Keohane, *International Institutions and State Power: Essays in International Relations Theory* (Boulder, Colo.: Westview Press, 1989), 158–82.

whereas constructivism can be seen, broadly speaking, as a synonym of reflectivism. I look at these three theoretical approaches and offer their respective answers to the problems described earlier.

Structural Realists as Pessimists and Optimists

Structural realism, or neorealism, has been labeled "the most prominent contemporary version of realpolitik."[10] There are several slightly different accounts in the general framework of structural realism. The most renowned version of structural realism, associated with theorists such as Kenneth Waltz and John Mearsheimer, can be seen as a natural null hypothesis of regime analysis or any discussion about international cooperation. According to this account, although states may occasionally operate through international institutions, these institutions (regimes, organizations, alliances, etc.) are only a superficial reflection of the distribution of power in the world and are constituted by the self-interested calculation of the great powers. In this frame, international cooperation is difficult to achieve. According to Waltz, the structure of international politics restrains cooperation between states in two ways. First, a state "worries about a division of possible gains that may favor others more than itself," and even the prospect of large absolute gains for all parties does not enhance cooperation as long as each one is concerned about "how the other will use its increased capabilities." Second, a "state also worries lest it become dependent on others through cooperative endeavors"; that is, states are mostly concerned about maintaining independence and autonomy, about widening the scope of their control and striving for greater self-sufficiency.[11]

Norms and rules, especially those related to military security, are of little importance and do not have independent leverage in this framework. Thematic issues are treated as if they were hierarchically related to one another and to military security at the top; security is seen as the field most immune to genuine cooperation. Although cooperation in security affairs clearly exists, for example, alliance formation, it is not to be interpreted as important evidence of cooperation. Under the conditions of Cold War bipolarity, alliances did not really matter. "Alliance leaders need worry little about the faithfulness of their followers." In multipolar systems, the problem of the tactical spirit of any cooperation is always present, because

10. See Patrick James, "Structural Realism and the Causes of War," *Mershon International Studies Review* 39 (1995): 181–208.

11. Kenneth N. Waltz, *Theory of International Politics* (New York: Random House, 1979), 105, 106.

the "flexibility of alliances" makes "everyone's estimate of the present and future relation of forces uncertain," and cooperation remains at best temporary.[12] International systems are thus self-help systems by nature. Therefore, were one to start to answer the questions raised in the introduction to this chapter about the impact or influence of international norms and rules, the premises of this mode of structural realism alone would make us respond negatively to them all. Mearsheimer put it succinctly: international regimes or other institutions have only "minimal influence on state behavior"; they "are not an important cause of peace but matter only on the margins." Consequently, the institutionalist theories "are all flawed" and "find little support in the historical record."[13]

Most structural realists do not take such a dim view of the role of cooperative regimes or of international cooperation in general, and in some of its forms, structural realism can even be seen as part of regime analysis itself. The approach put forward by Joseph Grieco, for instance, is a slightly modified version of structural realism, which suggests that while worrying about other states gaining more from cooperation, a state also focuses, at least to some degree, on its absolute gains from that cooperation. Moreover, by focusing especially on political economy, Grieco introduced arguments to the effect that international institutions or regimes do make a difference in enhancing international cooperation and helping states to overcome some relative gain problems.[14] From the viewpoint of Grieco's modified structural realism, institutions or regimes affect state policies more than only "marginally."[15]

Nevertheless, in this account as well, the problem of relative gains under the conditions of international anarchy remains the most important factor shaping state behavior. Anarchy means not only the absence of a common interstate government, but also the absence of overarching au-

12. Waltz, *Theory of International Politics*, especially 168, 169.

13. Mearsheimer, "The False Promise of International Institutions," 7. To mention Waltz and Mearsheimer in the same breath as focusing on relative power is perhaps not completely wrong, but they have serious differences in their emphases as well. Strictly speaking, Waltz did not claim that states try to maximize relative power, whereas Mearsheimer did. See the discussion in Charles L. Glaser, "Realists as Optimists: Cooperation as Self-Help," in Benjamin Frankel, ed., *Realism: Restatements and Renewal* (London and Portland, Ore.: Frank Cass, 1996), 122–63, especially 144–45.

14. Joseph M. Grieco, *Cooperation Among Nations: Europe, America, and Non-Tariff Barriers to Trade* (Ithaca: Cornell University Press, 1990), especially 233; Grieco, "Realist Theory and the Problem of International Cooperation: Analysis with an Amended Prisoner's Dilemma," *Journal of Politics* 50 (1988): 600–624, especially 614–20.

15. Hasenclever, Mayer, and Rittberger, "Interests, Power, Knowledge," 204.

thority to prevent states from using violence against other states, or at least to prevent them from threatening to do so. Consequently, states may have interests that can be fostered by cooperation, that is, they often have absolute gains independent of the gains of others, but "individual well-being is not the key interest of states." Instead, Grieco claimed, "*survival* is their core interest."[16] For this reason, states seek to prevent increases in other states' relative capabilities, but this behavior, which Grieco called "positional," does not amount to aggressiveness. On the contrary, state positionality is more "defensive" than "offensive" by nature.[17] In such a world, the prospects for cooperation remain fairly bleak, because concerns about relative gains restrain cooperation. In contrast to the Waltzian approach, the goal of this somewhat modified structural realism is not to lead the debate from the possibility of cooperation, but to offer it a more realistic framework. "Thus, with its understanding of defensive state positionality and the relative gains problem for collaboration," Grieco wrote, "realism may provide guidance to states as they seek security, independence, and mutually beneficial forms of international cooperation."[18] Grieco usually positioned his theory in a dialogue with neoliberal institutionalism, and in his own view, his approach "offers a more complete understanding of the problem of international cooperation" than neoliberal institutionalism, because it emphasizes not only individual or absolute gains, but relative gains as well.[19]

In the recent in-paradigm debates of structural realism, one can trace a tendency whose goal is openly proclaimed to be to correct the flaws that are seen in structural realism without sacrificing its basic assumptions. In other words, many structural realists apply the *methodological decision* that anomalies must *not* lead to changes in its "hard core," but to the enlargement of the protective belt around this core. This approach is more or less explicitly founded on Imre Lakatos's principle: "We may rationally decide not to allow 'refutations' to transmit falsity to the hard core as long as the corroborated empirical content of the protecting belt of auxiliary hypotheses increases."[20] Although there is no consensus among structural realists

16. Grieco, "Anarchy and the Limits of Cooperation: a Realist Critique of the Newest Liberal Institutionalism," in Charles W. Kegley Jr., ed., *Controversies in International Relations Theory: Realism and the Neoliberal Challenge* (New York: St. Martin's Press, 1995), 151–71, quotation 160. (Originally published in 1988.)

17. Grieco, "Anarchy and the Limits of Cooperation," 161, 162.

18. Grieco, "Anarchy and the Limits of Cooperation," 167, 168.

19. Grieco, "Anarchy and the Limits of Cooperation," 158.

20. Imre Lakatos, "Falsification and the Methodology of Scientific Research Programmes," in Lakatos and Alan Musgrave, eds., *Criticism and the Growth of Knowledge* (Cam-

about what elements constitute the hard core, three components—anarchy, functional homogeneity, and relative capabilities—are usually included in all definitions.[21] From the point of view of the subject of this chapter, the protective belt is often enlarged to be able to deal more fully with empirical cases of institutionalized cooperation. For instance, Grieco, again referring mainly to the field of political economy, claimed that states may prefer further institutionalization because it can provide them with a greater opportunity to influence decision-making processes than can market-oriented conditions. He maintained that this conclusion is still in accord with the "hard-core assumptions" of structural realism.[22]

Another version that is claimed to develop structural realism in the frame of its basic assumptions is put forward by Charles Glaser. His "contingent realism" refers especially to security cooperation. Glaser argued that the benefits of competition—specifically gaining military advantages—must be weighed against those of cooperation. "Structural realism properly understood predicts that, under a wide range of conditions, adversaries

---

bridge: Cambridge University Press, 1970), 91–196. Some critics of structural realism, such as John Vasquez, argue that instead of falsifying earlier theories in structural realism's research program by producing content-increasing versions of it, as would be the Lakatosian concept of scientific development, structural realists are producing more and more theories that include *contradictory* arguments. In that way it is easy to show that there always exists some version of (structural) realism that can explain the anomalies of another version, keeping all the versions alive, however. Vasquez sees that realism is therefore a degenerating research program, in terms of Lakatos's concept of theory choice. John A. Vasquez, "The Realist Paradigm and Degenerative Versus Progressive Research Programs: An Appraisal of Neotraditional Research on Waltz's Balancing Proposition," *American Political Science Review* 91 (December 1997): 899–912. Naturally, Vasquez was heavily criticized by realists, for misunderstanding Lakatos, realism in its different versions, or both. See the following replies in the same issue of *American Political Science Review* 91 (December 1997): Thomas J. Christensen and Jack Snyder, "Progressive Research on Degenerating Alliances," 919–22; Waltz, "Evaluating Theories," 913–19; Stephen M. Walt, "The Progressive Power of Realism," 931–35; Colin Elman and Miriam Fendius Elman, "Lakatos and Neorealism: A Reply to Vasquez," 923–26; Randall L. Schweller, "New Realist Research on Alliances: Refining, Not Refuting, Waltz's Balancing Proposition," 927–30.

21. See, for instance, Stephen D. Krasner, "Towards Understanding in International Relations," *International Studies Quarterly* 29 (1985): 141–48, especially 143. Other realists defined the neorealist hard core differently, adding additional assumptions to it, which makes the definition of this particular research program questionable. See, for instance, Elman and Elman, "Lakatos and Neorealism: A Reply to Vasquez," *American Political Science Review* 91 (December 1997): 923–26; Schweller, "New Realist Research on Alliances: Refining, Not Refuting, Waltz's Balancing Proposition," *American Political Science Review* 91 (December 1997): 927–30.

22. Grieco, "State Interests and Institutional Rule Trajectories. A Neorealist Interpretation of the Maastricht Treaty and European Economic and Monetary Union," in Frankel, *Realism*, 261–306.

can best achieve their security goals through cooperative policies, not competitive ones, and should, therefore, choose cooperation when these conditions prevail."[23] In other words, in situations where the risks of competition exceed the risks of cooperation, states should direct their self-help efforts toward achieving cooperation. Glaser's points of reference focus on alliance formation and the efforts to avoid arms races. The essence of this structural realism is to claim that the theory should not be specified primarily in terms of power, but should bring in offense–defense variables and shift from balance-of-power theory to a military-capabilities theory. The offense–defense balance means that one should calculate whether it is more advantageous for the opponent to invest in forces that support offensive missions, or for the threatened state to answer this offensive activity by investing the required amount in defense, or the other way round.[24] Starting from the offense–defense theory and treating a state's ultimate goal as security rather than relative power, Glaser concluded that, contrary to standard structural realist argument, a competitive arms race policy is preferred to less competitive policies only under rather narrow conditions: "when offense has the advantage and is indistinguishable from defense, and when the risks of being cheated . . . exceed the risks of arms racing."[25] The latter, in turn, depends mainly on the quality of monitoring capabilities. International cooperation is thus possible and indeed widespread, but Glaser claimed that it is not an end in itself. Cooperation is only a means to increase a nation's security. The relative gains problem is not a major problem here in terms of force sizes, because military assets are only instruments of policy, and security is the end. Furthermore, he argued that "contrary to the problem identified by the relative-gains logic, if cooperation increases a country's security, then increases in the adversary's security are usually desirable, whether or not they exceed increases in the defender's security."[26] Thus states often focus on absolute security gains offered by

23. Charles L. Glaser, "Realists as Optimists: Cooperation as Self-Help," *International Security* 19 (Winter 1994/95): 50–90, quotation 51.

24. For a detailed discussion of the offense–defense theory, see especially Glaser and Chaim Kaufmann, "What Is the Offense–Defense Balance and Can We Measure It?" *International Security* 22 (Spring 1998): 44–82. See further Glaser, "Political Consequences of Military Strategy: Expanding and Refining the Spiral and Deterrence Models," *World Politics* 44 (July 1992): 497–538; Jack S. Levy, "The Offensive/Defensive Balance of Military Technology: A Theoretical and Historical Analysis," *International Studies Quarterly* 28 (1984): 219–38; Stephen Van Era, "Offense, Defense, and Causes of War," *International Security* 22 (Spring 1998): 5–43; Robert Jervis, "Cooperation Under the Security Dilemma," *World Politics* 30 (January 1978): 167–214.

25. Glaser, "Realists as Optimists," 140.

26. Glaser, "Realists as Optimists," 150.

security cooperation, but institutions do not play an important role here (as they do in neoliberal institutionalism to be discussed below). Although institutions may make cooperation more desirable, they are nevertheless in principle like technology for monitoring or increases in force sizes: if they are needed, states create them.[27] In this way, Glaser argued that his variation of structural realism "reclaims much of the territory that the standard argument unjustifiably gave to neoinstitutionalism."[28]

Yet another power-based theory deserves mention, one that is often put forward as a slightly detached school of thought in the paradigm of structural realism—the hegemonic stability theory. The origins of this theory lie in economics, although it has also been applied in security regime analysis.[29] Charles Kindleberger's studies of the early 1970s are usually seen as the first formulations of this theory,[30] but it was not Kindleberger but rather his neoliberal critics who introduced or used the term *hegemony*.[31] Kindleberger himself responded that what he meant was not hegemony, which brings to mind force, threat, or pressure, but a certain leadership and responsibility. Kindleberger used the metaphor of the "father of a family" who often has important responsibilities, even though he is usually not considered a leader or hegemonic. More important, Kindleberger argued, the difference goes beyond semantics; ethics, morality, principles of justice, and obligation are important—not power alone.[32] As I see it, Kindleberger's approach was far removed from realism or structural realism and closer to early constructivism. Those in international relations who came close to this theory in the meaning of hegemony, such as Robert Gilpin, can perhaps be more accurately considered as representatives of a hybrid of realism or structural realism. Gilpin's approach can be crystallized by stating that he acknowledged the importance of international regimes to understand international politics, but that he argued that in every

27. Glaser, "Realists as Optimists," 157–60.

28. Glaser, "Realists as Optimists," 158.

29. For instance, in Schimmelfennig, "Arms Control Regimes."

30. See, for instance, Charles Kindleberger, *The World in Depression, 1929–1939* (Berkeley and Los Angeles: University of California Press, 1973), especially chapter 14; and Kindleberger, "Systems of International Economic Organization," in David Calleo, ed., *Money and the Coming World Order* (New York: New York University Press, 1976), 15–39.

31. Keohane, *After Hegemony: Cooperation and Discord in the World Political Economy* (Princeton: Princeton University Press, 1984).

32. Kindleberger, "Hierarchy Versus Inertial Cooperation," *International Organization* 40 (Autumn 1986): 841–47, especially 841, 842, 844.

social system the dominant actors assert their rights and impose rules on lesser members to advance their particular interests.[33]

Structural realism in its different forms would formulate slightly different responses about international cooperation through institutions and regimes. Nevertheless, the point of interest should be focused on quantitative rather than qualitative factors (perhaps with the exception of the Glaser-type approach, where a state's motives play a role). Another feature that all structural realists share is the emphasis on the limits of the potential independent effect of international institutions or regimes. One can perhaps crystallize the claims of structural realism by saying that Russia cooperates through institutions and regimes or that it complies with regime norms and rules if its self-interest does not suggest otherwise. Conversely, if Russia chooses not to cooperate, it violates norms and rules limiting its freedom of action, unless it can be compelled to comply and cooperate. The more flexible versions of structural realism can explain various forms of security-related cooperation where Russia is involved, but they emphasize that cooperation is itself not a goal, but a means to increase Russia's relative power and influence.

The Neoliberal Agenda: "How and Under What Conditions Regimes Matter"

Neoliberal institutionalism argues that cooperation is possible under certain fairly well defined conditions. As Robert Keohane and Joseph Nye explained: "These conditions include the existence of mutual interests that make joint (Pareto-improving) gains from cooperation possible; long-term relationships among a relatively small number of actors; and the practice of reciprocity according to agreed-on standards of appropriate behavior."[34] Neoliberal institutionalism does not suggest that international cooperation is easy to reach or easy to continue even under these conditions; cooperation, even when beneficial, can be blocked if, for instance, states suspect one another of cheating, if they disagree over the best possible cooperative solution, if some of them are sure that they will benefit from public goods regardless of whether they cooperate, or if they are uncertain about one

33. See, for instance, Robert Gilpin, *War and Change in World Politics* (Cambridge: Cambridge University Press, 1981), especially 35, 36.

34. Keohane and Joseph S. Nye, "Introduction: The End of the Cold War in Europe," in Keohane, Nye, and Stanley Hoffmann, eds., *After the Cold War: International Institutions and State Strategies in Europe, 1989–1991* (London: Harvard University Press), 1–19, quotation 4, 5.

another's preferences and rationality.[35] Here international institutions come into the picture, because they "can facilitate such a process of cooperation by providing opportunities for negotiations, reducing uncertainty about others' policies, and by affecting leader's expectations about the future. In this sense, international institutions can affect the strategies states choose and the decisions they make."[36] These human-constructed institutions vary historically and across issues, in nature and in strength. Thus, institutionalization is a variable rather than a constant, and the degree of institutionalization influences state behavior and cooperation between the states.[37]

Although under structural realism regimes are understood as usually synonymous with institutions and no clear distinctions are made between different types of cooperation, neoliberal institutionalism is more cautious with its definitions in this sphere. In Keohane's account, for instance, international regimes are understood in a fairly limited way, as institutions with explicit rules agreed on by governments. Instead of questioning whether regimes matter in international politics—as structural realists do, thereby limiting the focus on the distinction between the relative and absolute gains—most neoliberal institutionalists today are interested in raising more intricate questions, such as how regimes matter, under what conditions, through what mechanisms, to what degree, and so on. In addition to the general features of international institutions outlined above, Keohane has proposed a number of detailed characteristics. International regimes can affect both the capabilities and interests of states; they can alter bureaucratic practices or habits, promote an understanding of cause-effect relations, alter ideas about the legitimacy and value of practices, become embedded in higher-level normative networks, increase the political salience of certain issues, change the balance of political influence in domestic politics; they can enhance the political or administrative capacity of government or nongovernment organizations in countries.[38]

This list alone demonstrates that international regimes are regarded as crucial in explaining the outcomes of international politics from a neolib-

35. For a good example, see Lisa L. Martin, "Interests, Power, and Multilateralism," *International Organization* 46 (Autumn 1992): 765–92. Martin discusses the problem of cooperation from the point of view of prisoner's dilemma, battle of sexes, a suasion game, and an assurance game (stag hunt).

36. Keohane and Nye, "Introduction," 4, 5.

37. See, for instance, Keohane, *International Institutions and State Power*, 2, 3.

38. See Keohane, "The Analysis of International Regimes: Towards a European-American Research Programme," especially 29, 30.

eral perspective. As far as international *security* regimes are concerned, security as a subject of study was originally something of an anomaly in neoliberal research. Early neoliberalism[39] explicitly focused on "low politics" and nonsecurity cases, that is, on those issue areas where the use or threat of military force was seemingly irrelevant and the overall power structure could not adequately explain the behavior of actors and results of bargaining. The field of security was consequently left to realists, supposing that realism is better suited to that specific field. By the late 1980s, however, there were neoliberal-oriented security regime analyses, especially in German studies,[40] in Nye's chapter about nuclear learning,[41] and in Keohane's suggestion that *alliances* should be studied from a neoliberal perspective.[42] Subsequently it has become quite common for analyses located in the framework of neoliberal institutionalism to focus on security regimes in particular. John Duffield, for instance, challenged the balance-of-power theory and the public good theory when he explained the stability of North Atlantic Treaty Organization (NATO) conventional forces as relying largely on neoliberal institutionalism. In a characteristically neoliberal fashion, he argued that "a satisfactory account of the history of NATO conventional force levels must include institutional as well as structural factors."[43] Later, Duffield attempted to explain the long peace in Europe by emphasizing the importance of regional security regimes, especially the network of those associated with the Western alliance, which he regarded as the condition that linked U.S. military power and potential to Western Europe in a credible way and which also helped to address the threat to stability posed by Germany's still substantial military power.[44] Contemporary neoliberal institutionalism claims to offer the tools to understand and explain the existence and impact of security regimes.

What exactly is the essence of neoliberal argumentation compared with other accounts of regimes? In view of the broad list of regime conse-

39. Keohane and Nye, *Power and Interdependence* (Boston: Little, Brown, 1977).

40. See especially the series *Tübinger Arbeitspapiere zur internationalen Politik und Friedensforschung*. Up to the present, this series contains about twenty studies, of which some ten studies deal with international (mainly East–West) security regimes. See also the study edited by Beate Kohler-Koch, *Regime in den internationalen Beziehungen* (Baden-Baden: Nomos, 1989).

41. Nye, "Nuclear Learning and U.S.-Soviet Security Regimes," *International Organization* 41 (Summer 1987): 371–402.

42. Keohane, *International Institutions and State Power*, 15.

43. Duffield, "International Regimes and Alliance Behavior: Explaining NATO Conventional Force Levels," *International Organization* 46 (Autumn 1992): 819–55.

44. Duffield, "Explaining the Long Peace in Europe." See also the security-related 1993 volume edited by Keohane, Nye, and Hoffmann, *After the Cold War*.

quences put forward by Keohane, it becomes somewhat difficult to locate contemporary neoliberal institutionalism with regard to other approaches in international relations. First, neoliberal institutionalism is often seen as an effort to create a synthesis of structural realism and traditional liberal models. With regard to the former, neoliberal institutionalists see structural realism as "too narrow and confining"; it is "underspecified because it fails to theorize about variations in the institutional characteristics of world politics," and neoliberalism includes all that structural realism proposes but adds some important insights by its institutionalist emphasis.[45] Such statements might be interpreted to mean that neoliberal institutionalism, too, relies on the Lakatosian concept of theory choice and claims to produce a content-increasing version of structural realism. Keohane, for instance, explicitly relied on Lakatos (although not "without modification") to empathetically criticize structural realism. He has tried to show that although one should "seek to build on this core," it is possible to add, for example, more emphasis on change, institutions, and norms and to study the effect of variations in information or interdependence.[46] Indeed, in the 1980s, no longer "were realism and liberalism 'incommensurable'—on the contrary they shared a 'rationalist' research programme, a conception of science, a shared willingness to operate on the premise of anarchy (Waltz) and investigate the evolution of co-operation and whether institutions matter (Keohane)."[47]

As was shown above, some variations of structural realism do take institutions and regimes into account, however. What distinguishes neoliberal institutionalism from this kind of structural realism is that the existence of cooperative institutions in international politics is not only acknowledged but their importance is *emphasized*. One should add, however, that this is so only if a specific issue area or an international system, say in Western Europe or another part of the world, is "highly institutionalized." In such cases, neoliberal institutionalism would assert that state behavior is "to a considerable extent governed by rules"[48] and would suggest proceeding by

45. Keohane, *International Institutions and State Power*, 8, 9.

46. Keohane, "Theory of World Politics: Structural Realism and Beyond," (originally published in 1983) reprinted in Keohane, *International Institutions and State Power*, 35–73. Waltz, in his turn, has condemned neoliberalism by claiming that Keohane and Nye implicitly rely on traditional (non-Lakatosian) positivism in their search for "reality"; Waltz, "Evaluating Theories," 913.

47. Ole Wæver, "The Rise and Fall of the Inter-Paradigm Debate," in Steve Smith, Ken Booth, and Marysia Zalevski, eds., *International Theory: Positivism and Beyond* (Cambridge: Cambridge University Press, 1996), 149–85.

48. Keohane and Nye, "Introduction," 2.

studying empirically and concretely how those rules affect such behavior. Structural realism thus better explains state behavior in cases of less institutionalized situations, as was put forward more distinctly by early neoliberalism. In other words, in this mode of neoliberalism, the question of which of the theories should be applied always remains to some extent empirically open.

The relation between the traditional liberal models[49] that stress the role of institutions, interdependence, domestic policies, and transnational actors and neoliberal institutionalism has also remained vague. Originally, neoliberalism—or the well-known model of complex interdependence of Keohane and Nye—perhaps even stressed that states are not the only key units in the world and are not internally coherent in their relations with one another.[50] Neoliberal institutionalism, as propounded by Keohane, however, soon distanced itself from traditional liberal models by maintaining that states are central to neoliberal interpretations.[51] More recently, neoliberal institutionalists have again started to pay limited attention to the role of other actors, such as domestic bureaucracies and nongovernment activities.[52] The question of to what extent or in which cases one should pay attention to domestic policies has remained unanswered and is not fully clarified by the following extracts from Keohane's and Nye's more recent work: "Institutionalist analysis is consistent with elements of both realism and liberalism. It is consistent with aspects of realism since states are viewed, in both approaches, as the principal actors in world politics, and their relative power capabilities are considered to be crucial determinants of their behavior." However, "institutionalists recognize, with liberals, that states are not the sole significant actors in world politics: relationships of economic and ecological interdependence, and the nongovernment activities associated with them, also affect patterns of cooperation and the impact of international institutions." Keohane and Nye further stated that institutionalists focus neither on the structure of the international system emphasized by realism nor on the interactions between domestic politics and international relations on which liberalism fo-

---

49. See Michael W. Doyle, "Liberalism and World Politics Revisited," in Kegley, *Controversies in International Relations Theory*, 83–106; Mark W. Zacher and Richard A. Matthew, "Liberal International Theory: Common Threads, Divergent Strands," in Kegley, *Controversies in International Relations Theory*, 107–50.

50. Keohane and Nye, *Power and Interdependence*, chapter 2.

51. See Keohane, *International Institutions and State Power: Essays in International Relations Theory*, 8.

52. See especially Keohane, "The Analysis of International Regimes"; Keohane and Nye, "Introduction," especially 5.

cuses. "The principal focus of institutionalists is on international political processes."[53]

Those scholars who draw from both neoliberal institutionalism as well as other, more domestic policy-oriented approaches emphasized the "need for integrating domestic and international levels of analysis" or "interaction between international and domestic-level variables."[54] This approach of "two-level games," popularized especially by Robert Putnam's 1988 chapter, suggests that it is fruitless to debate "whether domestic politics really determine international relations, or the reverse" because the answer is clearly that both do sometimes. Therefore, the more interesting questions are When and How?[55] It seems that to develop a theory that successfully deals with the questions proposed here, a more explicit connection with the institutionalist insights at an international process level, on the one hand, and at the level of domestic policy, on the other, is needed. Although a "two-level games" approach may offer some clues toward this solution in neoliberal institutionalism's paradigm, such a comprehensive theory remains to be constructed. At the moment, the demarcation line of and the interaction between the level of international system and that of domestic politics remains obscure.

The problem of the factors to focus on becomes even more complicated because some of Keohane's suggestions about the impact of regimes verge on those of constructivism. What is the basic difference between neoliberal institutionalism and constructivism? First, some institutionalists come closer to the constructivist or cognitivist side of the dispute than others. As was mentioned, in the late 1980s, Nye, one of the founders of the neoliberal approach, introduced "learning" as an important factor that may lead to the creation of regimes and may crucially affect security relations among states. He made a distinction between simple learning, which uses new information merely to adapt means, and complex learning, which "leads to new priorities and trade-offs." Nye showed that complex learning led the Soviet Union and the United States to change their "declared position" about the usability of nuclear weapons, although he was careful not to tell us how this change affects the "operational doctrine."[56] Similarly, Duffield, who most of the time relied on basic neoliberal concepts and the

53. Keohane and Nye, "Introduction," 4, 5.

54. Jeff Checkel, "Ideas, Institutions, and the Gorbachev Foreign Policy Revolution," *World Politics* 45 (January 1993): 271–300, especially 274, 275.

55. Robert D. Putnam, "Diplomacy and Domestic Policy: The Logic of Two-Level Games," *International Organization* 42 (Summer 1988): 427–60.

56. Nye, "Nuclear Learning and U.S.-Soviet Security Regimes," especially 380, 386, 387.

rational-actor model, stressed, however, that although "it might be tempting to view compliance with regime rules simply as a rational response to the external opportunities and constraints created by the regime, the outcomes of cost–benefit calculations are ultimately profoundly influenced by the values that the decision makers hold and their beliefs about the likely consequences of different factors."[57] Keohane, too, did not deny the importance of the questions raised by constructivism and has, among others, recently started to consider subjects emphasized by constructivists, such as the role of ideas and identity in foreign policy and international politics.[58] For this reason, some theorists usually associated with the neoliberal rationalism-oriented paradigm, Keohane included, have lately been labeled "weak" cognitivists in regime analysis.[59]

Nevertheless, in widening the realm of study to ideas, Keohane and most neoliberals do not accept the position of constructivists, who hold that interests cannot be evaluated apart from ideas or identities. Neoliberal institutionalists recognize that ideas and interests are not phenomenologically separate and that all interests involve beliefs. In trying to gain something from rationalism and at the same time from reflectivism, one should keep ideas and interest analytically separate to find out how ideas or identities matter *beside* egoistic interests. Keohane and Judith Goldstein, for instance, maintained that they can understand "the significance of ideas" without challenging "the premise that people behave in self-interested and broadly rational ways."[60]

Thus, despite the recent interest among neoliberals in widening both the scope of actors to be studied and the scope of explaining variables, the basic assumption of neoliberal institutionalism—with the reservation that there are clear differences in the neoliberal approach or paradigm— remains unchanged: the motive for cooperation among states is that of

57. Duffield, "International Regimes and Alliance Behavior: Explaining NATO Conventional Force Levels," 844.

58. Judith Goldstein and Keohane, "Ideas and Foreign Policy: An Analytical Framework," in Goldstein and Keohane, eds., *Ideas and Foreign Policy: Beliefs, Institutions, and Political Change* (Ithaca and London: Cornell University Press, 1993), 3–30.

59. Hasenclever, Mayer, and Rittberger, "Interests, Power, Knowledge," especially 206–10. They refer to the study edited by Goldstein and Keohane, *Ideas and Foreign Policy*, where ideas are understood as "road maps" and "focal points." Other "weak" cognitivists, according to their classification, are those who emphasize learning, epistemic communities, limits of rationalism, etc. For these approaches, see, for instance, Peter M. Haas, "Epistemic Communities and the Dynamics of International Environmental Co-Operation," in Rittberger, *Regime Theory*, 168–201. Constructivists, such as Hurrell, Kratochwil, Wendt (see the text below), are called "strong" cognitivists in this classification.

60. Goldstein and Keohane, "Ideas and Foreign Policy," 5, 6.

potential gains from cooperation. Regimes operate through reciprocity in a tit-for-tat fashion.[61] This cooperation might under certain circumstances go at least beyond immediate calculations of reciprocal benefits; to understand those conditions better, as Keohane suggested, one should counterfactually study especially those cases where compliance is inconvenient, that is, where regime rules conflict with governments' perceptions of what their self-interest would otherwise suggest.[62] Duffield, in turn, offered some points of departure for this neoliberal research design by putting forward three ways of how states that might be inclined to violate certain norms or rules in some cases might nevertheless be led to think that "noncompliance may redound to a state's disadvantage." First, it is likely to "damage the state's reputation, causing its partners to be more skeptical of its promises and commitments in the future." Second, "a disregard of accepted standards of behavior may prompt other participants to exclude that state from some of the benefits provided by the regime or to take various other forms of punitive action." Third, noncompliance "may cause other states to question the merits of their own continued compliance," resulting in a weakening or collapse of the regime.[63] In being open to other models in addition to that of the rational, self-interested state actor, Duffield emphasized the role of "internal sources of compliance," such as institutionalized habits that "may acquire roots in the very beliefs and values."[64] As I have pointed out, how these additions can be combined with neoliberal institutionalism's basic assumption of rationality is somewhat obscure.

Neoliberal institutionalism can offer a fairly positive setting for answering the questions posed in this chapter. International institutions, regimes, or norms and rules are important in explaining the outcomes of international politics, the field of military security included, and the only task at hand is to study more precisely and empirically how and under what conditions norms and rules influence state behavior, or, here, the behavior of Russia. Russia should be treated as a self-interested rational state actor who makes cost–benefit calculations whenever it decides whether to cooperate or to comply with commonly accepted norms and rules. The crucial point is that the violation of a rule may have longer term costs or wider implica-

61. For a thorough treatment of this approach, see Robert Axelrod, *The Evolution of Cooperation* (New York: Basic Books, 1984).

62. See Keohane, "The Analysis of International Regimes," especially 29–33.

63. Duffield, "International Regimes and Alliance Behavior: Explaining NATO Conventional Force Levels," 836, 837.

64. Duffield, "International Regimes and Alliance Behavior: Explaining NATO Conventional Force Levels," 837, 838.

tions that should be taken into account, and therefore we should expect that Russia is constrained by these costs even if noncompliance seems to offer beneficial short-term results. The principal assumption that when making decisions Russia calculates a cost–benefit ratio is also consistent with structural realism's rationalism, but the difference is that in the world depicted by neoliberal institutionalism, institutions change this ratio crucially by enlarging "the shadow of the future."[65] In this context, our task is to define the degree of institutionalization of the environment where Russia is acting and to study empirically how these institutional networks affect its behavior. On the basis of this neoliberal assumption, one may hypothesize that the more institutionalized Russia's behavioral environment is in general and in specific issue areas, the more institutional networks influence its cost–benefit calculations and, consequently, its behavior.

Constructing International Norms and Rules

During the last years, constructivism has established itself as one of the mainstream approaches in international relations, and one can even trace a genre of constructivist-oriented, reflectivist regime analysis. Many constructivists see themselves in relation to rationalist approaches in largely the same way that neoliberal institutionalists see themselves in relation to structural realism. "Constructivism asks a different set of questions and attempts to fill in the gaps that rationalist approaches leave unexplained,"[66] especially in adding the role of ideas and identity to the agenda. On the other hand, representatives of conventional or mainstream constructivism often claim to cover not only the gaps of other research programs; constructivism includes the other international relations theories' ontology as its own special cases and sees itself—again in Lakatosian terms—as a more comprehensive theory of the same phenomena than structural realism or neoliberalism.[67]

---

65. For theoretical treatment of this concept, see Axelrod, *The Evolution of Cooperation*, 126–33.

66. Richard Price and Nina Tannenwald, "Norms and Deterrence: The Nuclear and Chemical Weapons Taboos," in Peter J. Katzenstein, ed., *The Culture of National Security: Norms and Identity in World Politics* (New York: Columbia University Press, 1996), 114–52.

67. David Dessler, for example, refers to the structural realist explanatory model, based on one level of analysis, as positionalist and offers his own alternative, based on agency–structure interaction, as a transformational model: *"Because the transformational model of structure provides a more comprehensive ontology than the positional model and is capable of grounding discussion of wider range of phenomena than any positional theory, it provides a more promising basis for progressive theoretical research."* David Dessler, "What's at Stake in the Agent–Structure Debate?"

Replying to the neoliberal institutionalists' claims that they can approach the role of ideas without using constructivist theory, constructivists for their part claim that one cannot "relax the basic assumption of rational egoism" and at the same time consider the role of normative factors "without the overall force of the rationalist project being undermined."[68] Indeed, a constructivist account of cooperation, institutions, regimes, or compliance with accepted norms and rules differs greatly from accounts committed to rationalism. The issue "becomes one of trying to understand how states relate to each other in terms of their identities, rather than in terms of their interests, which are epiphenomenal, or in terms of relative power, which underdetermines."[69] From the point of view of constructivism, realism and neoliberal institutionalism both fail because they are committed to rationalist models of explanation, starting from the assumption that states' goals, preferences, and interests should be taken as given, at least for analytical purposes.

It is worth considering precisely where the thread of this dispute between rationalism and reflectivism leads. Constructivists such as Andrew Hurrell admit that rationalist models may indeed explain how international cooperation, for example, is possible, once parties have come to believe that they constitute part of a shared project or community with common interests that can be furthered by cooperative behavior.[70] Friedrich Kratochwil's notion is that positivistic methodology provides elegant and powerful explanations when specialized institutions make interpretations of action problem free.[71] Alexander Wendt noted that social identities and interests may be relatively stable in certain contexts, in which case it can be useful to treat them as given.[72] In his foreign policy action model, Walter Carlsnaes

---

International Organization 43 (Summer 1989): 441–73. Cf. Wendt's "continuum of international systems" in Wendt, "Anarchy Is What States Make of It: The Social Construction of Power Politics," *International Organization* 46 (Spring 1992): 391–425, especially 400; and the 2X2 matrix in Ronald L. Jepperson, Wendt, and Katzenstein, "Norms, Identity, and Culture in National Security," in Katzenstein, *The Culture of National Security: Norms and Identity in World Politics*, 33–75.

68. Andrew Hurrell, "International Society and the Study of Regimes: A Reflective Approach," in Rittberger, *Regime Theory*, 49–72.

69. Ted Hopf, *Identity Politics: Constructing States at Home and Abroad* (quotation from unpublished manuscript, 275).

70. Hurrell, "International Society and the Study of Regimes," 61.

71. Friedrich Kratochwil, *Rules, Norms, and Decisions: On the Conditions of Practical and Legal Reasoning in International Relations and Domestic Affairs* (Cambridge: Cambridge University Press, 1989), 261.

72. Wendt, "Collective Identity Formation and the International State," *American Political Science Review* 88 (June 1994): 384–96.

distinguished three "dimensions"—intentional, dispositional, and structural—and wrote that "an explanation in terms solely of the intentional dimension is fully feasible. . . . [T]his dimension essentially indicates the explanatory parameters for all types of 'rationalistic' analyses of action."[73] In principle, rationalistic models of explanation therefore seem to form part of the complete picture of a constructivist explanation. One can also find suggestions made by constructivists or reflectivists that rationalism itself is not enough even when preferences, interests, or goals are given, because in social life political choices always take place under conditions of bounded rationality[74] one should explore the limits of human rationality.[75]

Constructivists do not usually include forms of rationalism in their empirical analyses and instead have tended to study a more profound puzzle: how a certain rationality has been created in intersubjective environments. *One* of the theoretical starting points used here is the linguistic speech-act theory, put forward especially by Kratochwil (referring to John Searle). His discussion of this theory is worth summarizing here because it illustrates how constructivism approaches the role of norms and rules in social behavior. The core of this theory is that a meaningful action is created by placing an act in an intersubjectively understood context. One should therefore study not only observable facts but also intentions. Because the meaning of an act is sometimes a matter of convention as well as intention, a correct analysis must capture both the intentional and the conventional aspects of acts. With regard to norms and rules, this means, first, that one of the most important functions of norms and rules in the world is to reduce the complexity of the choice situations in which actors find themselves. Second, means allow people to pursue goals, share meanings, communicate with one another, criticize assertions, and justify actions. Norms and rules thus influence choices through the reasoning process, which is why the processes of deliberation and interpretation deserve further analysis, which cannot be done by relying on rational choice models.[76]

The crucial distinction between this kind of thinking and that of neoliberalism is, as I see it, that neoliberal institutionalism emphasizes the role of institutions, regimes, norms, and rules in certain cases and under some specific circumstances as constraints for a rational actor, whereas construc-

73. Walter Carlsnaes, "The Agency–Structure Problem in Foreign Policy Analysis," *International Studies Quarterly* 36 (1992): 245–70.

74. Kratochwil, *Rules, Norms, and Decisions*, 260.

75. Christer Jönsson, "Cognitive Factors in Explaining Regime Dynamics," in Rittberger, *Regime Theory*, 202–22.

76. Kratochwil, *Rules, Norms, and Decisions*, introduction, section 2, and chapter 1.

tivism emphasizes that one cannot understand human behavior in the first place without taking into account the role of norms and rules. This implies that the definition of a norm or rule is much more penetrating in constructivism than is usually the case in regime analysis. Everything, even "anarchy," includes norms and rules that constitute its meaning.[77] From the viewpoint of constructivism, it is therefore pointless to consider only explicit and formal norms and rules. On the other hand, to understand the meaning and role of an explicit norm or rule, one must look beyond its letter. In other words, from the constructivist point of view, neither compliance nor noncompliance proves anything without a subsequent interpretation. Nicholas Onuf stated that rules "govern the construction of the situation in which choices are made intelligible. . . . [P]eople have always a choice, which is to follow rules or not."[78] As Richard Price and Nina Tannenwald stressed: "*Norms structure realms of possibilities; they do not determine outcomes.*"[79] Concerning noncompliance in particular, Kratochwil suggested that precisely because the means of peaceful change in the international arena are few, the violation of a legal norm (or threat to do so) is often "not a pure act of lawlessness, but rather a larger bargaining game for change." Norms and rules are often used for justifying actions in terms of broader principles, as demands for justice, and in that way they offer an instrument of peaceful change.[80]

Thus, norms and rules are used as a basis for, and as, tools of communication. Kratochwil adopted this basic starting point when he discussed specifically what to examine in regime analysis, referring especially to security regimes.[81] He emphasized that even explicit norms and rules are in themselves insufficient to make the regime work, but that there has to be some tacit understanding about the meanings of key terms or a relevant characterization of a particular action. In criticizing regime analysis, he referred to the famous 1983 "consensus-definition" according to which regimes are sets of implicit or explicit principles, norms, rules, and decision-making procedures around which actors' expectations converge in a given area of international relations.[82] Kratochwil argued that what is missing here is precisely an explanation of this convergence.

77. Wendt, "Anarchy." It should be noted here, however, that Wendt differs from most constructivists in that he adopts a statecentric position in analyzing international politics.

78. Nicholas Greenwood Onuf, *World of Our Making: Rules and Rule in Social Theory and International Relations* (Columbia: University of South Carolina Press), 261.

79. Price and Tannenwald, "Norms and Deterrence," 148.

80. Kratochwil, *Rules, Norms, and Decisions*, 256.

81. Kratochwil, *Rules, Norms, and Decisions*, chapter 2.

82. Krasner, "Structural Causes and Regime Consequences: Regimes as Intervening Variables."

Here we come to the issue of the importance of values and shared beliefs in the efforts to understand compliance or regime impact in general. Some constructivists approach this question from a distance. Kratochwil, for instance, said that our attitudes toward norms in a society are largely formed by our respect for the "law," which was inculcated during socialization. He added that although we may object to one law or another, compliance with norms is significantly shaped by our values, among which deference to law is one of the most important. Thus, in studying social systems, it is important to take into account both norms and values. This same perspective can also be applied to the international system, although here the question of shared values, or their absence, comes into the picture. In his study published on the eve of the momentous events of 1989, Kratochwil stated that the "time when the international arena might move from a 'negative community' to a conception of a 'global community' still seems far off."[83]

In an article published in 1993, Hurrell adopted a more optimistic stance.[84] He argued that the weakness of rational models lies in their developing the idea of self-interest and reciprocal benefits; that is, by claiming that regimes are created and that states obey the rules embodied in them because of the functional benefits they provide, these models have downplayed the traditionally significant role of community and the sense of justice and morals. This prevents us from seeing that a good deal of compliance leverage of international rules is derived from an interaction between individual rules and the broader pattern of international relations. States follow specific rules, even when inconvenient, because they have a long-term interest in the maintenance of a legally based international community and also because a sense of justice and morality plays an important part. Therefore, Hurrell claimed, the functional benefits of specific rules are only one part of the picture. A more essential element is the legitimacy of rules, which comes from the sense of being part of a community and which serves as the crucial link between the procedural rules of behavior and the structural principles that define the character of the system and the identity of the players. Once states see themselves as having a long-term interest in participating in an international legal system, the idea of obligation and the normative nature of rules can be given a tangible form and can acquire a degree of distance from the immediate interests or preferences of states. In such a situation, a law is based not on

83. Kratochwil, *Rules, Norms, and Decisions*, 63–67, quotation 67.
84. Hurrell, "International Society and the Study of Regimes," especially 57–69.

external sanctions or the threat of them, but rather on the existence of shared interests, common values, and patterned expectations.

How should one analyze the issues raised by constructivism? Constructivism is often claimed to be methodologically underdeveloped, and its critics have argued that it lacks a working research program.[85] A number of methodological propositions and, more recently, applications can be found, however. Hurrell stated that constructivism, or reflectivism, suggests the need for "a hermeneutic or interpretivist methodology that seeks to re-create the historical and social processes by which rules and norms are constituted and a sense of obligation engendered."[86] This is basically what Price and Tannenwald meant by their "genealogical approach," which "focuses on understanding how norms are constituted through social and discursive practices and how these discourses normalize or delegitimate forms of behavior." Their other approach, which is used in parallel with the first, has a "social construction perspective" as its analytical focus and incorporates "the interaction between norms and the constitution identities and interests involved."[87] These methodological solutions try to grasp one of the basic ideas of constructivist regime analysis: international regimes are intersubjective phenomena. That is, they are created, obeyed, and changed in the interrelation of their subjects, and they are mutually constructed and are not only abstract, static norms and rules with a life of their own. In this connection, the importance of practice is often emphasized.

Constructivists maintain that only very few norms and rules are simply constraining, but that many of them are rather enabling, and, therefore, actors are not only programmed by norms and rules but they reproduce and change by their practice the normative structure, which in turn shapes their behavior. Therefore, the practice of actors is one of the most important sources of change; by acting in existing normative frameworks actors create new ones at the same time.[88] In this process of change, the first steps may well be motivated by egoistic reasons, but cooperation and the practice of the actors may, in the best case, transform essentially egoistic reasoning into collective identity.[89]

85. Goldstein and Keohane, "Ideas and Foreign Policy," 6.

86. Hurrell, "International Society and the Study of Regimes," 64.

87. Price and Tannenwald, "Norms and Deterrence," 124, 125.

88. Wendt, "Constructing International Politics," 81; Hurrell, "International Society and the Study of Regimes," 64; Kratochwil, *Rules, Norms, and Decisions*, 61; Kratochwil and John Gerard Ruggie, "International Organization: A State of the Art on an Art of the State," *International Organization* 40 (Autumn 1986): 753–75.

89. Wendt, "Anarchy," 418; and Wendt, "Collective Identity Formation and the International State."

Thus, constructivists seek explanations from sources completely different from those drawn on by structural realists or neoliberal institutionalists. The constructivist account does not exclude the role of power and interest in understanding state behavior. Hurrell, for instance, pointed out that the rules of a system that depends on self-enforcement must be sufficiently close to the power and interests of states if they are to have any meaningful political impact, although he added that if a regime's political impact is to be significant, international norms cannot be an automatic and immediate reflection of self-interest.[90] Constructivists make use of the realist or rationalist concepts without accepting the notion of given meaning and the use of these concepts by realists. The crucial point of the constructivist account is captured in the ingenious sentence: the account is "defining," not "defending" national interest.[91] The constructed nature of national interest is the element that needs to be understood in studying national security affairs. For example, without understanding the socially constructed nature of the nonuse norm of nuclear weapons, "it would be difficult to explain why the Soviet Union did not resort to nuclear weapons to avoid a costly and humiliating defeat in Afghanistan."[92]

Most constructivists have also emphasized the role of domestic processes, although they are not alone in doing so.[93] Hurrell explained this by saying that the international community cannot be separated from the character of domestic political systems; moreover, if we focus on implementation and compliance, domestic factors become even more critical. He introduced three aspects of this question. First, there is the role of international law and norms and rules in the policy-making process, about which we should study how the sense of obligation plays out in detail. Second, technical linkages between international law and domestic legal systems become important when implementation is studied. Third, many political costs of violating international rules have a domestic impact, because the leaders in their need for domestic political support—especially in "hard" security cases—are unwilling to offer the domestic political opposition a chance to mobilize around the claim that the leaders do not follow legal rules.[94] Without detracting from the spirit of constructivism, one can per-

90. Hurrell, "International Society and the Study of Regimes," 53.

91. Katzenstein, "Introduction," in Katzenstein, *The Culture of National Security: Norms and Identity in World Politics*, 2.

92. Price and Tannenwald, "Norms and Deterrence," 149.

93. See, for instance, a neoliberal-oriented theoretical treatment of this issue in Michael Zürn, "Bringing the Second Image (Back) In: About the Domestic Sources of Regime Formation," in Rittberger, *Regime Theory*, 282–311.

94. Hurrell, "International Society and the Study of Regimes."

haps add to the last point that there are not necessarily only political costs incurred through noncompliance, but also many domestic benefits. In Kratochwil's writings, too, the domestic and international dimensions are not sharply separated. Kratochwil remarked that it is "important that regime analysis shall more explicitly examine decision-making procedures and more systematically link domestic bureaucratic structures and international regimes."[95] Notions of the importance of the domestic context in studying the role of international norms and rules, however, remain very general, and it is unclear how a constructivist study of these domestic processes differs from the empirical applications of the traditional decision-making or bureaucratic policy models.

To return to the questions presented at the beginning of this chapter, in using a constructivist viewpoint, we would answer Yes to all of them. The importance of international norms and rules is obvious from the above discussion; any attempt to understand human behavior needs to take normative elements into account. Whether explicitly stated norms and rules can in turn prevent and contain the unilateral behavior of Russia and persuade it to resort to cooperative and nondiscordant forms of behavior depends on robust normative frameworks, especially about the meaning of those norms and rules, and on the degree to which they are shared and accepted. The sense of community and obligation to that community is an essential precondition in understanding Russia's compliance with international norms and rules, but noncompliance should not be interpreted to the effect that such norms and rules do not matter to Russia. Constructivists see no qualitative distinction between different spheres of behavior; according to them, norms and rules are as important in military security issues as in any other issues. Thus, constructivism would claim that international norms and rules, explicit and implicit, formal and informal, have a crucial and manifold impact on the behavior of Russia in security affairs.

RUSSIA, CHECHNYA, AND THE OSCE: THREE INTERPRETATIONS OF RUSSIA'S BEHAVIOR

The points raised so far have drawn together the main lines of the theoretical disputes around international cooperation, institutions, regimes, norms, and rules and have produced rival answers to the questions posed

---

95. Kratochwil, *Rules, Norms, and Decisions*, 93.

in the introduction. Because this analysis has been pitched at a general level. I therefore concretize and deepen this debate with one brief but illustrative security-related case study and interpret it from the three perspectives discussed above.

As was mentioned earlier, the impact of OSCE norms and rules on Russia's policy toward Chechnya in 1994–1995 involves two theoretically interesting problems. The first is connected with Russia's decision to resolve the crisis in Chechnya by starting a large-scale military operation on December 11, 1994, and the nature of that operation. Although this decision was formally recognized by the international community as a Russian internal matter, various accounts describe the *international* regimes and human rights conventions that were violated by this decision and during the ensuing crisis.[96] As for OSCE norms and its rules, some stipulations of the Vienna Document of 1994 in the Confidence and Security Building Measures (CSBM) regime were contravened. The violated rules in question concern *the forty-two days' previous notification* and provide an opportunity for observa-

---

96. Usually in the *Russian* discussion, first, the fairly general articles on human and basic rights in Russia's constitution of 1993 have been referred to; see Articles 20, 21, 22, 35, 40, 56, etc. Concerning the international human rights conventions, the Geneva Convention of August 12, 1949, and its additional protocols of August 12, 1997, which restrict the methods of warfare and introduce guarantees to protect civilian populations in the course of military conflicts, were mentioned. In some writings, the International Covenant on Civil and Political Rights and especially its Articles 3 and 4 were also referred to. See *Moscow News* 13–19 January 1995; *Moscow News* 27 January–2 February 1995; *Nezavisimaya gazeta* 10 January 1995. Some Russian newspapers raised the question of the CFE treaty violation; see the interview with Istvan Gyarmati in *Moscow News* 20–26 January 1995. That treaty was not violated in the beginning of the mission, because it came into force in these respects only in November 1995, and after that Russia managed to negotiate for itself a three-year additional period before the flank restrictions were to be implemented. *International actors*, such as the EU, referred in resolutions and statements to "the serious violations of the human rights and the international human conventions," and it was recalled that the relations between the EU and Russia "should be based on the common principles of the UN and the OSCE in the form as they are defined in the Partnership Agreement"; see the statements of the EU of January 17, 1995, and January 23, 1995, for instance: *Bulletin of the European Communities* 1–2 (1995): 96, 97. In these statements, the EU referred to the Partnership Agreement's Article 2, which says: "Respect for the democratic principles and human rights as defined in particular in the Helsinki Final Act and the Charter of Paris for a New Europe underpin the internal and external policies of the Parties and constitute an essential element of partnership and of present Agreement." The Partnership Agreement itself was not in force, however, and "sources" from the commission informed journalists in December 1994 that because of this, appeal could not be made to the articles of the agreement referring to human and minority rights; see *Agence Europe* 6385, 23 December 1994, 6. Furthermore, the EU resolutions and statements referred to "the OSCE action rules and the additional protocol of the 1948 Geneva Convention"; see the resolutions of February 6, 1995: *Bulletin of the European Communities* 1–2 (1995): 97. See also: *euro-east*, no. 29 (18 January 1995).

tion of certain military activities.[97] All the figures mentioned in that document were clearly exceeded when Russia suddenly moved its troops. Another OSCE document obviously violated in Chechnya was the Code of Conduct on Politico-Military Aspects of Security.[98] This document was signed at the Budapest summit on December 5 and 6, 1994, only one week before Russia launched its operation in Chechnya. Chapter 36 refers to "internal security missions," and its essence is that the "armed forces will take due care to avoid injury to civilians or their property." The tactics of the Russian military, which included attacks using heavy weapons against civil targets, were evidently exactly the opposite of those propounded by the code of conduct.

The second problem, which in a way reveals the paradoxical nature of our case, chronologically follows the clear violations of and contempt for OSCE norms and rules. Why did Russia, after a period of negotiations, allow the OSCE to become a legitimate party in the conflict settlement in its own territory in the form of a long-term permanent mission and thereby for the first time officially break with the principle of telling others not to *interfere* in Russia's internal national security affairs? Why did Russia accept "the presence of the OSCE in a conflict which it regards as a domestic matter," as is currently continually referred to and celebrated in any context where the OSCE's role is mentioned?[99] OSCE mission activity as a whole can also be seen as a regime, although one with no clear explicit or formal basis, even if some general principles on political consultation were included in the Helsinki Document in 1992.[100] That document provided the basis for such activity, but long-term missions were brought into play only later, in autumn 1992, when the first missions were established in Kosovo, Sandjak, and Vojvodina. Later, the OSCE also became active in the former Soviet Union, but when Russia, in the name of consensus, agreed to the establishment of the new OSCE regime, it scarcely considered that its own territory would soon be host to a mission. From January 1995, the OSCE delegation discussed Chechnya altogether seven times in Moscow, and on four occasions, it was allowed to visit the crisis region. In March of that year, the OSCE and the Russian government finally agreed that a permanent OSCE mission would be established and that the OSCE would participate in the

97. The Vienna Document of 1994, especially Articles 36 and 38.1.1 as well as 45.5.
98. The code of conduct can be found as the fourth chapter in the CSCE *Budapest Document of 1994.*
99. "The OSCE's increasing responsibilities in European security," *NATO Review*, no. 6 (November 1996): 7–12, quotation 9.
100. Chapter 3.

negotiations for the short-term and long-term solutions for the crisis. This mission, called exceptionally the Assistance Group, started its work in Chechnya on April 26, 1995. No limitations to the duration of the group's work were set a priori.[101]

We, therefore, have a situation of noncompliance and of compliance and cooperation in the same package. Does our case confirm or diconfirm some of the theories detailed earlier? How might the different theoretical approaches explain the case? Can these theories offer some insight to help us understand Russia's somewhat paradoxical behavior?

Ignoring the Case, Stressing the Autonomy of Decision, or Looking for a Power-Based Explanation

I see at least three ways to deal with this case study from *structural realism's* perspective, while staying true to its basic assumptions and (meta)theoretical commitments: to ignore the case, to stress the autonomy of decision, or to look for a power-based explanation. The first possibility is most clearly related to "strong" structural realism, especially to the theory advanced by Waltz. This theory immediately brings us face to face with a crucial problem: is it legitimate to hypothesize on the basis of Waltz's systemic theory in studying the issues we are dealing with here? What should a theory of international politics tell us? What kinds of cases should it explain? A theory at "one level of generality cannot answer questions about matters at a different level of generality," Waltz explained, and one should not "mistake a theory of international politics for a theory of foreign policy"[102] (or for that matter, state or domestic policy). Waltz stated that system-level theories "tell us a small number of big and important things," and the importance comes from the fact that systemic theories "focus our attention on those components and forces that usually continue for long periods." At the same time, he admitted that his theory can handle only some problems that concern international politics and that structures never explain all we want to know.[103]

We can take several attitudes toward this self-limitation of Waltzian structural realism. We can accept that our case falls outside the realm of

101. The establishment of the Assistance Group took place at the sixteenth permanent council meeting, April 11, 1995, decision (a).

102. Waltz, *Theory of International Politics*, 121, 122.

103. Waltz, "Reflections on *Theory of International Politics:* A Response to My Critics," in Keohane, ed., *Neorealism and Its Critics* (New York: Columbia University Press, 1986), 322–45, especially 329.

structural realism, that it moves at a different level of generality, and that the puzzles it embraces do not concern the core problems in Waltz's theory as they do not concern great power rivalry or a case of international war. This position leaves the explanatory potency of this form of structural realism untouched, and we can conclude that this theory is appropriate for a different level of explanation. Thus, Russia's behavior in this case cannot be explained by Waltz's theory, and we can leave our subject to theories of other levels.

This is one possible interpretation of our problem and of the scope of structural realism in general, perhaps the only one from a Waltzian perspective. While bearing this interpretation in mind when proceeding further, we might note, however, that this position is not very complimentary to structural realism. Our case may be somewhat odd from structural realism's perspective, but it is highly illustrative of post–Cold War international politics. To ignore it is tantamount to saying that structural realism has nothing to say about most things that happen in international politics today. We should at least try to find some well-grounded reasons that this case is not important. Moreover, should we ignore this case, we face the dilemma of how to discuss structural realism's strong claims about cooperation empirically in the first place if some forms of state cooperative and uncooperative behavior are excluded from the agenda. Keohane has, I think rightly, noted that Waltz himself looked at only those cases that are consistent with his theory instead of all possible cases that seem to have something to do with his theoretical claims.[104] From this point of view, it is legitimate to continue, to find out how far we can go when relying on structural realism's basic assumptions, including Waltz's theory. We can also adopt a more aggressive attitude and claim that our subject, with its focus on norm-based cooperation, represents a principal example of one of the "small number of big and important things" that structural realism really claims to explain. It is justified to expect to find some guidance from structural realism in explaining Russia's behavior in our case and in doing so to put it to the test.

As far as Russia's noncompliance is concerned, at first glance, structural realism has no great difficulty in offering an explanation. Although the different variations of structural realism disagree with one another in their accounts of cooperation in general, all of them clearly imply that the case of Russia's noncompliance with OSCE rules is not an exception but a rule. In reference to the violation of the CSBM rules, structural realism in princi-

104. Keohane, *International Institutions and State Power*, 45, 46.

ple can explain the very existence of this regime in the first place. From a Waltzian viewpoint, there naturally exist many institutions in which Russia is involved, but they need not be essential to an understanding of Russia's behavior. From a more flexible structural realist viewpoint, the CSBM can be understood in terms of norms and rules that do not affect the relative power or relative security of participants. In this case, the risks of cooperation are fewer than under the conditions of arrant anarchy in this area, which could more easily lead to over-reaction or false alarms; all regime participants may benefit from these rules without losing anything in terms of relative power or security.

It is not therefore surprising that Russia adheres to these regulations in normal situations, but in the case of Chechnya, no structural realist expects the previous notification rule to be followed. The unifying feature in all accounts is clear: structural realism stresses the importance of the autonomy of decision—Russia's striving for independence—especially where such things as Russia's decision making on Chechnya is concerned. This basic point of departure, in turn, offers simple solutions to our puzzle.

I specify this by first introducing a commonsense explanation and then comparing it with the one of structural realism. With a little historical inquiry,[105] commonsense logic easily brings us to the same conclusion that

105. As it later turned out, the decision to begin an open military operation in Chechnya was already made at the security council meeting of November 29, 1994. This was recounted by the secretary of the security council, Oleg Lobov. See *Interfax*, 27 December 1994. The deputy secretary Valery Manilov said the same thing in a later interview; see *Izvestiya*, 16 February 1995; see also Grachev's speech: *Nezavisimaya gazeta*, 1 March 1995. The participants at the security council meeting of November 29, 1994, were President Boris Yeltsin, Prime Minister Viktor Chernomyrdin, the Speakers of both chambers of the Parliament Ivan Rybkin and Vladimir Shumeiko, Foreign Minister Andrei Kozyrev, Defense Minister Pavel Grachev, Minister of the Interior Viktor Yerin, Minister of Justice Yuri Kalmykov, Head of the FSK Sergei Stepashin, Head of the Foreign Intelligence Services Yevgeni Primakov, Deputy Prime Minister Sergei Shakhrai, Minister of Emergency Situations Sergei Shoygu, Minister of Nationalities and Secretary of the Security Council Oleg Lobov; see *Nezavisimaya gazeta*, 30 November 1994. For information on voting, see *Izvestiya*, 16 February 1995 (Manilov's interview): according to the "sources" of *Izvestiya*, Kalmykov was against, and Primakov and Kozyrev were "hesitative"; Kalmykov was dismissed or quit his office on December 7, and he confirmed his negative position on the decision; see *Nezavisimaya gazeta*, 8, 10, 22 December 1994, *Itar-Tass*, 10 December 1994. See also State Duma Deputy Vladimir Lysenko's article in *Moscow News*, 9–15 December 1994: "On the other hand, the 'war party' still remains 'unpersonified.' We know, for example, that the votes of the Security Council members were divided nearly in half when deciding the question of bringing military pressure to bear on Chechnya. But the verbatim report of the Security Council's meeting is inaccessible to the deputies. We do not know exactly who spoke, nor in favor of what." Vladimir Rubyanov, the deputy secretary of the security council at that time, later said that everyone, except Kalmykov, "signed" the decision anyhow (interview with the author, Moscow, September 25, 1996). Two more decisions, made

structural realism implies. The strategic choice to use force in Chechnya was made less than two weeks before the operation started; in other words, forty-two days before (the previous notification time) the operation was launched, the Russian leadership had not decided and was unwilling to deploy an open, large-scale military operation. In view of that fact, to comply with the previous notification rule of the CSBM would have meant canceling or postponing the whole operation. The decision was made in a clear crisis decision-making situation, and had the previous notification rule been taken literally, it would have precluded the option of large-scale troop deployments in Chechnya when they were needed. Also, in the light of the extreme secrecy surrounding the decision when it was finally made, the very idea of complying with the previous information rule is unrealistic and even naive. The plans and decisions were made in a tight circle in and around the Security Council of the Russian Federation; they were kept secret from even the majority of Russian government officials; the Presidential Council and the Analytic Center of the President, consultative organs in the president's administration, meant to deal with such questions, were openly misled.[106] Even a deputy defense minister, who had earlier criticized the possibility of using force in Chechnya, announced afterward that he was not informed about the plans to use the army to solve the crisis.[107] This secrecy in the Russian leadership makes it easy to infer that Russia's leaders did not turn, officially or unofficially, to the leaders of other countries or international organizations in advance. Thus, compliance with the previous notification rule was seemingly out of the question. Although we do not know for sure, it seems more likely that Russia's decision makers never even thought of it or at least did not put it on the agenda of the security council when it took its decision. The only norms and rules that were seemingly discussed in the security council were those connected with the constitutional legitimization for the use of force.[108]

---

by the security council, can be seen as crucial. On December 7, the strategy was confirmed, because Dudayev did not show any signs of complying with Russia's demands. On December 26, the decision to attack Grozny by using all forces available was made. For a detailed treatment of these decisions, see Christer Pursiainen, *Modelling Russia's Crisis Decision-Making: The Case of Chechnya* (UPI Working Papers, no. 2, 1997).

106. See *Izvestiya*, no. 1, January 1995.

107. See Deputy Defense Minister Gromov's interview in *Moscow News*, 13–19 January 1995.

108. According to Vladimir Rubyanov, the deputy secretary of the security council at that time (interview with the author, Moscow, September 25, 1996). In fact, the question of whether the decision was made in accordance with the constitution of the Russian Federation became a lengthy matter of dispute. In the constitution, Articles 87 and 88 deal with martial law and the state of emergency, and according to Article 102 the implementation of these

What is the meaning and function of structural realism in this context, and how does it differ from the commonsense explanation depicted above? Structural realists, in particular those inspired by Waltz, would say that their approach differs by virtue of its being a theory, which means that it has certain advantages over a commonsense explanation of a specific case. In our case, this means that a structural realist would not even consider such "detailed" information as was referred to above—the details of rules, the behavior of individual officials and politicians, the question of who was misled and who was not or even of who made the decision. In this way, structural realism necessarily loses something when compared, for example, with a historical account, but theory is not history. Thus, Waltz, for instance, admitted that any radical simplification conveys a false impression of the world. He added that this is just the way it should be. The function of a theory is to simplify complexity; it is a means of dealing with complexity and can be useful for this reason only.[109] In our case, this complexity can be reduced by stating that details or unit-level factors do not really matter when larger questions, such as territorial integrity—which in Russia's case could easily be interpreted as a synonym for the state's survival, the "core interest" of a state in structural realism's discourse—are at stake. From this point of view, I believe it reasonable to state that structural realism would clearly predict this materialized outcome: Russia does not care about any international norms and rules that limit its autonomy when it defends its vital interests, at least if there is no power to compel it to do so. Russia would not let its autonomy be restricted by international norms and rules when it takes decisions of this kind.

This same simplicity is applicable to the question of the cruelty of the methods used by Russia in Chechnya. This again is something that at first

---

articles would involve informing the State Duma and the Federation Council, and the consent of the latter. The negative reactions of both houses of parliament to the rumors of a possible military operation might have led to the decision not to proclaim a state of emergency, which thus "allowed for" the ignorance of parliament. Because the security council of the Russian Federation is not a constitutional organ empowered to take this decision alone, however, the mission was formally legitimized by the order of the president on December 9, 1994. In that order, Yeltsin demanded that the government "with all means at the state's disposal" should guarantee the security of the state, the human rights and freedom of the citizens, and the legal order of the society and should undertake the fight against criminality and the disarmament of all illegal groupings. Yeltsin has justified the decision by referring to Article 13, Clause 5, 80, and Article 114 of the constitution. For more details, see, for instance, *Moscow News*, 13–19 January 1995. The decision was proclaimed as legal *post factum* by different Russian juridical organs.

109. Waltz, "Realist Thought and Neorealist Theory," in Kegley, *Controversies in International Relations Theory: Realism and the Neoliberal Challenge*, 67–82.

glance does not belong to the realm of structural realism, and yet this behavior becomes part of international politics, even "high politics," because
Russia's behavior was conspicuously at variance with what was solemnly
promised to the international community when President Yeltsin signed
the code of conduct only a few days earlier. This is not to say that Russia
would not opt to follow the code of conduct in internal crises. Again, we
can provide more detailed information. The statements of Russian officials
as well as the original plans of the operation made public afterward[110] seem
to imply that no real large-scale war was anticipated. The plans were apparently based on the assumption that civilians would leave Grozny, a large
number of the Chechen rebels would lay down their arms, and the rest
would be either easily defeated or would escape to the mountains when
they realized the hopelessness of their situation. The southern part of the
city was deliberately left open for these reasons. Evidence from different
sources suggests that according to the original plan the army was not supposed to take Grozny by storm.[111] Rather, the takeover should have been
performed by special troops from counterintelligence; two commando
troops, altogether 120 men, should have "neutralized" Dudayev, the rebel-
lious leader of Chechnya.[112] The army's task was merely to show that Dudayev had no chance of winning the battle and to prevent forces outside
Chechnya, groupings in the Caucasus hostile toward Russia, from interfering in the operation. In launching the operation, Russia apparently did
not expect to meet massive and effective resistance. Faced with a war they
had no prospect of winning, it was assumed that the Chechen rebels would
surrender en masse.[113]

How can structural realism help us simplify this complexity of events?
The course of events in this case would have been impossible to predict

110. According to the plan, the mission would include four phases. The first phase (November 29–December 6) was aimed at mustering the troops and preparing the whole mission;
during the second phase (December 7–9), the troops would advance through Chechen territory and blockade Grozny; during the third phase (December 10–13), the administration and
communication buildings would be taken, and the Chechen troops located there disarmed;
finally, the last phase (December 14–) was for stabilizing the situation in five to ten days and
handing over the responsibility and command to the troops of the ministry of the interior.
See Grachev's speech in *Nezavisimaya gazeta*, 1 March 1995.

111. See, for example, the "reliable sources" of a Russian newspaper: *Nezavisimaya gazeta*,
17 December 1994. Also Emil Pain, a member of the Analytic Center in the administration of
the president, who specialized in Chechnya, said that according to his sources there would be
no large-scale attack on Grozny: *Nezavisimaya gazeta*, 14 December 1994.

112. *Nezavisimaya gazeta*, 14 December 1994.

113. Cf. Franz Walter, "Militärische Aspekte des Tshetschenien-Kriegs," *Osteuropa* 45 (August 1995): 691–708.

from structural realism's perspective, but structural realism does not claim to be able to do so. Most of the factors described above are not relevant to structural realists, whose perspective can be outlined without presenting detailed information. In view of the role of national security affairs at the top of its discourse hierarchy, one can hypothesize that the violation of human rights conventions follows when these clash with vital national security interests. National security interests dominate state behavior, not international norms and rules or moral judgments.

The second aspect of our problem, Russia's adaptation to become a subject of the OSCE mission in its internal national security affairs, appears more difficult in considering the same basic structural realist assumption that can be advanced when explaining Russia's noncompliance. We have hypothesized that a state does not let its autonomy be restricted if there is a way of avoiding it. There are no firm reasons to believe that Russia was compelled to accept the establishment of the OSCE Assistance Group. The decision had to be made on the basis of consensus in the organs of the OSCE, that is, with Russia's acceptance. At first sight, structural realism therefore seems to suggest that Russia should have behaved not as President Yeltsin agreed to behave, supported by his foreign minister, but as the Russian military advised, which, as later discussed in detail, was apparently opposed to the OSCE's or any other factor's interference in Russia's internal national security affairs.

Why did Russia comply? I see at least two possibilities to approach this question from a structural realist perspective. The first possibility is to refer again to the nature of the question from structural realism's point of view. We can simply ignore it by saying that the question is unimportant, that it did not matter whether there was an OSCE mission in Chechnya. From this point of view, we are dealing with a case totally different from that of the previous notification rule. Complying with that rule would have affected Russia's behavior in a crucial way and would have led to canceling or postponing the whole operation. In accepting the OSCE's interference, one can claim, Russia did not curtail its autonomy, and OSCE intervention did not change the basic course of events, because a group of some six mediators or observers could not stop the war and make Russia behave against its self-interests. From this perspective, all the diplomacy around the dispute was only superficial. Although this issue appears more interesting when seen in the news media or from the point of view of practitioners of international politics, it had nothing to do with those elements of international politics that should be explained by international relations theorists. This, I think, is the correct interpretation of Waltzian structural realism in our case. In Waltz's metaphor,[114] Russia's behavior may be seen as the wayward path of a falling leaf that neither challenges the theory of gravity nor can be explained by it. From the Waltzian perspective, therefore, it does not matter whether the leaf goes up or down, whether Russia complied or not with the OSCE's demands.

When we consider the more flexible variations of structural realism, we may pay attention to the power factor at a more general level. Inspired by structural realists such as Grieco, for instance, we can try to find a power-based explanation for Russia's behavior or explanations that emphasize the pure tactical use of international institutions by a self-interested state actor. First, Russia's attitude toward the aspirations of the OSCE should be seen in the broader context of a rationalist policy. Its general line toward security matters in Europe has been to propose a collective security system based mainly on the OSCE structures as an alternative to NATO enlargement. Although this foreign policy line is most obviously related to institutions from the perspective of (this brand of) structural realism, it should be interpreted in terms of the search for a balance of power, as an effort by Russia to maximize its influence and relative power. The question of the OSCE's role in creating a balance of power that was more favorable for Russia was highly topical at that time. In the beginning of December 1994, Russia had dramatically refused to endorse its individual participation program in NATO's Partnership for Peace regime, and at the Budapest OSCE summit the same month, it made clear its wish to strengthen the organization.[115] To sound credible in demanding an enhanced role for the OSCE in European security affairs—that is, for Russia, too—Russia could not simply ignore the demands of the OSCE with regard to Chechnya. It was not beneficial for Russia's general purposes to undercut the organization and demonstrate that it was ineffectual.

Second, there was a risk that the OSCE "by its very presence could provide implicit legitimization for Russia's action. . . . Russia's unexpected willingness to support the OSCE resolution condemning the massive violations of human rights in Chechnya could be just a tactical maneuver in this game."[116] This interpretation perhaps goes too far. Nevertheless, Russia seems to have had some expectations different from those of the interna-

114. Waltz, *Theory of International Politics*, 121, 122.
115. For details, see Michael Mihalka, "Restructuring European Security," *Transition* 1 (June 30, 1995): 3–9; and Heather Hurlburt, "Russia Plays Double Game," *Transition* 1 (June 30, 1995): 10–17.
116. Pavel Baev, "Drifting Away from Europe," *Transition* 1 (June 30, 1995): 30–37, quotation 32.

tional community about the role of the OSCE in Chechnya. The attitude of the Russian leadership was that the international community had reacted too sharply to events in Chechnya; the international community had not understood the situation and the nature of the enemy. Russian actions were necessary and correct because of the cruelty and uncompromising line of Dudayev's troops. The task of the OSCE, Russian leaders thought, should be to verify these points and transmit this aspect of the war to the international community. As a result, the international community would accept, or at least understand, the necessity to use force, and Russia would avoid additional international pressure.[117] From this tactical perspective, Russia's behavior—the fact that it altered its position and started to comply in part with the OSCE's demands—fits well into structural realism's overall picture. Russia did not lose anything; its real autonomy of decision and behavior was not constrained by the presence of the OSCE Assistance Group, as seen also with the other crisis in the Commonwealth of Independent States (CIS) where the OSCE was involved[118]; in fact, it could make some propaganda to its advantage by acting in a cooperative way.

Despite our case being somewhat outside the conventional realm of structural realist analysis, I have here offered an interpretation of Russia's behavior while trying to keep in the framework of this theoretical approach. I leave the evaluation of this experience, its theoretical and practical implications, to the concluding section of this chapter, and now look at our case from the perspective of the other approaches discussed above.

The Effects of an Institution

Although structural realism unequivocally focuses on other questions about international politics, our subject with its complicated institutional networks may appear better suited to a *neoliberal institutionalist* interpretation. Some neoliberal institutionalists may find it easy to accept structural realism's account of the first part of our puzzle, that of Russia's noncompliance, but may also ask about the degree of institutionalization that is sup-

117. As an example of this kind of attitude, see the reaction of the head of the president's administration, Sergei Filatov, to the decision of the CE to freeze Russia's application for membership. According to Filatov, the CE did not understand the methods Russia used in Chechnya when it tried to restore the legal order. He felt that when the OSCE mission took place, this weakness in judgment would be corrected. *Nezavisimaya gazeta*, 24 January 1995.

118. In reference to crises in Moldova and Georgia, "CSCE missions were never granted the access to Russian peacekeeping operations that the mission mandates, accepted by Russian diplomats, guaranteed." Heather Hurlburt, "Russia, the OSCE, and European Security Architecture (1)," *Helsinki Monitor*, no. 2 (1995): 6.

posed to influence state behavior. In our case, neoliberal institutionalists would most probably explain that there is clearly a highly institutionalized environment in which Russia's behavior should be expected to be governed to a considerable extent by norms and rules. On the other hand, as was demonstrated in connection with structural realism, our subject is one where regime rules seem to be in conflict with Russia's perceptions of what its self-interest suggests. Thus, noncompliance becomes understandable because neoliberal institutionalism does "not assume that states can be forced to act against their own interest" when they act in international institutions and regimes.[119]

This is only part of the story from neoliberal institutionalism's perspective. Starting from my earlier diagnosis of the problem, I try to interpret Russia's behavior on the assumption that it is a rational self-interested actor in an institutionalized environment. Neoliberal institutionalism does not claim to have great predictive power; instead, neoliberal institutionalists see one of the most important functions of a theory as its ability to act as "a set of questions" that help us to get more out of empirical cases, to focus our attention on the crucial points. Neoliberal institutionalists do not claim that their theory is sufficiently precisely formulated to permit the rigorous testing of hypotheses. Rather, they claim that they can offer tools for understanding "the roles that international institutions have played in affecting state strategies and the outcomes of interstate negotiations."[120] I elucidate these tools, or sets of questions, to understand Russia's behavior more comprehensively.

It can be assumed from a neoliberal institutionalist perspective that Russia *should* at least have considered the consequences of its noncompliance. This leads us to a different understanding of interests than that in structural realism's framework. The realist assertion that states carry out regime or treaty commitments only when it is in their interest to do so "seems to imply that commitments are somehow unrelated to interests." This claim goes further by suggesting that the opposite is true, because the state need not usually enter into a treaty that does not conform with its interests. It is also true "that a state's incentives at the treaty-negotiating stage may be different from those it faces when the time for compliance rolls around," and a state may have reason to seek to escape the obligations it has undertaken. Nevertheless, the very act of making commitments

119. Celeste A. Wallander and Jane E. Prokop, "Soviet Security Strategies Toward Europe: After the Wall, with Their Backs up Against It," in Keohane, Nye, and Hoffman, *After the Cold War*, 63–103.

120. Keohane and Nye, "Introduction," 7.

"changes the calculus at the compliance stage, if only because it generates expectations of compliance in others that must enter into the equation."[121] I believe that neoliberal institutionalists would be happy to underwrite this statement. Thus, Russia should have calculated what its noncompliance would cost; that is, it should have considered the consequences.

We can find several possible consequences for Russia to consider from the toolbox of neoliberal institutionalism. Some potential consequences are directly related to Russia's wish to cooperate through institutions or regimes in general; others emanate from the fact that a noncompliance may be reflected far from its original subject or issue area through issue linkages. Russia should have taken into account that noncompliance with OSCE norms and rules would result in a weakening, or even collapse, of the regimes in question, for example, in the sense that they would be rendered "dead-letter regimes." Russia should also have been worried about its reputation, because its noncompliance would cause others to be more skeptical of its commitments in the future, which again undermines some regimes that Russia is interested in or even the role of the OSCE as a whole. Neoliberal institutionalism would also expect Russia to consider that its behavior that violates the jointly agreed-on standards may prompt other participants to take various forms of punitive action in other areas, such as trade relations.

Let us assume that consideration was given to the future effectiveness of regimes. In that case, Russia's noncompliance may be approached as a cooperation problem, for which neoliberal institutionalism, inspired by game theory, can offer several explanations. For instance, Russia's behavior can be interpreted in terms of free riding. In this case, the CSBM, or the previous notification rule in it, and the code of conduct are public goods from the point of view of Russia. Russia probably appreciates the existence of the regimes included in the OSCE framework and generally welcomes others' compliance with the accepted regime norms and rules. Russia benefits from these regimes, but its own noncompliance becomes understandable if one takes into account that it was perhaps sure or calculated that its behavior, in this very limited case at least, would not jeopardize the existence of the regimes in question and would not lead to the violation of the norms and rules by other regime participants. On the other hand, as far as Russia's tarnished reputation and possible issue-area linkages are concerned, these would make us question whether Russia or its leaders calcu-

---

121. Abram Chayes and Antonia Handler Chayes, "On Compliance," *International Organization* 47 (Spring 1993): 175–205, quotations 179, 183, 184.

lated the gross price of violating the rules in question in terms of trade relations, for example, and then considered the net value of noncompliance. Because noncompliance took place anyway, we should conclude that in our case the benefits of noncompliance were apparently seen to exceed the costs.

Is there any evidence to show that Russia really thought along those lines? Can one say that free riding was part of the picture in the sense that Russia clearly wishes to benefit from the OSCE's public goods, but was not willing to pay the whole price? In the case of the transgressed CSBM rules, available data do not provide any evidence of such calculations having been made or discussed by the Russian leadership. As a matter of fact, to my knowledge, Russian leaders made no mention of these rules in this connection before the decision or soon after it, and as we see below, when these rules were discussed later in March 1995, the Russian attitude seems to imply that they never thought they had violated the rules. These rules simply did not matter in this case, but we should not necessarily conclude that they do not matter in general. From neoliberal institutionalism's point of view, the CSBM rules produce institutional limits to Russia's behavior, but these institutions were not effective enough; they did not include such mechanisms and automatic penalties that in this case would have persuaded Russia from its course. Thus, Russia follows the previous notification rule in normal situations, in maneuvers, but not in real situations. The outcome is the same in both structural realism and neoliberal institutionalism, but although in the former perspective it is largely determined, the latter is more cautious in claiming that in the future Russia's rational approach in all similar cases would be to violate these rules.

Although the norms and rules created in the framework of the OSCE apparently had little impact on Russia's behavior in our case, if we look at the code of conduct and the overall role of the OSCE in Russian politics from the same point of view, we see a slightly different picture. First, the code of conduct differs in one crucial way from the CSBM: with regard to the CSBM, the decision to comply or not to comply with the previous notification rule, if this dilemma was ever discussed, was a one-time decision, whereas the violation of the code of conduct, the cruelty of the war against the civilian population, was an ongoing process, and the costs of violation seemed to grow day by day. More generally, the price of Russia's uncooperative line grew. This, in turn, offers us an important starting point to discuss the other part of our case, namely, Russia's compliance with the OSCE's demands to participate in conflict management, which went far beyond what it had agreed to in any documents.

To interpret Russia's behavior from a neoliberal institutionalist perspective, we need more information. István Gyarmati, a personnel representative of the chairman in office (Hungary's foreign minister) of the OSCE, stated in January 1995: "We first heard an unequivocal 'no' from the Russian side to any cooperation attempts. Later, we probably managed to make it clear that we were not intent on putting Russia on trial, and that our only goal was to help."[122]

Thus, there was a *change* in Russia's attitude. Why did it take place? Aside from the OSCE, one of the most active entities that tried to influence Russia was the European Union (EU). From the beginning, the EU energetically criticized Russia's behavior, although at first mostly verbally and in the form of secret diplomacy. On December 29 and 30, 1994, the eve of the bloody attack on Grozny, official negotiations were held between a delegation of the EU and Russia. Nevertheless, the issue discussed was not Chechnya but the so-called Interim Agreement between the EU and Russia, which was aimed at accelerating the implementation of the trading and commercial parts of the general Agreement on Partnership and Cooperation between the EU and Russia. It was announced that the Interim Agreement would come into force in March 1995.[123] In January, however, the EU line became stricter. On the same day the OSCE opened official negotiations in Moscow, on January 5, 1995, the Commission of the EU also declared that it would not forward the Interim Agreement, as would have been the usual process. Instead, the commission first wanted to discuss freezing the whole matter among EU countries as a protest against Russian action in Chechnya.[124] By January 10, 1995, the vigor of the international reaction had increased. The Council of Europe (CE) announced that it would put a hold on Russia's membership application for the time being. According to news agency information, the French foreign ministry had sent all EU countries a list of possible measures to be taken in case the situation persisted. Sanctions against Moscow were also considered.[125] On January 19, 1995, the European Parliament adopted a resolution, which confirmed the commission's position not to sign the Interim Agreement.[126] On the other hand, by the middle of January, the commission had come

---

122. *Moscow News*, 20–26 January 1995.

123. On December 30, it was announced that the Interim Agreement was "initialed," that is, "once an accord has been initialed it means the end of the negotiations and their outcome." On the negotiations, see *Bulletin of the European Communities* 12 (1994): 113, 1.3.53. On the implementation of the Interim Agreement, see *Agence Europe* 6389, 30 December 1994, 7.

124. *Agence Europe* 6392, 6 January 1995, 5, 6; *Financial Times*, 6 January 1995.

125. *Agence Europe* 6395, 11 January 1995, 5.

126. *Bulletin of the European Communities* 1–2 (1995): 117, 1.4.100; *Official Journal of the European Communities* (20 February 1995): C43.

to the conclusion that it was not wise to go too far in freezing relations with Russia. The upshot was that although the Interim Agreement would not be signed, the bilateral and Tacis programs were to continue.[127] On March 9, 1995, the EU troika, led by France, visited Moscow and discussed matters with President Boris Yeltsin and Foreign Minister Andrei Kozyrev. The troika informed Russia that the implementation of the Interim Agreement depended on four conditions: a cease-fire, progress in the political settlement of the crisis, free access for humanitarian aid, and the establishment of a permanent OSCE mission in Chechnya. After the negotiations, the foreign ministers of France and Germany told the press that Russia was now in principle ready to comply with the demand for the active participation of the OSCE.[128]

Meanwhile the OSCE itself had been active. As was mentioned above, a turning point in the international dimension of the Chechen crisis took place on January 5, 1995. On that day, the EU sharpened its line, and the host country of the OSCE, Hungary, together with the other troika countries of that time, Switzerland and Italy, started negotiations between the Moscow-based ambassadors of the troika and the Russian foreign ministry. The starting point of the OSCE was the absolute recognition of the territorial integrity of Russia. According to the OSCE, the government of Russia reacted positively to the OSCE initiatives and invited a personal representative of the chairperson of the organization to discuss its participation in the resolution of the conflict.[129]

This initial phase, naturally, had to be already accepted by Russia, its foreign ministry, or Russia's representative in the OSCE, and the Russian foreign ministry could have ended the negotiations at the beginning had it chosen to do so. Apparently the foreign ministry was lobbying for the participation of the OSCE to avoid a more serious crisis in Russia's foreign relations. As briefly noted above, the Russian military originally opposed any interference. Such was the situation in January when the negotiations between Russia and the OSCE started. The personal representative of the chairman in office of the OSCE, István Gyarmati, arrived in Moscow on January 9, 1995, but during this first mission, the official meetings took place only between him and the representatives of the Russian foreign min-

127. *European Report*, no. 2009 (21 January 1995): V external relations, 3.

128. *Bulletin of the European Communities* 3 (1995): 85–86, 1.4.73.

129. The official OSCE document: Press-reliz deystvuyushchego predsedatelya organizatsii po bezopasnosti i sotrudnichestvu v Yevrope, minindel Vengrii L. Kobacha: K sobytiyam v Chechne, 5 Yanvarya 1995 goda. (Perevod s angliyskogo.) 5 January 1995 [OSCE press release by the foreign minister of Hungary, L. Kobach: The situation in Chechnya, January 5, 1995].

istry. Gyarmati said in an interview during his first mission: "So far, we have been denied admission to Russia's Defense Ministry and we have been unable to meet with a single representative of the Defense Ministry or the General Staff. . . . We requested a meeting, but to no avail. This means that we have no accurate information."[130]

In a period of two weeks, something changed in the attitude of Russia; probably the foreign ministry had got the president on its side. The OSCE five-person mission led by Gyarmati arrived in Moscow on January 24, 1995, and this time the reception was warm. The representatives of the OSCE were able to discuss matters not only with the representatives of the foreign ministry, but also with those of different bureaucracies, including the military. They met human rights activists and representatives of the Chechen diaspora in Moscow. The mission to the actual region of the conflict lasted two days.

In the first phase of the crisis, Russia received expressions of "concern" rather than condemnation or reprimand. Then the international community hardened its stance. Finally, after a hard bargaining process, Russia agreed to the permanent OSCE mission in Chechnya, which started its work in April 1995. Here are those elements that we need to construct an interpretation of Russia's behavior from a neoliberal institutionalist perspective.

From this process, during which Russia's behavior toward the OSCE's demands changed, neoliberal institutionalism would point to a self-interested and rationally calculating Russia, encircled not only by other states trying to influence Russia, but also by institutions and regimes, *through which* states act. First, the OSCE itself is an institution, and since January 1995 an organization that includes several regimes. Neither Germany nor the United States nor Finland was allowed to interfere in the crisis in Chechnya. International intervention was made possible through an institution that was itself a product of a process of institutionalization. Wilhelm Höynck, Secretary-General of the OSCE, has described this general process as follows:

> The "old'" CSCE was mainly an instrument of conference diplomacy, a framework for negotiation and linkage of interests to achieve decisions and ascertain implementation. The common basis was still much too fragile to allow for operational activities of the CSCE as such. The participating States used to decide on their com-

---

130. *Moscow News*, 20–26 January 1995.

mitments by consensus, but implemented them individually—each State on its own account. No institutional structure existed, except for conference secretariats set up on an ad hoc basis for each meeting. Now missions in the field belong to the hard-core of the CSCE conflict prevention inventory.[131]

In other words, the OSCE was an institution that had some earlier agreed-on general mechanisms, based on certain principles and norms, which allowed this sort of intervention and enabled negotiations with regard to such intervention in the first place. The OSCE was acceptable to Russia for a number of reasons. First, Russia was a member. Second, there was the specific nature of the OSCE as an organization: it was based on a strict principle of consensus; it was understood as not having supranational aspirations; it had no punishment mechanisms or coercion means of its own. In fact, these institutional weaknesses suggest that cooperation through institutions is more complex than a pure reflection of the "degree of institutionalization." It has been noted (with reference to the fact that the OSCE was at one time the only international organization allowed to be stationed in Chechnya) that "paradoxical though it may seem, these weaknesses may also turn out to be its strengths."[132] The OSCE was probably more desirable from Russia's point of view than, for example, the United Nations. It was a European organization whose position in European security affairs Russia wanted to enhance. Russian leaders might have concluded that if someone should be allowed to interfere in Russia's internal affairs, it should be the OSCE, because Russia could also win some benefits with its compliance in strengthening the organization.

This, in turn, was understood in the international community. The role of an all-European actor toward Russia in the case of Chechnya was thus delegated to the OSCE because of previously existing institutional linkages. The Russia–OSCE level of institutionalization gave other European actors, such as the EU, the CE, individual countries, and also some domestic pressure groups in Russia, a legal basis of reference in their efforts to put pressure on Russia's leaders.

Russia would perhaps never have accepted the OSCE's interference for the above reasons alone. The institutional linkages were important precon-

131. Wilhelm Höynck, "CSCE Missions in the Field as an Instrument of Preventive Diplomacy: Their Origin and Development," in *The Challenge of Preventive Diplomacy: The Experience of the OSCE* (Stockholm: Ministry for Foreign Affairs, 1994) 55–73, quotation 56.

132. "The OSCE's Increasing Responsibilities in European Security," *NATO Review*, no. 6 (November 1996): 7–12, quotation 9.

ditions, but we should expect Russia to have calculated that cooperation in this case was more beneficial than pursuing an uncooperative line. It was shown above that the price of this line grew in the course of time, and neoliberal institutionalism would expect Russia to consider it and change its behavior accordingly. The development described above would have caused Russia to make serious cost–benefit calculations. Although the OSCE did not have any punishment retribution of its own, other actors performed on its behalf, most importantly the EU and the CE. Any "real" sanctions were not expected by Russia, however. Foreign Minister Kozyrev said at the end of January that "common sense tells that the USA or the EU will not adopt economic sanctions against Russia."[133]

Such sanctions need not have been strictly material. One of Russia's openly declared main goals in Europe was to be integrated into the all-European framework of cooperation, and Russia was vulnerable from this point of view. With regard to the CE, Russia was seeking membership that was already promised to it (Russia eventually became a member in February 1996). With regard to the EU, it was a matter of closer institutional and trade partnership. The OSCE participation in the conflict settlement was one of the four conditions for the signing of the Interim Agreement; the other conditions were fulfilled by the temporary cease-fire and negotiations that started after the Budyonnovsk drama, and the Interim Agreement was signed in July 1995. Although the pressure of the international community cannot be seen as decisive in the cease-fire and peace negotiations in Chechnya then or in retrospect, without doubt it was a decisive factor that made Russia adopt a flexible line toward the OSCE's aspirations. The indirect consequences of Russia's uncooperative line, especially its spoiled reputation, which would hinder that country's integration goals, were seen as serious setbacks for Russia by the Russian foreign policy elite.[134] Although one can easily see Russia's desire for a strengthened position in European affairs as the basis for all these goals, neoliberal institutionalism would point to the crucial role of institutions in Russia's policy and in the policy of others toward Russia. Despite the "sanctioning problems" that the international community faced vis-à-vis Russia in this case, the complex institutional framework undoubtedly raised the costs associ-

133. *Rossiyskaya gazeta*, 28 January 1995.

134. See, for instance, V. Nikonov, head of the subcommittee of international security of the State Duma, article in *Nezavisimaya gazeta*, 12 January 1995, or V. Lukin, head of the committee for international affairs of the State Duma, interview in *Nezavisimaya gazeta*, 14 March 1995.

ated with Russia's noncompliance with jointly accepted norms and rules and an uncooperative line in general.[135]

As has been mentioned in passing, bureaucratic struggles in Russia also played a role.[136] Although neoliberal institutionalism sees states as the principal actors and analytical entities in interstate relations, in our case some neoliberal institutionalists would perhaps point out that the OSCE was not only supported by Russia's foreign ministry, but that to some extent it offered the ministry an instrument in its efforts to fulfill its task. The establishment of the OSCE Assistance Group would at least partially stabilize the somewhat spoiled relations between Russia and the international community and make it easier for the ministry to fulfill its declared task of integrating Russia more closely with European institutions. Neoliberal institutionalism does not offer us precise tools for dealing with this domestic dimension. For that, any traditional bureaucratic policy model provides a much better starting point.

Meaning of the Rules and Changing Normative Context

From *constructivism's* perspective, the meaning of norms and rules, and the shared and unshared beliefs behind them, should be taken seriously in interpreting Russia's and other actors' behavior. Moreover, we might also be encouraged by constructivism to hypothesize that the possibility of changes in the normative context of behavior should be considered. Thus, instead of trying to understand the behavior of Russia and other actors as such, we are encouraged to study how "social and discursive practices normalize or delegitimate forms of behavior."[137] Starting once more with the previous notification rule, constructivists might agree with the commonsense interpretation presented above that the question of complying with these rules did not even come onto the agenda of the security council. Instead of saying that this is a natural conclusion without offering a detailed consideration, constructivism would question the role of these rules.

Previous notification rules, as mentioned above, are routine rules, according to which the regime participants inform one another, usually once a year, about major military maneuvers they are going to perform. Practice (especially in the former Soviet Union and the former Yugoslavia) clearly

---

135. See the discussion of "tit-for-tat" strategies, "sanctioning problems," and "reputational effects" in Hasenclever, Mayer, and Rittberger, *Theories of International Regimes*, 35–37.

136. For more details, see, for instance, Hurlburt, "Russia, the OSCE, and European Security Architecture (1)."

137. Price and Tannenwald, "Norms and Deterrence," 124, 125.

suggests that these peacetime institutions usually, and not only in Chechnya, become hollow or dead as soon as it is a question of real war and not a maneuver.[138] There is, of course, no mention in the respective document that they should be limited to peacetime maneuvers only; that would be against the spirit of the whole CSBM. Nor is there any mention that the regime refers to external relations only. One might speculate, however, that the reaction of other states would have been more obvious and critical if Russia's troop movements had been made in connection with an interstate crisis between fellow OSCE members (between Russia and Ukraine or Russia and Estonia, for instance) as was originally the underlying point of reference in the CSBM regime.

Constructivism would not take this state of affairs as given. It would ask whether there was a tacit understanding among the regime participants that these rules are not applicable to "real" situations or "internal crises." Although some Western and Russian newspapers as well as some scholars have raised this issue,[139] in some cases immediately after the operation started, in general this violation was *originally* not emphasized by other regime participants. Official references to noncompliance with OSCE rules, except those of the human dimension, were extremely rare, especially during the first months of the crisis.

Later, when the OSCE participation in principle was already accepted by Russia, this matter was included in the agenda. In the Stockholm International Peace Research Institute's (SIPRI's) Yearbook 1996, one can read an enlightening report of the attitudes expressed at the Annual Implementation Assessment Meeting (AIAM), held March 13 to 15, 1995:

> [C]oncern was expressed about Russian military activities in Chechnya in the light of its Vienna Document obligations. The Russian delegation considered CSBM provisions on notification and the invitation of observers to be inapplicable during the domestic crisis and argued that transparency about the conflict was ensured by the mass media coverage; that the aim of military action in Chechnya was to defend Russia's territorial integrity and it did not endanger the security of any state; and that the allegedly stabilizing situation

138. See Schimmelfennig, "Arms Control Regimes." Schimmelfennig refers to the CSBM and CFE treaty with regard to wars between Armenia and Azerbaizan and in former Yugoslavia.

139. See, for instance, *Financial Times*, 14 December 1994. See also Eberhard Schneider, "Moskaus Entschluss zum Tschetschenien-Krieg," *Aussenpolitik*, no. 11 (1995): 155–65, especially 163, 164.

in Chechnya made it possible to provide military information. These arguments were questioned and rejected on all counts by other OSCE delegations. They stressed the applicability of CSBM in "all-weather" conditions, including internal crisis situations, and considered mass media coverage to be no substitute for Vienna Document notification. The claim that no security threat exists was considered counter to the principle of indivisibility of security in the OSCE area. Nevertheless the discussion at the AIAM was reported to have been "constructive and cooperative."[140]

In questioning the above notions and evidence, constructivism would suggest that the meaning of a norm or a rule is a matter of mutual construction, there being no definite or permanent definition of any norm. In fact, one might claim that the meaning of the previous notification norm has gradually changed and that the crisis in Chechnya accelerated this change. The early Western and Russian newspaper comments and scholarly interest in Russia's violation of the letter of the CSBM in this context can be interpreted as legalistic misunderstanding of the contemporary meaning of the rules, but they might be understood also as parts of a game to change the meaning of the rules in question so that they should also be applied to such crises as Chechnya. Were this to become true, it would give more options for preventive diplomacy. In fact, when discussing the OSCE's conflict prevention tools, the representatives of the participant states often refer to these rules.[141]

How should we then interpret the originally weak diplomatic reaction to and lack of protests about Russia's violation of the previous notification rule, and why was this question then raised at the AIAM in March 1995? Three possible alternatives come to mind. First, we can see it as proof that there was originally a tacit understanding of the fact that these rules were not expected to be applied in a real crisis, especially in a domestic one, and the opposite attitude or interpretation was developed only later. In other words, this alternative implies that there was, in the end of 1994, a widely shared meaning of the previous notification rule as governing peacetime maneuvers only and not covering domestic security crises. The other alternative would be to interpret it so that the diplomatic silence in

140. Zdzislaw Lachowski, "Appendix 16A: The Vienna CSBM in 1995," in *SIPRI Yearbook 1996: Armaments, Disarmament, and International Security* (Stockholm, International Peace Research Institute: Oxford University Press, 1996), 740–44.

141. Margaretha af Ugglas, "Conditions for Successful Preventive Diplomacy," in *The Challenge of Preventive Diplomacy: The Experience of the OSCE*, 11–54.

reaction to Russia's violation, which could not be retracted, was part of the effort to pursue a more important and more topical aim: the OSCE's participation in conflict management in Chechnya. This alternative would imply that the meaning of the rule was contested and that Russia was expected to follow it in any situations of large troop movements, even though this was not emphasized by other regime participants for tactical reasons in the beginning of the crisis. The third alternative would be to emphasize that in a way the other regime participants followed the bureaucratic rules of the procedure and raised the question only at the annual implementation meeting. All these interpretations are possible on the basis of available evidence, although a combination of the two last alternatives draws a more appropriate picture, if we retrospectively ask this question of the regime participants themselves.

The crucial theoretical point here, from constructivism's point of view, is that the meaning of a rule cannot be defined once and forever; it is a matter of mutual construction, and its violations can consequently be open to varying meanings. Nevertheless, in violating the previous notification rule, Russia did deviate from the generally expected standards of behavior, but not so much as it did in violating human rights. Russia's violation of human rights in Chechnya was obviously seen as an altogether different and more serious matter than the violations of the CSBM rules.

This dimension prompts us first to consider more precisely the question of the autonomy and sovereignty of a state in the OSCE framework. From constructivism's point of view, we should notice that in the background there was a mutually constructed and reproduced understanding during the whole process about Russia's territorial integrity. Chechnya's right to independence was denied, and through that the whole puzzle was constituted: it was a question of an internal Russian affair. This, however, was not as self-evident as it may appear. The right of Chechnya to declare independence according to the previous and present constitutions of Russia, as well as with regard to international law, was disputable. The international community could have chosen to recognize the independence of Chechnya by referring to the so-called de facto situation or by interpreting the aspirations of Russia as colonial and the struggle of the Chechens as a struggle for national liberation.[142] This was not the case, and it was noticed in Russia. This becomes clear in retrospect, from a letter drawn up in Feb-

142. See Walter, "Militärische Aspekte des Tshetschenien-Kriegs" (1995), 696, n. 9 and the literature mentioned in it. Cf. the comments of Urban in "Nochmals: Militärische Aspekte des Tschetschenien-Kriegs (Replik: Thomas Urban; Entgegnung: Franz Walter)," *Osteuropa* 45 (November 1995): 1064–66.

ruary 1995, containing the reply of the Russian foreign ministry to the State
Duma committee: "No country in the world, not a single international organization, has reacted positively to these claims [of Chechnya's right to
independence]. It has always been confirmed that the Chechen Republic
is an integral part of the Russian Federation, and it has always been stressed
that the national borders of Russia are inviolable. (The only exception is
the well-known decision of the Estonian MPs.)"[143]

Russia's motives for these starting points can be well understood, and
its position in this principal question of Chechnya "as an integral part of
the Russian Federation" had remained stable.[144] The motives of the international community, or the OSCE, for coming to the same understanding
about the basic parameters of the problem as Russia can be interpreted in
many ways; they respected a stable Russia or a stable international system
as a whole, or perhaps they had "learned" from Yugoslavia's experience.
From the viewpoint of the OSCE, this was probably seen as a constructive
and pragmatic position, because any other position would have hindered
the OSCE from intervening in the first place.

Motives aside, constructivism would emphasize that in the course of
this process, the case of Chechnya was constructed or reconstructed as an
"internal affair" of Russia. Constructivism would also stress that what this
"internal affair" meant was mutually constructed. Here we can find a clear
change in attitudes. Although this "internal affair" had for a long time
been understood as tantamount to "do not interfere" or "do not pay too
much attention," this became less so as the process unfolded. At first, even
those organizations that later were active in trying to put pressure on Russia, such as the EU, the CE, or the OSCE, did not raise any questions,
although the crisis in Chechnya had started in 1991. It was not only that
there was no information. At the research level, one can find sources that
early on raised the possibility that the crisis could end with the large-scale
use of force by Russia.[145] Nevertheless, defined as an internal Russian prob-

143. The letter is signed by Deputy Foreign Minister Kolokolov, 20 February 1995. A copy
of it can be found in *Gosudarstvennaya Duma: Komissiya po rassledovaniyu prichin i obstoyatelstv
vozniknoveniya krizisnoy situatsii v Chechenskoy Respublike: Itogovyj otchot* [State Duma: Commission for the study of the reasons for and conditions of the emergence of a crisis situation in
the Chechen Republic: The results] (Moscow: Izdanie Gosudarstvennoy Dumy, Oktyabr
1995), 105, 106.

144. Although the negotiations of the status of Chechnya have been postponed for the
time being, this has remained the official position of the Russian leadership. In Russian
media, there can be found some rare exceptions on this question in 1995. See, for instance,
A. Illiarionov's and B. Lvin's article in *Moscow News*, 24 February–3 March 1995.

145. Uwe Hallbach, *Russlands Auseinandersetzung mit Tschetschenien, Berichte des Bundesinstu-

lem, the crisis was not included on the agenda when Russian politicians and officials met with other actors of the international community. The principle of not interfering in the internal affairs of other countries seemed to be especially delicate in relations between Russia and other countries; Russia was apparently blocking all such efforts, and this was accepted without further questions. Although one can find many similar crises and many places mentioned and discussed in the public abstracts of the minutes of the CSCE meetings, Chechnya was not among them before the war actually began.

A brief look at some of the facts illustrates this point. Although kept secret until December 11, 1994, the strategic choice to use force to achieve the stated goals in Chechnya was made by Russia's security council on November 29.[146] By that time, the situation in Grozny was extremely tight because of fighting between Dudayev's troops and the Chechen opposition, helped unofficially and secretly by some Russian troops. When such a crisis happens in the area of the OSCE, the organization usually reacts in some way. The Committee of Senior Officials of the OSCE, one of the most important preventive diplomacy tools of the organization, held an emergency meeting between November 28 and December 1, at the time when the danger of large-scale war in Chechnya was growing. This meeting was not convened to discuss the acute situation in Chechnya, however, but the situation in Bosnia-Herzegovina.[147]

In other words, although the OSCE had a set of mechanisms for early warning and preventive diplomacy,[148] which perhaps could have changed the course of events or at least offered room for international consultation, these mechanisms were not or could not be applied to the case of Russia-Chechnya. The OSCE's mechanisms were not correct or effective enough to deal with such things as Russia's problem with Chechnya, an argument that also basically suits a neoliberal institutionalist analysis. On the other

---

tuts für ostwissenschäftliche und international Studien 61(1994), especially 35, 36; Elainen M. Holoboff, "Russian Views on Military Intervention: Benevolent Peacekeeping, Monroe Doctrine, or Neo-Imperialism," in Lawrence Freedman, ed., Military Intervention in European Conflicts (Oxford: Political Quarterly, Blackwell), 154–77, especially 169, 170.

146. See note 105 above.

147. See: Fourth Emergency Meeting of the Committee of Senior Officials, Journal (CSCE), Budapest November 28–December 1, 1994. I have not found any mention of Chechnya in the official published minutes of meetings of the OSCE in 1994.

148. See, for instance, The Role of the High Commissioner on National Minorities in OSCE Conflict Prevention: An Introduction (Foundation on Inter-Ethnic Relations: June 1997); Consolidated Summary of the CSCE: Seminar on Early Warning and Preventive Diplomacy (Warsaw: January 19–21, 1994).

hand, this could be changed to a constructivist argument by saying that during the first months of the crisis, from December 1994 onward, this internal crisis of Russia was mutually constructed so that it allowed for OSCE intervention although there were no major institutional changes in the OSCE mechanisms. The product of this development was clearly a new dimension for OSCE practice, and the activity of the new host country of the OSCE from the beginning of 1995, Hungary, as well as Russia's foreign ministry's responsive attitude, was essential in creating this new practice.

Russia was constrained by many norms and rules of the OSCE, but as was shown above, neither the previous notification rule nor other rules were able to make international intervention possible *in advance*. Later, human rights issues appear to have justified OSCE intervention. In his speech on January 26, 1995, the Secretary-General of the OSCE, Wilhelm Höynck, discussed Russia's violation of the OSCE norms and rules without mentioning the Vienna Document of 1994 or the CSBM. Instead, he said that "for the relationship between one OSCE state and another as well as for the relationship between the OSCE and Russia as a participating State, the reference to an 'internal affair' as a 'killer argument' can *no longer* be invoked under international law." He referred to two ways in which this applies to Chechnya, namely the human dimension principles of the 1992 Helsinki Summit and the Code of Conduct of the Budapest 1994 Summit.[149]

One reason that the OSCE and the international community were more concerned with human rights violations than previous notification violations may have been that the norms connected with the former have a much longer standing in just war theory in the form of an age-old prohibition against disproportionate harm to civilian noncombatants, as incorporated into international law. This belief was shared to some extent also by the Russian leadership. According to one Russian newspaper, Gyarmati told a press conference on January 10, 1995, that Foreign Minister Kozyrev had admitted that human rights violations in Chechnya were not a "special internal affair of Russia"—which in the words of the newspaper took place "for the first time officially at this level after the beginning of the operation in Chechnya." At the same time, Kozyrev added that the restoration of constitutional order in Chechnya was a matter for Russia alone.[150] Nevertheless, Russia thereby accepted that the OSCE has a mandate to monitor human rights questions in Chechnya.

149. Wilhelm Höynck, "Contributions of the OSCE to the New Stability " (speech in Bonn, January 26, 1995). Emphasis added.
150. *Nezavisimaya gazeta*, 12 January 1995.

On January 12, 1995, Russia received an official statement from the OSCE, prepared on the basis of the results of Gyarmati's first mission to Moscow, which contained a demand that the OSCE be allowed to take an active part in the settlement of the crisis and in the restoration of democratic institutions. The territorial integrity of Russia was recognized, but the grave violations of human rights that had occurred were condemned.[151] Soon after this, the first OSCE mission to the conflict area was organized. On the basis of that experience, Gyarmati reported that human rights were being violated both by the Russian forces and Dudayev's troops. As far as Russia was concerned, this involved the bombing of Chechen towns and villages and the resulting civilian casualties. In his meetings with Russian military leaders, Gyarmati commented that he received no answer as to how these tactics would be changed.[152]

This, in turn, seems to imply that in the military's view the OSCE had no right to interfere in these questions. In other words, although the OSCE seemingly had found a partner in Russia's foreign ministry, at the practical level the military did not take the OSCE's presence into account. Later, in April, Gyarmati stated this more clearly: "It is interesting to note the difference between two facts. On the one hand, the continuation of the war using methods that have been condemned, and on the other hand the very open attitude of Russia's leadership to cooperation with the OSCE. It is as though there were two separate states."[153]

This could be interpreted mainly as Russia's tactical behavior, but also as a difference between the normative framework of the Russian military and that of its foreign policy leadership about what constituted OSCE intervention. Although the OSCE's right to monitor human rights questions in Chechnya was accepted by the president and the foreign ministry, the military saw it as interference in Russia's internal affairs.

Nevertheless, the permanent mission was established. When it is stated that Russia realized that "the constitution of a group of this kind is in the

151. The official OSCE document: Zayavlenie predsetatelya postoyannogo soveta OBSYe po situatsii v Chechenskoy Respublike, Rossiyskaya Federatsiya, 12 Yanvarya 1995g. (Perevod s angliyskogo.) [Announcement of the representatives of the permanent council of the OSCE about the situation in the Chechen Republic, Russian Federation, January 12, 1995.]

152. The official OSCE document: Doklad lichnogo predstavitelya deystvuyushchego Predsedatelya OBSYe o vizite v Rossiyskuyu Federatsiyu, Chechenskuyu Respubliku. (3.02.)1995. [Presentation of the personal representative of the chairman-in-office of the OSCE about the visit to the Russian Federation, the Chechen Republic, February 2, 1995.] See also *Nezavisimaya gazeta*, 31 January 1995.

153. *Nezavisimaya gazeta*, 14 April 1995.

best interests of Russia itself,"[154] constructivism prompts us to point out that this interest was by no means given; it was defined during the process. In arriving at a deeper view of why this was the first time that Russia let an international organization interfere in such a crisis in its territory, we can point out the changes in the normative context in the long run. In light of the developments in the Soviet and Russian understanding of international norm-based cooperation, the overall tendency seems to have been a growing importance ascribed to international law and international norms, despite the standoff of the Cold War.[155] This general development in the normative context can be seen as a precondition for the actual decisions analyzed here.

Another way to approach these more fundamental changes is to show that the role of the OSCE itself has developed over the years and that its interference in Russia's internal affairs depends on its mutually constructed role in European politics, not only on institutional solutions, which are in a way surface phenomena. The present identity of the OSCE developed from sharply conflicting expectations. The thesis was the self-interested need of the Soviet Union, which wanted the West to finally recognize the Soviet Union's postwar political and territorial gains, to promise not to violate the existing borders in Europe, and to recognize the German Democratic Republic. The antithesis was the suspicious West, which finally came to the conclusion that it could benefit from the process and in doing so decided to use the institution to open the socialist camp to a flow of ideas and people and, as a result, to promote the erosion of Communist ideology. Moreover, the Western motive was to urge the Warsaw Pact to limit its disproportionate number of troops. It recently became known that an influential part of the Soviet leadership "had grave doubts about assuming international commitments that could open the way to foreign interference in our political life."[156]

In the Soviet bureaucratic and ideological struggles, the more positive attitude won. Bearing in mind the constructivist emphasis on practices, we

154. "The OSCE's Increasing Responsibilities in European Security," *NATO Review*, no. 6 (November 1996): 7–12, quotation 9.

155. See Christer Pursiainen, "Pacta Sunt Servanta? The Development of the Sense of Community and the Principle of Obligation in Soviet and Russian Doctrines of International Law," *Journal of Communist Studies and Transition Politics* 14 (September 1998).

156. The words of a former Soviet diplomat, Anatoly Dobrynin, *In Confidence: Moscow's Ambassador to America's Six Cold War Presidents (1962–1986)* (New York: Times Books, Random House, 1995) 345. The same argument has been put forward by another former Soviet diplomat, Yuri Kashlev, "SBSJe v politike Sovetskogo Soyuza" [CSCE in the politics of the Soviet Union], *Mezhdunarodnaya zhizn*, no. 11–12 (1995): 74–81.

can point out that the history of the organization is a good example of how practices, together with norms and rules, can produce change. In our case, the synthesis is the new identity of the OSCE, which from contemporary Russia's viewpoint should represent the normative framework for all-European cooperation and which has the right to interfere in many affairs of Russia previously defined as purely domestic or internal in nature.[157] Without this development in the mutually constructed role of the organization and its present identity, as Russia sees it, the presence of the OSCE in Chechnya cannot be understood.

One can also refer to shorter term changes in normative contexts and behavioral practices and claim that before Chechnya the fact that the organization had similar missions in the CIS area can be seen as a precondition that helped to extend the practice into Russia itself. This experience enabled Russia to evaluate what this mission activity involved, to measure its limits, and to allow it finally to cross the threshold, with the adoption of this practice in a crisis in Russia itself. Thus the practice of the actors was one of the most important sources of the change in Russia's attitudes toward the OSCE's role and scope.

IMPLICATIONS FOR THEORY AND PRACTICE

It is time to clarify the theoretical and practical implications of our experience. The theoretical conclusions become crystallized in the comparison of the three theoretical approaches used here, and the conclusions drawn at the practical level in turn depend largely on which theoretical approach is considered superior to others.

What is decisive when the relative superiority of the theories is to be evaluated? Each of the theories considered is committed to certain criteria on the question of what the standards for theory choice should be and to a certain philosophy of science. True, the idea that "students of international politics should justify their theories in terms of Imre Lakatos's . . . criteria for distinguishing progressive research programs from degenerative ones"[158] is widespread and as referred to in passing, very often relied on in realist, neoliberal, and constructivist international relations de-

---

157. This is the line of argumentation of Kashlev, "SBSJe v politike Sovetskogo Soyuza."
158. Christensen and Snyder, "Progressive Research on Degenerating Alliances," 919.

bates.[159] If we accept Lakatos's criteria, we should look for a theory "with a higher corroborated content," in terms of discovery of "novel facts"; in other words, a theory that explains the same data as another theory along with something more is superior to the latter.[160] According to Alexander Motyl, however, this approach seems to be useful "in larger theoretical families," but it does not tell us how to resolve the competition among theories with "different paradigmatic foundations,"[161] or as Stephen Krasner put it, across research programs. Lakatos's sophisticated methodological falsificationism's "analytic utility is impeded by at least partial theory incommensurability."[162]

The point of reference in these remarks is, of course, Thomas Kuhn's notion of incommensurable paradigms; according to him, when paradigms (or theories) enter into debate about paradigm choice, their role is circular, because each school uses its own paradigm to argue in that paradigm's defense and uses its own criteria that it dictates for itself.[163] Paul Feyerabend's argument is that the content of incommensurable theories "cannot be compared" (although for him this fact, leaving room for aesthetic judgments and judgments of taste, makes science an attractive enterprise).[164]

Nevertheless, without going deeper into this metatheoretical discussion,[165] in this chapter the conscious point of departure for the comparison

159. For the discussion of Lakatos in terms of the "realist research program," see the literature mentioned in note 20 above. For the neoliberal claim that Lakatos's formula should be applied to the study of international politics, see Keohane, "Theory of World Politics: Structural Realism and Beyond"; for constructivist analyses that rely on the Lakatosian concept of theory comparison, see the literature mentioned in note 67 above.

160. Lakatos, "Falsification and the Methodology of Scientific Research Programmes," especially 116, 118.

161. Alexander Motyl, "The Dilemmas of Sovietology and the Labyrinth of Theory," in Frederic J. Fleron and Erik Hoffmann, eds., Post-Communist Studies and Political Science: Methodology and Empirical Theory in Sovietology (Boulder, Colo.: Westview Press, 1993), 77–104.

162. Krasner, "Towards Understanding in International Relations," 144.

163. See Thomas Kuhn, The Structure of Scientific Revolutions (Chicago: University of Chicago Press, 1970), especially section IX.

164. Paul Feyerabend, "Consolations for the Specialists," in Lakatos and Musgrave, Criticism and the Growth of Knowledge, 197–230, for this point especially, see 227–29. Feyerabend is often given the responsibility for articulating the "anything goes" type of relativism in the philosophy of science; see Feyerabend, Against Method (London: Verso, 1988).

165. For the treatment of the incommensurability thesis in contemporary international relations literature from rival perspectives, see Colin Wight, "Incommensurability and Cross-Paradigm Communication in International Relations Theory: 'What's the Frequency Kenneth?' Millennium 25, 2 (1996): 291–319; Mark Neufeld, The Restructuring of International Relations Theory (Cambridge: Cambridge University Press, 1995), especially 50–69; Wæver, "The Rise and Fall of the Inter-Paradigm Debate."

of the various theories has been the assumption—while taking the Kuhnian incommensurability thesis seriously—that the theories in question can be compared with each other, at least to some degree, because they claim to offer alternative solutions to the fundamental problems of international cooperation that I have tried to encapsulate by the main questions raised at the beginning of this chapter. The theories presented here clash, but they also share an area of referential overlap and can be compared, albeit "under their own descriptions."[166]

For the purpose of our comparison, I emphasize the instrumental (in terms of tools or set of questions) and heuristic value of the theories. Theories always concern a large body of cases, but where the focus is on empirical questions in the light of rival theories, the actual empirical case has to be investigated: can the theories used here identify, describe, and explain those elements that were crucial in determining Russia's behavior in the situation described earlier? Do they draw our attention to issues or factors that would otherwise be difficult to bring to light, and do we discover something that without them we could not find? These questions can be generalized by asking whether these theories have something new to give to the study of Russian foreign policy in general, something that the field has not attained using other approaches.

The interpretation of Russia's behavior from structural realism's perspective was based on three variations. The first variation was to ignore the case by referring to structural realism's metatheoretical commitments, and this is one way to approach all puzzles it contains. The second possibility was to refer to the basic assumption that Russia is not restricted by international norms and rules when its self-interest suggests otherwise. This was best applicable to the first puzzle in our problem; were this to be accepted as a legitimate argument of structural realism, Russia's noncompliance was to be predicted. If this interpretation is accepted as a plus for structural realism, if Russia ever goes against its self-interest, it would indicate a failing in the predictive power of structural realism. The second puzzle we looked at came close to such a situation, but as was shown, one could evade it by opting for an explanation rooted in a possible power-based impulse or again by ignoring the case altogether by saying that variations in Russia's behavior are irrelevant to structural realism's perspective.

In other words, it seems that structural realism provides us with two

166. The term *referential overlap* and the claim that the clashing theories must be put to the test "under their own description" come from Bhaskar's modification of Kuhn's problem and Lakatos's solution; see Roy Bhaskar, *Scientific Realism and Human Emancipation* (London: Verso), chapter 1, section 6 ("Incommensurability and the Refutation of Superidealism").

dubious alternatives. In the first case, it tells us to base an explanation on a single factor—the autonomy of decision or power—without bothering to question such a basic assumption. Yet even if Russia's behavior was determined by this single factor, the approach does not contain elements that could not be captured just as well by other models in or outside the rationalistic paradigm and does not deepen and call into question this explanation by considering other possible sources of behavior. Single factor theories appear rather unpromising for the study of Soviet/Russian foreign policy, which has, since the early 1960s, tried to escape from these orientations toward more manifold explanations.[167] Second, to accept the other alternative and leave cases like ours unexplained would mean that structural realism gives us no tools, instruments, or predictive power for cases like ours. Parsimony of this kind is not much help from the viewpoint of detailed Russian foreign policy studies, and the message is again clear: find another theory to suit our purposes.

As for the practical message, structural realism promises a rather pessimistic prospect for the efforts of integrating Russia with the international institutions. Russia is not constrained by any rules of the game based on self-enforcement, and it is always ready to choose unilateralism over cooperation whenever its self-interest so demands. Such surface phenomena of international politics as the OSCE mission in Chechnya do not change this axiom, because they do not have a tangible effect on Russia's behavior.

Both instrumentally and heuristically, neoliberal institutionalism has more to offer. This is, of course, understandable, because our research questions originated largely from institutional approaches. Neoliberal institutionalism focuses our attention on the institutional constraints that might have affected Russia's behavior and encourages us to speculate about the degree of these constraints, starting from the assumption that Russia behaves rationally and calculates cost–benefit ratio in making decisions. If the suggestions of neoliberal institutionalism are considered against the background of the history of the field of Soviet/Russian foreign policy studies, one can note that this theory offers to some degree a new perspective; although in international relations in general the questions related to the impact of institutions on state behavior have been widely discussed, these questions are not emphasized in any of the main approaches that constituted sovietology. Neoliberal institutionalism appears to offer several ways to deepen our understanding of Russia's behavior,

167. Christer Pursiainen, "The Heritage of Soviet Foreign Policy Studies," *Idäntutkimus/ The Finnish Review of East European Studies* 2, 2 (1995): 7–31.

although in focusing on institutional constraints, neoliberal institutionalism alone seems to be insufficient to deal with the complexity of Russian foreign policy behavior. Nevertheless, neoliberalism as a theory of interests may, if developed further, offer an overall framework to be applied to the pragmatic needs of empirical research on Russian foreign policy.

In any case, we might find that the reasoning presented above supports the claims made by neoliberal institutionalists. Institutionalization is a variable, and the changes in that variable may affect state behavior, although the experience of the OSCE can suggest that the connection between an institution's ability to enhance cooperation and the formality of an institution is by no means linear. The experience of the OSCE may give cause to study more precisely the role of loose or weak institutions in enhancing cooperation or in overcoming thresholds in difficult cases of cooperation. Our experience speaks in favor of the assumption that institutions may enhance cooperation by their very existence, although this cooperation is not necessarily easy and in many cases not automatic. In other words, the fact that Russia may allow an organization of which it is a member and which it sees as on the whole beneficial to interfere in its internal security matters greatly supports neoliberal institutionalism's basic assumptions about the nature of the international system and the role of institutions in it.

Were the picture outlined by neoliberal institutionalism to be accepted as the point of departure, the OSCE's achievement—its participation in the conflict management in an internal crisis in Russia—can be appreciated. In this light, OSCE rules violations cannot be seen as a proof of Russia's immunity to international norms and rules, but as a challenge to develop the organization further toward a more effective institutional framework that also has independent impact on state behavior.

The last of our three approaches, constructivism, draws our attention to questions that seem to have been left under the surface in the rationalistic explanations. To sum up the constructivist interpretation I have put forward, the concrete day-by-day action of the players in the drama may have had many causes, but constructivism suggests that the normative context constituted the frames of that play. In our case, the normative framework did not determine the lines of the players or the exact plot of the events, but it constituted the language and theme of the state of the play. With regard to the violations of OSCE rules, I focused attention on the meanings of these rules for different actors and emphasized that these meanings are subject to change. This is not enough to explain Russia's and other actors' behavior, but it helps us to see the parameters of this behavior. My constructivist interpretation of Russia's positive attitude toward the OSCE mission began by questioning the concept of an internal affair. In the course of the process, the role of the OSCE as an actor with regard to Russia was reconstituted in such a way that this new role legitimized the OSCE's concern about Chechnya, which in turn enabled the establishment of the OSCE Assistance Group. A more general frame for this decision worked through the role of the OSCE that was constituted over the last twenty years as an actor whose mandate extends to Russian affairs that are traditionally regarded as domestic concerns by that country. If the things that constructivism inspires us to pay attention to are considered against the background of the field of Soviet/Russian foreign policy studies, we can perhaps say that constructivism systematizes the issues that traditional study of history and of Soviet/Russian foreign policy thinking or ideology has widely dealt with and offers clearer and more explicit arguments about the relation between behavior and normative frameworks. In this sense, constructivism easily links theoretical and empirical levels in the study of Russian foreign policy.

As far as practical conclusions are concerned, constructivism offers conclusions that complement those of neoliberalism. The unhappy war in Chechnya perhaps brought about a new practice in the relation between Russia and other European countries. In Chechnya, this practice has had an important role even if it has not been decisive. The role of the OSCE Assistance Group has been one that offers "good services" in terms of neutral facilities and mediation, rather than functioning as a decision maker in conflict settlement. In the negotiations after the cease-fire following the Budyonnovsk hostage drama of June 1995, as well as in the negotiations that started in August 1996 and resulted in a temporary rearrangement of the Russian-Chechen relationship, the OSCE played a role but was not an initiator. It could not stop the Russian military from using outlawed methods in prosecuting its war; Russia continued to violate the code of conduct through the crisis. Despite that, the OSCE has been useful even in this form, and it has secured and legitimized an international place at the table when discussing Russia's behavior in Chechnya. Moreover, constructivism leads us to consider that in the best case this kind of third-party intervention can be the start for a developed practice in which the OSCE functions more fully as a tool of preventive diplomacy in potential future crises of a similar nature involving Russia.

The epigraph to this chapter quotes President Yeltsin, and it is perhaps appropriate to close with him and to reveal the meaning of the quotation. Russians hate to obey all sorts of rules, laws, instructions, and directives, we read. Be that as it may, the point of reference was not international law, and even less the norms and rules of the OSCE, but "all the niceties of protocol—where to step, where to stop?" At first, Yeltsin, by his own account, stumbled a lot when he met with representatives of other countries, but, he said, he soon learned the "proper behavior by looking at what my neighbors were doing." Perhaps norms and rules matter after all, even for Russia.

4

Russia and the Democratic Peace: The Decision to Use Military Force in Ethnic Disputes

Andrea M. Lopez

The democratic peace theory is arguably the most discussed theory on war and peace in international relations. The theory has been examined and re-examined, tested and retested. Its basic premise that although stable democracies are as war prone as nondemocracies, they do not war with one another has withstood numerous critical studies. Yet interstate war is by no means the most common state military venture. Instead, states are more likely to militarily intervene in the domestic politics and civil conflicts of other states and to avoid a large-scale interstate war. Russian behavior since the collapse of the Soviet Union is indicative of this tendency. Although not fighting open wars with other countries, Russia has become involved in many ethnic, religious, and political disputes in the other former Soviet republics. In several cases, including Moldova, the military has intervened by forcibly assisting rebel groups against the government. In other cases, as in Estonia, the Russian military has not become involved.

Does the democratization of Russia and the democratization of the other former republics explain the different Russian behavior in these two cases? For more than twenty years, democratic peace[1] theorists have postulated that democracies do not fight one another and that a world system populated by democracies would be without war. Indeed, numerous studies have shown that democracies, although as prone as nondemocracies to go to war, do not fight one another.[2] "This absence of war between democracies comes as close as anything we have to an empirical law in international relations."[3] Put simply, the democratic peace theory assumes that the government of a democracy, because of its reliance on a large and diverse constituent base for its political survival, is constrained by the needs, desires, and fears of that base. In foreign policy, and particularly in the desire to go to war with another country, the constituency's needs and desires are largely founded on its opinion of the opposing country. According to the democratic peace theory, if the other country is a democracy, the constituents see it as an extension of the desires of its population and therefore legitimate. Such legitimacy, coupled with the internalized belief in compromise, leads to increased negotiations and to the notion that the crisis can be averted through nonviolent means. On the other hand, the lack of legitimacy bestowed on nondemocracies often leads to a crusader complex in the democracy and results in the conviction that war is the only answer.[4]

Yet Russia's active foreign policy has been directed toward the decision of whether to intervene in any of the numerous ethnic and political conflicts on its borders. Analysts have rarely sought to apply the democratic

1. The term *democratic peace theory* is problematic as there have been numerous versions put forth. The definition of democracy itself changes from author to author. Moreover, some authors focus on liberalism and others on democracy. Nonetheless, "democratic peace theory" is used here to describe the group of theories that have emerged to explain why democracies do not fight one another.

2. See Michael W. Doyle, "Kant, Liberal Legacies, and Foreign Affairs," *Philosophy and Public Affairs* 12 (Summer 1983): 205–35; Zeev Maoz and Nasrin Abdolali, "Regime Types and International Conflict, 1816–1976," *Journal of Conflict Resolution* 33 (March 1989): 3–35; Bruce Russett, *Grasping the Democratic Peace: Principles for a Post–Cold War World* (Princeton: Princeton University Press 1993); and Melvin Small and J. David Singer, "The War-Proneness of Democratic Regimes, 1816–1965," *Jerusalem Journal of International Relations* 1 (Summer 1976): 50–69.

3. Jack S. Levy, "Domestic Politics and War," *Journal of Interdisciplinary History* 18 (Spring 1988): 653–73.

4. Doyle, "Kant, Liberal Legacies, and Foreign Affairs, Part 2," *Philosophy and Public Affairs* 12 (Fall 1983): 323–53.

peace theory to the decision to intervene. The theory, however, may hold in those instances where intervention in opposition to an established government is considered. If democracies view other democracies as legitimate, then interference in the others' domestic affairs should be kept at a minimum. If the other states are democracies, then the intervening party should become involved on the side of the government, as a nonpartisan peacekeeper, or not at all.

This chapter seeks to test this proposition by examining Russian behavior in the "near abroad" in two cases: the intervention in Moldova and the lack of intervention in Estonia. Can this difference in behavior be attributed to the relative levels of democracy in Moldova and Estonia? Is it better understood through an examination of other factors affecting the Russian perception of the legitimacy of both the Moldovan and Estonian governments and their respective opposition groups?

I argue that, although the Russian behavior in Moldova and Estonia is consistent with the democratic peace theory, the institutional arm of the theory is unsupported. Instead, a legitimacy-based theory is better able to explain Russian involvement in the "near abroad." Such a legitimacy-based theory, premised on the presence of shared ideologies and national groups, political and territorial cohesion, and international recognition, is better suited to predicting the conditions under which Russia intervenes as well as on whose behalf, the government or the opposition, the intervention occurs.

RUSSIAN INTERVENTION

There has been remarkably little work on explaining when countries, including Russia, intervene in the civil wars, ethnic disputes, or internal crises of other states, and there has been little attempt to apply the existing theories of war and peace to intervention.[5] What literature there is on intervention tends to be focused on the moral, normative, and legal limitations of intervention or on prescriptions for successful interventions. There has

5. Among those who do attempt to apply more traditional analyses of war to military intervention in civil conflicts, see Gregory A. Raymond and Charles W. Kegley, Jr., "Long Cycles and Internationalized Civil War," *Journal of Politics* 38 (May 1987): 481–99; Morton A. Kaplan, "Intervention in Internal War: Some Systemic Sources," in James N. Rosenau, ed., *International Aspects of Civil Strife* (Princeton: Princeton University Press, 1964), 92–121.

been little creation or application of theory and even less systematic examination of conflicts and the likelihood of interventions.[6]

As for Russian intervention in particular, few works are devoted to examining the conditions leading to, or the causes of, intervention, largely because the country has not yet enjoyed even ten years of independence. It is widely recognized that Russia is active in the territories of the former Soviet Union. Russian interventions, often as peacekeeping forces,[7] have occurred in Georgia, Tajikistan, and Moldova. To a lesser extent, Russia continues to be involved in events beyond the borders of the former superpower, including the deployment of troops in Croatia and Bosnia-Herzegovina. What circumstances encourage Russian behavior, however, are not agreed on. According to Elaine Holoboff:

> There seems to be general agreement that military intervention can be justified as long as it fulfills one or more of the conditions below.
>
> i.   contributes to the maintenance of Russia' [sic] great power status;
> ii. protects Russians residing in the "near abroad" (blizhnyeye zarubyezhye), including military personnel and their families;
> iii. prevents the spread of instability, especially to regions of Russia itself;
> iv. looks after Russia's geopolitical interests, for example, protecting Russia's southern borders and preventing the spread of Islamic fundamentalism;
> v.   coincides with nationalist public opinion.[8]

6. For the purposes of this chapter, intervention is limited to military intervention, defined as "the movement of troops or military forces by one independent country, or a group of countries in concert, across the border of another independent country (or colony of an independent country) or actions by troops already stationed in the target country." Frederic S. Pearson, "Foreign Military Interventions and Domestic Disputes," *International Studies Quarterly* 18 (September 1974): 261. This definition, and this chapter, ignores solely economic or diplomatic interventions.

7. Coupled with the lack of theory on interventions is a failure to create a consistent definition. Many definitions rely on a normative explanation of intervention, indicating improper interference in violation of another state's sovereignty. Such definitions claim that peacekeeping, which is traditionally and by law conducted only with the agreement of all warring factions, is not an intervention. The above definition of intervention, however, is not contingent on the legality of the action or the motives of the intervening power. For this reason, peacekeeping operations are included under a heading of military intervention.

8. Elaine Holoboff, "Russian Views on Military Intervention: Benevolent Peacekeeping, Monroe Doctrine, or Neo-Imperialism?" in Lawrence Freedman, ed., *Military Intervention in European Conflicts* (Cambridge: Blackwell, 1994), 156.

Goltz saw a far more sinister plot behind Russian behavior. He believed Russia seeks to retain total control and to deny sovereignty to the nations of the former Soviet Union. Any instability is used as a justification to intervene in the domestic affairs of the states.[9] Instability itself may be exacerbated by Russian intervention to force the acquiescence of the government. Both Holoboff and Goltz offered underlying causes for Russian intervention, and Holoboff provided some indicators likely to signal involvement in a civil dispute by Russia, but their analyses do not lend themselves to a wider explanation of Russian intervention beyond the "near abroad" or provide an explanation of when to expect intervention by other states.

Can the democratic peace theory provide some insight into which disputes Russia is likely to enter on the side of the opposition forces? Moreover, can findings about Russia and the democratic peace theory be applied elsewhere? The examination of Russian military involvement in civil wars offers an opportunity to assess the applicability of the democratic peace theory to military interventions. Military intervention on the side of the opposition resembles interstate war in several respects. Active intervention on the side of the opposition is, in essence, an attack by the intervener on the government of the target country. The intervening power seeks to wrest territory or control from the existing government either for its own benefit or for the benefit of the opposition group it assists. Military intervention by large numbers of troops is likely to result in the intervener's troops meeting the warring government's forces on the battlefield. In many cases, this intervention (especially when marked by the involvement of large numbers of troops) overwhelms the actual civil war. The focal point of the conflict is likely to shift from government versus opposition groups to government versus the intervening state. In Lebanon, what began as a civil war quickly took on aspects of an interstate conflict when Syria invaded to assist the Palestine Liberation Organization (PLO) against the Lebanese government. Vietnamese intervention against the government of Cambodia quickly became a war between the two states. "More simply, when the intervener in a civil war comes to the aid of the opponents of the legitimate government, and when the intervener comes to play the dominant role in the war, an internationalized civil war becomes an interstate war."[10]

9. Thomas Goltz, "Letter from Eurasia: The Hidden Russian Hand," *Foreign Policy* 92 (Fall 1993): 92–116.

10. J. David Singer and Melvin Small, *Resort to Arms: International and Civil Wars, 1816–1980* (Beverly Hills, Calif.: Sage, 1982), 220.

Therefore, intervention on the side of the opposition forces is discussed here. Intervention on the behest of the government or as a neutral party presents issues that are not discussed by the democratic peace theory, however tangentially: when does a democracy come to the aid of another and when do states intervene as neutral peacekeepers or peacemakers? These questions, although relevant to the understanding of military intervention, are not likely to be explained by the democratic peace theory and are therefore not the focus of this study.

THE DEMOCRATIC PEACE THEORY

In 1964, Babst showed a lack of war between democracies although finding that democracies are, on average, as war prone as nondemocracies. Later studies supported these findings.[11] Since then, there have been numerous attempts to demonstrate that the cause of the peace is not found in democracy itself. Other variables, including wealth (democracies tend to be wealthier and therefore less warlike), contiguity (historically there have been few democracies and they have rarely bordered on one another), and alliances (since World War II, democracies have largely been grouped in a single alliance against a large, powerful enemy), have been put forward as possible sources of the findings. Yet, most studies controlling for such variables have shown that they do not explain the lack of war among democracies.[12]

Beginning with the 1983 articles by Doyle, numerous authors have sought to explain the phenomenon of democratic peace by looking at what mechanisms internal to democratic regimes act to shape state behavior. From Doyle's work and others, two inter-related arguments have emerged to explain the democratic peace. The first is a normative argument with two main branches. Derived largely from Kant, the first leg of the argument is the idea that liberal regimes are inextricably linked with freedom of the

11. See David A. Lake, "Powerful Pacifists: Democratic States and War," *American Political Science Review* 86 (March 1992): 24–37; Maoz and Abdolali, "Regime Types"; Maoz and Bruce Russett, "Normative and Structural Causes of Democratic Peace, 1946–1986," *American Political Science Review* 87 (September 1993): 624–38; and Small and Singer, "War-Proneness."

12. See Spencer R. Weart, "Peace Among Democratic and Oligarchic Republics," *Journal of Peace Research* 31 (August 1994): 299–316; Small and Singer, "War-Proneness." For an alternative view arguing that these findings lack statistical significance, see David E. Spiro, "The Insignificance of the Liberal Peace," *International Security* 19 (Fall 1994): 50–86.

individual and with a respect for the rights of the individual.[13] Liberal regimes in turn see other liberal states as legitimate and as respecting the rights of their citizens. Moreover, liberal regimes respect the political independence and territorial integrity of other states.[14] Because these regimes see one another as legitimate, their demands also retain legitimacy, and therefore there is greater reliance on negotiation and compromise. In practice, illiberal states are seen as lacking such legitimacy and therefore do not have the right to nonintervention. "If the legitimacy of state action rests on the fact that it respects and effectively represents morally autonomous individuals, then states that coerce their citizens or foreign residents lack legitimacy."[15]

A second branch of the normative argument relies on the idea that, in a democracy, decisions are made based on negotiation. Politics are not zero sum as they are in nondemocracies where winning factions can literally eliminate their opposition. Democratic decision makers expect like governments to behave as they do and therefore expect other democratic states to engage in negotiation and compromise. On the other hand, nondemocracies are expected to use violence and threats and are seen as unpredictable and possibly dangerous.[16]

Both these branches of the normative argument lead to the conclusion that democracies are far more likely to negotiate with countries seen as democratic and to avoid military confrontation. "Once liberals accept a foreign state as a liberal democracy, they adamantly oppose war against that state."[17] On the other hand, those states seen as nondemocratic are expected to be more warlike and less willing to negotiate. Therefore, there appears little reason to engage in negotiations that are unlikely to succeed. Studies have shown that the perception of democracy or liberality in other regimes may be as important a factor in behavior as whether the opposing state *is* a democracy.[18]

The second component of the democratic peace theory is a structural or institutional one. This institutional theory is based on the idea that the

13. Doyle, "Kant," 207.
14. Doyle, "Kant, Part 2," 325.
15. Doyle, "Kant, Part 2," 325.
16. For a discussion of politics in democratic and nondemocratic states, see Maoz and Russett, "Normative Structural Causes"; John M. Owen, "How Liberalism Produces Democratic Peace," *International Security* 19 (Fall 1994): 87–125. Russett, *Grasping the Democratic Peace;* and Weart, "Peace."
17. Owen, "How Liberalism Produces Democratic Peace," 95
18. Owen, "How Liberalism Produces Democratic Peace," 90; and Russett, *Grasping the Democratic Peace,* 53.

more constrained the executive, the less able it is to involve itself in military ventures, partially because the need to mobilize general public opinion and the need to overcome the checks and balances of a democratic system take time. Democracies, realizing other democracies are also slow in coming to a decision, need not fear surprise attack. On the other hand, because swift decisions can presumably be made in nondemocracies, democratic regimes fear such attack and may therefore forgo the attempt to coalesce support and may engage in preemptive strikes.[19]

A more widely touted version of the institutional theory is based primarily on the idea that the populace, because it bears the brunt of any war, is less eager for war than the high officials making decisions. The population of the country, more so than the elites, suffers the restrictions of rationing and the sacrifices of conscription and forced government acquisition. Elections inherently tie officials to the interests of the populace and make them answerable for their foreign policy decisions. This dependence on domestic support acts as a constraint on the ability to go to war. Moreover, the system of checks and balances in a democratic political system means that policies must appeal to a broad range of institutions and constituencies and therefore radicalism tends to be mitigated.

According to the democratic peace theory, neither normative nor institutional constraints can alone account for the democratic peace. If institutional constraints alone were to explain the lack of military conflict between democracies, the population of a country should always be unwilling to go to war, whether the opponent is a democracy or not. This is clearly not the case; there are several examples, not least of all the United States before the Spanish-American War and Great Britain before the Crimean War, where belligerent populations pushed reluctant leaders to war. The normative bias against nondemocracies, however, explains this willingness to fight against those states seen as untrustworthy and unwilling to recognize the basic individual rights afforded by democracies.

Moreover, a state's institutions are inexorably linked with its norms. The beliefs of leaders and people alike help shape the institutions that govern a society. The existence and perpetuation of these institutions in exchange affect the norms of those governing and governed. It is thus necessary to take into account both norms and institutions in any creation of a model of the democratic peace theory.[20]

19. Maoz and Russett, "Normative Structural Causes," 626; and Russett, *Grasping the Democratic Peace*, 40–53.
20. T. Clifton Morgan and Valerie L. Schwebach, "Take Two Democracies and Call Me in the Morning: A Prescription for Peace?" *International Interactions* 17 (1992): 318; Owen, "How Liberalism Produces Democratic Peace," 89; and Russett, *Grasping the Democratic Peace*.

State 2

State 1	Democracy	Nondemocracy
Democracy	Negotiation/peace	Possible war
Nondemocracy	Possible war	Possible war

Figure 4.1 Democratic peace theory.

As noted above, the democratic peace theory has been supported by numerous studies that have found war does not occur between democracies, but there has been little attempt to apply the theory to interventions. One such study found that, of interventions occurring from 1974 to 1988, 42 percent of interventions by democracies targeted at other democracies were conducted *against* the target government.[21] This finding suggests that the democratic peace theory is not as compelling for interventions as for interstate war.

In addition, the democratic peace theory cannot explain such interventions as peacekeeping forces or partisan forces in support of other governments. It is therefore useful to create a theory, related to the democratic peace theory, better able to predict in which direction intervention occurs. It is as important to understand the form of an intervention as it is to understand whether it occurs at all. This new theory, premised on the legitimacy of other states and groups, is detailed in the following sections. The question of whether a legitimacy-based theory better explains Russian interventionist behavior than does the democratic peace theory is examined in the study of Estonia and Moldova.

LEGITIMACY, WAR, AND INTERVENTION

As discussed earlier, the normative branch of the democratic peace argument suggests that if a democracy views another state as democratic, it sees the state as legitimate and as having legitimate and justifiable demands. This raises an important question. Does the view of the other state as legitimate deter a state from war? Is a shared democratic nature simply an ingredient in determining the relative legitimacy of other states? If so, then

21. Cited in Margaret G. Hermann and Charles W. Kegley, Jr., "Ballots, a Barrier Against the Use of Bullets and Bombs: Democratization and Military Intervention," *Journal of Conflict Resolution* 40 (September 1996): 440.

perhaps the democratic peace is a manifestation of a broader theory. In this section, such a legitimacy-based theory is described, what is meant by and what determines legitimacy is detailed, and how shared legitimacy leads to peace and nonintervention is discussed.

The legitimacy-based theory, derived from the normative branch of the democratic peace theory, argues that one country's belief that another is legitimate and that its position on the issue in dispute retains some degree of legitimacy may lead to negotiation and to a decreased likelihood of war. On the other hand, a lack of legitimacy bestowed on the second state and its demands is unlikely to provide any grounds for discussion and increases the chance of conflict. Legitimacy is a quality or state of "conforming to or in accordance with established rules, standards, or principles."[22] "[L]egitimacy beliefs [are considered] as part of the 'intrinsic interests' of an actor, the moral aspect that determines the relative rightness and wrongness of his own and his opponent's aim and actions."[23] Legitimacy is ultimately a subjective determination by that actor, who in turn behaves according to its views of the world and of the legitimacy of other actors.

Two forms of legitimacy are important for the purposes of war and intervention. The first, issue legitimacy, is based on the view of the opponent's position as justifiable. "A special aspect of value structures is the legitimacy the parties ascribe to each other's claims. By *legitimacy* we mean not only legality but the broader and more subjective beliefs about the justice of one's own and the opponent's cause."[24] The legitimacy ascribed to the other state's claims, is, in large part, dependent on the view of the other state. This is the second form of legitimacy, state legitimacy. It is this form of legitimacy that is of greater importance for the purposes of this chapter. A belief that the other state, or its leaders, is legitimate inherently increases the possibility that the position the state takes on an issue is also legitimate.

Legitimacy Bestowed

Whether legitimacy is bestowed by one state on another or on a group is contingent on a number of issues. Constructivists argue that the continuing

22. David B. Guralnik, ed., *Webster's New World Dictionary of the American Language*, 2d ed. (New York: Prentice-Hall, 1986), 807.

23. Glenn H. Snyder and Paul Diesing, *Conflict Among Nations: Bargaining, Decision Making, and System Structure in International Crises* (Princeton: Princeton University Press, 1977), 184–85.

24. Snyder and Diesing, *Conflict Among Nations*, 184.

relations between states create and refine each state's view of the other.[25] Thus, a state's legitimacy directly depends on its previous interactions with the determining state. Past negotiations that resulted in agreements that were consistently adhered to are likely to yield to a greater expectation that the state will again abide by treaties. On the other hand, a state that has undertaken terrorist actions or failed to comply with earlier agreements is unlikely to be trusted again. Although a careful examination of states' relations with one another is the surest way to determine whether legitimacy is bestowed, three factors are believed to be especially important in influencing the level of legitimacy. Shared ideologies and governing nationalities are expected to increase legitimacy by increasing the sense that the other state is part of the same group and shares the same interests. The political cohesiveness of a state indicates its ability to fulfill any agreements made and enhances the perception of legitimacy by increasing the view of the state as a viable, stable entity. A fourth factor, international recognition, acts to reinforce and enhance the view of a state as legitimate.

Ideology "establishes the intellectual framework through which policy makers observe reality."[26] Shared ideology implies a shared view of reality between decision makers of the two countries. Different ideologies increase the view that the other side is illegitimate. Often contradictory views are translated into negative stereotypes.

Democracies, in line with the democratic peace theory, are perhaps especially prone to see states as legitimate on the basis of their ideology. The importance attributed to the rights of the individual in democracies provides a reasonably clear benchmark against which to measure other states. States seen as violating what are believed to be universal individual rights are seen as inherently different and inferior.[27]

People and policy makers in democratic societies have internalized the need for negotiation and the reliance on legal resolutions[28] and seek negotiation with those from whom they expect similar treatment. Like criminals, who because of their refusal to abide by the norms and laws of society are open to coercion,[29] those states seen as not abiding by legal decisions

25. Alexander Wendt, "Anarchy Is What States Make of It: The Social Construction of Power Politics," *International Organization* 46 (Spring 1992): 391–425. See also Heikka, Chapter 2, for a fuller description of constructivism.

26. K. J. Holsti, *International Politics: A Framework for Analysis,* 4th ed. (Englewood Cliffs, N.J.: Prentice-Hall, 1983), 325.

27. Doyle, "Kant, Part 2."

28. Gregory A. Raymond, "Democracies, Disputes, and Third-Party Intermediaries," *Journal of Conflict Resolution* 38 (March 1994): 27.

29. Weart, "Peace," 309.

and as violent and unpredictable are viable targets for coercion and military intervention.[30] For democracies, "[i]lliberal states are seen as *prima facie* as unreasonable, unpredictable, and potentially dangerous."[31] On the other hand, democratic states are expected to desire negotiations and to be willing to abide by the decisions reached in the bargaining. Democracies, therefore, are far more willing to negotiate with their ideological brethren and are, indeed, loathe to fight those states viewed as democracies.[32]

Democracies do not hold a monopoly on the view that different governments lack legitimacy or that opposing governments are less likely to abide by one's own norms and rules. "The propensity of two states to fight each other may be linked to the degree of difference *between* their two political systems."[33] Indeed, democracies are not alone in their reluctance to fight others of the same ideology. Well-established oligarchies have also rarely made war against one another.[34]

Similarly, states that have the same governing (or at least influential) nationalities are seen as more legitimate than those who do not. A shared nationality implies a shared history, language, and culture and hence the same building blocks of a worldview. Commensurate with ideology, a shared governing nationality suggests a similar vision of reality, especially in states that are newly democratizing[35] or that have long histories of domestic ethnic tension. Here, belligerent nationalism can take the place of ideology and can be used to foment war.

The political and territorial cohesion of a state or group affects the legitimacy of the actor as one who can fulfill the obligations of agreements. The control over population and territory suggests an ability to mobilize support for a given government decision. A government unable to control its territory or the population in that territory is less likely to be able to enact or abide by a treaty. When discussing issues of intervention, the role of cohesion is of particular importance. The ability of a state to control its own territory signifies to outside governments the degree to which the state retains the right to sovereignty, a fundamental tenet in international politics, which strictly limits the permissibility of intervention. A government

30. Doyle, "Kant, Part 2," 325.

31. Owen, "How Liberalism Produces Democracy," 96.

32. Owen, "How Liberalism Produces Democracy," 95.

33. Greg Cashman, *What Causes War? An Introduction to Theories of International Conflict* (New York: Lexington Books, 1993), 129.

34. Weart, "Peace," 303.

35. Edward D. Mansfield and Jack Snyder, "Democratization and the Danger of War," *International Security* 20 (Summer 1995): 6.

that has no control has lost its legitimacy and hence has no right to non-intervention in its territory.[36] The cohesion of the opposition groups is also important in the assessment of their legitimacy. Groups seeking secession or autonomy but that lack territorial unity or are spread among other populations often fail to garner much legitimacy. Their demands for independence are weakened by the lack of a consolidated territory and by the demands of others in that territory for a continued union with the state. Moreover, groups divided over issues and goals often lack the political cohesion necessary to present a single front to a possibly intervening ally.

Legitimacy is bestowed by a number of actors on a state or opposition group. The most important of these actors is the state deciding whether to go to war with another or to intervene in its domestic affairs. Because legitimacy, as discussed above, is an inherently subjective measure of another actor's justification and worth, a state acts on its own beliefs, not necessarily those of others. Nonetheless, other actors can affect the state's beliefs.

Third-party states and international organizations can increase the group's legitimacy by recognizing its rights and the importance of its concerns. States themselves are accorded sovereign status only by the recognition of other states, particularly the major powers. For this reason, the Serbian government was condemned and sanctions applied against it for its involvement in Bosnia, which had been recognized by Germany and other major states. Chechnya, which arguably was more independent from Russia than Bosnia was from Yugoslavia, lacked the recognition bestowed by other countries, and Russia was not censured as was Serbia.[37]

The role of international organizations is both that of a bestower of legitimacy and of a reinforcing agent for the legitimacy given by a particular state. International organizations reflect the opinions of their members and therefore are reflections of individual states' beliefs in legitimacy. Moreover, international organizations can strengthen the perception of legitimacy, often by according membership or similar status, which presents the state or group with considerable international legitimacy.[38] The PLO, for example, had its position vis-à-vis the Israeli government strengthened

36. Michael Walzer, *Just and Unjust Wars* (New York: Basic Books, 1977), 32.

37. Although this is clearly a simplistic argument and many other factors played into the decision to condemn Serbian and not Russian actions, the position of Chechnya as an internal part of Russia and Bosnia-Herzegovina as an independent state cannot be ignored.

38. The same holds true for states. The inclusion of states as small as Palau and the Marshall Islands bestows on these states the status of full members of the international system. The exclusion of Yugoslavia (Serbia and Montenegro) from the UN detracts from its claim to be the successor state to the former Communist state and limits its status in the international system.

by its inclusion in the United Nations (UN) as the sole representative of the Palestinian people. International organizations can also reinforce one state's beliefs that another is legitimate by attending to particular issues or including the other in negotiations.

In summary, legitimacy is measured on four points: the presence of ideological similarities, shared nationalities, cohesion, and international interest or recognition.

Legitimacy and War

"People act and react according to their *images* of the environment."[39] The view of others as legitimate or illegitimate shapes these images. Legitimacy creates, in the minds of policy makers, an ingroup and an outgroup. Those in the ingroup are seen to share the norms and laws of the society and are expected to abide by them. Those failing to abide by the norms and laws, or who by ideology or nationality are believed to hold different norms, are often viewed as beyond the scope of normal behavior and are placed in an outgroup.[40] This creation of an outgroup allows for the deindividualization and the enmification of the people in the group.

Once this belief that a state or faction belongs in either an ingroup (one of us, legitimate, with justifiable demands, abides by the rules) or an outgroup (one of them, illegitimate, demands often unjust, does not follow the norms and rules) is created, it has a powerful pull on the behavior of policy makers. The existing view of a state as legitimate or illegitimate is likely to lead to an expectation of particular behavior by that state. Stress, often a major factor in the periods leading to war, exacerbates this view and produces an increase in oversimplification, cognitive rigidity, stereotyping, and "we–they" thinking.[41]

In other words, policy makers who see another state or group as illegitimate and unwilling to abide by negotiation respond accordingly and generally refuse to engage in negotiations. On the other hand, when the other state or group is seen as legitimate and willing to abide by negotiation, policy makers are predisposed to seek agreements and outside mediation. For this reason as much as for institutional limitations on the ability to go to war, democracies that see similar states as abiding by the norms of

39. Holsti, *International Politics,* 319–20.
40. Weart, "Peace," 209.
41. Cashman, *What Causes War?* 47; Holsti, "Crisis Management," in Betty Glad, ed., *Psychological Dimensions of War* (Newbury Park, Calif.: Sage, 1990), 125.

compromise and legality do not war with one another.[42] Those states dissimilar in ideology, however, are seen as unpredictable and therefore unlikely to negotiate seriously or to abide by any agreement reached. When opposite beliefs are held, war is most apt to occur.[43]

Moreover, the view of the other state and its position as legitimate provide common ground on which negotiations can begin and on which they can be resolved. When one actor sees the other's position as legitimate, it raises doubts about its own position and increases the likelihood of compromise.

As with the democratic peace theory, however, it cannot be inferred that simply because one state faces another it sees as illegitimate, there will be war. Instead, external military and political issues must be incorporated in the model to determine the actual likelihood of conflict. If states are rational actors, war is likely only when the costs of victory are expected to be light or the need for victory is great. When the costs of war overwhelm the possible gains from a victory, negotiation is likely if the issue in dispute is of fair importance.

The role of legitimacy is especially important in situations with a great power imbalance, including the cases described in this chapter. Where there is a large military power differential, the larger state has little impetus to engage in negotiations as it can resolve the situation in its favor using its strength.[44] The presence of a belief that the other side and its demands bear legitimacy may counteract the tendency to resort to force against a clearly weaker power.

| | State 2 | |
State 1	Legitimate (seen by State 1)	Illegitimate (seen by State 1)
Legitimate (seen by State 2)	Negotiations/peace	Possible war
Illegitimate (seen by State 2)	Possible war	Possible war

Figure 4.2 Legitimacy-based theory and war.

42. Raymond, "Democracies," 26.
43. Snyder and Diesing, *Conflict Among Nations,* 498–500.
44. Arthur Lall, *Modern International Negotiation: Principles and Practice* (New York: Columbia University Press, 1966), 136.

Legitimacy and Intervention

When discussing intervention,[45] the role of legitimacy in influencing policy makers' decisions is similar to that in war, but the model becomes more complex as the view of the opposition groups as legitimate or illegitimate becomes important. Only with this interaction of the beliefs in the legitimacy of the target state and of the opposition group is a legitimacy-based theory effectual in determining both the likelihood and the direction of intervention.

As with interstate war, a belief in the legitimacy of the target state, of the opposition groups, or of both is expected to increase the likelihood of negotiation with those parties and empathy with their positions. When the possible intervener believes both the target state and the opposition groups to be legitimate, the possible intervener will urge negotiations on the other two parties, seeking a compromise between two parties whose positions the possible intervener feels have merit. Intervention, if any, would be as a nonpartisan peacekeeping force and would occur *only* if requested by all legitimate factions.

On the other hand, when neither the target state nor the opposition parties are seen as legitimate, there is little chance of the possible intervener seeking negotiations. As with interstate war, when no legitimacy is bestowed on parties, little common ground is seen between them and the possible intervener and there is little expectation that the parties will abide by an agreement even if reached. Intervention occurs if the benefits are likely to outweigh the military and political costs; such intervention is likely to be as a partisan force seeking to install a new government, unaffiliated with either the illegitimate target state or the illegitimate opposition groups.

The picture becomes somewhat more convoluted when the possible intervener views one party as legitimate and the other as illegitimate. In view of low expected military and political costs of involvement, intervention is expected to occur in opposition to whichever group is held to be illegitimate. When the target state is believed legitimate and the opposition illegitimate, intervention, if it occurs, is partisan and on behalf of the gov-

45. A note about terminology is necessary here. The target state is the state undergoing some domestic issue that raises the possibility of outside intervention. In this chapter, the two target states are Estonia and Moldova. The possible intervener (Russia) is the state deciding whether or not to become involved in the conflict. Opposition groups are those groups in the target state in a dispute with the government of that state (for simplicity's sake, the model assumes only one opposition group).

ernment. Similarly, when the target state is seen as illegitimate and the opposition group as legitimate and intervention is expected to be simple and lack political and military costs, intervention is likely to occur on the side of the opposition.

With two theories outlined, the democratic peace and the legitimacy-based theories, it is possible to examine Russian behavior in the "near abroad." Can Russia's lack of intervention in Estonia and its involvement in Moldova be explained by the institutional mechanisms of the democratic peace theory, or is it better explained by a focus on the degree of legitimacy Russia bestowed on the two countries and their respective opposition groups? First, however, it is necessary to determine whether Russia is in fact a democracy. If it fails this litmus test, then the democratic peace theory itself cannot be applied.

As seen by possible intervener

	Opposition group	
Target state	Legitimate	Illegitimate
Legitimate	Three-way negotiations/ possible intervention as peacekeepers with all factions' permission	Possible intervention on side of government
Illegitimate	Possible intervention on side of opposition	Possible intervention to install new, unaffiliated government

Figure 4.3   Legitimacy-based theory and intervention.

RUSSIA: DEMOCRACY OR AUTHORITARIANISM IN DISGUISE?

It is possible to analyze Russia under a framework of the democratic peace theory partly because the definitions of democracy vary tremendously. Part of the discrepancy is whether the focus should be on the liberal nature of the regime or on the presence of democratic institutions. The definitions used by Owen and Doyle emphasize the importance of the liberal nature of a regime. Owen's definition of a liberal regime is a state in which there is free speech and regular, competitive election of officials (empowered to declare war).[46] According to Doyle, a liberal regime is one in which citizens

46. Owen, "How Liberalism Produces Democratic Peace," 102.

possess juridical equality and other civil rights; the effective sovereigns of the state are the elected legislatures; there are market and private property economies; and the polities are externally sovereign. Moreover, the representative government must be internally sovereign, especially over the military, and must have been in existence for at least three years.[47] Russia clearly fails to qualify as a liberal regime under this definition as it had not existed for three years during the 1992–93 period under examination.

Other authors have focused primarily on the level of institutionalized "democracy." Small and Singer used a three-part definition: periodic, scheduled elections with free participation of opposition parties; at least 10 percent of adult population able to vote; a parliament enjoying either superiority over or parity with the executive branch. These different definitions have not resulted in different results. The democratic peace theory continues to hold for the broad statistical examination of a variety of conflicts and thus counters authors who question whether only a highly limited definition of a democratic regime allows the democratic peace theory to prevail.[48] Russia's standing as a democracy is less tenuous under Small and Singer's definition as there was widespread suffrage and participation in the period in question. Several opposition parties challenged the government. If parliament was not pre-eminent, at least the Congress of People's Deputies was able to prevent the Russian president from acting against its wishes.

Still other authors have argued that democratization is not the dichotomous variable provided by the previous definitions but can be measured along a continuum. It is this measurement that is most applicable in the case of Russia and other newly democratizing states. Maoz and Russett examined the institutional aspect of democracy on a twenty-five-point scale looking at four issues: the degree of executive constraint, the centralization of the political system, the scope of government action, and the degree of "one-man rule" or monocratism.[49] When using this framework to examine the level of Russian democracy in 1992–93, Russia is classified as a weak democracy.

For the first issue, the level of executive constraint, it is important to understand that even states widely accepted as democracies vary tremendously in their levels of executive power. In fact, the United States is among the most constrained and decentralized of states, especially in foreign pol-

---

47. Doyle, "Kant," 212.
48. Spiro, "Insignificance," 51.
49. Maoz and Russett, "Normative and Structural Causes," 629.

icy. Intrinsic tensions between the Pentagon, the State Department, and a more powerful Congress limit the ability of the executive to make unilateral decisions.[50] Moreover, the executive is legally constrained in its ability to go to war. In other countries, there is noticeably less restraint on the government. In France, the making of foreign policy is plainly the *domaine reserve* of the president of the Republic, despite several chapters of the Fifth Republic's constitution, which "make it clear that the president must share his foreign policy responsibilities and collaborate closely with the parliament and government."[51]

Indeed, Russia has been compared to the Fifth Republic. Both needed to create a constitution and political structure to deal with a "deeply divided society."[52] Russia's 1993 constitution was modeled on the "Gaullist Constitution that established the Fifth Republic. This Constitution, while providing for a system of checks and balances among the branches of government, [created] a powerful yet constrained executive subordinate to the will of the people."[53]

The second issue is the level of centralization in the government. Maoz and Russett argued that federal systems, even on foreign policy issues, restrict the ability of the government to mobilize its economic and political resources. Moreover, the federal system "also provides an institutionalized base from which regional political leaders can challenge government policy."[54] Even before the December 1993 ratification of the Russian constitution officially institutionalized the existence of the federation, it was clear that Russia was governed by a federal system. The numerous republics, regions, and oblasts hold considerable power in their ability to tax and otherwise control their own domestic societies. The Federation Treaty of March 31, 1992, encouraged Russia's regions to claim considerable sovereignty as long as they maintained the historical unity with Moscow.[55]

The scope of government action or how far into the lives of its citizens the government reaches is the third issue affecting the level of democracy. Russia's press displayed noticeably less government control by 1992. In that

50. Thomas Risse-Kappen, "Public Opinion, Domestic Structure, and Foreign Policy in Liberal Democracies," *World Politics* 43 (July 1991): 487.

51. Mark B. Hayne, "The Quai d'Orsay and the Formation of French Foreign Policy in Historical Context," in Robert Aldrich and John Connell, eds., *France in World Politics* (London: Routledge, 1989), 197–98.

52. Nicolai N. Petro. *The Rebirth of Russian Democracy: An Interpretation of Political Culture* (Cambridge: Harvard University Press, 1995), 153.

53. Petro, *Rebirth of Russian Democracy*, 151.

54. Maoz and Russett, "Normative and Structural Causes," 629.

55. Petro, *Rebirth of Russian Democracy*, 166.

year, there were 339 daily newspapers and nearly 4,500 other papers published less frequently.[56] Between early 1992 and 1993, the Russian economy's autonomy increased, with privatization of enterprises continuing. At the same time, however, Russian government control had not ended. Thousands of larger enterprises remained under government control, and price controls on some goods and products remained. In October 1993, President Boris Yeltsin closed fifteen opposition newspapers and banned the antigovernment television program *600 Seconds*.[57]

The fourth issue, monocratism, is based on the issue of how widely spread is decision making. In 1992 and most of 1993, the claim that Russia was led by a one-man government is overstated. Although the legislature was limited in its ability to pass and enact laws, it was able to limit Yeltsin's power. He was limited in his ability to act throughout 1993 by the Congress of People's Deputies. Economic reforms were stymied by a reticent parliament. Yeltsin's attempt to have the reformist Yegor Gaidar confirmed as premier in December 1992 was vetoed by a 486 to 67 vote in the Congress of People's Deputies.[58] "One change from the Soviet system is that the Russian legislative branch has acquired real decision-making authority."[59]

According to this four-point definition, Russia can be classified as a weak democracy. The constraint on the executive was limited, but the legislature had gained greater power in relation to the presidency. The existence of a federation among the Russian republics and regions increased the breadth of constituencies that the federal government must appeal to and decreased the ability of the federal government to directly affect its population. Finally, the government's attempt to affect the population had declined. Its control of the economy and press had lessened. On the other hand, although the press was nominally free, the government still banned opposition press.

Freedom House has identified democracies on a thirty-six point scale, later collapsing it into a seven-point measure. Through its analysis of nine issues, Freedom House determined that between 1992–94 Russia was a "partly free" state, falling one point outside the "free" category in which the United States and Estonia reside. The "partly free" categorization,

56. UNESCO, *Statistical Yearbook, 1995: Reference Tables* (Lanham, Md: UNESCO Publishing and Bernan Press, 1995), 7–104, 7–110.

57. *Facts on File* 1993, 812.

58. *Facts on File* 1992, 936.

59. Charles H. Fairbanks, Jr., "The Legacy of Soviet Policymaking in Creating a New Russia," in Leon Aron and Kenneth M. Jensen, eds., *The Emergence of Russian Foreign Policy* (Washington, D.C.: United States Institute of Peace Press, 1994), 55.

however, does not necessarily deny that Russia is a democracy.[60] The issues on which freedom is measured, when collapsed, provide a three point checklist from which to discuss the level of democracy in Russia.

1. Were the head of state and legislators elected through free and fair elections? It is widely acknowledged that the 1991 elections in which Russian President Boris Yeltsin was elected were free and were also highly attended by those eligible to vote. Here, Russia rates high on a measure of democracy. The legislature is less clearly an accurate representation of the voters' choices. In 1992 and most of 1993, the majority of the Congress of People's Deputies was a holdover from the Soviet Union. The vast majority of legislators were elected before the collapse of the Soviet Union, in elections in which many of the seats were set aside for Communist Party members. Parties representing nearly all segments of society, however, were allowed, and the parliament did represent a broad variety of opinion. In 1992–93, however, this freedom was diminished as Communist parties were outlawed by the Russian government.

2. Was there significant opposition to the head of state, and did people have the opportunity to join opposition groups? The answer to both is Yes. In both 1992 and 1993, the parliament was a clear division of ideologies with roughly 250 liberals, 350 centrists, 350 hard-liners, and 90 independents.[61] As discussed in the previous section, the power of Yeltsin was limited by the parliament. People joined or created numerous political parties and unions throughout the later Soviet and post-Soviet eras, several of which were competitors for power in both the parliament and the presidency. As noted earlier, however, the formal Communist parties were outlawed by a federal decree. After a ruling by the Constitutional Court, the Communists were able to participate at the local level but were still prevented from national-level organization. By the end of 1993, the opposition to the president gained numerous seats in the parliament as the Liberal Democratic Party of Vladimir Zhirinovsky won more than 20 percent of the vote.

3. Are local and regional administrations led by freely elected officials? Do religious, ethnic, and other minorities have reasonable levels of autonomy and self-determination? Despite the fact that most local administrators were appointed by Yeltsin, as discussed above, the regions and republics have considerable autonomy, with the ability to collect taxes and influence

60. Freedom House, *Freedom In the World: The Annual Survey of Political Rights and Civil Liberties, 1993–1994* (New York: Freedom House, 1994), 671.
61. *Facts on File*, 1992, 936.

their own populations. Many of these republics, Ingushetia and Chechnya among others, are largely defined along ethnic boundaries and retain conspicuous autonomy.

As with Maoz and Russett's definition of a democracy, the Freedom House checklist allows for a determination that Russia is a weak democracy. The existence of freely elected officials, reasonable power and opposition in the legislature, and a federal system have created the beginnings of institutionalized democracy. Nonetheless, we must be careful not to overstate the democratic nature of Russia. The lack of constraint on the executive and on Yeltsin in particular has allowed Russia to retain many of its autocratic characteristics. The lack of constraint on the executive, however, does not totally negate Russia's membership in the community of democracies. Indeed, words used to describe France are equally applicable to Russia in 1992 and 1993: "The rules included in the Constitution to strengthen the French government against the legislature seem formidable. . . . The National Assembly under the Fifth Republic is therefore often regarded as one of the weakest legislatures in any modern democracy."[62]

Although institutionally Russia is a democracy, albeit weak, it largely lacks the normative basis of democracy. Maoz and Russett measured democratic norms through an examination of the period of political stability and the level of violent social and political conflict.[63] As a new democratic state, Russia lacks the time needed to develop democratic norms. Its long history of authoritarian rule in fact leads one to believe that the opposite norms are likely to have been instilled in the people and governing bodies of Russia. The level of political and social violence in 1992 and until the fall of 1993 was very low, with the first violent demonstrations since the collapse of the Soviet Union occurring in May 1993.[64] Nonetheless, the violence between elements of the Congress of People's Deputies and the executive in October 1993 clearly demonstrated that the almost two years of domestic peace did not allow for the installation of the democratic norms of nonviolence and negotiation. The lack of a strong civil society weakens the development of democratic institutions.[65]

> Traditional (Soviet-) Russian political culture and the political consciousness of major sections of the population are still hindering the

---

62. John D. Huber, *Rationalizing Parliament: Legislative Institutions and Party Politics in France* (Cambridge: Cambridge University Press, 1990), 2.

63. Maoz and Russett, "Normative and Structural Causes," 630.

64. Freedom House, *Freedom in the World*, 470.

65. Fairbanks, "Legacy," 57.

development of a civic society. The pertinacity of a paternalistic view of the state favours the inclination toward authoritarian rule. Though democracy and a state based on the rule of law is the officially declared goal of the Russian constitution and its present leadership, the political decision making process is becoming highly centred toward the Security Council and the rather opaque presidential apparatus.[66]

RUSSIAN INTERVENTION: ESTONIA AND MOLDOVA

The cases of Estonia and Moldova were chosen for a variety of reasons. First, both are small countries whose respective militaries and populations are unlikely to pose a threat to a focused Russian offensive. Estonia, with a population of 1.6 million, had an active military force numbering only two thousand in 1992. Moldova had a greater number under arms—twelve thousand of its 4.3 million population.[67] Neither country possessed or possesses nuclear weapons. Each posed a relatively small threat to Russian security, and both presented the Russian government with the prospect of a limited war. These factors are important in the examination of the democratic peace theory as, in democracies, decisions to engage in "[l]imited wars . . . (1) involve multiple actors; (2) take a considerable amount of time to reach a conclusion, [and] (3) involve conflicting goals on what a policy is supposed to accomplish."[68] These potential interventions, therefore, were not a situation, such as an invasion by foreign troops, which demanded crisis-situation decision making. In this case, the decision making "very much resembles authoritarian decision-making: Policies are determined by a relatively small number of actors who must act with dispatch and unity."[69]

A second issue involved is that the considered intervention by Russia in both countries was in opposition to the sitting government of the state.

66. Hans-Georg Ehrhart, Anna Kriekemeyer, and Andrei V. Zagorski, "Introduction," in Hans-Georg Ehrhart, Anna Kriekemeyer, and Andrei V. Zagorski, eds., *Crisis Management in the CIS: Whither Russia?* (Baden-Baden: Nomos, 1995), 12.

67. *The Military Balance, 1992–1993* (London: Brassey's for the Institutional Institute for Strategic Studies, 1992), 75, 80.

68. John Spanier and Eric M. Uslaner, *How American Foreign Policy Is Made* (New York: Holt, Rinehart and Winston/Praeger, 1978), 167.

69. Spanier and Uslaner, *How American Foreign Policy Is Made,* 168.

As touched on earlier, intervention as an opposition force to a standing government takes on many of the attributes of an international war, with which democratic peace theory deals explicitly. Two governments are pitted against each other, the conflict tends to be conventional rather than guerrilla or low-intensity warfare, and the enemy is usually clearly defined. Moreover, it is often easier to determine the level of democracy in a government than in an opposition group.

Third, the concern in each of the two former republics was over the treatment and autonomy of Russian nationals. In other examinations of Russian behavior,[70] the presence of, and threats to, Russian nationals has been a strong indicator of Russian interventionary behavior. In fact, in every case where there have been Russian nationals involved, however tangentially, in a civil war, the Russian government has intervened, often as part of a peacekeeping force. The Soviet Union, too, in Afghanistan, where there were shared nationalities (Tajiks and Uzbeks), intervened in the conflict. The presence of nationals encourages intervention for two reasons. First is the spillover effect. The creation of large numbers of refugees threatens to destabilize the states to which they flee. Russians fleeing from civil war were most likely to flee to Russia (from Tajikistan, for example) and to increase the demands on the already strained Russian economy. Second, claims by the Russian nationals of human rights abuses provide direct motivation for intervention for the government of Russia and other states. Growing nationalist pressures on the government call for the protection of Russian nationals wherever they live. Such claims also offer convenient legitimacy for the intervention. It is often easier to legitimize an intervention to the domestic population when the purported cause is to "save your brothers and sisters" than when the true reason may be rooted in economic or security issues.

Finally, Estonia and Moldova are at different levels of democracy. On the basis of the Freedom House ratings, Estonia from 1992 through 1994 was rated a "free" state, higher on the scale of political rights than Russia. In 1992, Estonia ratified its new constitution and held elections.[71] Moldova, however, was rated "partly free." Its status was two points lower than Russia's and bordered on a "not free" rating. Causes for this rating included the lack of free elections and no new constitution or independent judiciary.[72]

---

70. See Holoboff, "Russian Views."
71. Freedom House, *Freedom in the World*, 250.
72. Freedom House, *Freedom in the World*, 406.

If the democratic peace theory is an adequate explanatory tool for Russian interventionist behavior, the Russian parliament should be concerned with the issue, and the Russian executive should generally respond to the desires of the population, represented by the demands of parliament. The population should be generally opposed to intervention and should act as a check on the expected aggressive tendency of the government. The public and the government should be especially reluctant to intervene in democratic Estonia. Thus, for the democratic peace theory to be considered a successful explanatory model for Russian behavior, several conditions need to be met if the democratic peace theory holds:

There should be no intervention against the democratic government, but the nondemocratic faces possible intervention.

The Russian people, and its parliament, should be generally less belligerent than the executive. This desire to avoid involvement is heightened when confronted with another democratic state.

There should be negotiations held with the democratic state but few if any with the nondemocratic state.

There should be considerable discussion in the press and in the government on intervention in both cases.

The legitimacy-based theory, however, does not demand that the Russian parliament or public play a role. Instead, a cohesive, democratic Estonia should lend itself to increased negotiations with Russia. Moldova, because of its different political system and inability to control its own territory, should be largely excluded from negotiations, and intervention should occur on behalf of the largely Russian opposition groups. For the legitimacy-based theory to be considered a convincing tool, the following conditions need to be met if the legitimacy-based theory holds:

There should be no intervention against the government held legitimate, but intervention may occur against an illegitimately viewed state. This legitimacy is measured by shared nationalities, ideologies, and strong political and territorial cohesion of the state or group.

There should be negotiations held with the state perceived to be legitimate and little if any with the illegitimate state.

Russia will seek to assist any opposition groups it perceives legitimate, intervening if the government is perceived as illegitimate.

Russia will seek to incorporate international organizations as mediators between a state and opposition group if both are perceived as legitimate.[73]

Estonia

Nearly 30 percent of Estonia's 1.6 million people are ethnic Russian, and relations between the Baltic state and Russia have largely revolved around the relations between the Estonian government and the Russian minority. In 1992 and 1993, tensions between the two states increased as a number of laws were passed in Estonia focusing on citizenship rights, as heavily Russian-populated towns voted for autonomy, and as sporadic conflicts between Russian troops and Estonian forces left several dead. Nonetheless, and despite the fact that Russia had several thousand troops stationed in Estonia, the Russian government limited its response to political statements and a short, five-day cutoff of natural gas. Indeed, Russian troops pulled out in August 1994. Can the level of democracy in Estonia explain this behavior? First, it is necessary to set the scene.

On August 20,1991, Estonia formally declared its independence from the Soviet Union. The Supreme Soviet acquiesced on September 6, 1991, and ended a fifty-year rule begun by the Soviet invasion during World War II. After independence, several regulations were passed affecting the lives of Russians. In 1992, the Estonian parliament re-established the 1938 citizenship law. People without a claim to citizenship during the independent period of 1920–40 were required to submit to a naturalization process mandating a two-year residency, Estonian language proficiency, and a permanent source of income. Moreover, there was a one-year waiting period from the date of application before citizenship could be granted.[74] The differentiation between Estonian citizens and noncitizens living in Estonia was further clarified by the May 1992 Rules for the Issuing of Visas.[75] Because of these laws, the overwhelming majority of the Russian-speaking population was unable to participate in the June 1992 referendum on the Estonian constitution or in the September 1992 parliamentary elections.

---

73. A fifth option, that Russia would intervene in a state where both the government and opposition groups are perceived as illegitimate, is omitted here as neither case falls into this category.

74. U.S. Congress, Commission on Security and Cooperation in Europe, *Human Rights and Democratization in Estonia* (September 1993), 11.

75. Michael Geistlinger, "The Legal Status of Russians in Estonia in the Light of Public International Law," in Michael Geistlinger and Aksel Kirch, eds., *Estonia—A New Framework for the Estonian Majority and the Russian Minority* (Vienna: Braumuller, 1995), 101.

In 1993, other laws, viewed by many Russians as violations of human rights, were passed by the Estonian parliament. In February 1993, a separate law on the Estonian language requirement was passed, including an examination fee equaling 15 percent of the monthly minimum wage. In July 1993, parliament passed a law calling for the employment of the Estonian language as the language of instruction in grades ten through twelve by the year 2000. The most controversial law passed was the June 21, 1993, Law on Aliens. It defined those who had arrived after 1940 and their descendants as aliens, requiring them to apply for residence within one year of the law's adoption.[76] The law would force most Russians in Estonia to apply for Estonian citizenship or repatriate.[77]

These laws were ameliorated in part by the May 1993 Law on Local Elections allowing noncitizens with five years' residency to vote in local elections. Estonian President Lennart Meri also refused to sign the Law on Primary and Secondary Schools on the grounds that it was contradictory.

Nonetheless, tensions in Estonia ran high. On July 27, 1992, Russian and Estonian troops exchanged shots, reportedly when Estonian soldiers attempted to take control of a Russian navy building in Tallinn. A Russian officer and a civilian were injured. In other incidents, "a paramilitary organization calling itself the Forest Brothers (after an anti-Soviet guerrilla force that had been active in Estonia in the 1940s and 1950s) . . . intercepted a Russian army truck convoy" and seized several Russian officers at gunpoint. These officers were later released unharmed. In a separate incident, Estonia claimed that thirty drunken Russian soldiers crossed into Estonia and assaulted Estonian border guards.[78]

On June 20, 1993, ethnic Russians in the northeast city of Narva demonstrated against the Law on Aliens, and the next day, demonstrations were held in Tallinn. On June 28, the Narva city council, a town 95 percent Russian, voted to hold a referendum calling for autonomy. Estonia immediately called the plebiscite illegal. Although annulled by Estonia's national court, both Narva and nearby Sillamae held the July 16–17 referendum, with more than 97 percent of the voters supporting autonomy from the central government.[79]

Russia's government, too, reacted harshly. In several statements on July 24, 1993, Yeltsin accused Estonia of practicing "ethnic cleansing" and

---

76. U.S. Congress, *Human Rights,* 14.
77. Geistlinger, "Legal Status," 104.
78. *Facts on File,* 1992, 594.
79. *Facts on File,* 1993, 635.

"apartheid."[80] He told the Estonian leaders, that, "if the Russian-speaking population expresses the natural desire to protect itself from crude discrimination, Russia will not be able to remain in a position of indifferent onlooker."[81] Moreover, Estonia had "forgotten some geopolitical and demographic realities" of which Russia could "remind" Estonia.[82] Yeltsin's adviser Sergei Stankevich warned that "Russia has the right to defend its citizens, without making use of the services of international defenders of human rights."[83]

Despite these threats, Russia's only actions were to halt natural gas deliveries for five days to all three Baltic states, ostensibly for unpaid bills, and to delay the withdrawal of Russian troops. Why, despite the tensions between the Russians living in Estonia and the Estonian government, did Russia do little more to affect overall Estonian behavior? Why did Russia, who as of March 1, 1993, still had 7,600 troops, more than 200 tanks and armed personnel carriers, and another 166 infantry fighting vehicles in Estonia,[84] not mobilize these troops to support the autonomy of the Russians living in Estonia? Does the democratic peace theory explain Russian behavior or is the legitimacy-based theory more compelling?

The Democratic Peace: Estonia as Democracy

Estonia was considered a democracy by several western analysts. Freedom House, citing the 1992 constitution, an institutionalized multiparty system, and independent judiciary, categorized Estonia as a "free state." Moreover, Estonia retained a free press and freedom of religion and conscience in both law and practice.[85] Estonia had sixteen radio stations, including fifteen local FM commercial bands[86] and fifteen daily newspapers and 169 less frequently printed.[87] The ethnic laws passed did not negate Estonia's position as a democracy, especially after the May 1993 law allowing all residents to vote in local elections. The "ethnic democracy" in Estonia, although it did accord the Estonians a superior status beyond their numerical proportion, extended certain collective rights to ethnic minori-

80. U.S. Congress, *Human Rights*, 15.
81. *Facts on File*, 1993, 530.
82. U.S. Congress, *Human Rights*, 15.
83. U.S. Congress, *Human Rights*, 15.
84. *Nezavisimaya gazeta* in *Current Digest of the Post-Soviet Press*, 5 May 1993.
85. Freedom House, *Freedom in the World*, 252.
86. Freedom House, *Freedom in the World*, 252.
87. UNESCO, *Statistical Yearbook 1995*, 7–104, 7–109. Daily newspapers are 1992 statistics. Radio stations and nondaily papers are from 1993.

ties and retained civil and political rights enjoyed by all.[88] In April 1993, the Conference on Security and Cooperation in Europe (CSCE) High Commissioner on National Minorities found no systemic prosecution of national minorities. In February of that same year, Marrack Goulding, UN undersecretary for political affairs, concluded that the Estonian constitution and the language and citizenship laws were compatible with the International Covenant on Civil and Political Rights and the Covenant on Economic, Social, and Cultural Rights.[89]

Russian Politics

As noted above, Russia was a weak democracy in 1992 and 1993, marked by an increasingly free press, widespread party representation in the parliament, and a federal system. The press and opposing parties were more belligerent than was the executive in the case of Estonia. The status of the press as largely undeveloped and unprofessional led to a strong emphasis on nationalist causes.[90] The general population of Russia was more hostile toward Estonians than toward other groups, including Caucasians, Muslims, and Ukrainians.[91] Nearly all parliamentary members demanded decisive action from the president to protect Russians abroad. Charges of apartheid against the Estonians were leveled in 1992 by nationalist leaders.

The threats made by Yeltsin and Stankevich in 1994 reflected the charges and statements made by opposition parties in 1992. The delayed response indicates that the chief executive was not overly concerned with parliamentary or public opinion. Moreover, there appears to have been little discussion in the executive or between the executive and legislature on the possibility of intervention. This may suggest that, as was the case in Moldova, the government sought to exclude the legislature from the decision on whether to intervene. There was a lack of the checks and balances called for by the institutional branch of the democratic peace theory. On the other hand, the lack of discussion may suggest that intervention had

88. Graham Smith, Aadne Aasland, and Richard Mole, "Statehood, Ethnic Relations, and Citizenship," in Graham Smith, ed., *The Baltic States: The National Self-Determination of Estonia, Latvia, and Lithuania* (New York: St. Martin's Press, 1994), 190.

89. Geistlinger, "Legal Status," 106, 110.

90. Jack Snyder, "Democratization, War, and Nationalism in the Post-Communist States," in Celeste A. Wallander, ed., *The Sources of Russian Foreign Policy After the Cold War* (Boulder, Colo.: Westview Press, 1996), 35.

91. Alex Pravda, "The Public Politics of Foreign Policy," in Neil Malcolm, Alex Pravda, Roy Allison, and Margot Light, *Internal Factors in Russian Foreign Policy* (New York: Oxford University Press, 1996), 192.

been rejected immediately, as leaders recognized that the West would retaliate with economic and political reprisals, the costs of which would overwhelm any potential gains from intervention. This suggests the fairly low priority placed on national ties by the Russian government and further implies the greater aggressiveness of the public and parliament.

Legitimacy: A Shared Ideology?

Estonia was, according to Freedom House and others, a democracy. Similarly, Russia can be described as a democracy, albeit weak. Perhaps more important than their actual status, however, was each country's desire to become more closely tied to the West. Estonia desperately wanted to "rejoin Europe" and be included in European organizations and trade.[92] Russia, too sought close ties with the West to democratize and to create a stable free market. Financial and technological aid was needed from the Western powers. The heavy focus on defense expenditures during the Cold War needed to give way to a focus on domestic reform. To this end, Yeltsin and his foreign policy team, most notably Andrei Kozyrev, focused almost entirely on emphasizing a "new solidarity with the West."[93] Both countries aimed at becoming "Westernized" and part of the European society. This shared aspiration incorporated mutual beliefs in what was needed to become part of that society, including respect for human rights and a willingness to abide by treaties and laws.

Russian Nationalities

Even more than in Moldova, the opposition forces in Estonia were of Russian nationality. The groups seeking autonomy were almost exclusively Russian, whereas the Estonian government was almost totally Estonian in nationality. The laws forming the heart of the disagreement effectively divided government and opposition along national lines. As already discussed, the fact that the Russian government and the opposition forces shared a nationality increased the Russian perception that the opposition was legitimate. They were brothers and sisters and shared the same language and history and, presumably, the same goals and desires.

92. Lowell William Barrington, "To Exclude or Not to Exclude: Citizenship Policies in Newly Independent States" (Ph.D. diss., University of Michigan, 1995), 142.
93. Neil Malcolm, "The New Russian Foreign Policy," *The World Today* 50 (February 1994); Alexei D. Boguturov, head of Section for Comparative Political Studies, Institute of the USA and Canada, interview by author, Moscow, September 23, 1996.

Estonian Cohesion

In Estonia, the cohesion of the state and the Estonian government's control of its territory was hardly in doubt. Although up to 95 percent of the urban population in the northeast region of the country was Russian, they were not well organized. Individual cities were marked by different parties and groups seeking autonomy with only limited interaction. Additionally, the Russian minority failed to exert control over even the northeast region where numerous Estonians made up a large portion of the rural population. This lack of organization and the local flavor of many protests prevented the Russian minority from having a large effect on the Estonian government or its policies.[94]

Role of International Organizations

There was considerable negotiation between the two governments during 1992 and 1993, largely under the auspices of the UN. Moreover, international organizations, including Helsinki Watch, the Council of Europe, and the CSCE, stepped in, seeking to mediate the dispute over the Estonian citizenship policies. Indeed, Russia appealed to the European states to become involved and initiated the studies conducted by the CSCE and others.

Assessment of the Nonintervention in Estonia

Both the democratic peace theory and legitimacy-based theory were supported in their general expectations: no intervention in Estonia. Both also predicted numerous negotiations between Russia and the state. This was similarly upheld as Russia negotiated at the highest levels with the Estonian government and held numerous meetings.

There was limited support for the institutional branch of the democratic peace theory, however. The public and its representatives in parliament, despite the arguably democratic nature of Estonia, were more bellicose than the government, violating an expectation of the democratic peace theory (that the Russian people, and its parliament, should be generally less belligerent than the executive). Furthermore, the government failed to go along with its public as would be predicted by the institutional branch of the theory. On the other hand, the bellicose speeches of Yeltsin and Stankevich may have been an effort to placate the population and to convince them that the government was taking a hard-line stance.

94. Barrington, "To Exclude," 135–37.

The legitimacy-based theory provides a better explanation for Russian behavior. As detailed above, when one state believes another legitimate, intervention is unlikely but negotiations are likely to occur as it is believed the target state will abide by the outcome. The importance to Russia of Estonia's pro-Western ideology and the importance of Estonia's ability to control its own territory led to a view of the Estonian government as legitimate and thus largely eliminated the likelihood of intervention.

Russia, however, did not intercede on behalf of the government because the opposition was likewise viewed as legitimate. The opposition groups gained legitimacy largely for their national character: the autonomy-seeking parties were Russian. Because both sides were viewed as legitimate, Russia sought to settle the issue by negotiation. The incorporation of external mediating organizations by Russia indicated its perception that the government of Estonia was a legitimate state that could be dealt with through international law. Moreover, the use of the international organizations suggested that Russia thought Estonia, as well as the opposition forces in Estonia, would abide by decisions reached by the CSCE and other organizations.

As previously discussed, international organizations can have a reinforcing effect on the legitimacy of a state. By its involvement in the crisis and Estonia's close cooperation, the CSCE further strengthened the view that Estonia was a part of Europe and was a legitimate state.

Moldova

Unlike the case of Estonia, where Russian involvement was limited to a short-lived cessation of natural gas exports, the Russian Fourteenth Army intervened in Moldova. The 1991–92 rebellion by many of those living on the left bank of the Dniester River resulted in the involvement of the Russian military force and the death of more than six hundred people.

The Moldovan conflict had its recent roots in the end of the Soviet era. In 1989, the Moldovan parliament passed a number of language laws that enshrined the Moldovan-Romanian language as the state language and called for the gradual transition from the Cyrillic alphabet to the Latin script. On the left bank, however, even the Moldovans had used Cyrillic since the fourteenth century.[95] In early 1990, in partial reaction to the threat of unification with Romania, referenda were held in Bendery and

95. Pal Kolsto and Andrei Edemsky with Natalya Kashnikova, "The Dniester Conflict: Between Irredentism and Separatism," *Europe-Asia Studies* 45 (1993): 980–81.

other towns in Dniester, similar to that held three years later in Estonia, to call for the creation of an autonomous territory. After 90 percent voted in favor of autonomy, the Dniester Moldavian Soviet Socialist Republic (later called the Dniester Moldavian Republic or PMR) was declared in September 1990.

Throughout 1991, military confrontations between the Moldovans and citizens of the PMR increased. In June 1992, the conflict came to a head. Clashes in Bendery involving separatist forces, Moldovan government troops, and members of the Fourteenth Army cost several hundred lives. When pressed, Yeltsin admitted that soldiers had entered Bendery to "defend people and stop the bloodshed."[96] Witnesses, however, reported that the Fourteenth Army openly sided with the separatists. In addition to the direct military assistance, the Fourteenth Army also provided more than twenty thousand firearms to the PMR forces and assisted in instructing the Trans-Dniester forces.[97]

Before continuing with the analysis, it is imperative that a caveat be included. The assumption here is that the Russian government had foreknowledge of the pro-PMR activities of the Fourteenth Army and either tacitly or explicitly supported the actions. Reaction by the Yeltsin government following the Moldovan conflict hinted strongly at its support of the actions taken by the military forces. Medals and commendations were subsequently given out to soldiers in the unit. Presidential adviser Sergei Stankevich and others have echoed the belief that the Russian government supported the Fourteenth Army's involvement.[98] Several Western analysts have cited the fact that the intervention by Russia is one facet of the pattern of Russian involvement in the domestic affairs of the other former Soviet states and therefore not an anomalous act.[99] Two years after the incident, the Russian paper, *Rossiiskie vesti*, concluded: "Only now, summing up all the facts, we have come to understand: every step of [Lebed in Moldova] was authorized by the hierarchy of Russia's Ministry of Defense."[100]

Why did Russia become involved in the Moldovan conflict, even as it refrained from action in Estonia? Was it because Moldova lacked a demo-

96. *Facts on File*, 1992, 649.

97. Gerald B. Solomon, "Peacekeeping in the Transdniester Region: A Test Case for the CSCE," Draft Special Report, [Online]. Available INTERNET http://www.intnet.net/pub/COUNTRIES/Moldova/Moldova.conflic.data, November 1994.

98. Vladimir Socor, *RFE-RFL Daily Report* 24 [Online]. Available http://www.missouri.edu/ras/ref/refmoldova.html, 4 November 1994.

99. See Goltz, "Letter from Eurasia"; Johnathan Sunley, "The Moldovan Syndrome," *World Policy Journal* 11 (Summer 1994); and Solomon, "Peacekeeping."

100. Quoted in Socor, *RFE-RFL Daily Report*.

cratic regime or because the Moldovan government was seen as an illegitimate force unable to control its own territory?

Democratic Peace: Moldova as Nondemocracy

As with the case of Estonia, the democratic peace theory appears, on the
surface, to provide an explanation for the intervention. There is little question that Moldova was not, in 1992, a democracy. Moldovan President Mir-
cea Snegur ran unopposed in 1991. There were several political parties,
but their existence was not institutionalized. There was no independent
judiciary, and human rights violations were reported throughout 1992.
Through August 1992, a state of emergency was imposed on the country.
Furthermore, newspapers were still constrained by their reliance on government subsidies, and government employees and those in essential services were not allowed to strike.[101] Corresponding with the democratic
peace theory, there was little negotiation between Russia and the Moldovan
government, reflecting perhaps the lack of legitimacy bestowed on the Moldovan government by Moscow.

Russian Politics

There was little discussion in the parliament about the potential intervention. The key to the institutional branch of the democratic peace theory is
that the public and the legislature act as a constraint on federal behavior.
Actions outside the public view and hidden from the eyes of parliament
subvert the role of a legislature in a democracy. The Russian government
did not seek the parliament's approval either before or after the intervention in Moldova, but, as with the Estonian case, the members of parliament
were consistently more aggressive than the chief executive.

Legitimacy: A Lack of Shared Ideology

Unlike Estonia, there was little movement by Moldova to the West. As discussed above, Moldova had made little progress toward democracy. Moldovan intransigence coupled with Russia's turn to the West signaled a
difference in belief systems between the two states. Because Moldova arguably followed different norms and rules, Russia did not expect the state to

---

101. Freedom House, *Freedom in the World*, 406.

abide by negotiations and was not likely to think that a settlement could even be reached.

Shared Nationalities

The Moldovan government, like the Estonian, was primarily populated by non-Russians. In the Trans-Dniester region, Russians made up only 25 percent of the population.[102] Despite this relatively small percentage, Russians were over-represented in the leadership of the PMR. This presence of Russians as leaders and spokesmen for the organization increased the perception that the PMR was, indeed, a Russian organization. Moreover, the PMR was openly pro-Russian, interested in closer ties with Russia. Such an organization could be expected to appeal to the Russian sense of right and wrong as the perceived members shared history and ideology with the Russian people and government. Indeed, the PMR gained support from both liberal and nationalist forces in Russia.

A Moldovan Lack of Cohesion

Unlike the Estonian government, the Moldovan government could not control its own territory. The left bank of the Dniester was largely under PMR, not government, rule. By September 1991, the PMR had established its own republican guard, which eventually reached twelve thousand. By spring 1992, Cossack mercenaries had begun to come to the PMR to support the struggle for autonomy.[103] Assisted by members of the Fourteenth Army, the PMR gradually gained control over the institutions of the left bank, including courts, administration, police, and army.[104] The inability of Moldova to control its own territory signaled an inability to live up to any possible agreement. On the other hand, the PMR, because of its ability to control its territory, was likely to retain the ability to fulfill any obligations made to Russia.

Role of International Organizations

International organizations were active in the Moldovan situation as intermediaries, much as in Estonia. The CSCE set up a mission in Moldova

---

102. Solomon, "Peacekeeping."
103. Kolsti and Edemsky, "Dniester Conflict," 987.
104. Solomon, "Peacekeeping."

following the Moldovan government's request in mid-1992 to seek a peaceful settlement between the three parties. The role of the CSCE in attaining peace, however, was only partial; it had failed, largely because of PMR reticence, to negotiate the withdrawal of Russian troops. The endorsement of Moldova's territorial integrity by the CSCE did little to assist the reintegration of the Trans-Dniester region.[105]

The involvement of international organizations differed considerably in two ways from the involvement in Estonia. First, the mediation was largely limited to post-Russian intervention as opposed to Estonia where there was early intervention, before military involvement by Russia. The second and more important difference is that the CSCE became involved in Estonia on Russia's request and in Moldova on behalf of that government's appeals. The fact that Russia did not itself seek CSCE involvement before allowing the Fourteenth Army to become involved in Moldova suggests that Russia did not believe the illegitimately viewed Moldovan government warranted such international attention. Moreover, it suggests that Russia did not believe Moldova would uphold any agreement or decision that was made.

Assessment of the Intervention in Moldova

As with the Estonian case, both the democratic peace theory and the legitimacy-based theory are supported by Russia's decision to intervene in Moldova. Moreover, there were few negotiations between the Russian and Moldovan governments, again supporting both theories. Beyond this, however, the underlying expectations of the democratic peace theory are not supported. There was little discussion in the press or government about a potential intervention. Again, the population and parliament were more bellicose than the executive, which violated the expectation that the public acts to check state behavior.

Instead, the legitimacy-based theory again appears better suited to explain Russian intervention. As with the democratic peace theory, the lack of negotiations is consistent with the legitimacy-based theory. Russia viewed the Moldovan government as illegitimate because of a lack of shared nationalities between the two governments, Moldova's lack of a Westernizing, democratizing ideology, and its inability to control its own territory. Moreover, the legitimacy-based theory can explain why Russia supported the PMR. The PMR was viewed as legitimate because of its shared Russian view-

---

105. Solomon, "Peacekeeping."

point and leadership and its own ability to control the territory it possessed. The legitimacy bestowed on the opposition group and the lack of legitimacy for the government predicts the likelihood and direction of Russian intervention.

INTERVENTIONS: RUSSIA, DEMOCRACY, AND LEGITIMACY

The democratic peace theory has limited ability to explain the intervention in Moldova and the lack of intervention in Estonia. Although the failure of Russia to intervene in democratic Estonia and its involvement in the nondemocratic state corresponds to the predictions of the democratic peace theory, its institutional framework fails to explain the mechanisms by which intervention did or did not occur. In both cases, the population and parliament were more aggressive than the chief executive and failed to act as a constraint on state behavior. There was little discussion between the executive branch of government and the population, which heightened the failure of the institutional branch to explain Russian behavior.

On the other hand, the normative branch of the theory appears to hold. The desire to negotiate and cooperate with democratic Estonia was greater from the government standpoint than the desire to negotiate with the nondemocratic government of Moldova. This is a surprising outcome as many proponents of the democratic peace theory argue that it holds only when the democracies are stable.[106] Time is needed for traditional democratic beliefs to become internalized. Indeed, cases abound where newly or weakly democratizing states war with others, including the War of 1812 and the recent wars between Croatia and Serbia and Armenia and Azerbaijan.

Closely linked with the normative assessment of Moldova and Estonia, the legitimacy-based theory, incorporating ideology, nationalities, and territorial cohesion, is far better at explaining Russian behavior. In addition to predicting when intervention may occur, it also allows predicting the direction in which it occurs. The shared goals of Western inclusion and the ability of Estonia to control its own territory increased Russian views of Estonia as a viable state, likely to uphold agreements on which it settled. The presence of a Russian opposition group similarly was held as legitimate

---

106. Snyder, "Democratization," 21–22.

because of the perception of shared ideals and goals. Russia saw both government and opposition group as legitimate and vigorously pursued negotiations and outside mediation. In Moldova, on the other hand, the view of
the Moldovan government as a non-Western-facing state and one unable
to defend its internal integrity led to the perception of Moldova as illegitimate and both unwilling and unable to abide by outside mediation. Coupled with the Russian character of the opposition force and its ability to
control the land on which it was based, Russian views of legitimacy turned
toward the PMR. Not expecting the Moldovan government to abide by outside agreements, the Russian government did not seek outside mediation
and instead turned toward intervention against the Moldovan state.

What do the above findings herald for the future of Russia? Although
it is clear that Russia is more democratic than during the days of the Soviet
Union, it is not clear whether Russia is now a true democracy or is even on
its way to becoming one. In some ways, democratic norms have diminished.
The violent resolution of the standoff between members of the Congress
of People's Deputies and the president in October 1993 and the formulation of the new constitution giving more power to the presidency signaled
a shift away from democratic ideals. The acceptance of democratic norms
too have appeared to have declined. "Between 1992 and 1994 support for
democratic values such as a competitive party system, popular participation
in politics, the right to organize opposition to government policies, and
the protection of minority rights receded."[107]

On the other hand, the 1996 presidential elections clearly demonstrated that Yeltsin faces strong competition. The December 1995 parliamentary elections showed a continuation of the competitive, multiparty
elections held in 1993. In 1995, Vladimir Zhirinovsky's Liberal Democratic
Party won only one-half of its 1993 total, with 11 percent of the vote. The
Communists won with 22 percent of the vote, and the party supporting
Yeltsin came away with only 55 Duma seats to the Communists' 157.[108]

Perhaps more significant than the actual level of democracy, in view of
the importance of the legitimacy-based theory, is the direction that the
Russian government is taking and its particular form of democracy and
ideology. The turn away from a Westernizing focus and toward a more
regional, "Russified" aim may decrease the legitimacy Russia bestows on
those states seeking to become more like Western Europe. This move may

---

107. Arthur H. Miller, William M. Reisinger, and Vicki L. Hesli, "Understanding Political
Change in Post-Soviet Societies: A Further Commentary on Finifter and Mickiewicz," *American
Political Science Review* 90 (March 1996): 160.
108. Bruce W. Nelan, "How Dark a Red Is He?" *Time*, 8 January 1996, 44.

herald an increase in the importance of nationality in the determination of legitimacy as Russian nationalism and regionalism increase in importance.

Ironically, the effects of a democratic society have come to fruition in the war in Chechnya. The government became increasingly more constrained by the public's vocal desire to withdraw from the conflict, which resulted in Yeltsin's 1996 announcement that Russian forces would withdraw. The impact of the population has grown from the early 1980s when similar military losses in Afghanistan were hidden in the Soviet machinery.

A different version of the institutional branch of the democratic peace theory may, in fact, play a role in Russian behavior. Some have linked Yeltsin's military actions in Russia and the "near abroad" to an attempt to rally public opinion and gain support for himself and his policies. When he discovered such actions were detrimental to his own public standing and, indeed, endangered his own election chances, he was willing to seek peace. Unlike the apparent inability of the legislative branch to constrain the executive, presidential elections may indeed play a role in institutionally limiting the president's ability to act.

This indicates a second issue. The finding in the earlier sections of this chapter that institutional constraints seem to matter little is weakened by the fact that the constitutional and political system of Russia scarcely changed between the Moldovan and the Estonian case. In fact, there was overlap in the time examined for the two periods. This lack of variation of the independent variable makes it difficult to determine its role in affecting state behavior. Moreover, this chapter deals with states that are newly democratizing and that have lacked the time to develop the institutions and ingrained beliefs that are hallmarks of democracy.

Despite these shortcomings, it is clear that the democratic peace theory, although not disproved, does not successfully explain Russian behavior toward Moldova and Estonia. The institutional branch of the theory is fully rebuffed as there was little attempt by the parliament or public to check the government, and, indeed, the two bodies were more bellicose than the Russian executive. Furthermore, the historical evidence has shown that democracies are likely to intervene against other democracies. United States' involvement against elected governments in Guatemala and Costa Rica and Russian involvement against the elected government in Azerbaijan are but three examples. These facts point to a need for a theory better suited to intervention. The legitimacy-based theory, with its inclusion of nationalities and political cohesion with ideology, appears a better predictive tool for Russian intervention and is far better suited to explaining when and how military interventions occur.

5

Politics and Economics in Russo-Japanese Relations

Hiroshi Kimura

Evgenii Primakov paid his first official visit to Tokyo as Russian foreign minister on November 14–17, 1996, when President Boris Yeltsin was still recovering from the operation that he had undergone on November 5. The Russian foreign minister tried to impress on the Japanese people that the Yeltsin government regarded the improvement of Russo-Japanese bilateral relations as one of the most important foreign policy objectives.

Primakov formally proposed that Japan and Russia conduct "the joint *economic* development" *(sovmestnoe khoziaistvennoe osvoenie)* of the disputed islands off Hokkaido during his meeting with his Japanese counterpart, Yukihiko Ikeda, as well as with former Prime Minister Yasuhiro Nakasone and the Liberal Democratic Party policy chief Taku Yamazaki.[1] In his an-

---

1. *Japan Times, Asahi Evening News, Mainichi Daily News,* 16 November 1996; *International*

nual state-of-the-union address to Parliament on March 6, 1997, Yeltsin reiterated the same proposal that the foreign minister had made.[2] Primakov had proposed that joint economic projects be conducted in areas such as fishing, fish canneries, building up the infrastructure for tourism on the islands, and improving the transportation system. He had also emphasized that joint economic cooperation on the islands would bring the two neighboring countries closer. He cited the example of the Falkland Islands (Malvinas), where Great Britain and Argentina, although disputing the territorial ownership of the archipelago, conduct joint economic activities. Yet, the responses made by the Japanese side to Primakov's proposal were not very positive. Why?

Put simply, Japan is concerned that its assent to this proposal could be interpreted as recognition of Russian sovereignty and thereby could adversely undermine Japanese claims to the four disputed islands. The disputed islands, known to Japanese as the Northern Territories and to the Russians as the Southern Kuril Islands, include Etorofu, Kunashiri, Shikotan, and the Habomai group of islets, which were seized by Soviet troops immediately after the end of World War II. Japan maintains that these four islands are not part of the Kuril Islands, which Japan renounced in the San Francisco Peace Conference in 1951, but are historically an integral part of Japan's territory. Japan has long demanded the return of these islands. In his reply to the Russian foreign minister's proposal, Japanese Foreign Minister Ikeda said that he was willing to discuss economic development but added that the sovereignty issue could not be shelved simply for the purpose of furthering economic development in the disputed islands.

Both foreign ministers clearly viewed the proposed joint economic projects in different political contexts. Primakov indicated that cooperation between Russia and Japan in *economic* and other areas would contribute to a possible solution of political conflicts, including the territorial dispute. In marked contrast, Ikeda and Japanese officials believed that the establishment of a legal *political* framework through signing a peace treaty, thereby improving the political atmosphere between the two nations, would inevitably lead to active intercourse in economic and other areas. The debate boils down to the question of whether economic factors should determine political factors or vice versa and, therefore, whether Japan and Russia

---

Herald Tribune, 17–18 November 1996; *BBC Monitoring: Summary of World Broadcasts (Part I, Former USSR),* 11 November 1996, B15–16.

2. *Poriadok vo vlasti—poriadok v strane (O polozhenii v strane i osnovnykh nagrtavleniiakh politiki Rossiiskoi Federatsii)* [Order in power—order in the country (on situations in the country and fundamental policy of the Russian Federation)] (Moscow: Rossiiskaia Federatsiia, 1997), 60.

should start to improve their bilateral relations in the political or economic arena. With regard to this question confronting both nations, I discuss in this chapter the relative significance of politics and economics in current Russo-Japanese relations.

To what extent does geographic proximity determine Russo-Japanese relations? Is there economic interdependence between Russia and Japan? If there is, what kind of interdependence is it, and which of the two countries is more dependent on the other? Likewise, is there economic complementarity between the two countries? If so, how has it changed over time? Which country, then, has more economic leverage to influence the political behavior of the other? To what extent has Japan's linkage policy of economics and politics been consistent? If there have been inconsistencies, when and how did they arise, and for what reasons? In the linkage of economics and politics, how do Russo-Japanese relations differ from Sino-Japanese relations, and what accounts for the differences? Why has Russia not been very successful in exploiting its huge stock of natural resources with the aim of obtaining diplomatic concessions from Japan? Conversely, why has Japan been unable to use its financial and technological clout as a bargaining leverage to achieve its foreign policy objectives vis-à-vis Russia?

GEOGRAPHIC PROXIMITY

Non-Japanese and even some Japanese seem to misunderstand the relation between geographic proximity and economic development. Because of the geographic proximity and economic complementarity between Japan and Russia, some think that these two nations have developed and should continue to develop good political and economic relations. Some argue that Japan, a resource-poor nation, should, in an effort to diversify her energy resources, cooperate more positively with Russia in the economic development of Siberia and the Russian Far East. Such an effort may eventually lead to Japan's getting back the Northern Territories. Along the same lines, others argue that Japan should help Russia's reform more positively than other Group of Seven (G-7) nations have done, if Japan is serious about its demands for reversion of the islands. These arguments are neither entirely incorrect nor correct. One reason for the incorrectness stems from the simplistic conception of the relation between economics and politics, which is not as simple, straightforward, direct, or unilinear in nature as one might imagine. Of course, economics is an important determining factor of politics, and vice versa. No matter how important it may be, however, economics is only one determinant of politics.

Geographically, Japan and Russia are neighbors. In my view, the customary proposition that geographic proximity leads to, or should lead to, good relations (a conclusion carelessly or deliberately drawn by many Russian commentators and by some Japanese) warrants criticism. Japanese politicians and journalists frequently make the point that Japan has no choice but to be friendly toward, and live peacefully with, Russia, regardless of ideological differences and subjective preferences. Russian spokespeople frequently quoted a statement made in 1973 by the former Japanese prime minister Kakuei Tanaka: "Though the distance between the capitals of Tokyo and Moscow may be great, the USSR and Japan nevertheless are close neighbors *(blizkie sosedy)*."[3] Therefore, it is not surprising, Soviet spokespeople continued, "that both Moscow and Tokyo attach much importance to the expansion of Soviet-Japanese relations."[4] Elaborating further, Russian spokespeople drew the bold conclusion that "geographic proximity" *(geograficheskaia blizost')* "necessitates" or provides "objective conditions" (N. Nikolaev and A. Pavlov) or the "objective necessity" (G. Krasin, V. Dal'nev, O. V. Vasil'ev) for adopting a policy of *good neighborliness* and mutual cooperation between Russia and Japan.[5] Mikhail S. Gorbachev also underlined the importance of the geographical proximity between the Soviet Union and Japan, stating: "We are in favor of improving our relations with Japan, and we are confident that this is a possibility. This possibility stems from the simple fact alone that both countries are immediate neighbors *(priamye sosedy)*."[6]

Unfortunately, however, our complex experiences in international relations have revealed that geographic propinquity does not necessarily lead to neighborly or friendly relations. Occasionally, such good relations do

---

3. *Pravda*, 30 March 1973.

4. N. Nikolaev, "Rassirenie sovetsko-iaponskikh sviazei" [Expansion of Soviet-Japanese ties], *Mezhdunarodnaia zhizn'* (hereafter in this chapter *MZ*), no. 7 (July 1972): 43.

5. N. Nikolaev and A. Pavlov, "SSSR-Iaponiia: Kurs na dobrososedstvo i ego protivniki" [USSR-Japan: Course to good neighborliness and its opponents], *MZ*, no. 7 (July 1982): 31; G. Krasin, "Sovetsko-iaponskie otnosheniia" [Soviet-Japanese relations], *MZ*, no. 4 (April 1976): 36. In an article written two years later, however, Krasin noted: "Our countries [the Soviet Union and Japan] are neighbors . . . [and] always have a subject for discussion." Krasin, "Uglubliala doverie" [Trust deepened], *Novoe vremya*, no. 4 (January 20, 1978): 7; V. Dal'nev, "Chto meshaet razvitiiu Sovetsko-iaponskikh otnoshenii" [What prevents the development of Soviet-Japanese relations], *MZ*, no. 1 (January 1981): 50; O. V. Vasil'ev, "Nekotorye problemy vneshnei politiki Iaponii v 1980 g." [Some problems of Japanese foreign policy in 1980], *Iaponiia 1981: Ezhegodnik* [Japan 1981: Yearbook] (Moscow: Nauka, 1982), 63.

6. *Pravda*, 28 November 1985.

occur among neighbors (e.g., Canada and the United States),[7] but this is not always the case. At times, even the opposite occurs. Just as close relatives may sometimes dislike one another, neighboring countries sometimes disagree more harshly than they do with more remote states, partly because they compete for the same objectives. Geographic contiguity tends to facilitate conflict.[8] As demonstrated by history, disputes over territorial boundaries between geographically adjacent nations have constituted one of the most significant sources of international conflicts. Some specialists of international affairs have gone so far as to regard conflicts over boundaries as "the most important single cause of war between states in the modern world."[9] Research by Lewis F. Richardson revealed that the numbers of frontiers that a country shared with other countries was *positively correlated* to participation in wars.[10] This should not, of course, be taken to mean that states sharing common territorial borders always fight with one another. As Bruce M. Russett put it, such states have "the *opportunity* to fight because they are close. Proximity becomes the catalyst."[11] In his appearance on a Japanese television program on Nippon Hōsō Kyokai, the Japanese Broadcasting Society, on March 5, 1997, Alexander Panov, Russian Ambassador to Tokyo, stated: "Although Russia and Japan are *geographically close* to each other, these two nations are *psychologically very remote* from each other" (emphasis added).[12]

ECONOMIC INTERDEPENDENCE
AND FOREIGN POLICY

The theoretical distinction between two concepts of international relations, interconnectedness and interdependence, proposed by Robert O.

7. Former Canadian Prime Minister Pierre E. Trudeau was once quoted as having said (March 1969) that, for Canada, being the United States' neighbor "is in some ways like sleeping with an elephant. No matter how friendly and even-tempered is the beast, if I can call it that, one is affected by every twitch and grunt." Quoted in Louis Turner, *Invisible Empires* (New York: Harcourt, Brace, Janovich, 1971), 166, and W. H. Pope, *The Elephant and the Mouse* (Toronto: McClelland and Stewart, 1971), vii.

8. In writing this passage, I am obliged to Lloyd Jensen's *Explaining Foreign Policy* (Englewood Cliffs, N.J.: Prentice-Hall, 1982), 208–9.

9. Evan Luard, *Conflict and Peace in the Modern International System* (Boston: Little, Brown, 1968), 111.

10. Lewis F. Richardson, *Statistics of Deadly Quarrels* (New York: Quadrangle/New York Times Books, 1960), 176 (emphasis added).

11. Bruce M. Russett, *International Regions and the International System* (Chicago: Rand McNally, 1967), 200.

12. Quoted from Ambassador Panov's statement in the NHK television program entitled "Recent Japan-Russian Relations," March 5, 1997.

Keohane and Joseph S. Nye, is useful for discussing a major point of this chapter. When Country A imports from Country B such commodities as furs, jewelry, perfume, and other luxury goods, there exists an economic *interconnectedness* between the two countries. On the other hand, when Country C imports almost all its oil and other energy resources, which are indispensable for the survival of its national economy, from Country D, then the dependence on a continual flow of these resources creates an *interdependence* between Countries C and D.[13] Between Japan and Russia, there is economic interconnectedness rather than economic interdependence. In most cases, economic interconnectedness or interdependence leads to politically friendly and secure relations among nations, but among economically interconnected or interdependent nations, political difficulties and other problems cause friction. Sometimes, not despite but rather precisely because of the existence of such close economic relations, conflicts and feelings of insecurity arise in the relations between countries.

To measure the degree of power in economic interdependence, Keohane and Nye further distinguished between the two dimensions of sensitivity and vulnerability. *Sensitivity* means the liability to costly effects imposed from outside *before* policies are altered to try to change the situation. *Vulnerability* can be defined as the liability to suffer costs imposed by external events even *after* policies have been altered.[14] Sensitivity interdependence is less important than vulnerability interdependence in providing power resources to countries.[15]

Since, or even before, the time when these definitions and distinctions were proposed by Keohane and Nye, the concept of dependence or interdependence in world politics has stimulated lively scholarly debate.[16] One debate centers on the definition of the concept of *interdependence* itself. One school of thought includes in the concept the two meanings of *interdependence: sensitivity interdependence,* defined in terms of mutual effects, and *vulnerability interdependence,* defined in terms of the opportunity costs of disrupting the relation. The other school argues that only the second meaning, *vulnerability interdependence,* corresponds to everyday and academ-

13. Robert O. Keohane and Joseph S. Nye, *Power and Interdependence: World Politics in Transition* (Boston: Little, Brown, 1977), 9.
14. Keohane and Nye, *Power and Interdependence,* 12–13.
15. Keohane and Nye, *Power and Interdependence,* 15.
16. See, for example, David A. Baldwin, "Interdependence and Power: A Conceptual Analysis," *International Organization* 34 (Autumn 1980): 471–506; Janice E. Thomson and Stephen D. Krasner, "Global Transactions and the Consolidation of Sovereignty," in Ernst-Oho Czempiel and James N. Posenau, eds., *Global Changes and Theoretical Challenges* (London: MacMillan, 1989), 319–39.

ically meaningful usage.[17] Another debate revolves around the relation between interdependence of economic transactions and sovereignty of the state. One school of thought argues that interdependence has undermined the effective sovereignty of the state by underlining the following causal sequence: technological change leads to increased economic flows, which erodes state control.[18] In contrast, realists like Kenneth Waltz have argued that growing interdependence has been a function of political power and political choice.

Vulnerability can be reduced to a certain degree by a country's efforts to change its policies.[19] Japan's efforts, for instance, lowered its 99 percent dependence on other countries for its oil supplies to 78 percent. As far as Japan's heavy dependence on other countries for oil is concerned, however, "Japan is a fragile superpower."[20] Even before the energy crisis of 1973, Japan's policy was not to depend too much on the Soviet Union as a source of oil and other energy resources but to try to diversify its sources of natural resources as much as possible. This policy was made clear by Shigeo Horie, former president of both the Bank of Tokyo and *Sotooboo* (the Japan Association for Trade with the Soviet Union and Central-Eastern Europe), who stated in 1970 that "the maximum share of major raw materials imported by Japan from the USSR in the 1980s must be limited to within the following percentages: 9–10 percent for nonferrous minerals, 10 percent for coal, 12–15 percent for timber, and 3 percent for oil."[21] This is an excellent example of "planned interdependence."

Furthermore, as mentioned later in more detail, in the wake of the "oil shocks" of the 1970s, Japan successfully undertook a structural transformation of its economy from a highly energy- and resource-intensive economy to a less raw-material-intensive one. Japan's economy now depends less than before on energy and other mineral resources from Russia. In addition, with its present large supply of hard currency and high-quality products, Japan is now in the rather fortunate position of having a large degree of freedom in choosing its trading partners.

17. Baldwin, "Interdependence and Power," 486, 489.
18. Thomson and Krasner, "Global Transactions," 320.
19. Keohane and Nye, *Power and Interdependence*, 15.
20. Frank Gibney, *Japan: The Fragile Superpower*, rev. ed. (New York: New American Library, 1979), 65, 293; See also Zbigniew Brzezinski, *The Fragile Bloom: Crisis and Change in Japan* (New York: 1972).
21. Quoted from Keisuke Suzuki, *Shiberia Kaihatsu to Nisso Keizai Kyōryoku* [Development of Siberia and Japan-Soviet economic cooperation] (Tokyo: Nikkan Kōgyo Shimbunsha, 1977), 223.

MYTH OF ECONOMIC COMPLEMENTARITY

Russian and some Japanese specialists on Russo-Japanese relations tend, or at least tended in the past, to overemphasize the role that *economic complementarity* played in the relations between Russia and Japan. Some even went so far as to argue that, on these grounds alone, these two countries are almost destined to develop and expand their good *political* relations. The assumptions, logic, and conclusions of such an argument, however, are not necessarily correct.

According to the late Dmitrii Petrov, the concept of economic complementarity *(ekonomicheskaya vzaimodopolnitel'nost')* stems from "the difference in natural and other specific conditions of each respective national economy."[22] Japan, on one hand, is a resource-poor and insular nation that relies heavily on imports of energy and all raw materials for her survival; yet Japan is also an industrial superpower in fields of advanced technology, capital, and other financial capabilities, second only to the United States. In striking contrast, the economy of Russia, which is one of the world's richest nations in terms of potential energy and other natural resources, remains, because of its lack of technology, capital, and transportation capabilities (except in space and military fields), in a sluggish or even stagnant "developing"-country stage. In 1984, one year before the start of Gorbachev's perestroika, Marshall Shulman, then a noted specialist on Soviet affairs at Columbia University, regarded the Soviet Union as "the most developed of the undeveloped countries or the least developed of the developed countries."[23] Be that as it may, Viktor B. Spandar'ian, chief Soviet representative of trade and commerce in Tokyo, clearly underlined the existence of an economically complementary relation between the Soviet Union and Japan in 1973:

> The USSR exports to Japan the following commodities: timber, petroleum products, cotton, coal, non-ferrous metals, platinum, potassium salts, whale meat, and fish products, all of which are essential for the Japanese economy. . . . For its part the USSR imports from

22. Dmitrii D. Petrov, *Iaponiia v mirovoi politike* [Japan in the world politics] (Moscow: Mezhdunarodnye otnosheniia, 1973), 240.

23. Cited from Leslie H. Gelb, "What We Really Know About Russia," *New York Times Magazine,* 28 October 1984, 76; Serge Schmemann, who completed a second assignment as Moscow bureau chief of the *New York Times,* wrote in February 1994 that "Russia is not an 'underdeveloped' or a 'developing' country. It is a misdeveloped country." *International Herald Tribune,* 21 February 1994.

Japan goods that are necessary for its economy: ferrous metal products including steel pipes, rolled ferrous metals, tinplate, engineering equipment, and chemical textile goods."[24]

No doubt such an economic complementarity existed in the past, and still exists today to a certain extent, between Russia and Japan. With such economic complementarity (and geographic proximity) between Russia and Japan, these two countries appear to be ideal trading partners. In fact, many Russians and some Japanese have argued that Japan and Russia should be more actively engaged not only in trade and other economic exchanges but also joint economic development of Siberia and the far eastern part of Russia.

Soviets who were directly or indirectly engaged in trade and other economic intercourses between the Soviet Union and Japan showed enthusiasm in their exaggerated arguments about the existence of economic complementarity between their country and Japan. For example, V. N. Berezin of the Soviet Ministry of Foreign Affairs stated: "The mutual economic complementarity between Japan and the Soviet Union is of a kind that is *very rare in the world.*"[25] Spandar'ian added: "Such mutually supplementary relations provide an *objective condition* for the successful development of Soviet-Japanese ties in the long term and on an extensive scale."[26] P. Dolgorukov, head of the Japanese Economy Section at the Institute of Soviet Trade, stated: "Because of this complementarity, the Soviet Union and Japan have transformed themselves into important trade partners and can no longer regard one another in a *secondary or reserve capacity.*"[27] Petrov also emphasized that "mutual complementarity between these two econo-

24. V. B. Spandar'ian, "Sovetsko-iaponskie torgovo-ekonomicheskie otnosheniia [Soviet-Japanese trade-economic relations]," *Problemy dal'nego voskoka* [Problems of the Far East] no. 3 [35] (1980): 91–92.

25. *Pravda*, 19 October 1973; V. N. Berezin, *Kurs no dobrososedstvo i sotrudnichestvo i ego protivniki: Iz istorii normalizatsii otnoshenii SSSR s poslevoennoi Iaponiei* [Course to goodneighborliness and cooperation and its opponents: From the history of normalization of relations between the USSR and postwar Japan] (Moscow: Mezhdunarodnye otnosheniia, 1977), 123. Berezin is a pseudonym of some high officials in charge of Japanese affairs at the Soviet Ministry of Foreign Affairs.

26. Spandar'ian, "Sovetsko-iaponskie torgovo-ekonomicheskie otnosheniia," 91.

27. P. D. Dolgorukov, "Tolgovo-ekonomicheskie otnosheniia SSSR s Iaponiei" [Trade-economic relations of the USSR with Japan], *SSSR-Iaponiia: K 50-letiiu ustanovleniia sovetsko-iaponskikh diplomaticheskikh otnoshenii (1925–1975)* [The USSR-Japan: Toward the 50th anniversary of the establishment of Soviet-Japanese diplomatic relations (1925–1975)] (Moscow: Nauka, 1978), 108.

mies *creates extraordinarily favorable prospects* for further development of mutual relations in the future."[28]

Although Soviet specialists correctly pointed out the existence of an
economic complementarity between Japan and the Soviet Union, the logic
of their further reasoning and the conclusions they drew from this fact are
not necessarily correct. Starting from the existence of economic complementarity, they tended to jump to a premature conclusion that Japan and
the Soviet Union were almost inevitably destined to become ideal trading
partners.

Russia is not the only country that has economic complementarity with
Japan. All the countries that provide Japan with energy and other natural
resources and/or purchase Japanese products can be regarded as countries
having economic complementarity with Japan. With regard to its choice of
trading partners, Japan is in a fortunate position to be able to choose rather
freely, from a long list of possible candidates, those countries that can provide the most favorable conditions for Japan. Russia is only *one* of a long
list of candidate countries with the potential to become good trading partners for Japan.

Furthermore, economic complementarity constitutes an important precondition for nations to become good trading partners with one another,
but economic complementarity alone does not necessarily provide a sufficient condition. Many other conditions and factors besides economic complementarity play significant roles in determining whether any two nations
actively develop their economic exchanges: geographic proximity, the size
of the gross national product, the amount of foreign currency reserves,
and even politicodiplomatic factors. Only the results of the complex dynamics of all these factors can answer the question of whether two nations
develop good economic relations. It is therefore short-circuited logic or
politically oriented reasoning to jump to the conclusion, based only on the
existence of economic complementarity between Russia and Japan, that
these two countries should be actively engaged in trade and economic relations.[29]

LOW LEVEL OF TRADE AND OTHER
ECONOMIC EXCHANGES

The level of trade between Russia and Japan has never been very high. At
one time in the 1970s, Japan became the second largest trading partner

28. Petrov, *Iaponiia v mirovoi politike*, 240.
29. *Izvestiya*, 11 August 1978.

among Western nations of the Soviet Union, next only to West Germany, in terms of total volume of trade. In the wake of the Soviet invasion of Afghanistan in 1979, however, economic sanctions imposed on the Soviet Union by the United States,[30] as well as other economic, political, and international developments, caused Japan's trade with the Soviet Union to drop to third (after West Germany and Finland), fourth (after Italy), and even fifth (after France) among Western nations. Since the collapse of the COMECON economic bloc in 1989 and of the Soviet Union in 1991, Japan has occupied eighth place (after the United States, Britain, and Canada) in the entire list of trading partners of the Russian Federation. In 1997, Japan's trade with Russia totaled U.S.$5 billion and accounted for a mere 0.66 percent of Japan's total world trade (see Table 5.1). In contrast, Japan's trade with the United States and the People's Republic of China accounts for about 25 percent and 8.4 percent, respectively, of its total world trade.

Following a peak of U.S.$6.1 billion in 1989, bilateral trade between Japan and Russia plunged to U.S.$3.5 billion in 1992, and then gradually, but modestly, increased to U.S.$4.7 billion in 1994 and to more than U.S.$6 billion in 1995,[31] but again decreased to U.S.$5 billion in 1996. In 1996, Japan's trade with mainland China and the United States was about 13.5 and 46.3 times, respectively, more than that of Japan's trade with Russia.

As far as the number of joint ventures with Russia, Japan occupied ninth place in 1995, after Germany, the United States, Finland, Austria, England, Switzerland, France, and Sweden. As an investor in Russia, Japan ranks only eleventh, with about U.S.$330.6 million as of January 1998, amounting to 0.1 percent of its total investments in foreign countries.[32]

The one enduring exception to the low level of economic relations between Japan and Russia may be fisheries. The Japanese love eating fish and have not yet found any way to dramatically increase their catch, even with advanced technology. Thus, Russia is tempted to exploit the fisheries issue with the aim of gaining ground in other areas. Moscow used the fisheries issue to force Tokyo to enter into negotiations on a number of diplomatic issues pending between Japan and the Soviet Union, especially the conclusion of a peace treaty, and advocated that the time is "not yet ripe"

30. Gary Clyde Hufbauer, Jeffrey J. Schott, and Kimberly Ann Elliott, *Economic Sanctions Reconsidered: History and Current Policy*, 2d ed. (Washington, D.C.: Institute for International Economics, 1990), 163–74.

31. S. V. Nozdrev and A. P. Rodionov, "Rossiisko-iaponskie torgovo-ekonomicheskie otnosheniia v 90-e gody" [Russo-Japanese trade economic relations in the 1990s], *Iaponiia: Ezhegodnik (1995–1996)* (Moscow: Nauka, 1996), 97–99.

32. *Japan Times*, 16 April 1998.

Table 1   The Soviet Union's and Russia's trade with Japan (Russia only in 1992, 1993, 1994, 1995, 1996, 1997).

	Total		Imports		Exports	
	Volume (US$ million)	Percentage of Japan's Total	Volume (US$ million)	Percentage of Japan's Total Imports	Volume (US$ million)	Percentage of Japan's Total Exports
1977	3,356	2.2	1,934	2.4	1,422	2.0
1978	3,944	2.2	2,502	2.6	1,442	1.8
1979	4,372	2.0	2,461	2.4	1,911	1.7
1980	4,638	1.7	2,778	2.1	1,860	1.3
1981	5,280	1.8	3,259	2.1	2,021	1.4
1982	5,581	2.1	3,899	2.8	1,682	1.3
1983	4,277	1.6	2,821	1.9	1,456	1.2
1984	3,912	1.3	2,518	1.5	1,394	1.0
1985	4,180	1.4	2,751	1.6	1,429	1.1
1986	5,122	1.5	3,150	1.5	1,972	1.6
1987	4,915	1.3	2,563	1.1	2,352	1.6
1988	5,896	1.3	3,130	1.2	2,766	1.5
1989	6,086	1.2	3,082	1.1	3,005	1.4
1990	5,918	1.1	2,563	0.9	3,351	1.4
1991	5,430	1.0	2,114	0.7	3,317	1.4
1992	3,480	0.6	1,077	0.3	2,403	1.0
1993	4,270	0.5	1,501	0.4	2,769	1.2
1994	4,657	0.7	1,167	0.3	3,490	1.3
1995	5,933	0.7	1,170	0.3	4,763	1.4
1996	4,953	0.7	1,021	0.2	3,932	1.1
1997	5,009	0.7	1,009	0.2	4,000	1.2

SOURCE: *Tsūsho Hakusho: Kakuron [White Paper on International Trade]*, vol. 2 (Tokyo: MITI, 1977–98 editions).

for talks on the fisheries issue and that diplomatic issues should be settled first.[33]

The best example of such an exploitation of the "fisheries card" occurred in 1956. When, because of the territorial dispute, Soviet-Japanese negotiations on diplomatic normalization of state relations fell into an impasse, the Kremlin suddenly imposed new restrictions on Japanese fishing rights in northern waters. This tactic worked successfully, because Japanese fishermen, desperate for a speedy conclusion to fisheries agreements, pressed the Tokyo government hard to enter into negotiations with Moscow on the fisheries issue. In the agreement reached with Moscow, Tokyo

33. Rajendra Kumar Jain, *The USSR and Japan 1945–1980* (New Delhi: Harvester Press, 1981), 101.

had no alternative but to acquiesce to the unilateral Soviet action in controlling fishing in what the Soviet Union considered to be their waters. Moreover, the Soviets were careful to make sure that the fishing agreement went into effect only after diplomatic normalization of relations between Moscow and Tokyo had been agreed on in 1956.

With the enforcement of 200-nautical-mile exclusive fishing zones in 1976–77, however, fishing rights ceased to play such an important role. The Soviet Union was actually more adversely affected by the implementation of 200-mile fishing zones than Japan was.[34] Consequently, the Soviet Union was no longer in a position to be able to take a generous stance toward Japan on the issue of fishing quotas in its coastal waters. Based on the so-called "principle of equal quotas," Moscow and Tokyo agreed to exactly the same quota: 600,000 tons and 150,000 tons in 1985 and 1986, respectively (see Table 5.2). In 1987, an agreement was made on a 300,000-ton quota for Japan and a 200,000-ton quota for the Soviet Union, with Japan paying a sizeable fee of 1.29 billion yen in exchange for the 100,000-ton difference in the hard currency, which the Soviet Union certainly badly needed. Since that time, the same rule has been applied. In 1998, for example, Japan and Russia agreed on the same mutual quota of 95,000 tons, and Japan had to pay 480 million yen for an additional 11,000 tons.[35]

Table 5.2 Fishing quotas in the 200-nautical-mile exclusive fishing zones of Japan and the Soviet Union (1,000 tons).

Year	Japan	Soviet Union	Year	Japan	Soviet Union
1977	455	355	1988	310	210
1978	850	650	1989	310	210
1979	750	650	1990	217	182
1980	750	650	1991	217	182
1981	750	650	1992	212	182
1982	750	650	1993	189	171
1983	750	650	1994	118	100
1984	700	640	1995	118	100
1985	600	600	1996	109	100
1986	150	150	1997	100	100
1987	300	200	1998	95	95

SOURCE: *Nisso-gyogyō-kankei shiryō* [Data on Japanese-Soviet Fishing] (Tokyo: Fishing Agency, July 1989), 7, 77.

34. Hiroshi Kimura, "Soviet and Japanese Negotiating Behavior: The Spring 1977 Fisheries Talks," *ORBIS* 24 (Spring 1980): 47.
35. *Nihon Keizai Shimbun*, 13 December 1997.

Thus, it seems that the time has come when Japanese must buy fish from Russia at almost twice the price they pay to the United States. The conclusion may be made that Japan has been squeezed by Russia to such an extent that the fishing issue has simply become a normal item on the business agenda, an item no longer exploited by the Russians to manipulate Japanese diplomatic behavior.

REASONS FOR THE LOW LEVEL OF TRADE AND ECONOMIC EXCHANGES

What are the reasons for the recent low level of trade and economic activities between Japan and Russia? Economic and political factors seem to be involved.

The first reason is purely economic. For a start, the element of mutual economic complementarity between the two countries has been diminishing and almost ceased to exist by the late 1970s to early 1980s, mainly because of domestic and economic conditions in both Japan and the Soviet Union. The so-called oil shocks in 1973–74 led the Soviet leadership to the misleading conclusion that the Soviet Union, as an energy-rich nation, was in a stronger position to gain political concessions from Japan on their territorial disputes. This assumption turned out, however, to be premature and even wrong. In the wake of the two successive oil shocks in the 1970s, Japan successfully steered the structural transformation of its economy from a "smokestack," heavy manufacturing-based economy to an economy based more on high-quality information, knowledge, and value-added industries, such as electronics, robotics, new materials, bioengineering, and supercomputers. Japan no longer depends, or at least depends less than before, on energy and other raw materials from resource-rich countries such as Russia. On the other hand, Russia, with its abundant supplies of energy and raw materials, was very slow to recognize the need to undertake such a systemic transformation of its economic structure. The development of Siberia and the Russian Far East has become less attractive to Japanese businesspeople, who, in turn, tend to refute the assumption that the Russian and Japanese economies are mutually complementary.

Furthermore, the perestroika began by Mikhail Gorbachev and the reforms initiated by Boris Yeltsin led to deepening economic confusion, chaos, and crisis in Russia, and resulted in a great reduction of the country's economic capabilities as a trading partner. To make matters worse, the international market price of oil dropped in the middle of the 1980s and again in the late 1990s, resulting in a drastic reduction in income revenue and an increase in foreign currency debt for Russia. Russia's unpaid debt to Japan in 1995 amounted to U.S.$3.59 billion, more than 75 percent of the total exports (U.S.$4.76 billion) from Japan to Russia. Under such circumstances, it is understandable for Japanese corporations to refrain from engaging in trade with, particularly exports to, Russia and other Commonwealth of Independent States (CIS) countries. Japanese businesspeople and investors have frequently complained about the slow development of Russia's economic reforms in such fields as taxes, custom duties, decentralization, nontransparent statistics, and financing. Deficiencies in infrastructure, frequent changes in Russian legal regulations, and a huge outflow of capital despite a domestic shortage of hard currency are other items on their list of complaints.

To make matters worse, the State Duma, the lower house of the Russian parliament, on February 21, 1997, passed in the first reading a draft federal law, which aimed to restrict direct foreign investment in Russia with the clear purpose of protecting Russia's national interests. When this law is enforced, bans and restrictions will be applied to foreign investments in areas relating to Russia's national security such as extraction of uranium and delivery and distribution of electric power through federal networks, railway services, and the production of drugs and medical goods.[36] This law is thought to be a response to patriotic concerns that Russia's industries and marketplace would be taken over by foreign capital. Such concerns may be justified in light of the fact that more than 98 percent of the commodities on the shelves at GUM, the largest department store in Moscow, are imports. No doubt, however, foreign investment in Russia will be further discouraged by this law, at a time when the total amount of U.S. foreign investment in Russia is only U.S.$6.6 billion, less than one-half of that in Hungary.

The second reason for the recent low level of trade and economic activ-

36. BBC Monitoring, 22 February 1997, C2. David Rubin, chairman of Trans-World Group and one of Russia's largest foreign investors, published an open letter to U.S. Vice President Albert Gore and Russian Prime Minister Viktor Chernomyrdin in the 7 March 1997, issue of the *International Herald Tribune,* protesting that the Russian government has recently begun "the takeover campaign" of certain foreign investments and facilities, confiscating them without due process. According to him, Anatolii Kulikov, the Russian interior minister, demanded control of the aluminum industry for national security reasons and made an allegation as his rationale that "curtailing foreign capitalists' independence and retaking control of the aluminum industry is essential for Russia's survival." *International Herald Tribune,* 7 March 1997, 7.

ity between Russia and Japan is political. A series of incidents and events that contributed to the stagnation and even deterioration of Soviet-Japanese relations took place in the later half of the 1970s: Leonid Brezhnev's speech to the Twenty-Fifth Communist Party Congress in 1976, in which the general secretary clearly reconfirmed the Soviet Union's unwillingness to return the Northern Territories to Japan; the MIG-25 incident in 1976, in which a Soviet pilot, Lieutenant Victor Belenko, landed at Hakodate Airport; arduous negotiations over fishing rights in the 200-mile fishing zones in 1976–77; Tokyo's signing of a peace treaty with Beijing, with its "antihegemony" clause directed against the Soviet Union, in 1978; and the incursion of Soviet troops into Afghanistan in 1979.

Mikhail Gorbachev's ascent to power in 1985, was, of course, welcome also in Japan, and yet, unlike in the United States, Germany, and other G-7 member nations, where "Gorbymania" was witnessed, there was no "Gorbachev fever" in Japan either in academic circles or among the general public.

Why were Japanese decision makers and the Japanese public so little impressed with Gorbachev's perestroika and the new political thinking? In an attempt to answer this question, Peter Berton, one of the leading authorities on Soviet/Russian-Japanese affairs, listed the following reasons: long-standing Japanese animosity toward their northern neighbor; anti-Soviet sentiment as the natual reaction to the Soviet declaration of war on Japan after the dropping of an atomic bomb on Hiroshima, which was seen by the Japanese as a stab in the back in the light of the existence of the Japanese-Soviet Neutrality Pact; the continuous, illegal Soviet occupation of the Northern Territories and Russian unwillingness to return them to Japan; and the military threat that the Soviet Union posed to the security of Japan.[37] Berton concluded that the answer to the question of Japanese indifference to perestroika was probably "a combination of all of these factors" and added that "a solid majority of the Japanese believe that the territorial issue is the major reason why relations between the two neighbors are not good."[38] I fully agree with both Berton's observations and conclusion. Tokyo was the slowest among Western capitals to acknowledge the changes taking place in the Soviet Union under Gorbachev. Japanese leaders insisted on a resolution to the Northern Territories dispute before serious discussion on wider global issues could begin. For many Japanese,

37. Peter Berton, "The Impact of the 1989 Revolution on Soviet-Japanese Relations," in Young C. Kim and Gason J. Sigur, *Asia and the Decline of Communism* (New Brunswick, N.J.: Transaction, 1992), 137.

38. Berton, "Impact."

the four islands have a symbolic significance far beyond their actual value: as long as these islands illegally seized by Soviet troops remain in the hands of the Russians, the Cold War does not seem to have really ended for the Japanese.

How strong and united are, then, the Japanese with regard to the demands of the Northern Territories? It is difficult to accurately gauge the complex opinions of the Japanese, particularly in view of the fact that Japan is a pluralistic society, where all kinds of opinions exist. Yet, one can discuss a few general trends prevalent among the Japanese.

First, the Japanese have constantly held a negative image of the Soviet Union/Russia. Opinion polls conducted in postwar Japan have shown one constant trend: Japanese people have consistently singled out the Soviet Union/Russia as the most disliked foreign nation. The only exceptions have been during the brief two-year peak of the Chinese Cultural Revolution (1966–67), when the People's Republic of China replaced the Soviet Union as the most disliked nation, and the past nine years (1988–96), when, since the shooting down by North Korea of South Korean Airlines Flight 858 in December 1987, the Democratic People's Republic of Korea (DPRK) was listed as the nation most disliked by the Japanese public. As demonstrated by public opinion surveys regularly conducted by the *Jiji* press, the number of Japanese people who dislike the Soviet Union increased during the 1980s (see Table 5.3). Although the dislike started to decline after Gorbachev came to power, it has begun to rise again since Yeltsin came to power. In a similar poll conducted by the Cabinet Office of the Japanese prime minister, respondents have been asked, "How do you feel about the Soviet Union (Russia)?" As shown in Table 5.4, there has been a steadily high rate of unfavorable responses, ranging from 77.7 percent in 1979 to 84.5 percent in 1997. Favorable responses have remained abysmally low, ranging from a high of 12.7 percent in 1979 to a low of 11.2 percent in 1997. Approximately 60 percent of those respondents, who in a similar survey replied that Soviet/Russian-Japanese relations were not good, said that "the Soviet Union/Russia is not willing to settle the issue of Japanese Northern Territories."[39]

Furthermore, all the political parties in Japan across the political spectrum from right to left, including the Japanese Communist Party (JCP), have been unanimous in condemning the Russian occupation of the Northern Territories and in demanding the return of these islands from the Soviet Union/Russia. Such unanimity is very rare in Japan. With regard

39. Berton, "Impact."

Table 5.3 "Which foreign countries do you dislike the most? (Name three countries)" (%).

Year	Soviet Union	China	North Korea	South Korea
1966	37.4	38.0	—	30.4
1967	36.8	41.5	—	29.2
1968	37.1	37.1	—	24.0
1969	39.2	36.4	—	23.6
1970	32.8	30.9	18.9	15.9
1971	29.4	21.6	24.1	12.5
1972	26.6	10.3	19.0	11.3
1973	24.9	5.9	16.6	12.4
1974	24.1	7.1	18.8	20.4
1975	27.0	8.3	25.3	25.0
1976	30.1	9.6	25.2	22.7
1977	38.3	9.8	25.7	22.6
1978	41.3	8.7	25.9	21.1
1979	43.9	8.0	28.0	22.6
1980	55.4	5.1	30.6	25.9
1981	53.2	5.8	29.6	22.7
1982	50.9	5.7	29.3	21.4
1983	49.0	5.2	27.1	20.2
1984	59.0	4.0	33.1	16.7
1985	55.0	4.0	33.6	16.8
1986	52.5	4.0	33.1	19.0
1987	51.2	4.6	36.2	19.2
1988	46.1	4.5	47.2	16.7
1989	40.8	15.3	44.7	19.1
1990	36.1	17.9	44.7	19.8
1991	35.6	14.3	44.4	19.2
1992	36.0	13.0	46.6	21.1
1993	47.6	11.2	49.8	18.6
1994	44.3	12.9	56.1	18.0
1995	45.2	12.9	51.8	16.7
1996	41.3	17.0	54.3	23.0
1997	40.3	15.8	61.9	22.1

SOURCE: Surveys conducted regularly by the *Jiji-tsu-shin-sha*, Tokyo.

Table 5.4   "How do you feel about the Soviet Union?" (%).

Response:	Favorable	Relatively Favorable	Relatively Unfavorable	Unfavorable	Don't Know	Total
1979	3.0	9.7	36.4	41.3	9.6	100
1980	1.9	6.0	36.9	47.5	7.7	100
1981	1.3	5.9	34.1	50.1	8.6	100
1982	1.3	6.7	38.5	44.6	8.9	100
1983	1.3	7.6	36.8	45.5	8.8	100
1984	1.2	6.4	37.2	48.4	6.8	100
1985	1.5	7.1	40.5	43.2	7.7	100
1986	1.9	7.0	39.9	44.0	7.2	100
1987	2.1	7.7	41.3	43.2	5.7	100
1988	3.1	11.0	43.6	36.1	5.4	100
1989	2.5	10.7	37.0	44.1	5.7	100
1990	3.8	19.5	43.9	26.9	5.9	100
1991	4.7	20.7	42.3	27.2	5.1	100
1992	2.8	12.4	36.5	43.1	5.2	100
1993	2.3	8.7	42.0	42.8	4.2	100
1994	2.6	9.1	38.7	45.5	4.2	100
1995	1.5	8.4	36.6	49.8	3.7	100
1996	1.4	8.9	39.0	45.8	4.8	100
1997	2.0	9.2	39.7	44.8	4.4	100

SOURCE: *Gaiko-ni kansuru Seron-chôsa* [Survey on public opinion concerning foreign policy] (Tokyo: Cabinet Office of the Prime Minister 1998), 46.

to the extent of the territories that should be returned to Japan, the JCP has been the maximalist: it demands the reversion of not only the four Northern Islands but also the entire Kuril Islands *(zen-chishima)*, all the way to the Kamchatka peninsula.[40]

In April 1991, Gorbachev paid an official visit to Japan as the Soviet president and the Communist Party general secretary, but this visit was very belated—the last among his visits to G-7 nations—and only four months before his virtual downfall in August of the same year. Russian President Boris Yeltsin's official visit to Tokyo in October 1993 was also received less enthusiastically than were his visits to other G-7 nations. This visit to Japan came almost one year after the sudden cancellation of his original plan to visit Tokyo in September 1992, which greatly infuriated the Japanese. One

40. Berton, "Soviet-Japanese Relations: Perceptions, Goals, Interactions," *Asian Survey* (December 1986): 1269; Joachim Glaubitz, *Between Tokyo and Moscow: The History of an Uneasy Relationship, 1972 to the 1990s* (London: Hurst and Company, 1995), 92.

reason that these two Russian "reformers" are not so popular in Japan is obviously because both of them accomplished far less than the Japanese had expected them to do vis-à-vis Japan particularly with regard to the territorial dispute.

LINKAGE OF POLITICS AND ECONOMICS

The relation between economics and politics in general and foreign/security policy in particular is very complicated, so complicated that its study is an almost permanent theme for all social scientists. The relation between economics and politics can be compared with that between an egg and a chicken. Politics are determined by economic factors and other substructures, although this relation has been overstated by Karl Marx, W. W. Rostow, and others. In return, the economy is determined to a great degree by politics, as frequently exemplified by practices of the Soviet Union and other "communist-oriented" countries with a dictatorial leadership. Thus, economics and politics affect each other.

There are two distinct approaches to linking economics and politics in Russo-Japanese relations. The distinction revolves around which should come first in Russo-Japanese relations: a settlement of the territorial dispute and a conclusion of a peace treaty or the expansion of bilateral economic cooperation. Debate has long been waged about whether the reversion to Japan of the Russian-held islands should be envisaged as a precondition to the development of economic exchanges or as a consequence of improved economic and other bilateral relations.

The former of the above two approaches, known as *iriguchi ron* ("entrance" approach), is the more conservative and has usually been the choice of Japanese governments, especially since the decline of Japanese interests in Soviet energy resources in the late 1970s to early 1980s. This position argues that both the Japanese and the Russian governments should do their utmost to solve the largest stumbling block, the Northern Territories problem, which has prevented these two countries from concluding a peace treaty. If the two governments successfully complete this task—this approach believes—Russia and Japan will thereafter inevitably develop and improve their relations in other fields. The second school, known as *deguchi ron* ("exit" approach), advocates, in contrast, that such thorny issues as the Northern Territories dispute between Russia and Japan cannot be solved in one single stroke but only by a gradual, step-by-step approach. This approach thus proposes that both countries first try to improve their bilateral relations in areas outside the territorial dispute, such as trade and other economic exchanges, fisheries, and cultural and personnel matters. The establishment of bilateral relations in such fields may, according to this school, eventually pave the way for a solution of the most difficult problem between Japan and Russia, boundary demarcation. The aforementioned proposal made by Russian Foreign Minister Evgenii Primakov during his visit to Japan in November 1996 to his Japanese counterpart Yukuhiko Ikeda can be regarded as a variant of the second approach.

In reference to these two possible approaches that can be adopted by the Japanese government, there are two caveats. First, when it comes to the nongovernment (i.e., private) sector, the matter is quite different. Although the Japanese government has been unable to take a very enthusiastic role in promoting economic relations with a country with which Japan has not yet established fully normalized diplomatic relations, such a self-restrained attitude has not necessarily been the case in Japanese private business sectors. Generally speaking, whenever a business opportunity presents itself, Japanese businesspeople seem eager to go anywhere in the world, whether to Africa or Siberia. They are willing to promote the establishment of close economic relations with Russia as long as they can make profits. This basic business philosophy is the norm for Japanese businesses, especially small- to middle-sized businesses. One ugly example of such a simple business philosophy is the so-called Toshiba Machine Company affair, which came to light in May 1987. In clear violation of the Coordinating Committee on Multilateral Export Controls (COCOM) regulations, Toshiba Machine Company sold to the Soviet Union precision-milling equipment to make quieter propellers for its nuclear submarines. Recently, however, without assistance or guarantees offered by the Japanese government, private companies in Japan are not so eager to conduct economic transactions with Russia. This is understandable in light of the fact that Russia's debts to Japan have grown to as much as U.S.$8 billion, if we include all of Russia's debts to Japan at the so-called Paris Club, London Club, and Tokyo Club. (Russia's external debt to all foreign countries is now estimated to be about U.S.$127 billion.)[41]

As long as the problem of the Northern Territories remains unsettled, there will always be resentment or ill-feeling among the Japanese people

---

41. Eleena Chinyaeva and Peter Rutland, "Profile: Viktor Chernomyrdin," *Transition* 3 (7 March 1997): 37; according to the June 4, 1995, issue of the *Washington Times*, the total debts amounted to U.S.$130 billion. *Washington Times*, 4 June 1995, A14.

toward Russians. Although most Japanese accept that Russia, which currently finds itself in the midst of chaos, is not now in a position to immediately return all four islands to Japan, they still feel unhappy about the fact that the Russians have not shown much serious intention to resolve this dispute with Japan. This unwillingness on the Russian side can be illustrated by a statement made by President Yeltsin after the devastating earthquake in May 1995 in the city of Neftegorsk, northern Sakhalin. The president stated that he would not welcome Japanese aid, because he feared that it would give the Japanese the leverage to demand the return of the islands.[42]

This psychological dissatisfaction among Japanese over Russia's attitude toward Japan about the dispute cannot fail to influence the Japanese government. The Tokyo government has been reluctant to use official government funds collected from Japanese taxpayers for the purpose of promoting economic relations between Russia and private business sectors in Japan. This accounts at least in part for the Japanese government's less enthusiastic attitude compared with other G-7 member states over the issue of economic assistance to the Soviet Union under Gorbachev and to Russia under Yeltsin. In terms of financial assistance to Russia, Japan, an economic superpower, occupies third place, behind Germany and the United States. Japan has lately been providing Russia with financial assistance of U.S.$6.1 billion.[43] Without the support of the Japanese general public for aid to Russia, the Tokyo government cannot become enthusiastic about providing a huge amount of economic assistance to Russia, particularly when the Tokyo government itself is suffering from its own huge national deficit.

Another caveat in reference to the above-mentioned theoretical distinction between the two approaches in linking political and economic aspects in Russo-Japanese relations ("entrance" and "exit" approaches) has in practice been blurred. The Japanese government has shown a tendency to interpret either very tightly or loosely the principle of the "inseparability of politics and economics" (*seikei fukabun*) depending on circumstances. More precisely, the Japanese government has chosen to assume a position somewhere between the "entrance" and "exit" approaches. For example, from the late 1960s to mid-1970s, when Prime Minister Kakuei Tanaka intended to promote economic cooperation between Japan and the Soviet Union, the Japanese government in fact loosened the ties of economic

---

42. BBC Monitoring, 1 June 1995.
43. Based on the publication as of January 1998 of the Russian Assistance Division, European and Oceanic Affairs Bureau, the Japanese Ministry of Foreign Affairs, Tokyo.

relations to the Northern Territories and other political issues. Tanaka, a pragmatic, economically minded politician, considered that for its fast-expanding economy, Japan needed the vast natural resources of Siberia and the Soviet Far East. The oil shocks in the mid-1970s justified Tanaka's judgment. Tanaka very likely also considered that the expansion of bilateral economic ties between Japan and the Soviet Union would help to soften Moscow's tough stand on the territorial question. Be that as it may, based on such considerations, five to seven large Japanese-Soviet joint projects dealing with economic cooperation in Siberia and the Soviet Far East were started, both before and after Tanaka's visit to Moscow in October 1973 to discuss the Northern Territories issue in his summit meeting with Soviet leader Leonid Brezhnev. These projects included the development and exploration of coal and natural gas in Yakutia and prospecting for oil and gas on the continental shelf off Sakhalin.

From the late 1970s to early 1980s, however, there were no new large projects between Japan and the Soviet Union because of domestic and international economic circumstances. In the wake of the two oil shocks in the mid-1970s, as already mentioned, Japan succeeded in restructuring its economy and reducing its dependence on the Soviet Union for energy and other raw materials. The mid-1980s also saw a dramatic decline in the international market price of oil. The reduction by Japan in its dependence on imported natural resources and the drop in international oil prices resulted in an ironic reversal of the positions of Japan and the Soviet Union. In their new positions, it was not Japan but the Soviet Union that needed to develop economic cooperation. The Soviet-Japanese economic relation revolved around Japanese credits, investment, and technological transfer to the Soviet Union. With its growing financial clout, Japan had ample funds that could have been made available to the Soviet Union. In the absence of any possibility of a settlement of the territorial dispute, however, the Japanese government did not consider a massive infusion of funds into the Soviet Union necessary. At any rate, through these developments, the Japanese government became freer to pursue the principle of linking economic and political issues in its relation with the Soviet Union.

With the ascent to power of Gorbachev in 1985, the new political thinking in foreign policy making generated a new expectation among the Japanese that Soviet leadership might seek a breakthrough to the long-standing dispute over the Northern Territories. Probably with an optimistic viewpoint, Sosuke Uno, Japanese foreign minister, made a diplomatic initiative in May 1989 in announcing a new Japanese approach, "expanded equilibrium" (*kakudai kinkō ron*). The important point in this new approach was that the Tokyo government still regarded the conclusion of a peace treaty for the solution of the Northern Territories dispute as its major objective, but at the same time it would give humanitarian, intellectual, technological, financial, and other economic aid to the Soviet Union in proportion to the degree of progress made on the territorial dispute. Uno's proposal indicated a willingness on the Japanese side to take the initiative in loosening the linkage of economic cooperation and assistance with progress on the territorial dispute, in the hope that such a slight modification in Japan's stance would better serve its ultimate political objective vis-à-vis the Soviet Union.

It is not completely clear, however, whether and to what extent this new approach or tactics represented a revision of Tokyo's traditional principle of "the inseparability of politics and economics": that is, no significant Japanese economic assistance to the Soviet Union without progress on the territorial dispute and a linkage between the amount of aid and the extent of Soviet concessions on the territorial issue. In contrast, however, Primakov's proposal of Russo-Japanese joint economic activities in the disputed Northern Islands, which the Russian foreign minister made to Ikeda during his stay in Tokyo in November 1996, can still be regarded as a variant of the "exit" approach. His proposal is based on the assumption that sovereignty of the disputed islands will not be transferred to Japan or even to joint ownership by both Russia and Japan, but will remain in Russian hands.

COMPARISON WITH CHINA

In many ways, post–World War II relations between Japan and the People's Republic of China contrast sharply with those between Japan and the Soviet Union/Russia. The policy of the inseparability of politics from economics is a good example. Japan has not tried to apply this policy to China in the way that it has vis-à-vis the Soviet Union. On the contrary, Japan has actually been trying for a long time in its relations with China to promote the opposite idea of the separability of politics from economics.

Why has Japan been pursuing these seemingly inconsistent, contradictory policies toward its two neighboring nations? There seem to be at least four major reasons for this.

The first reason is historical. Japan invaded China, whereas Japan was invaded by the Soviet Union. Japan started an aggressive war against China, a war in which many atrocities were committed by Japanese against Chinese. Many Japanese, particularly the older generation, still have deep feelings of guilt over their disgraceful conduct in China. In marked contrast, however, the Russians, in violation of the Soviet-Japanese Neutrality Pact, attacked Japan just after Japan had suffered the devastating atomic bombing of Hiroshima. This betrayal by the Soviet Union aroused very bitter feelings among the Japanese toward the Soviets. Moreover, the Soviet Union under Stalin took more than 600,000 Japanese as prisoners of war and used them for cheap labor, mainly in Siberia. About one-tenth of the 600,000 Japanese captured by the Soviet Union died while working under harsh conditions in frigid environments. The Soviet Union also seized the Northern Territories more than two weeks after Japan had accepted the Potsdam Declaration on August 15, 1945. In short, China was a victim of Japanese imperialism, whereas Japan was a victim of Russian expansionism. The Chinese side feels entitled to receive favorable treatment because of past wrongs from the war, for which it had not claimed reparations. It is natural that such a historical legacy would lead to two contrasting approaches by Japan vis-à-vis her two neighboring states.

The second reason that Japan's policy toward China greatly differs from that toward Russia has something to do with the de facto existence of the two Chinas, the People's Republic of China and Taiwan,[44] the republic of China (ROC). Japan's basic policy has been to try to maintain relations with both Chinas, which accords with history and with Japan's economic interests. Yet, the United States, whose foreign policy Japan usually follows, has, at least on paper, been taking a "one-China" policy. To make matters worse, U.S. policy has changed over time. Until the early 1970s, Washington recognized Taiwan as the only legitimate China and did not acknowledge the People's Republic. Then, early in the 1970s, it completely reversed its position. Each time, Tokyo had no choice but to faithfully follow Washington's China policy.

The third reason is economic or economically related. From Japanese businesspeople's point of view, China seems to offer a better economic partnership than does Russia. Traditionally, the Chinese market has been important for Japan. In the prewar years (1934–36), 23.8 percent of Japan's export trade and 14.1 percent of its import trade were with China.[45] Following the signing of the San Francisco Peace Treaty in 1951, Japan also con-

44. Michael Yahuda, *The International Politics of the Asia-Pacific, 1945–1995* (London: Routledge, 1996), 242.

45. Mikiso Hane, *Eastern Phoenix: Japan Since 1945* (Boulder, Colo.: Westview Press, 1996), 86.

cluded a peace treaty with Taiwan, but Japanese businesspeople also wanted to have trade and economic relations with the People's Republic, with which their government did not have diplomatically normalized relations. In response to such a request from Japanese businesspeople, the Tokyo government proposed a principle of "separability of politics from economics" (*seikei bunri*) for the People's Republic. For its part, China seemed intent on pursuing a principle of the "inseparability of politics and economics" in its effort to induce Tokyo to acknowledge it as the sole legitimate state of China. Beijing was in a difficult position to adhere strictly and consistently to this principle, because it was also interested in developing economic ties with Japan, particularly because Beijing's relation with Moscow began to deteriorate from the mid-1950s.

In the early 1970s, Tokyo switched its Chinese partnership from Taipei to Beijing, faithfully following the policy shift made by the U.S. diplomatic team headed by Nixon and Kissinger. When Tokyo concluded a peace treaty with Beijing in 1978, thereby establishing normalized bilateral relations, a territorial dispute over the sovereignty of a small group of rocky islands between Japan and the People's Republic, the Senkaku (in Chinese, Diaoyutai) Islands did not become a constraint to Tokyo at all. Tokyo and Beijing decided to leave debate over the sovereignty of the islands to future generations. The Tokyo government was not in a position to oppose the proposal to shelve the territorial issue, because an agreement to maintain the status quo of the islands was advantageous to Japan and was in accord with its national interests. It was not the People's Republic but Japan that had virtual control of the islands. In sharp contrast, a similar way of solving the Northern Territories issue will never be acceptable to Tokyo, because it is not Japan but Russia that currently controls the islands. As far as Japan's relations with both Chinas are concerned, a clever formula was found by which Japan established formal diplomatic relations with Beijing, while still maintaining an ostensibly unofficial mission in Taipei, through which Japan was able to continue to maintain trading, economic, cultural, and other relations with the Republic of China.

The fourth reason was that Japan is more eager to establish economic and other relations with China than with Russia lies with the complicated, even emotionally charged, mixed feelings of superiority and inferiority held by the Japanese, which stem from Japan's cultural indebtedness to China and Japan's greater economic modernization. To illustrate the difference in Japanese feelings toward Russia and China, compare the Japanese reaction toward Yeltsin's bombardment of the Russian White House on October 4, 1993, and Deng Xiaoping's killing of demonstrators in Tiananmen Square on June 4, 1989. Following the latter incident, the United States imposed three kinds of sanctions against China, including an end to high-level exchanges, a termination of concessionary loans and grants, and a call to halt all military exchanges and sales of military or military-related technology to the People's Republic.[46] The United States did not, however, react to the Russian leadership in the same way after Yeltsin's order to bombard the parliament building in October 1993 and after the military invasion of Chechnya in December 1994. Washington was criticized for adopting a double standard.[47] Japan, for its part, did not share U.S. enthusiasm for imposing sanctions on China following the Tiananmen Square massacre.

For whatever reasons, since 1993, Japan has become China's most important trading partner. In 1995, Japanese imports from China accounted for 10.7 percent of Japan's total imports, making it the second largest importer from China next to the United States (22.8 percent of total imports). In the same year, Japan occupied seventeenth place in the list of importers from Russia (only 0.3 percent of total imports). On the export side, Japan was the sixth largest exporter to China in 1995 (accounting for 5.0 percent of Japan's total exports) and the thirty-fourth largest exporter to Russia (1.4 percent of total exports). Japan was also the first of the G-7 countries to resume Official Development Assistance (ODA) to China. Since 1993, the People's Republic has occupied first place in the list of recipient countries of Japan's ODA, receiving more than 15 percent of Japan's worldwide total ODA.[48]

The fifth reason that Japan has adopted a different approach toward China is related to a tacit agreement about the division of labor among G-7 countries. There has recently been much debate in the West, particularly in Washington, about how the West should react to the increasingly expansion-oriented and even aggressive stance of China. The debate centers on whether the most appropriate policy toward Beijing should be one of "containment" or "engagement." As long as Beijing behaves itself reasonably, the West's policy is simple: the People's Republic should be encouraged as much as possible to become an active member of the world community. When Beijing does not behave itself—for instance, by massacring demonstrators in Tiananmen Square, repeatedly conducting nuclear experiments despite worldwide protest, and engaging in saber rattling in

46. Yahuda, *International Politics*, 282.

47. *Newsweek: International Herald Tribune*, 5 October 1993.

48. *Japan's ODA: Annual Report 1995* (Tokyo: Economic Cooperation Bureau, Ministry of Foreign Affairs, 1996), 10, 102.

the Taiwan Strait—Western industrialized countries are forced to demonstrate their disapproval of such misconduct by imposing economic sanctions and/or other appropriate measures against China.

In the latter situation, Japan's position is usually to try to resolve the dilemma by playing "dual roles."[49] On one hand, as a member nation of the G-7, Japan joins the West in condemning, and even in imposing sanctions on, Beijing, while on the other hand, Japan tries not to isolate China too much from the international community and even to pave the way for China's return to the community. Japan has shown its willingness to act as mediator between China and the Western world, by sending a message to the West that an isolated, chaotic China might bring more harm to the peace and security of the international community. To play such a role, Japan lifts its freeze on ongoing aid projects to China and may even approve new grants, thereby moving one step ahead of other nations in improving its relations with China and helping to create a climate for other nations to follow Japan's example.[50]

Japan is not completely immune from criticism, however. Some may veiw Japan as undertaking easy, comfortable, and even profitable tasks, while leaving the hard and dirty tasks to the United States and other Western countries. If every country chose to play the same role that Japan does, what results would be gained? One justification for Japan's stance, however, is that Japan would be the most severely affected by an unstable, chaotic China in terms of economic damage, a flood of refugees, nuclear fallout, and so on. In this respect, Japan's policy on China is similar to Germany's policy on Russia: both Japan's and Germany's policies toward their neighboring giants appear to be extremely lenient in the eyes of other nations.

THE EFFECTIVENESS OF POSITIVE
ECONOMIC SANCTIONS

When debating the impact of economic interdependence on politics and foreign policy, scholars once assumed that the Soviet Union, a resource-rich country, had political leverage over resource-poor Japan. Since the early 1980s, however, this situation has been reversed. Now, the appropriate

49. Quansheng Zao, *Japanese Policymaking: The Politics Behind Politics: Informal Mechanisms and the Making of China Policy* (Westport, Conn.: Praeger, 1993), 165–67.
50. Zao, *Japanese Policymaking,* 175.

point to discuss is how successfully Japan, the world's second largest economic power, can use its advanced technology, huge capital endowments, and other economic capabilities as bargaining leverage to achieve its foreign policy objectives.

As far as development of the Soviet Union as well as of Siberia and the far eastern part of the Soviet Union were concerned, the active participation of Japan was essential, according to Allen Whiting, who wrote as early as 1980:

> Japan must weigh heavily in Moscow's decision on the development of East Asia Siberia. Japanese capital and technology are essential in attaining the desired goals of resource extraction and economic expansion. Japan also offers the only market of significance for exports like timber, coal, and gas. Without that market the products of East Asian Siberia have little chance of earning foreign exchange to serve the overall Soviet economy. *Japan thus occupies a central position in Moscow's calculations, in inputs as well as outputs*[51] (emphasis added).

Such an essential role for Japan's economic and technological potentialities in the Soviet economy often tempted some Western observers to draw rather sweeping conclusions. In 1982, for example, Seweryn Bialer went so far as to make the bold prediction that the Soviets could court Japan by returning to the Japan-Soviet Joint Declaration of 1956, which would "allow the return of the southernmost Kurile Islands to Japan in return for a new Japanese agreement to help develop Siberia."[52] What an otherwise astute observer of Soviet conduct in foreign affairs overlooked when it came to Soviet behavior in the Far East was that the economy was not the sole determinant of Soviet foreign policy, precisely the point that Bialer made elsewhere.[53]

51. Allen S. Whiting, *Siberian Development and East Asia: Threat or Promise?* (Stanford: Stanford University Press, 1981), 112; and Marshall I. Goldman, *The Enigma of Soviet Petroleum: Half-Empty or Half-Full?* (London: George Allen and Unwin, 1980), 112.

52. *Christian Science Monitor*, 8 November 1982. In an interview with *Newsweek* magazine, when asked "Do you think the Soviets would be willing to consider giving the Kurile islands back to Japan?", Bialer replied: "Yes. Japan is one of the natural partners of the Soviet Union in developing the richness of Siberian resources. Their policy with regard to Japan has been very unimaginative, if not stupid. Maybe a new leadership will have the flexibility to try to reach some compromise with Japan that will enable Japan to have better relations with the Soviet Union and to invest in Siberia." *Newsweek*, 11 October 1982, 60.

53. Bialer, ed., *The Domestic Context of Soviet Foreign Policy* (Boulder, Colo.: Westview Press, 1981), particularly 409–41.

Later, a few specialists raised an interesting question. Why has Japan failed to use its economic clout to "purchase" the Northern Territories from the Soviet Union or Russia, in view of West Germany's successful de facto purchase of East Germany by which it finally achieved its objective of uniting the two parts of divided Germany?[54] The unification of Germany, the Northern Territories dispute, and the unification of the two Koreas—these are three major problems considered to be the most difficult issues to be resolved by the end of the twentieth century. Yet, the first problem was suddenly solved with the demise of the Cold War in 1989–91, whereas the remaining two are yet to be resolved.

Japan and Germany have many things in common: defeat in World War II; rapid recovery from ashes to economic prosperity; achieving the second and third largest economies in the world; a close alliance with the United States; and membership in G-7. These remarkable similarities tempt one to make a test case for studying the role of economic power in world affairs in general and the effective use of "positive economic sanctions"[55] against the Soviet Union/Russia in particular. Moreover, the question raised earlier about why Japan failed whereas Germany succeeded appears to be more justified when one takes into consideration the following two dissimilarities between Japan and Germany. First, in terms of recent relations with the Soviet Union, Germany was a military invader in World War II, whereas Japan was a victim of Soviet invasion in violation of the Soviet-Japanese Neutrality Pact. Second, in terms of the geographic sizes of the territories that Japan and West Germany requested or are requesting the Soviet Union/Russia to relinquish, East Germany is far larger than the total land area of the Northern Territories.

For these and other reasons, I agree with Tuomas Forsberg and Randall Newnham that a comparative study of Germany's success and Japan's failure may provide an interesting case study and even a useful lesson to Japan.

54. Tuomas Forsberg's unpublished paper titled "The Effectiveness of Positive Economic Sanctions: A Comparison of German Success and Japanese Failure Against the Soviet Union/Russia" (1994) and Randall Newnham's unpublished paper titled "How to Win Friends and Influence People: A Comparison of German and Japanese Linkage Policies" (1996) are two examples of studies focused on this question. Forsberg is currently the director of the Finnish Institute of International Affairs, Helsinki, who prepared the paper for the Sixteenth World Congress of the International Political Science Association, held in Berlin on August 21–25, 1994. Newnham is affiliated with Pennsylvania State University.

55. With regard to the kinds and roles of "positive economic sanctions" in influencing international actors, see, for instance, David Baldwin, *Economic Statecraft* (Princeton: Princeton University Press, 1985), 40–42; Russett and Henry Starr, *World Politics: The Menu for Choice,* 4th ed. (New York: Freeman, 1992), 171–175.

I especially consider very interesting both scholars' suggestion to Japan that the Japanese government should use its economic advantage in a more "subtle," "indirect" fashion with regard to its dispute with Russia over the Northern Territories, by expanding economic ties to Russia[56] "without explicit political preconditions (general linkage),"[57] because what the Russians are more concerned about than anything else is the loss of face. In this regard, the idea of Masamori Sase, Japanese specialist on German affairs at the National Defense Academy, is close to those of Forsberg and Newnham. Sase has acknowledged that the deutsche mark played an important role in contributing to Gorbachev's shift to a positive position with regard to two issues, unification and North Atlantic Treaty Organization (NATO) membership, for Germany. Sase has not, however, failed to underline the fact that Bonn acted extremely carefully so that Gorbachev[58] was not criticized at home for resolving the issues in return for deutsche marks.[59] The Russians were concerned that their assent to Japan's request for the reversion of the islands should not be interpreted domestically and internationally as their de facto capitulation to the Japanese yen. No wonder that in March 1991 Ichirô Ozawa, a powerful Japanese politician and secretary general of the Liberal Democratic Party (LDP) at that time, failed to make a deal with Gorbachev, when the former was reported to have made a proposal to the latter on Japan's de facto purchase of the disputed islands from the Soviet Union for 26–28 billion yen.[60]

Despite these excellent points, Forsberg's and Newnham's attempts to compare Germany and Japan do not seem to be very meaningful; the experiences of these two countries vis-à-vis the Soviet Union/Russia do not really have a great deal in common. The point with which I most disagree is their association of the former West Germany's economic assistance to the Soviet Union with the political result of sudden unification of Ger-

56. Newnham, "How to Win Friends," 15, 18–19.

57. Newnham, "How to Win Friends," 3–4.

58. At that time, Gorbachev was cautioning German leaders and saying: "We must use a wise word, in order to be received." Theo Waigel and Manfred Schnell, *Tage, die Deutschland und die Welt veränderten: Vom Mauerfall zum Kaukasus: Die deutsche Währungsunion* (Munich: Bruckmann, 1994), 46.

59. Masamori Sase, "Doitsu-tōitsu to 'ni purasu yon' Kōshō" [The German unification and "two plus four" negotiations], *Bōeidaigaku kiyō (shakai kagaku-hen)* (Yokosuka: National Defense Academy, no. 75, September 1997), 50–54.

60. Glaubitz, *Between Tokyo and Moscow*, 208; William F. Nimmo, *Japan and Russia: A Reevaluation in the Post-Soviet Era* (Westport, Conn.: Greenwood Press, 1994), 91; Hiroshi Kimura, *Sōketsusan Gorubachofu no Gaikō* [The final balance sheet of Gorbachev's diplomacy] (Tokyo: Kobundo, 1993), 272.

many. Although it may have facilitated or even accelerated the process of unification, I do not believe that West Germany's economic assistance to the Soviet Union was the major factor that initiated the unification process. Furthermore, I do not consider that German unity was a consequence of changes in Gorbachev's policy toward the German problem, although it did have something to do with the policy of perestroika that the Communist Party's general secretary started.[61] Rather, this development was, in my view, due to almost unpredictable and even accidental events.[62] The dynamism generated behind perestroika went beyond the bounds of what individual political leaders, such as Mikhail Gorbachev or Helmut Kohl, understood as perestroika.[63] Residents of East Germany had been conducting day and night demonstrations, which developed into an unstoppable, never-ending flow of people who suddenly realized that they were on the western side of the Berlin Wall. This was the true nature of the event, which political leaders were forced to acknowledge as a fait accompli.[64] Gorbachev, as well as Western leaders, failed to anticipate the nearly inevitable outcome that followed in the wake of the opening of the Berlin Wall and German unification.[65] The Gorbachev government repeatedly reacted too timidly and too late without a defined position or a policy dealing with the

61. For a similar view, see, for example, the following: Mikhail Gorbachev, *Zhizn' i reformy* [Life and Reform] (Moscow: Novostii, 1995), vol. 2, 150–79; Hannes Adomeit, *Imperial Overstretch: Germany in Soviet Policy from Stalin to Gorbachev* (Baden-Baden: Nomos, 1998), 215–71, 441–46; Philip Zelikovsky and Condoleezza Rice, *Germany Unified and Europe Transformed: A Study in Statecraft* (Cambridge: Harvard University Press, 1997), 33, 62, 88, 109; Avril Pittman, *From Ostpolitik to Reunification: West German-Soviet Political Relations Since 1974* (Cambridge: Cambridge University Press, 1992), 160–65.

62. In his memoirs, Gorbachev acknowledged that he was surprised by the course of events in Germany in the late 1980s: "I should be less than sincere if I said that I had foreseen the course of events and the problems the German question would eventually create for Soviet foreign policy. As a matter of fact, I doubt whether any of today's politicians (in either East or West) could have predicted the outcome only a year or two beforehand. After the radical changes that had taken place in the German Democratic Republic, the situation developed at such breathtaking speed that there was a real danger that it would get out of control" Gorbachov, *Zhizn' i reformy*, vol. 2, 150; Gorbachev, *Memoirs* (New York: Doubleday, 1995), 516; Adomeit, *Imperial Overstretch*, 215.

63. When Helmut Kohl was asked in October 1988 whether Gorbachev might someday offer unity to the Germans, Kohl was scornful. "I do not write futuristic novels like [H. G.] Wells," he replied. "What you ask now, this is in the realm of fantasy." Zelikoysky and Rice, *Germany Unified*, 62.

64. Adomeit also argued that "it was essentially the force of events that persuaded him [Gorbachev] to act as he did but even then, at no time . . . did he actively *promote* German unification" (Adomeit's italics). Adomeit, *Imperial Overstretch*, 218.

65. Adomeit also observed that "Gorbachev's reactions were shaped by wishful thinking and an astounding misreading of developments." Adomeit, *Imperial Overstretch*, 445.

issue of German unity.[66] It was thus forced to settle for a small fraction of the financial assistance that could have been realized as a result of unification.[67] In short, Forsberg and Newnham were hasty in their tendency to link economics with politics; they neglected other factors, as a result of which their view is another version of the simplistic fallacy of economic determinism.

KRASNOYARSK AND AFTER

The unofficial Japanese-Russian summit held on November 1–2, 1997, at Krasnoyarsk, an eastern Siberian city, halfway between Tokyo and Moscow, turned out to be an epoch-making event in recent bilateral relations between Japan and Russia. On that occasion, two important agreements were reached by Japanese Prime Minister Ryutaro Hashimoto and Russian President Boris Yeltsin.

The first is an agreement to make maximum efforts to conclude a peace treaty by the year 2000. This agreement marked a diplomatic victory on the Japanese side. The Japanese and even many Russians understand that a peace treaty would contain a clause about the demarcation of national borders, thereby putting an end to the territorial dispute (in the case of a Russo-Japanese peace treaty resolving the Northern Territories). Yeltsin was not opposed to Hashimoto's understanding that a peace treaty between Japan and Russia should be concluded on the basis of the Tokyo Declaration, which pleased the Japanese side. It was also a pleasant surprise for the Japanese side that no one other than the Russian president himself took

66. Adomeit, *Imperial Overstretch*, 448–49.

67. Before West Germany's "acquisition" of the German Democratic Republic in 1990, West Germans were making under-the-table payments to buy freedom for East Germans at an average price of $50,000 per immigrant. At the moment of reunification, there were some sixteen million people in East Germany. At the going price, that totals $800 billion. Land and other physical assets were severely damaged, but at auction they could have commanded a price in the hundreds of billions. As it happened, Gorbachev delayed negotiations about money to cover the costs, distributions, and national losses from Soviet withdrawal from East Germany until after the outcome was no longer in doubt. From gratitude and the need to relocate 370,000 Soviet troops stationed in Germany, the German government provided approximately only $34 billion in economic assistance.
In July 1991 at Zheleznovodsk, Koh/ and Gorbachev announced that Germany could join NATO in exchange for West Germany's economic concessions to the Soviet Union. It seems that West Germany pledged aid to the Soviet economy totaling five billion deutsche marks. Pittman, *From Ostopolitik to Reunification*, 164; Sase, "Doitsu-tōitsu," 51; Horst Teltschik, *329 Tage Innenansichten der Einigung* (Berlin: Siedler, 1991), 314, 325.

the initiative in setting a concrete deadline for the future conclusion of a peace treaty, the year 2000. This initiative amazed many Japanese, who are used to believing that the Russians are not usually fond of working in a definite timetable, but instead postpone almost endlessly.

Another significant agreement reached at Krasnoyarsk was the so-called Hashimoto–Yeltsin Plan. Although this plan covers a wide range of political, economic, and financial dimensions of Russo-Japanese bilateral cooperation, a pledge for Japan to provide Russia with economic aid to a more positive degree and on a more massive scale than before has a central place. There is no need to add, therefore, that this part of the Krasnoyarsk package of agreements pleased the Russians more than anything else. Assistance to be provided by Japan to Russia, according to the agreement, includes the following: the Japanese government's guarantee of protecting Japanese private sectors' investments in Russia; Japanese assistance with the managing and training programs of Russian business executives; Japan's cooperation for the modernization of the Trans-Siberian Railway.[68]

To recapitulate, a diplomatic breakthrough at the first-ever Russo-Japanese "meeting without neckties" at Krasnoyarsk was nothing but a package deal, consisting of two main parts: a *political* pledge to do their utmost for the conclusion of a peace treaty between the two neighboring countries, the part that the Japanese side is more excited about than the Russians, and a promise of more *economic* exchange, cooperation, and aid between these countries, the part that the Russian side is interested in. Here naturally a question arises; why did such a deal become possible at this time? There may be a number of answers to this question. Let us divide the factors that helped make the Krasnoyarsk agreement possible into three types: precipitating, intermediate, and deep.[69]

The most important precipitating cause of the Krasnoyarsk agreement was personal in nature, the match in "chemistry" between the two top leaders, Hashimoto and Yeltsin.

The deep historical forces driving the two leaders, particularly Yeltsin, to the acceptance of such package deals between Russia and Japan were perhaps due to the changes in the international environment taking place since the end of the Cold War in general, and hence in Russia's recent foreign policy orientation in particular. There is neither space nor need to

68. For more details of the Hashimoto–Yeltsin Plan, see, for example, BBC Monitoring Service, 3 November 1997, B/7–8.

69. On this kind of classification, I have borrowed Nye's useful system for the purpose of discussing the cause of the end of the Cold War. Nye, *Understanding International Conflicts: An Introduction to Theory and History* (New York: HarperCollins, 1993), 116–19.

dwell on the details of these changes here; a brief summary suffices. First, a shift in Russia's diplomatic orientation from "Atlanticism" to "Eurasianism"[70]: the Yeltsin leadership's disillusionment with the West became evident when NATO decided to expand eastward in the spring of 1997; finding itself alone and an outsider in Europe, Russia decided to seek new partners—in the East. Second, the Russians' uneasy feelings about China's growing economic and political power[71]: even though the current Russian administration is publicly pursuing amicable relations with the People's Republic of China, as illustrated by the catchphrase "Sino-Russian strategic partnership," there is a deep-rooted wariness or fear of China among the Russian people. The primary reasons are the geographic factor of a border of nearly 4,300 kilometers between Russia and China; a history of conflicts between the two nations accompanied by bloodshed; the huge disparity in population; the differences in the Chinese and Russian approaches to reform; and the difficulties and crises that will certainly result from China's future economic development, growth, and improvement in living standards, including the pressures that will be placed on Russian and worldwide energy resources and the consequent environmental problems.[72] Third, the trend in Russia toward putting more emphasis on economic calculations: the Yeltsin administration's recent foreign policy decisions are increasingly driven by considerations of economic gain and loss. Konstantin Sarkisov, the director of the Center for Japanese Studies, Institute of Oriental Studies, Russian Academy of Sciences, is essentially in agreement with this interpretation, when he wrote: "In exchanging our *romantic-democratic* slogans for *national-patriotic* ones, Russia does not gain anything. It is time to go over to a *pragmatic* conception of foreign policy—that is the only chance for survival" (emphasis added).[73]

For these three, and other reasons, Russian foreign policy under Yeltsin has recently shifted to one that aims to move closer to Japan and increasingly pays more attention to Japan's economic clout and even its politico-

70. For a discussion of "Atlanticism," "Eurasianism," their advocates, and the gradual shift of Yeltsin's diplomacy from the former to the latter, refer to Hiroshi Kimura, "The Russian Decision-Making Process Towards Japan," *Japan Review* (Kyoto: International Research Center for Japanese Studies), no. 7 (1996): 61–63.

71. For more detail on this point, see Hiroshi Kimura, "Russia's Eurasian Diplomacy and Japan" (unpublished paper read at the "International Symposium '97" held in Fukui, Japan, November 1997).

72. Mikhail Titarenko, "Kitai v postdenovskuiu epokhy i rosiisko-kitaiskie otonosheniia," *MZ*, no. 8 (August 1995): 27–36.

73. Konstantin Sarkisov, "Na vostochnom fronte bez peremen?" *Moscovskie novosti*, 8 October 1995, 5.

diplomatic utility vis-à-vis the West, headed by the United States, and China. Observing this change in Russia's policy orientation, the Hashimoto administration has been responding to Moscow's foreign policy catchphrase "Russia's Eurasian diplomacy viewed from the Atlantic," with the similar one, "Japan's Eurasian diplomacy viewed from the Pacific."

The intermediate reason that a package deal became possible had to do with a change in strategy or tactics, employed to achieve the ultimate objectives, particularly those of Japan. In his speech of July 24 1997, Japanese Prime Minister Hashimoto announced three guiding principles in Japan-Russian relations, "trust," "mutual benefit," and "a long-term perspective".[74] With regard to the territorial disputes between these two countries, he stated: "The Northern Territories issue is a matter which our nations have been unable to solve in fifty years. Obviously, it is very difficult to solve it." Lest his "long-term" principle be misinterpreted, the Japanese prime minister made it clear that the Northern Territories issue should not be left for the next generation. Nonetheless, without paying much attention to this part of Hashimoto's speech, some Russians have gone so far as to intentionally or unintentionally interpret this speech as a turning point to separate the Northern Territories problem from other issues and to temporarily shelve the territorial dispute and give preference to economic exchange and cooperation.[75]

Are politics and economics now under Hashimoto's administration decoupled, as some Russians interpret it, or still linked with each other? My answer is that these two areas are no longer linked in a direct, tight fashion and yet are still linked in an indirect, more sophisticated way. The Tokyo government has perhaps picked up a lesson from Forsberg and Newnham. Immediately on his return to Tokyo on November 3, 1997, Hashimoto went out of his way to contact the German chancellor, Helmut Kohl, to convey the Japanese prime minister's appreciation for the German chancellor's advice about how to deal with the Russian president.[76] This episode reveals that the Japanese prime minister has tried to learn a valuable lesson from the German experience. At any rate, since the Krasnoyarsk meeting, the Hashimoto administration has been fulfilling with enthusiasm and promptness the Hashimoto–Yeltsin Plan—even to such an extent that Sergei Yastrzhembskii, Yeltsin's presidential press secretary, expressed gratitude to

74. The Russian translation of Hashimoto's speech appeared in the 12 August 1997 issue of *Nezavisimaya gazeta*.

75. For example, *Nezavisimaya gazeta*, 29 July, 30 July and 12 August 1997; *Komsomol'skaya pravda*, 29 July 1997, and *Izvestiya*, 16 August 1997.

76. *Asahi Shimbun* and *Yomiuri Shimbun*, 4 November 1997.

the "Japanese side and to the Japanese government for practical steps to implement the Yeltsin–Hashimoto plan, which is not only on paper but is being implemented."[77] The Hashimoto government has been doing so intentionally in the hope that then, and probably only then, the Yeltsin government will be deprived of an excuse for sitting idly with folded arms, not concluding a peace treaty by 2000. In this sophisticated way, the Hashimoto government has been linking its *economic* cooperation to Russia with its *political* objective. Furthermore, it is also understood that Tokyo's generous offers of economic assistance and cooperation to Russia will continue only until 2000. For example, an untied loan granted by the Export-Import Bank of Japan to Russia in the amount of U.S.$1.5 billion is effective only during the years of 1998 and 1999, not beyond that—that is to say, if the possibility of concluding a treaty should fade away.

The second informal "no-necktie" summit between Hashimoto and Yeltsin was launched at the seaside resort town of Kawana, Shizuoka prefecture, 130 kilometers southwest of Tokyo, on April 18–19, 1998. The meeting was not expected to achieve a breakthrough, because the two leaders had already made a major breakthrough in Japanese-Russian relations at Krasnoyarsk. Yet the Kawana summit also proved to be an important event in bilateral relations in the following sense. To begin with, it further deepened personal ties between the two leaders. The fact that the Russian president went out of his way to visit Japan, despite his much-needed presence in Moscow during a period of political uncertainty and confusion, underlines the importance that Yeltsin places on relations with Japan. Thanks to his visit, the momentum for a high-level exchange between these two countries has been maintained. Furthermore, Japan and Russia seem to be successful in making proposals that help make their positions more acceptable to, or their requests stronger vis-à-vis, each other.

On the Japanese side, the following three actions may be counted as achievements: Both leaders confirmed their previously made agreement that Japan and Russia would do their utmost to conclude a peace treaty by the year 2000, based on the Tokyo Declaration. This time, Hashimoto not only repeated the above pledge but also made one important additional remark clear: the Japanese-Russian peace treaty should contain the settlement of the ownership issue over the four islands, which will be based on the second clause of the Tokyo Declaration. The second clause of the Tokyo Declaration, which was signed by President Yeltsin and then Prime Minister Morihiro Hosokawa, in October 1993, reads as follows: "Both na-

---

77. BBC Monitoring Service, 26 January 1998, B/16.

tions [Japan and Russia] agree to the early conclusion of a peace treaty through the resolution of the issue [concerning ownership of Etorofu Island, Kunashiri Island, Shikotan Island, and the Habomai group of islets], based upon law and justice." Yeltsin said that the efforts toward the conclusion of a peace treaty lagged behind the progress achieved by the two leaders on the bilateral relation. He even indicated that he will give a political push to Russian officials involved in working-level negotiations on the proposed treaty. To be sure, these statements by Yeltsin may be interpreted as lip service, yet it cannot be completely ruled out that he uttered what he really thinks. Most important, Hashimoto made to the Russian president a new serious proposal about a peace treaty. Although both leaders declined to elaborate on its details, the gist of the proposal appears to be this: the demarcation line between Russia and Japan is to be set north of the group of four disputed islands; Russia can continue to exercise administrative powers over the islands for a specified period, during which Japan and Russia can run joint economic activities on the islands. The thrust of this proposal is psychologically more acceptable to Russians than the previous outright call by Japan for the immediate return of sovereignty. The Russian president said that he would "seriously study this proposal," adding further that he had an "optimistic feeling" about it.

Seen from the Russian side, the Kawana talks turned out to be a great success as well. The Japanese side agreed to the Russian proposal that a peace treaty should be made more comprehensive—to such an extent that it will cover not only settlement of the territorial dispute but also a broader range of issues, such as economic and cultural cooperation. As a result, the peace treaty will be called a treaty of peace, friendship, and cooperation; Yeltsin's new proposal for joint economic activities on the disputed islands was also accepted de facto by Hashimoto, on the condition that Japan consider the project "in parallel with" negotiations on the peace treaty. As an example of such joint activities, the Russian president mentioned large-scale facilities for processing marine products, infrastructure, roads, ports, and airports on the disputed territories. Yeltsin obtained from Hashimoto the assurance of more actively fulfilling the Hashimoto–Yeltsin Plan, including the release of U.S.$600 million in commercial loans to Russia in 1998 as part of a plan, announced in February 1998, to lend $1.5 billion over the next two years.

Finally, how is what happened at the Kawana summit meeting related to the central theme of this chapter: the relation between politics and economics? Put simply, Japanese Prime Minister Hashimoto became confident in applying in a more sophisticated fashion the Japanese traditional strategy of the inseparability of politics and economics. While further loosening the linkage of the Northern Territories issue and economic cooperation and assistance, Hashimoto did not demonstrate any intention to decouple these two fields. In the joint press conference after the Kawana meeting, the Japanese prime minister said: "Japan would not subscribe to the kind of relationship where we say, 'You do this for me and then we do that for you.' "[78] What Hashimoto implied was that Japan would not base its relations with Russia on a "land for money" attitude.[79] At the same time, however, Hashimoto did not fail to add the following words: "Our relationship would be the kind of the one, where 'I will do this and you will do that, so that we shall build the better future.' "[80] What Hashimoto indirectly implied was that Japan does not request an immediate return of the disputed islands from Russia, and yet without cooperative efforts from Russia, Japanese-Russian relations will not be improved. It remains to be seen whether Hashimoto's strategy of more sophisticated linkage between politics and economics is successful in the near future.

78. *Asahi Evening News,* 20 April 1998.
79. *Asahi Evening News,* 20 April 1998.
80. *Asahi Shimbun,* 20 April 1998.

6

Explaining Russia's Interest in Building Security Mechanisms in the East Asia Region:

Realism and Neoliberal Institutionalism

Eunsook Chung

A new era of transition in the East Asia region offers epistemological challenges to international relations scholars who are attempting to define when and under what conditions cooperation occurs. In the case of Russia, how can we explain its increased interest in building regional security institutions in the East Asia region? Scholars' responses to this question differ according to the underlying basic assumptions of their theoretical orientations.

In recent years, there has been a vigorous debate about the problem of international cooperation. In the United States, this debate has involved realist theory, as articulated by scholars such as Robert Gilpin, Kenneth Waltz, and Stephen Krasner, and neoliberalism, the work of scholars such as Robert Keohane, Arthur Stein, Charles Lipson, and Robert Axelrod.[1] For realists, international anarchy fosters competition and conflict among states and inhibits their willingness to cooperate even when they share common interests. Hence, realism presents a pessimistic analysis of the prospects for international cooperation and of the capabilities of international institutions.[2] For neoliberal institutionalists, even if anarchy constrains the willingness of states to cooperate, states nevertheless can work together and can do so especially with the assistance of international institutions.

This chapter compares both schools' basic assumptions on cooperation to analyze Russia's increased interest in building regional security institutions in the East Asia region. Russia's adventure eastward began in the sixteenth century with its conquest of Siberia's Tatar Khan. Russia is a legitimate northeast Asian country; Siberia occupies almost one-third of the land mass of Asia, yet it has been isolated from regional contact and exchanges. First, its capitals (St. Petersburg and Moscow) are located far from the region. Second, during Cold War days, under military-strategic purposes, it was difficult to have normal development and participate in the regional integration as a Pacific country. Third, Russia culturally shares with European countries, not Asian countries, Christian civilization.[3] When

1. Robert Gilpin, *U.S. Power and the Multinational Corporation: The Political Economy of Foreign Direct Investment* (New York: Basic Books, 1975); Gilpin, *War and Change in World Politics* (Cambridge: University Press, 1981); Gilpin, *The Political Economy of International Relations* (Princeton: Princeton University Press, 1987); Kenneth N. Waltz, *Theory of International Politics* (Reading, Mass: Addison-Wesley, 1979); Waltz, "Reflections on Theory of International Politics: A Response to My Critics," in Robert O. Keohane, ed., *Neorealism and Its Critics* (New York: Columbia University Press, 1986); Stephen D. Krasner, "Global Communications and National Power: Life on the Pareto Frontier," *World Politics* 43 (April 1991): 336–66; Keohane, "The Demand of Regimes," in Krasner, ed., *International Regimes* (Ithaca: Cornell University Press, 1983); Keohane, *After Hegemony: Cooperation and Discord in the World Political Economy* (Princeton: Princeton University Press, 1984); Arthur A. Stein, "Cooperation and Collaboration: Regimes in an Anarchic World," in Krasner, ed., *International Regimes;* Charles Lipson, "International Cooperation in Economic and Security Affairs," *World Politics* 37 (October 1984): 1–23; Robert Axelrod, *The Evolution of Cooperation* (New York: Basic Books, 1984); Axelrod and Keohane, "Achieving Cooperation Under Anarchy: Strategies and Institutions," *World Politics* 38 (October 1985): 226–54.

2. For realism's pessimistic view of the human condition, see Hans Morgenthau, *Scientific Man Versus Power Politics* (Chicago: University of Chicago Press, 1946). Among the realists, however, some like Charles L. Glaser, envision the optimistic view of cooperation as self-help. See Charles L. Glaser, "Realists as Optimists: Cooperation as Self-Help," *International Security* 19 (Winter 1994–95): 50–90.

3. See, for details, Nicolai N. Petrov and Alvin Z. Rubinstein, *Russian Foreign Policy: From Empire to Nation-State* (New York: Longman, 1997), especially 210–11; John J. Stephan, *The Russian Far East: A History* (Stanford: Stanford University Press, 1994); Alan Wood, ed., *The History of Siberia from Russian Conquest to Revolution* (London: Routledge, 1991); F. G. Safronov,

the coup of the conservative-rightist coalition in Moscow in the summer of 1991 brought an end to the Soviet Communist system, Russia was emerging as a newly born neighbor not only postulating representative democracy and market economy as its new principles but also showing an interest in the security configuration in the post–Cold War East Asia region.

Because of the lack of experiences and measures for region-wide security cooperation in the East Asia region, which is different from the European context, this chapter sheds light on Russia's interest in regime formation from the beginning, unlike Chapter 3 in this volume, which tests the effectiveness and resilience of a previously constructed pan-European security regime, that is, to what extent Russia abides by the Organization for Security and Cooperation in Europe's (OSCE's) norms and rules. Although the main aim of this chapter is to test the persuasiveness of each theoretical framework, I do not intend to side with one theory against the other in a clear-cut manner. At the end of this chapter, a third approach to international cooperation, cognitivism, is briefly examined. Unlike rationalist theory (both realism and neoliberalism), cognitivism emphasizes the legitimacy of normative injunctions, the role of communication in forming intersubjective meaning, and the process of identity formation, all of which are beyond the reach of individual manipulation.

EVOLUTION OF THE TWO SCHOOLS

Thucydides, Machiavelli, Thomas Hobbes, and the mercantilists constitute intellectual ancestors of realism. They have emphasized international anarchy, reliance on self-help, the usefulness of military force, and the importance of balance-of-power calculations. Likewise, the ancient Stoics, the early Christian philosophers, and Woodrow Wilson have emphasized international economic interdependence, international law and institutions, international communications, and societal norms. These figures are regarded as the intellectual ancestors of contemporary liberal institutionalism.[4] When academic study of international relations emerged in the United States in the 1920s, a fundamental harmony of international inter-

---

Russskie na severo-vostoke Azii v XVII-seredine XIX v. [Russia in Northeast Asia during the 17th–mid-19th centuries] (Moscow: Nauka, 1978).

4. For the debate's historical roots, see David A. Baldwin, "Neoliberalism, Neorealism, and World Politics," in Baldwin, ed., *Neorealism and Neoliberalism: The Contemporary Debate* (New York: Columbia University Press, 1993), 11–15.

ests was assumed. In the 1930s, however, with the collapse of the post–World War I international order—the Japanese invasion of Manchuria, the signing of the Molotov–Ribbentrop agreement, and the failure of the League of Nations—the notion of harmony withered away, and modern realism was brought home. During the Cold War, the continued salience of U.S.–Soviet antagonism enhanced the status of realism as the dominant paradigm among international relations scholars. Hans Morgenthau's *Politics Among Nations: The Struggle for Power and Peace* (1948) served as a touchstone for realists in earlier days of the Cold War era.

Yet, challenges to realism continued to emerge in the form of functionalist integration theory as an approach to peace in the 1940s and early 1950s and neofunctionalist regional integration theory in the 1950s and 1960s.[5] The (neo)functionalists argued that international institutions can help states cooperate. Despite numerous events in the 1970s and 1980s, which appeared to support realist theory, the developed states in Europe achieved cooperation through international institutions in the fields of international finance, trade, energy, and high technology. Ultimately, neoliberal institutionalism emerged during the 1970s and 1980s as the major challenge to realism. The neoliberalism representatively presented by Robert O. Keohane and Joseph S. Nye, Jr., challenged realism with respect to the relative importance of military security on foreign policy agendas, the role of military force in international politics, and the fungibility of power resources among issue areas.[6] What is peculiar about neoliberal institutionalism is its claim that it accepts a number of core realist propositions, including the realist argument that anarchy impedes the achievement of international cooperation and that states are the major actors in world affairs as rational agents. Neoliberal institutionalists, however, hold firm to the core liberal argument that realism overemphasizes conflict and underestimates the capacities of international institutions to promote cooperation. Although neoliberal institutionalism prevailed during the 1970s and 1980s, neorealism and structural realism have also emerged on the realist side. Kenneth Waltz's and Joseph Grieco's works have become popular among the new realists.[7]

5. For functionalist international theory, see David Mitrany, *A Working Peace System* (Chicago: Quadrangle Press, 1966) [1943]. On neofunctionalism, see Ernst Haas, *The Uniting of Europe: Political, Economic, and Social Forces, 1950–57* (Stanford: Stanford University Press, 1958).

6. Keohane and Joseph S. Nye, Jr., "Introduction" and "Conclusion" in Keohane and Nye, eds., *Transnational Relations and World Politics* (Cambridge: Harvard University, 1972); Keohane and Nye, *Power and Interdependence: World Politics in Transition* (Boston: Little, Brown, 1977).

7. Waltz, *Theory of International Politics*; Joseph M. Grieco, "Anarchy and the Limits of Cooperation: A Realist Critique of the Newest Liberal Institutionalism," *International Organization* 42 (Summer 1988): 485–507.

Debates between realists who emphasize the constraints on international cooperation and neoliberals who stress the opportunities for such cooperation still continue in the post–Cold War world. Neoliberals call into question realism's relevance for understanding the post–Cold War world,[8] but realists maintain that their explanation of the Cold War's end and the relatively peaceful nature of the Soviet Union's decline is superior to explanations based on other theoretical traditions.[9] Today, although neoliberals argue that the renaissance of the European Union (EU) severely challenges realist theory, neorealists suggest that it is possible to "distill from realist theory an argument about international institutions that is based on the core realist assumptions."[10]

INTERNATIONAL COOPERATION IN NEOLIBERAL INSTITUTIONALISM

The Cheating Problem in the Prisoner's Dilemma Situation

Realists and neoliberal institutionalists agree that states exist in an anarchic international environment in which states are the major actors.[11] The diverging explanations for cooperation are attributed to how anarchy is understood as a condition shaping state behavior. Realists argue that the

8. See John Gerald Ruggie, "The False Premise of Realism," *International Security* 20 (Summer 1995): 62–70; Richard Ned Lebow, "The Long Peace, the End of Cold War, and the Failure of Realism," *International Organization* 48 (Spring 1994): 249–77; Rey Koslowski and Friedrich Kratochwil, "Understanding Change in International Relations: The Soviet Empire's Demise and the International System," *International Organization* 48 (Spring 1994): 215–47; Kratochwil, "The Embarrassment of Changes: Neo-Realism as the Science of Realpolitik Without Politics," *Review of International Studies* 19 (January 1993): 63–80; John Gaddis, "International Relations Theory and the End of the Cold War," *International Security* 17 (Winter 1992–93): 5–58; Richard Rosecrance and Arthur A. Stein, "Beyond Realism: The Study of Grand Strategy," in Rosecrance and Stein, eds., *The Domestic Biases of Grand Strategy* (Ithaca: Cornell University, 1993).

9. John J. Mearsheimer, "The False Promise of International Institutions," *International Security* 19 (Winter 1994–95): 5–49; William C. Wohlforth, "Realism and the End of the Cold War," *International Security* 19 (Winter 1994–95): 91–95.

10. Joseph M. Grieco, "Understanding the Problem of International Cooperation: The Limits of Neoliberal Institutionalism and the Future of Realist Theory," in Baldwin, *Neorealism and Neoliberalism*, 302.

11. Morgenthau, *Politics Among Nations: The Struggle for Power and Peace* (New York: Knopf, 1948), 10; Keohane, *After Hegemony*, 25; Waltz, *Theory of International Politics*, 95.

international environment is a self-help system. Because states often cannot afford to maximize their power to maintain their position, they choose to balance power.[12]

On the other hand, neoliberal institutionalists argue that the system is not as competitive and conflictual as realists suggest. Anarchy is the lack of common government in world politics and in areas where cheating is a problem.[13] Cheating is the greatest impediment to cooperation among rationally egoistic states, but international institutions can help states surmount this barrier to joint action. To develop this argument, neoliberals first observe that states in anarchy often face situations that can be depicted by the prisoner's dilemma. In the game, each state prefers mutual cooperation to mutual noncooperation, but also prefers successful cheating to mutual cooperation and mutual defection to victimization by another's cheating. In the absence of some other countervailing force to bind states to their promises, each state defects regardless of what it expects the other to do.

Cooperation Through Institutions

Neoliberals suggest that conditional cooperation is more likely to occur in the prisoner's dilemma if the game is highly iterated, because states that interact repeatedly find that mutual cooperation is their best long-term interest. Accordingly, neoliberal institutionalists see international institutions as a key instrument that states use to overcome the prisoner's dilemma and to achieve joint gains. In a prisoner's dilemma played over again by the same egoistic players, cooperation can be induced and maintained purely through a reciprocal strategy (tit for tat) as long as future gains and losses are not completely disregarded by the actors. Conditional cooperation is more attractive to states if the costs of verifying one another's compliance, and of sanctioning cheaters, are low compared with the benefits of joint action. Hegemonic power may be necessary to establish cooperation among states, but cooperation may persist after hegemony with the aid of institutions.

Absolute Gains for Atomic Actors

For neoliberal institutionalists, states are atomic actors. Keohane suggested that states in an anarchical context are rational egoists. According to Keo-

---

12. Waltz, *Theory of International Politics*, 126–27.
13. Axelrod and Keohane, "Achieving Cooperation Under Anarchy," 226.

hane, egoism means that their utility functions are independent of one another: "they do not gain or lose utility simply because of the gains or losses of others."[14] Cooperation occurs because states are concerned with individual absolute gains and are indifferent to gains achieved by others. In other words, absolute gains and common interests drive international cooperation. Neoliberal institutionalists believe that power and security are becoming less important to states in the era of nuclear weapons and economic interdependence.

INTERNATIONAL COOPERATION IN REALISM

Relative Gains Concern

Realists believe that neoliberals overstate the extent to which institutions are able to alleviate anarchy's constraining effects on interstate cooperation. Realists find that there is a barrier to international cooperation other than the cheating problem. Realists criticize neoliberals for ignoring the matter of relative gains and assuming that states desire only absolute gains.[15]

Positional Actors

Realists believe that states are positional and not atomic in character; states are concerned not only about cheating but also about other states gaining more in cooperative arrangements. Realism's identification of the relative gains problem for cooperation is based on its insight that states in anarchy worry about their survival as independent actors. Instead of individual well-being, survival is their core interest.[16] Driven by an interest in survival, states are sensitive to any erosion of their relative capabilities, which are the ultimate basis for their security and independence in an anarchical, self-help international environment. Kenneth Waltz suggested that "the first concern of states is not to maximize power but to maintain their position in

14. Keohane, *After Hegemony,* 27.
15. As a representatively well-organized critique on neoliberal institutionalism from a neorealist viewpoint, see Grieco, "Anarchy and the Limits of Cooperation," 485–507.
16. See Raymond Aron, *Peace and War: A Theory of Peace and War,* trans. Richard Howard and Annette Baker Fox (Garden City, NY: Doubleday, 1966), 7.

the system."[17] According to Grieco, the state of positionality is more defensive than offensive in nature, and only gaps in payoffs to the advantage of a partner, not any payoff achieved by a partner, detract from the state's utility.[18]

Table 6.1 A state's utility function in realism.

U = V − k (W − V)
U: a state utility
V: the state's individual payoff
W: partner's payoff
k: the state's coefficient of sensitivity to gaps in payoffs to either its advantage or disadvantage

Source: Adapted from Joseph M. Grieco, "Anarchy and the Limits of Cooperation: A Realist Critique of the Newest Liberal Institutionalism," *International Organization* 42 (Summer 1988): 485–507.

In sum, although both sides agree that international cooperation is possible, they differ as to the ease and likelihood of its occurrence. Realists view international cooperation as "harder to achieve, more difficult to maintain, and more dependent on state power" than do the neoliberals.[19] In the realist perspective, the motives and actions of states induced by anarchy impede efforts for cooperation, even when states share common interests.

Having presented realism's and neoliberalism's basic assumptions and conditions for international cooperation, I now address the case of Russia's interest in the post–Cold War security configuration in the East Asia region.

THE POST–COLD WAR EAST ASIA REGION SECURITY CONFIGURATION

Lack of Experiences in Multilateral Cooperation

During the Cold War era, security in the entire East Asia region was maintained on the basis of a network of bilateral security arrangements with

17. Waltz, *Theory of International Politics*, 126. For a similar connotation, see also E. H. Carr, *The Twenty-Years Crisis, 1919–1939: An Introduction to the Study of International Relations* (London: Harper Torchbooks, 1964), 111; Gilpin, *War and Change in World Politics*, 87–88.

18. Grieco, "Anarchy and the Limits of Cooperation," 500.

19. Grieco, "Understanding the Problem of International Cooperation," 302.

the United States playing the central role. Unlike Europe, no region-wide security regime was created in the East Asia region mainly because of the diverse histories and cultural roots and the peculiar local patterns of rivalry and enmity in the region. Although the arbitrariness in the regime concept still prevails in the field of international cooperation,[20] there has been a consensus among scholars and policy makers that, unlike Europe, the East Asia region has not experienced region-wide regimes.[21] The security dimension is worse than the economic dimension. There is nothing like an East Asia–region equivalent of the Organization for Security and Cooperation in Europe (OSCE; formerly CSCE), which stands alone, not just in the comprehensiveness of its geopolitical coverage (from the Atlantic to the Urals) and membership (fifty-three states), but in the scope of its lofty ideals and extensive agenda.

Association of Southeast Asian Nations (ASEAN) Regional Forum (ARF)

With the end of the Cold War, however, the regionalization of security policies and the growing importance of a cooperative approach to security became notable trends in the region. The Southeast Asia subregion has experienced some progress and embraced some positive region-wide security implications beyond the subregion: the ASEAN Post-Ministerial Conference (PMC) first held in 1991 is an approved forum for official dialogue, involving not only the six ASEAN member states but also the so-called seven dialogue partners (Australia, South Korea, Canada, the EC, Japan, New Zealand, and the United States).

More important, because of a need to develop an Asian mechanism for control and settlement of disputes and for prevention of armed conflicts throughout the region, the first ministerial conference on the issue of peace in East Asia, the so-called ASEAN Regional Forum (ARF), was held in 1994. It included nineteen member countries (the six ASEAN countries, their seven dialogue partners, and other individual countries including Russia, China, Vietnam, Cambodia, Laos, and Papua New Guinea). The

20. For details, see Andreas Hasenclever, Peter Mayer, and Volker Rittberger, "Interests, Power, Knowledge: The Study of International Regimes," *Mershon International Studies Review* 40, 2 (1996): 177–228.

21. Byung-Joon Ahn, "Regionalism in the Asia-Pacific: Asian or Pacific Community?" in Sung-Joo Hahn, ed., *The New International System: Regional and Global Dimensions* (Seoul: Ilmin International Relations Institution, 1996); Eunsook Chung, *Multilateral Security and Cooperation: The CSCE Process and Lessons for the Asia Pacific* (in Korean) (Seoul: Sejong Institute, 1993).

ARF was regarded by the Clinton administration as the security equivalent of the Asia Pacific Economic Cooperation (APEC), the premier institutional framework in the region. Yet, no single opinion about the speed and scope of confidence-building measures (CBMs) has been achieved as of now.

Table 6.2   Structure of the ASEAN Regional Forum (ARF).

Formation July 1994
Members —ASEAN: Brunei, Indonesia, Laos, Malaysia, Myanmar, Philippines, Singapore, Thailand, Vietnam —ASEAN's dialogue partners: Australia, Canada, China, European Union, India, Japan, New Zealand, Republic of Korea, Russia, United States —ASEAN's observers: Cambodia, Papua New Guinea
Primary objectives —To promote confidence-building measures —To develop preventive diplomacy —To develop approaches to conflict resolution

Organization
—Annual ministerial meeting
—Senior officials meeting (SOM)
—Three intercessional support groups (ISG)
  (a) on CBM
  (b) on Disaster Relief
  (c) on search and rescue
  (d) on PKO
—No permanent secretariat

Source: http://www.aseansec.org/history/asn_pol2.htm (16.04.99), Seo-Hang Lee, "Security Regionalism in Northeast Asia: Emerging Framework of Security Dialogue," *IFANS Review* 6 (December 1998): 65.

In the Northeast Asia subregion, where the interests of four major powers—China, Japan, Russia, and the United States—intersect, attempts to build meaningful subregional security institutions have failed, in spite of various proposals made by Russians, Koreans, Mongolians, Canadians, and others.

Track-Two Diplomacy

Besides ARF, which is the intergovernmental forum, the Council for Security Cooperation in the East Asia region (CSCAP) has also played an important role in the issue of security in the entire East Asia region at the level of track-two diplomacy. In the Northeast Asia subregion, in spite of the thriving track-two activities, including the Northeast Asia Cooperation Dialogue (NEACD) (1993–), the Hokkaido Conference on North Pacific Issues (1988–), the Multilateral Dialogue on Prospects for Stability and Cooperation in Northeast Asia (1993–96), and the United Nations (UN) Symposium on Northeast Asia (1995–), meaningful subregional security institutions fail to be born.

In sum, the East Asia region lacks a multilateral institutional basis of cooperation among countries in the region, when compared with Europe. Nevertheless, the collapse of the Soviet Union and the following security uncertainty of the region have been driving the countries in the region to construct region-wide security regimes or mechanisms for multilateral CBMs.

Russia's Membership

In spite of the failure to gain membership in APEC, Russia has been invited by ASEAN as an observer state to its PMCs since 1992 and to the ARF since its first session in 1994. Eventually, in July 1996, Russia, together with China and India, obtained dialogue partnership in ASEAN. This partnership entails Moscow's participation in all ASEAN discussions, both political and economic. On the occasion of gaining partnership, the Russian foreign minister Yevgeny Primakov expressed his hope that Russia will be one of the countries with open access to the ASEAN free trade zone, which will be created by 2003.[22]

Russia has also been a participant in various track-two multilateral meetings on the issue of cooperative security in the region, including CSCAP at the region-wide level, and the NEACD, the Hokkaido Conference on North Pacific Issues, the Multilateral Dialogue on Prospects for Stability and Cooperation in Northeast Asia, and the UN Symposium on Northeast Asia at the Northeast Asia subregional level.

Russia's Proposal for Security Arrangements in the East Asia Region

Since 1992 when Russia was first invited as a guest state to ASEAN-PMC, it has made various proposals for both region-wide and Northeast Asia subre-

22. *Kommersant-Daily*, 23 July 1996.

gional CBMs.[23] In July 1992, former Russian Foreign Minister Kozyrev spoke at the twenty-fifth ASEAN Foreign Ministers' Meeting in Manila as a special guest and declared that Russia intended to be *constructively engaged* in the East Asia region. He proposed a series of confidence- and security-building measures to limit naval exercises in designated zones of peace and suggested security cooperation with the ASEAN states. He also proposed to establish a security regime in the East Asia region. In November 1992, Boris Yeltsin, during his official visit to South Korea, called for a mechanism for multilateral negotiations in the East Asia region as well as in the Northeast Asia subregion. He also proposed a system of conflict regulation and regular discussions between regional security experts as a conflict prevention measure.[24] In July 1993, at the twenty-sixth ASEAN Foreign Ministers' Meeting, held in Singapore, Kozyrev proposed that Russia assume *the role of a guarantor* of an East Asia region security system to be developed over time. He declared that his aim at this meeting was to affirm Russia's role in the region in terms of maintaining a political stronghold for comprehensive Russian involvement in regional affairs. Kozyrev also suggested that a Russia–ASEAN committee be established.[25] In July 1994, when Russia was invited to the first region-wide security forum (ARF), Kozyrev proposed that a center for the study of conflict be established and called for greater transparency in arms sales and military doctrines. In 1994, during the UN Security Council debate over sanctions against North Korea, Russia proposed an international conference of key Asian players, to seek ways of defusing the crisis. The conference might involve eight actors, the two Koreas, Russia, the United States, China, Japan, the UN, and the International Atomic Energy Agency (IAEA). In May 1996, at a meeting of ARF where Russia was invited for the first time as a dialogue partner of ASEAN, Russia, together with China, offered joint proposals on principles ensuring security in the region.[26]

Specifically the following were discussed in an article in a Russian military journal as consolidating "Russia's peace initiatives" in the East Asia region[27]: *an agreement on limiting* the number of personnel, arms, and mili-

---

23. See Leszek Buszynski, *Russian Foreign Policy After the Cold War* (Westport, Conn.: Praeger, 1996), 170–213; Eunsook Chung, "Russia's Strategic Choice in Asia Pacific," in Eunsook Chung, ed., *Changes in Russia's Security and Strategic Environment* (Seoul: Sejong Institute, 1996), 153–73.

24. *Rossiiskaya gazeta*, 20 November 1996.

25. Buszynski, *Russian Foreign Policy*, 171.

26. *Sevodnya*, 12 May 1996.

27. N. M. Maslyayev, "On the Question of Russia's Military Security in the Asian Pacific Region," *Military Thought* (July–August 1994): 2–6.

tary equipment employed in military exercises, their scale and regularity, control of reservist callup, deployment of arms and military equipment bases, and movement and concentration of troops; *reciprocal notification* about military activity in the East Asia region—in the case of more than 15,000 land forces, more than 2,000 amphibious or air assault unit personnel, in a five-hundred-kilometer border zone, more than 200 battle tanks, more than 400 combat armored vehicles, more than 200 artillery systems of sixty- to one hundred-millimeter caliber, more than 100 artillery systems of one hundred-millimeter caliber; creation of *nuclear-free and demilitarized zones and limited military activity zones,* for instance, limiting or prohibiting naval activity in a five hundred- or one thousand-kilometer coastal zone, renunciation of actions against antisubmarine complexes and nuclear-powered ballistic-missile submarines in coordinated areas (for the Russian Pacific Fleet, the Okhotsk and Bering Seas; for the U.S. Navy, the Pacific area east of 14 degrees longitude west; for China's Navy, the Yellow Sea and the northeastern part of the South China Sea), limiting and banning the presence of U.S. air carriers in certain areas (for instance, in the Japanese Sea and the northwestern part of the Pacific closer than one thousand or fifteen hundred kilometers to the Russian coast), and conduct of military exercises in the proximity of the borders of other East Asia–region states, and early notification of the East Asia states concerned about the passage by ship units or separate single ships in coordinated areas (the Bering, Laperuz, and Korean Straits, as well as the straits linking the Philippines and the South and East China Seas); *consultations* with all states about preventing a regional arms race, defining the ceilings on the growth of the combat potentials of general purpose forces, and banning the creation of new military bases on foreign territories; *effective measures to verify* the observance of agreements: creation of international functional bodies to monitor the implementation of agreements on limiting military activity (a standing consultative commission and international centers for lessening military danger and deployment of international control and monitoring posts in potentially dangerous areas), and establishment of direct and regular contacts between military departments (invitation of military observers to large-scale exercises and maneuvers as well as conduct of joint seminars to discuss military doctrines, concepts for the organizational development of the armed forces, etc.).

In sum, Russia has continuously proposed to build multilateral security regimes in the East Asia region, which in principle are strongly guided by Gorbachevian multilateralism, the contents of which were spelled out in the Vladivostok speech of July 1986.

WHY RUSSIA CHOOSES TO ACTIVELY PARTICIPATE IN SECURITY CONFIGURATION IN THE POST–COLD WAR EAST ASIA REGION

Which explanatory framework for international cooperation is to be adopted? Which school is better equipped to analyze and explain Russia's interest in the security configuration of the post–Cold War East Asia region? It has long been argued that security cooperation is distinguished from cooperation in other issue areas because of the special peril of defection it contains.[28] Accordingly, neoliberal institutionalists concede that economic issues are more salient to their theory than security issues.[29] In their view, however, Russia's proposal for new security dialogue in the post–Cold War East Asia region is also an attempt for absolute gains based on common interests for a peaceful and secure East Asia region. In contrast, realists contend that power and security are still the motivating factors for Russia in the region in the post–Cold War era. Relative gains and positions in the international system determine Russian behavior.

The Neoliberal Institutionalist Explanation

For the neoliberal institutionalists, Russia's interest in confidence-building measures and participation in the region-wide ARF and CSCAP and other track-two security meetings in the Northeast Asia subregion prove Russia's acceptance of security cooperation with the countries in the region.

To integrate into the East Asia region: For neoliberals who see states becoming more concerned about the attainment of such national goals as growth and full employment and less concerned about power and security, Russia's proposal for regional security cooperation is a means of integrating it into the East Asia region. For them, the preoccupation of Russia with accelerating economic development and enhancing economic competitiveness has encouraged it to promote cooperative commercial relations with its neighbors. In other words, Russia's interest in regional security arrangements has been stimulated mostly by economic regionalism in East Asia, which has become the main source of dynamism in international trade and investment.

To minimize the negative effects of cheating: At the same time, in view of

---

28. Lipson, "International Cooperation in Economics and Security Affairs," 14.
29. Keohane, *After Hegemony*, 247.

"the lack of common government"[30] in regional politics, Russia's intention to cooperate in building security mechanisms is seen as a means of minimizing the negative effects of cheating in the prisoner's dilemma situation coming from regional anarchy. In neoliberal institutionalism, international institutions reduce verification costs, create iterativeness, and make it easier to punish cheaters. Keohane and Axelrod asserted that regimes incorporating the norm of reciprocity delegitimize defection and thereby make it more costly.[31] In neoliberal institutionalism, the functions of Russia's utility are independent of other states in the region. That is, Russia, as a rational egoist, cares only about its own gains and not about the gains or losses of the United States, Japan, China, Korea, thereby making cooperation more likely.

Side Evidence

Diminishing political barriers of cooperation: Neoliberals emphasize that with the end of the Cold War, the immense political barriers that for decades gave rise to distrust and hostility in the relations between Russia and other countries have collapsed. They argue that Russia can now cooperate with other countries in promoting peace and security in ways that were not possible while the Cold War existed. Russia has improved its relations with the United States and has become a partner for maintaining stability and peace in the East Asia region. Along with the improving U.S.–Russia relations, Russo-Japanese relations also show signs of reconciliation, including Yeltsin's visit to Tokyo in 1993 and the Japanese military minister's visit to Moscow in 1996, in spite of unresolved territorial disputes between the two countries.

Most notably, Russia's reconciliation with South Korea signifies a decisive turn toward a new era of regional cooperation, in view of the fact that throughout the Cold War era, Moscow maintained its formal relations only with Communist North Korea in the peninsula. In his first Asian visit to South Korea in 1992, Yeltsin signed the Treaty of Basic Relations between the Russian Federation and the Republic of Korea. According to this treaty, the two states would develop their cooperation in the interests of better

---

30. On the neoliberal definition of anarchy, see Axelrod and Keohane, "Achieving Cooperation Under Anarchy," 226; Keohane, *After Hegemony*, 7; Lipson, "International Cooperation in Economic and Security Affairs," 2.

31. Axelrod and Keohane, "Achieving Cooperation Under Anarchy," 250.

stability and prosperity in the East Asia region.[32] Russia and South Korea would refrain from the use of force or the threat of force and would solve all emerging bilateral disputes through peaceful means and in compliance with the UN charter. Yeltsin also assured Seoul that Moscow would discontinue military assistance to North Korea and expressed his intention to revise Russia's alliance relation with North Korea. Russia's relations with China have also improved further since the normalization achieved in 1989 in spite of ideological difference; both states have taken steps to reduce prospects for conflict and to assure each other about their peaceful intentions. In 1992, the Joint Declaration on the Principles of Relations between the People's Republic of China and the Russian Federation confirmed the two countries' intention not to use force or the threat of force against each other.

Economic cooperation:[33] Neoliberals emphasize that increases in Russia's economic transactions with the countries in the East Asia region need a stable and peaceful security atmosphere. For Russia, it is imperative to draw financial and technological assistance from neighboring countries to enter the world economy. Moreover, neoliberals see that because of its loss of European territory, Russia has a direct interest to cooperate with its East Asia–region neighbors. First, the Baltic and Black Seas are now foreign territory, and the importance of the Pacific has rapidly increased as an avenue for Russia to enter the world economy. Also, Russia lost natural resources once obtained from the former Soviet republics and now must develop natural resources in Siberia and the Russian Far East, for which its Pacific neighbors' assistance is necessary. Despite the crisis and turmoil following decentralization, the volume of Russian trade with Northeast Asia increased sharply, even showing a surplus. The major investors of the joint ventures in the Russian Far East are China, Japan, Korea, and the United States, who are developing oil in the Sakhalin shelf, gas in Yakutia, gold along Lake Baikal.

Russo-Chinese CBMs: Russia's recent experiences of achieving various confidence-building measures with China elevate neoliberal institutionalists' expectations for Russia to play a positive role in fostering peace and stability in the East Asia region. In 1993, a five-year agreement was ex-

32. For the text of the treaty, see Il Yung Chung, ed., *Korea and Russia* (Seoul: Sejong Institute, 1992), appendix, 435–39.

33. For a neoliberal view that economic cooperation provides an opportunity to generate greater trust and confidence in East Asia, see Ralph A. Cossa and Jane Khanna, "East Asia: Economic Interdependence and Regional Security," *International Affairs* 73 (April 1997): 219–34.

changed between the Russian defense minister Pavel Grachev and the Chinese defense minister Chi Haotian, prescribing regular consultations between top ministry officials, the establishment of direct ties between adjoining Russian and Chinese military districts, military exchanges between the two countries' armed forces at all levels, and an increase in the number of attachés posted in each other's capitals, informing each other of plans for military maneuvers in border districts, and exchanging information on military doctrine and military construction. In 1994, a joint communiqué between Yeltsin and Jian Zemin proclaimed that Russia and China would no longer target nuclear missiles against each other. At the same time, an agreement on the prevention of dangerous military activity was declared by the defense ministers of the two countries, including safeguards against an accidental missile launch, bans on the use of eye-damaging lasers, a prohibition against electronic jamming of communication, and early warnings. Impressively enough, Chinese officers have made first visits to regional detachments of the Russian armed forces, including the September 1994 visit by Jian Zemin to the Russian Transbaikal Military District.[34] Finally, in April 1996, a five-way agreement on CBMs in border areas was signed by the presidents of Russia, China, Kazakhstan, Kyrgyzstan, and Tajikistan, putting an end to the costly military standoff along the entire former Soviet-Chinese border.[35]

Awareness of unconventional threat: Neoliberal institutionalists view Russia, and other countries in the region, as aware of the fact that most unconventional threats to national security, such as the protection of the environment, the regulation of refugees, the prevention of international criminal activities, can be dealt with effectively only through regional and multilateral cooperation.

Prescription

Because of the lack of any multilateral institutions in the region, unlike in Europe, neoliberal institutionalists focus on a growing need to reduce political uncertainties in the East Asia region. For neoliberal institutionalists whose concern is to produce conditions under which cooperation is achieved in an anarchical international environment, Russia must be

34. James Clay Moltz, "Regional Tensions in the Russo-Chinese Rapprochement," *Asian Survey* 35 (June 1995): 519.
35. The data for Russo-Chinese CBMs are from various sources, including Taeho Kim, *The Dynamics of Sino Russian Military Relations: An Asian Perspective,* CAPS paper, no. 6 (1994), and Russian newspapers.

treated as a legitimate and prepared partner for countries in the region in building a multilateral security framework as a measure to enhance confidence and to dissipate possible tensions. It is necessary that the United States and its allies consider CBMs proposed by Russia in a sincere manner.

Neoliberals have found that Russia is making an effort to overcome the historical rivalries that constitute its legacy by developing harmonious relations with major regional and global actors, that is, an effort to decry military power and the balance of power, the pursuit of which would create tensions and conflicts with neighbors. In a word, the neoliberal prescription is to cooperate and negotiate with Russia on the basis of common interests like preventing arms races, conflicts in the region, and the emergence of regional hegemonic power and ensuring economic and environmental security.

The Realist Explanation

Realism specifies a wider range of systemic-level constraints for Russia on cooperation than does neoliberalism. In realism, anarchy is much more than a simple lack of a central agency to enforce promises. In anarchy, nothing can prevent wars, and therefore "force serves as the first and constant one."[36] Realism finds that survival is Russia's core interest rather than individual well-being and "other more noble goals such as truth, beauty, and justice,[37] which will be lost unless Russia makes provision for its security in the power struggle among groups." Russia's intent is to prevent other countries in the region—mostly the United States, Japan, and China—from achieving advances in their relative capabilities as much as possible. Believing in state positionality, realists think that Russia will decline to cooperate, even if it may have large absolute gains, if it expects that partners are likely to achieve relatively greater gains.

Decline in Russia's capability: In the realist perspective, interest in building a regional security regime is a means by which Russia has aimed at addressing relative gains concerns through the mechanism and operations of multilateral institutions instead of unilateral bargaining strategies. Since the last days of the former Soviet Union, Moscow, with the collapse of the economy, has become the weaker power in negotiations with the United States. At least for the near future, Russia will follow the path of unilateral

---

36. Waltz, *Man, State, and War: A Theoretical Analysis* (New York: Columbia University Press, 1959), 232; Waltz, *Theory of International Politics*, 113.

37. Gilpin, "The Richness of Political Realism," in Keohane, *Neorealism and Its Critics*, 305.

reductions even if they are not balanced by reciprocal U.S. reductions and although this unilateralism will cause serious domestic problems for the Russian administration. Alexei D. Bogaturov of the USA–Canada Institute of the Russian Academy of Sciences presented a notion of reasonable compression as Moscow's new approach to the Pacific, which is concerned with managing the inevitable withdrawal from East Asia.[38]

For Russia, the main destabilizing factor in the East Asia region is the superiority of the U.S. Navy over Russia's Pacific Fleet forces. Russia is in no position to change the existing balance by increasing the combat strength of its naval forces. A Russian military official assessed the fate of Pacific Fleet forces: "Having more than 60% of obsolete battleships and 70% of naval aviation aircraft, it will be forced to cut them unilaterally. . . . By the year 2000 Russia will unilaterally reduce the number of its submarines in the East Asia region by 25%, missile antisubmarine complex by 50%, surface ships by 40%, and sea aviation by 15%."[39] In this situation, Russian diplomacy should seek to use steps toward downsizing the navy on the principles of goodwill so that the other side resorts to analogous measures in response.

Existing U.S.–dominant security structure: At the same time, for realists, the legacy of the Cold War in the current alliance structure also drives Russia to build a multilateral security regime in the region. Despite Japan's influence in world politics and its economic power, Russo-Japanese relations remain a function of Russo-U.S. relations as they were several decades ago, and the position of the United States is still seen as an obstacle for Russo-Japanese military cooperation.[40] As with Japan, for Russia, military cooperation with South Korea is constrained by the U.S.–South Korea alliance relations. Russia has recognized South Korea's strategic role in East Asia security affairs, and during the first Russia–South Korea summit, the two ministers of defense signed a memorandum of understanding according to which the two countries were to start direct military contacts. The first exchange of naval unit visits was held in 1993. In compliance with the U.S.–South Korea treaty of alliance, however, U.S. armed forces are stationed on South Korean territory, and joint military exercises of broad scale and security consultations occur regularly.

Advantages of large numbers: Last, as realists argue, large numbers would enhance the likelihood that the relative achievements of gains favoring

38. Alexei D. Bogaturov, "The Yeltsin Administration's Policy in the Far East: In Search of a Concept," *Harriman Institute Forum* (August 1993): 2.

39. Maslyayev, "On the Question of Russia's Military Security," 4.

40. *Kommersant-Daily*, 23 March 1996; *Sevodnya*, 30 April 1996.

better positioned partners could be offset by more favorable sharing arising from interaction with weaker partners.[41] This could also be a reason
that Russia has been advocating the creation of new multilateral security
structures rather than negotiating exclusively with the United States on
bilateral terms.

Side Evidence

Re-emerging balance-of-power notion: With growing nationalism and anti-Western sentiment in Russia since around 1993,[42] the traditional balance-of-
power notion has re-emerged in Russia's security conceptions. Immediately
after the collapse of the Soviet Union, Yeltsin's and Kozyrev's foreign policy
line was hailed as "Atlanticism" or "pro-Westernism." Apparently, it favored neoliberalists in the debate of international theory scholars in the
United States. Because since around 1993 such terms as Eurasianism or
geopolitics began to appeal greatly to the Russian elite as well as to the
general public, realism has regained its momentum among international
relations scholars to describe Russia's external behavior. Although propos-
ing comprehensive CBMs in the East Asia region, N. M. Maslyayev asserted
a balance-of-power notion against the United States, which prevailed during the Cold War years: "In defining a scope, volume, and lines of military
and military-technical cooperation with countries in this region (Asia Pacific) . . . priority in cooperation should be given to China, India, Vietnam,
and Laos and also preserving military and military-technical cooperation
with North Korea to ensure a balance of power that would preclude a military solution of the Korean problem."[43]

   "Cold peace" with the United States at the global level: With regard to Russia's
relations with the United States, which have global implications beyond the
East Asia region, realists observe a "cold peace"[44] as a number of security
arrangements established between the former Soviet Union and the West
are threatened, such as ratification of the second Strategic Arms Reduction
Treaty (START II). The Open Skies Treaty is in a state of stagnation; there

41. Grieco, "Anarchy and the Limits of Cooperation," 506.
42. See Vladimir Zhirinovsky, *Poslednii brosok na yug* [Last throw at the south] (Moscow:
Rait 1994); Gennadi Zyuganov, *Derzhava* (Power) (Moscow: Informpechat' 1994).
43. Maslyayev, "On the Question of Russia's Military Security," 5.
44. On a newly emerging U.S.-Russian "cold peace," see Andrei Kozyrev, "Partnership of
Cold Peace?" *Foreign Policy* 99 (Summer 1995): 3–14; Dimitri Simes, "The Return of Russian
History," *Foreign Affairs* 73 (January–February 1994): 67–82; Andrei Kortunov, "Russia and
the United States," in Robert D. Blackwell and Sergei A. Karaganov, eds., *Damage Limitation
or Crisis? Russia and the Outside World* (Washington: Brassey 1994).

are new disagreements over the Anti-Ballistic Missile Treaty (ABM). With the possibility of North Atlantic Treaty Organization (NATO) expansion and the conflicts in the Caucasus, the Treaty on Conventional Armed Forces in Europe (CFE) is not fully implemented, and opposition to the final negotiations of the Comprehensive Test Ban Treaty (CTB) grows in Russia. For the West, Moscow's selling of nuclear and missile technologies to Iran, Iraq, and India has signified breaking the Treaty on the Non-Proliferation of Nuclear Weapons as well as the Missile Technology Regime.[45] Most notably, NATO expansion remains the most controversial foreign and security policy issue in Russia's domestic politics, despite the fact that President Yeltsin signed an agreement with President Clinton on the terms of its expansion in March 1997.

New military doctrine: Realists also emphasize that the importance of nuclear weapons as a deterrent against conventional as well as nuclear attack was reaffirmed in Russia's military doctrine adopted in November 1993. This modifies Moscow's previous no first-use pledge. According to Richard F. Staar, a document produced at the Institute for Defense Studies (*Institut oboronnykh issledovanii*), which has been considered the basis for a new military doctrine, would represent a much more dangerous threat than the current one for the West.[46] In this document, long-term threats to Russia's national security are interference in the internal affairs of Russia by the United States and its allies; political and economical penetration of Azerbaijan by Turkey, the United States, England, and Germany, with Azerbaijan serving as a bridgehead for future Western expansion into Central Asia, the Volga region, and the northern Caucasus; attempts to isolate and remove Russia from Europe through an expansion of NATO; unilateral disarmament of Russia by the West through financing the degradation of Russian strategic weapons systems and research and development centers, attempting to force acceptance of unequal treaties like START II, demanding amendments to the ABM agreements, and countering integration in the Commonwealth of Independent States (CIS).

Shift in Russia's Korea policy: Realists do not miss the point that with anti-Western sentiments growing in Russia, Russo–South Korean relations have also deteriorated. Roughly since around 1993, Russia has attempted to recover its leverage over North Korea by repairing the relations deeply hurt

45. See, for details, Alexei Arbatov, "Eurasia Letter: A Russian-U.S. Security Agenda," *Foreign Policy* 104 (Fall 1996): 102–17; Summer Benson, "Deep-Strike Weapons and Strategic Stability," *Orbis* 40 (Fall 1996): 499–515.

46. Richard F. Staar, "Moscow's Plans to Restore Its Power," *Orbis* 40 (Summer 1996): 375–89.

since the collapse of the Soviet Union. Eventually in April 1996, a Russian delegation headed by Deputy Prime Minister Vitaly Ignatenko visited Pyoungyang to hold the first meeting of the Intergovernmental Commission on Trade, Economic, Scientific, and Technical Cooperation.[47] In January 1997, a Russian delegation headed by Deputy Foreign Minister Grigori Karasin visited North Korea to negotiate a new treaty, which according to Karasin, replaces the old Soviet Union–North Korea treaty and is similar in content to the basic treaty signed by Russia and South Korea five years ago.[48] There are some reasons behind the policy shift from a Seoul-oriented to a two-Korea policy. First, having seen the U.S.–North Korea nuclear negotiations, Russia has begun to realize that the United States would ignore Russia.[49] It is Russia, not the United States, that has a border with North Korea not far from its main naval base at Vladivostok, and Russia would be directly affected by an economic collapse in North Korea, which could produce a flood of refugees or an outburst of violence on the peninsula with conflict or nuclear radiation spilling over the border. Second, Russia's proposal for a multilateral conference on the North Korean nuclear issue has been turned down by Washington, Tokyo, and Seoul. Moreover, Russia is not a member of the Korea Energy Development Organization (KEDO), the product of U.S.–North Korea negotiations held in Geneva in autumn 1994, and was not invited by a Seoul–Washington proposal in spring 1996 to four-way talks among the two Koreas, the United States, and China, for the purpose of concluding a peace treaty to replace the 1953 armistice agreement publicized in early 1996. To connote the sour relations between the two countries, a Russian newspaper stated that "the partnership between Russia and South Korea is undergoing an endurance test."[50] Alexander Zhevin of the Far Eastern Institute at the Russian Academy of Sciences and others who are in charge of Korean issues of the Russian Foreign Ministry expressed their views to this author at an informal meeting: according to these sources, for the past five years, Russia's Korean policy has been based on illusions and has done nothing to enhance Russia's position on the Korean peninsula.[51]

47. *Kommersant-Daily*, 13 April 1996.

48. An interview with Mr. Karasin by a research team including this author took place in Moscow on September 24, 1996.

49. These views are expressed by such influential scholars as Alexander Zhebin at the Far Eastern Studies Institute of the Russian Academy of Sciences. The interview was held by this author in Moscow on September 23, 1996.

50. Vladimir Nokiforov, *Nezavisimaya gazeta*, 23 May 1996.

51. A series of intensive interviews was held in Moscow in September 1996 for this article.

Relative capability concern as to Japan: At the same time, realists argue that many Russian experts increasingly begin to see Japan as a rising hegemon in the region even to the extent that they support the current U.S.–Japan security alliance as a constraint on Japan. Realists also observe territorial disputes between Russia and Japan as reinforcing their argument for relative capability concern. The Russian military has stressed the strategic significance of the disputed Northern Territories (the Japanese term for the Kuril Islands), which border the Sea of Okhotsk, as the main reason for their opposition to any territorial concession. In 1992, Major General Georgi Mekhov asserted that the dispute over the Kuril Islands is a more of a military-strategic than a political or economic problem:

> The Kurils, an archipelago of 30 big islands and a large number of small islands that separate the Sea of Okhotsk and the Pacific Ocean, are the only natural barriers that prevent offensive naval forces (nuclear submarines, aircraft carriers, amphibious-landing units, and aircraft) from having free access from the Pacific Ocean to the Sea of Okhotsk and directly to our coastline. . . . [T]here is a danger that if the four Southern Kurile islands were returned over to Japan, Washington and Tokyo might not agree to give them the status of demilitarized territories. It is quite probable that Japan and the United States, in the framework of their security treaty, would use the islands to create a forward base for naval operation.[52]

Deepening relations with China: Realists argue that contrast with its relations with the United States, Japan, and South Korea, Russia's relations with China have improved, from full normalization to what Yeltsin and other leaders now call constructive and even strategic partnership. From the realist perspective, because this trend was encouraged by the reorientation of Russian foreign policy away from Kozyrev's initial pro-Western emphasis, the improving relations with China present another sign of balancing behavior.[53] The following is a citation from a Russian daily:

> Shortsighted actions on Washington's part are prompting Moscow and Beijing to shift their emphasis from bilateral to geopolitical aspects of cooperation. A comparative analysis of the final documents

52. Georgi Mekhov, *Krasnaya zvezda*, 22 July 1992.
53. For a realist interpretation of Sino-Russian relations, see Rajan Menon, "The Strategic Convergence Between Russia and China," *Survival* 39 (Summer 1997): 101–25.

of the Russian-Chinese summit meetings in 1992, 1994, and 1996 reveals just such a trend. In their 1996 joint statement, Russia and China solemnly proclaimed their determination to develop an equal partnership based on trust and aimed at strategic cooperation in the 21st century. . . . [S]hort-sighted Western actions were what prompted the inclusion of the term "strategic cooperation." Moscow is concerned about efforts to extend NATO to Russia's present borders. Beijing is alarmed by attempts to lead an anti-Chinese thrust to the American-Japanese security system and to other bilateral military ties from the Cold War era. . . . [I]t pushes Moscow and Beijing to renew their alliance of the 1950s.[54]

Prescription

Realists have found in Russia's international behavior the importance of power and military strength. They also point to the Russian perception that the external environment is less than benign if not hostile. Unlike neoliberals, realists believe Russia is positional and worries not only about cheating but also about other states gaining more in cooperative arrangements. In the realist prescription, therefore, Russia is not a reliable partner with whom to discuss the post–Cold War East Asia security configuration. First, Russia would exit from the arrangement if gaps in gains came to favor the other major powers in the region. Second, Russia's proposal for a multilateral security mechanism in the East Asia region is not different from the traditional idea of balance of power. Russia wants to define the rules and procedures of possible security regimes in the region to pursue relative gains and to maintain a position of leading military power in the system. The Russian agenda for CBMs is to reduce U.S. regional maritime military superiority, which is an established fact and unlikely to be challenged.

In sum, the prescription from the realist side is as follows: first, there is no need to negotiate with Russia on the basis of its proposal for regional security and stability, as long as the interests of the United States and its allied countries are not fatally affected. Next, there is no need to help Russia recover from economic hardship, as long as a crisis in Russia would not harm the United States and its allies. Russia's economy is preferably to be maintained at a low level, given a realist assumption of issue linkage.

54. Vsevolod Ovshinnikov, *Rossiiskaya gazeta*, 20 August 1996.

CONCLUSION: TOWARD A SYNTHESIS

In this chapter, neoliberal institutionalism and realism, the two main-stream rationalist international theories of the twentieth century, were applied to the case of Russia's interest in East Asia security configuration. If we follow the neoliberal institutionalists' concession that economic issues are more salient to their theory than security issues,[55] the theoretical framework of this chapter can be called biased against neoliberal institutionalism from the outset. Moreover, neoliberals indicate two factors enhancing prospects for the achievement and maintenance of cooperation among the advanced democracies: a broad range of common political, military, and economic interests[56] and nesting in larger political-strategic alliances.[57] In the case of Russia, which had long been isolated and recently opened its doors, cooperation with East Asia–region countries would surely provide an opportunity for researchers to observe its behavior as confirming realist rather than neoliberal institutionalist expectations. Indeed, at least in terms of a number of examples of side evidence that this chapter illuminates, realism notably dominates over neoliberal institutionalism.

Nevertheless, as already shown, both schools could explain Russia's interest in an East Asia security configuration with ample evidence. Neoliberal institutionalists have focused on Russia's need for cooperation with countries in the East Asia region to facilitate its economic development and to minimize the negative effects of the cheating problem in the prisoner's dilemma situation as well. In contrast, realists argue that the goals of Moscow in maximizing power and balancing the United States and its allied countries have not changed with the end of the Cold War in the East Asia region. Only the methods to achieve these goals had to change because the Russian economy became too weak to support the former goals. Each argument seems correct and has its own merits in its prescription as well.

Yet a contextualized reading of Russia's security interest must be attempted instead of a reading rooted in and justified by only one paradigm. First, as international relations become more complicated, the distinction between realism and neoliberal institutionalism is often artificial. Although disagreement in each camp is increasingly noticeable, the latest version of the two schools seems to converge significantly. In Joseph Grieco's so-called

55. Keohane, *After Hegemony,* 247.

56. Keohane, *After Hegemony,* 6–7.

57. On the "nesting" of international regimes, see Keohane, *After Hegemony,* 90–91; Vinod K. Aggarwal, *Liberal Protection: The International Politics of Organized Textile Trade* (Berkeley and Los Angeles: University of California Press, 1985).

sophisticated neorealist perspective, unlike in vulgar realism, the suffering of relative loss in a relationship is weighed by the absolute gains, and international institutions can be instrumental in directly mitigating concerns about relative gains by way of using such methods as side payments.[58] Likewise, the rational approaches of today's neoliberal institutionalism are built on realism's assumption that states exist in an anarchic international environment in which states are the major actors.

Second, in the case of Russia, with the loss of superpower status, clarity and coherence are absent in its foreign policy. Over time, some opinion groups have been weakened, and others have been strengthened, as a result of political interaction and conflict. This may be the reason that the side evidence backing the realist arguments illustrated in this chapter comes mostly from events that occurred roughly since around 1993. Any categorization of Russian views of international cooperation cannot be rigid.

Third, besides realism and neoliberal institutionalism, a third approach to international cooperation, which is called cognitivism, might be taken seriously for the above-mentioned two reasons.[59] A massive attention to cognitivism was brought home in the study of international relations in the United States during the late 1980s and early 1990s. Unlike mainstream rationalist theory, which embraces both neoliberal institutionalism and realism, cognitivism premises that behavior cannot be explained solely on the basis of egoistic interests and relative power concerns without reference to idea. Russia's conceptions of self, others, and goals are in a constant process of formation in response to changing context.[60] Strong cognitivists argue that Russia's interests and identities are essentially the products of international interaction. From this perspective, better insights into Russia's interest in the East Asia security configuration needs to focus on normative injunctions, intersubjective meaning, and identity formation, that is, on necessary conditions for individuality and autonomy in international politics.[61]

58. Grieco, "Anarchy and the Limits of Cooperation," 507.

59. On cognitivism, see Alexander Wendt, "The Agent–Structure Problem in International Theory," *International Organization* 41 (Summer 1987): 335–70; Wendt, "Constructing International Politics," *International Security* 20 (Summer 1995): 71–81; Roy D'Andrade and Claudia Strauss, eds., *Human Motives and Cultural Models* (Cambridge: Cambridge University Press, 1992).

60. Wendt, "Collective Identity Formation and the International State," *American Political Science Review* 88 (June 1994): 385–86.

61. For details, see Hasenclever, Mayer, and Rittberger, "Interests, Power, Knowledge," 205–17.

In a contextualized reading, then, the following prescriptions can be made: first, as neoliberals argue, countries in the East Asia region should insulate Western-Russian relations in the region from what happens elsewhere especially since 1993 and see a number of shared interests and concerns with Russia in the region. Prevention of accidents between ballistic missile nuclear submarines potentially attacking in the Sea of Okhotsk and the potential rise of either China or Japan as regional hegemon are concerns shared by both Russia and other countries in the region. Second, as realists argue, to have successful negotiations with Russia, its sensitivity to the distributional aspects of cooperation must be taken into consideration. If we follow Grieco, who illustrated the conditions under which the coefficient for a state's sensitivity to gaps in payoffs is greater, the sensitivity coefficient must be high in the case of Russia in the East Asia region. That is, most of Russia's partners in the region are long-term adversaries rather than allies; Russia's relative power has been on the decline rather than on the rise; and the issue here is security rather than economic well-being.[62] The United States and its allies should identify methods by which Russia is able to address such concerns. Third, as cognitivists argue, it is important for the United States and its allies to admit the social fact that Russia already exists in international institutions. It is essential to acknowledge that despite economic decline and internal disorder, Russia continues to interact with countries in the East Asia region, while possessing its own individuality and autonomy.

---

62. Grieco, "Anarchy and the Limits of Cooperation," 501; Grieco, "Realist Theory and the Problem of International Cooperation: Analysis with an Amended Prisoner's Dilemma Model," *Journal of Politics* 50 (August 1988): 600–624.

List of Contributors

Eunsook Chung is a fellow at the Sejong Institute in Seoul, where she is responsible for assessing Russian foreign policy. She received her Ph.D. in political science from Ohio State University and has authored several monographs on Russian foreign policy toward the Koreas and East Asia more generally.

Henrikki Heikka is a research fellow at the Finnish Institute of International Affairs in Helsinki. He is a Ph.D. candidate at the University of Helsinki and is working on Russian-Western relations and international relations theory.

Ted Hopf is visiting associate professor of methodology and international relations in the Department of Political Science, Ohio University, Athens, and a research associate at the Mershon Center, Ohio State University, Columbus. He received his Ph.D. in political science from Columbia University and has taught international relations at the University of Michigan. He has written a book on deterrence theory *(Peripheral Visions)* and articles on international relations theory and Soviet/Russian foreign policy, which have appeared in the *American Political Science Review, International Security, Security Studies,* and *Global Decisions.*

Hiroshi Kimura is a professor at the International Research Center for Japanese Studies in Kyoto and is first vice-president of the International Council for Central and East European Studies. He received his Ph.D. in political science from Columbia University and previously was a professor and director of the Slavic Research Center at Hokkaido University. His most recent research has focused on Russian foreign policy toward Japan and his most recent book is *Beyond the Cold War to Trilateral Cooperation in the Asia-Pacific Region: Scenarios for New Relationships Between Japan, Russia, and the United States.*

Andrea Lopez is a Ph.D. candidate at the University of Michigan specializing in international conflict and conflict resolution. Her dissertation is entitled "Patterns of Intervention: Great Power Involvement in Civil Wars, 1945–1996.

Sergei Medvedev is a research associate at the Finnish Institute of International Affairs in Helsinki. He received his Ph.D. in religious history from Moscow University and has been a research associate in international affairs at Istituto Affari Internazionai in Rome and Stiftung Wissenschaft und Politik in Ebenhausen. Among his many published works in Russia and Europe are "USSR: Deconstruction of a Text," "Post-Soviet Developments: A Regional Interpretation," and *NATO Enlargement: Russian Perspectives.*

Christer Pursiainen is a Ph.D. candidate at the University of Helsinki and is a research fellow at the Finnish Institute of International Affairs. He has published works on Russian crisis decision-making and Russian political thought in Finland.

Index

Freedom House, 190–92, 194, 198
free riding, 147–48
Freud, Sigmund, 65, 66
  on causes of war, 70–71
  on group behavior and authority, 71–74
  on identity construction, 75
  on state of nature, 72
Fukuyama, Francis, 36

G -7 countries, relations with China, 237–38
Gaidar, Yegor, 42, 190
game theory, 147–48
geographic proximity
  boundary conflicts, 215
  relationship to economic development,
    213
  relationship to good relations, 214–15
Georgia, 45, 174
Germany
  financial aid to Russia, 232
  military power, 121
  reunification of, 35–36, 37, 240–43
  view of Russian actions in Chechnya, 150
  view of Slavic culture, 20
Gilpin, Robert, 118–19, 251
Glaser, Charles, 116–17, 118
Goldstein, Judith, 125
Goltz, Thomas, 175
Goncharov, Ivan, 16
Gorbachev, Mikhail, 37. See also perestroika
  as Communist Party leader, 33–34, 35 n.
    38
  foreign policy, 35–36, 38, 241, 263
  relations with Japan, 214, 226–27, 229–30,
    233, 241
  reunification of Germany, 35–36, 241,
    242–43, 242 n. 62
  Reykjavik summit, 35
Goulding, Marrack, 199
Grachev, Pavel, 267
Grieco, Joseph M., 114, 115, 116, 144, 254,
  258, 275–76, 277
Gromyko, Andrei, 35
Guatemala, 209
GUM, 225
Gyarmati, István, 149, 150–51, 160, 161

Hashimoto, Ryutaro, 243–44, 246, 247–49
Hashimoto-Yeltsin Plan, 244, 246–47, 248
hegemonic stability theory, 118–19

Helsinki Watch, 201
Hobbes, Thomas, 253
Hokkaido Conference on North Pacific Is-
  sues, 261
Holoboff, Elaine, 174, 175
Horie, Shigeo, 217
Hosokawa, Morihiro, 247–48
Höynck, Wilhelm, 151–52, 160
human rights abuses
  against Russian nationals in former Soviet
    republics, 194, 197
  in Moldova, 204
  Russian, in Chechnya, 135–36, 141–45,
    148, 157, 160–61
Hurrell, Andrew, 128, 131, 132, 133

identification
  ambivalent nature of, 71, 73
  dialectic, 74
  dissolution of transference, 106
  Freud's definition of, 71
  social order and, 71–74
  of subjects with state, 67, 72–74
identity construction, 77
  differences between constructivism and
    Lacanian theory, 80
  Freud on, 75
  in human development, 80–86
  hypernationalism and, 87, 88, 91
  internal split, 87
  Lacan on birth of ego, 80–86, 88
  master signifiers, 90, 91, 100–101
  mirror stage, 81–83, 83 n. 68, 89
  mirror theory of, 78–79
  psychoanalytical view, 80, 104–5
  role of desire, 88–93
  role of liminal groups, 96–97, 102
  role of other, 75, 81, 87–88, 91, 99–101,
    102, 103
  Russian, 11–13, 42, 43–44, 94–97, 99–101,
    102–3
  social, 83
  of states, 97
  symbolic interaction, 83–86
  Wendt on, 83
ideologies, shared, 181–82, 200, 204–5,
  208–9
Ignatenko, Vitaly, 272
Ikeda, Yukihiko, 211, 212, 231, 234
imaginary desire, 89, 95, 99

CPSIA information can be obtained
at www.ICGtesting.com
Printed in the USA
LVOW03s1536210318
570659LV00002B/551/P

9 780271 019154